THE ILLUSTRATED
★ Guide to ★
NO-LIMIT
TEXAS
HOLD'EM

Making Winners Out of Beginners *and* Advanced Players Alike!

DENNIS PURDY

SOURCEBOOKS, INC.®
NAPERVILLE, ILLINOIS

Published by Sourcebooks, Inc.

P.O. Box 4410, Naperville, Illinois 60567-4410

(630) 961-3900

Fax: (630) 961-2168

www.sourcebooks.com

Library of Congress Cataloging-in-Publication Data

Purdy, Dennis.
  The illustrated guide to no-limit Texas hold'em : making winners out
of beginners and advanced players alike! / Dennis Purdy.
      p. cm.
  Includes bibliographical references and index.
  ISBN-13: 978-1-4022-0724-2
  ISBN-10: 1-4022-0724-7
  1. Poker. I. Title.

GV1251.P868 2006

795.412--dc22

2006006322

Printed and bound in the United States of America

CH 10 9 8 7 6 5 4 3 2 1

Dedication

This book is dedicated to my new friend, Joe Wizan, who seems to get as much joy out of playing winning poker as he does producing hit movies in Hollywood. He's at the beginning of his third act—a poker career—which I hope will be long and satisfying.

Contents

Acknowledgments

Once again, I'd like to thank Robert "Doug" West, a true poker professional who took the time to read every one of the 150 situations to make sure they were as accurate as possible. Many times he stayed up until the early morning hours helping me to meet my deadline. He didn't find as many things to nitpick over in this book as he did in my first book on poker, but that's because over the last year I've gotten better...largely because of him.

I'd also like to thank my two youngest kids, Dennika and Dakota, who lost a lot of hours with Dad as he stayed up until the wee hours working on this book, and they never complained.

And I'd like to thank Kathy, my understanding, beautiful muse and longtime very good friend who has agreed to change her last name to mine in 2006. Together we have "no limit."

What This Book Is...and Isn't

"All in!"

With those two words, the chairs are pushed back and the players stand. The excitement fills the air as all eyes turn first to the two combatants, then to the board with eager anticipation of the cards to come. Like daggers and battleaxes, the cards are delivered, some amid shouts of triumph and exhilaration, others with groans of anguish and despair. The two gladiators each know and accept that one of them is duty-bound to fall, maybe for the last time.

And that, as they say, is no-limit Texas Hold'em, the king of poker games. There's nothing else like it. Fortunes (literal and figurative) can be won and lost on one hand, suddenly and without warning. As such, players of the no-limit game need to be acutely aware of what's going on at all times. While players of limit Texas Hold'em can afford the luxury of a mistake now and then because of the limited betting structure, players of the no-limit version risk losing it all if they miscalculate a situation; one flip of a card can—and often does—change everything.

No-limit Hold'em is the game you see played on numerous television networks, either by the pros or celebrities. While most of us will never play on television for hundreds of thousands, or even millions of dollars, there is a form of no-limit Texas Hold'em that we can all play regularly—tournaments on the Internet or in cardrooms and casinos across the country.

On the Internet, you can find a no-limit tournament at any hour of the night or day on more than one thousand poker sites. These tournaments have buy-ins as low as $1 and as high as $1,000, with a few even higher. Some no-limit tournaments are scheduled while others are sit 'n' go affairs (see glossary for explanation of both), and you can find one starting at almost any hour of the day or night, twenty-four hours a day, seven days a week. As for the cardrooms and casinos, most of them now have daily and nightly no-limit tournaments with variable entry fees.

The nice thing about most of these no-limit tournaments is that the entry fees are affordable and you're playing against non-professionals—although some of them will be very good players. You can compete with these very good no-limit players, and one step you can take to reach that level of play is to learn proper strategy techniques like those presented in this book.

Let me say from the start, this book does not deal with the strategy of limit Texas Hold'em. My first book, *The Illustrated Guide to Texas Hold'em*, presented in the same format as this book, concerns limit play and is available at bookstores everywhere. While the two games have some similar aspects, they are really quite different and you should have both books if you want to play both versions of Hold'em.

If you're new to Texas Hold'em, you'll find a most useful glossary in the back of this book. If you come across an unfamiliar word or phrase, take the time to check the glossary; chances are it's included. You will also notice several other useful charts, including the Relative Win Rates for All 169 Pocket Hands, which provides players with the relative strength of each starting hand compared to all other hands. You'll find an Odds Chart, in which I present the various odds (in easy-to-understand percentages) of a variety of occurrences common to Texas Hold'em play, an extremely useful tool for no-limit players since you often find yourself all in before the flop, and would like to know what your chances are of hitting a certain hand by the river.

This book also makes the assumption that you're either a beginner, somewhat new to the game, an intermediate player, or are fairly advanced at limit Hold'em and are now ready to branch out to the no-limit version; you've seen all the excitement on television and you're ready to take the plunge for yourself.

The meat of this book is the one hundred fifty illustrated situations that are presented in almost flash-card fashion. You'll find a situation/question on the left-hand page and either the correct or best answer on the right-hand page. This makes it much easier to visually grasp and retain the situation/problem. And, if you forget, you simply have to look at the pictures again. Ideally, what you should do is try to figure out the answer yourself before reading the answer I provide. Over the course of the book, you will begin to assimilate the strategies of hand analysis and proper play. You will learn how to quickly ascertain whether or not a hand is worth playing, either at the pocket stage, or later as the hand plays out.

There is no denying that anyone who takes up the game of Texas Hold'em–limit or no-limit–will have to go through the pains of the Texas Hold'em learning curve. How quickly you adopt the solid playing principles taught in this book will determine how painfully you make your way through the curve. It took me several years before I could consistently throw away small pairs, or Ace-6/7/8/9 unsuited in any position, and pocket Kings with an Ace on the board in the face of a large bet. I soon discovered that most of my losses at Texas Hold'em were the result of my own bad play. The intricacies of the game and nuances of betting strategy took me years to learn before I became a force in the limit games I engaged in. Once I made the move to no-limit Hold'em, I experienced that same learning curve of strategy and errors.

When I first decided I was going to play Hold'em, I, like virtually everyone else ever to play the game, bought a few books in order to teach myself the basics, and hopefully more. Unfortunately, I found these books hard to fathom. Their discussion of the intricacies of the game made my eyes glaze over. Once I finally grasped the game, I decided to write a book that beginners and intermediate players would find much easier to use and understand. In the year since my first book, *The Illustrated Guide to Texas Hold'em,* came out, I have received many emails, letters, and phone calls. The great majority have been from readers who told me they liked the visual format in which I presented the situations. They liked being able to read the situation on the left-hand page, visualize it using the illustrations, and then read the solution on the opposite page, going back and forth as often as necessary to grasp the principle until they understood it. Good. That was my intent, as I've always believed in the axiom that says people remember 10 percent of what they hear or read, 20 percent of what they see, and 70 percent of what they do. That principle alone makes this a better book from which to learn.

Most other poker books take a chapter-by-chapter approach to learning, with each chapter representing one facet of the game. In this book, poker strategy is discussed and illustrated, hand by hand, in situation format, as it is needed, as it develops, because the situations that come up in Texas Hold'em fluctuate, like an ebb and flow, when each new card comes on the board. You can start with pocket Aces, flop a 10-6-4 rainbow, turn a 6, and river an Ace with three cards of the same suit on the board and who knows what the heck has happened to everyone's hand. That's why you need to be able to think quickly and correctly about what has happened at each betting level of the hand and how you should proceed. Should you check or bet? Raise or fold? It can change with every card.

And it's also worth noting that the situations don't change just when cards are dealt. Sometimes the situations change when your position in the hand changes. Cards you might play in eighth position will be cards you should throw away in second position—or the other way around! Things can also change depending on what the players in front of you do, and what the players behind you are likely to do (or capable of doing). Are you frustrated yet? Have your eyes glazed over? Or are you still chomping at the bit to get going like I think you are and like I and everyone else who ever came before you in this game was? It is because of all these intricacies and complexities of Hold'em that I designed this book to allow you to more easily grasp the points of the game and the strategy being employed.

This book focuses on the no-limit version of Hold'em that you would typically find in your local cardroom or casino, or on any of the online poker sites, not the high-roller version you see on television. This is not a complicated book of poker theory targeted towards the sophisticated, established player, although I'm sure they, too, can pick up some useful pointers. This book is aimed at beginners and players early in their poker careers who desire more success than they've currently experienced.

This book is also very player friendly, as it takes the time to explain the intricacies of the game in easy-to-understand language. When I first learned to play Hold'em, I couldn't believe the number of new terms I'd never heard before, and I was a former professional gambler, albeit a blackjack player and sports bettor. That's why I especially wanted this book to incorporate the best glossary of any poker strategy book on the market. For the longest time, it seemed, I would be playing in a game and hear an unfamiliar term used by another player or the dealer and wouldn't have the slightest idea what they were talking about. And I certainly wasn't about to ask and reveal what a dunderhead I was!

Learning the game was costly, because I didn't possess all the knowledge and skill that I do now, years later. What I wanted to do with my first book–and this one–is to figuratively take a new player by the hand and walk him or her safely through the Hold'em jungles, something I wish had been available to me when I first started playing.

Chapter 1

The Basics of No-Limit Texas Hold'em

You've no doubt watched the no-limit version of Texas Hold'em on television with all its thrills and chills and whacky characters and are ready to take the plunge yourself. The main portion of this book is the one hundred fifty situations along with the correct/best solution to the questions posed in each situation. Before we get to that portion of the book, however, I will briefly go over the basics of Texas Hold'em for the unwashed among you.

Texas Hold'em is far and away the most popular game played in America today with an estimated seventy million practitioners. Yes, you can occasionally find a game of 7-card stud or Omaha, but by and large, if you want to hop on the Internet poker sites or go to your local cardroom or casino, Texas Hold'em is the game you're going to have to play.

Limit vs. No-limit Hold'em

While there are a few slight variations played at some establishments or on some Internet sites, there are basically two kinds of Texas Hold'em that you can play: limit and no-limit. Limit is the game played in 99 percent of the cardrooms and casinos on a daily and nightly basis. Typically, however, each of these cardrooms and casinos will sponsor a no-limit game sometime almost every day and/or night. This is done largely in order to attract poker players to their establishment with the hope that they will hang around after the tournament and join the limit games that are the meat and potatoes of their business. The cardrooms typically do not make any money on their no-limit tournaments, they're just a gimmick (sometimes at a loss) to get patrons on the premises. Many players will only play the tournament and then leave, often to another tournament at another establishment. Many, however, choose to stick around and play in the live games, which are almost always limit versions. This gives players the best of both worlds: they get the fantasy and action of playing in no-limit tournaments (even though the typical buy-in is only around $25 for 1,500 chips) and the safety of playing in limit games when the stakes are real.

In limit Hold'em, the betting is structured (i.e., the bets that are made are at required levels) and there is nothing the player can do to change it. For example, if you play in a "4-8" game, what that means is that you have to bet in $4 increments for the first two betting rounds and $8 increments for the last two betting rounds. There is a round of betting after the pocket cards are dealt, after the three-card flop is placed on the board, after the turn card (fourth board card), and after the fifth board card (called the river card) is dealt. Players are usually allowed to make one bet of the prescribed level and up to three raises.

In no-limit Hold'em, players have to start off at a certain minimum amount, but then are allowed to bet anything over that any time they wish, up to and including everything they have. When you bet everything, it is called "going all in." A player simply has to announce he's going all in and he is considered to have made a bet representing all his chips, whether or not he actually pushes all his chips into the pot. In this book, we will only be discussing no-limit strategy and play.

Playing the Game

Texas Hold'em is not a game played against the casino, like blackjack. Hold'em is played against other players with a house dealer. The typical Hold'em table will seat either nine or ten players, but occasionally eleven, with ten being the most common.

The player positions at the table are referred to by seat numbers. The player to the immediate left of the dealer is Seat 1. To his left is Seat 2, to his left Seat 3, and so on until you circle the table to Seat 10, the seat to the immediate right of the dealer. For the instructional purposes of this book, we're going to assume that each of the illustrated situations used occurs at a ten-handed table. Occasionally, some situations are presented with empty seats at the table, a frequent occurrence in no-limit tournaments. These seat number references will be used throughout the book, so be sure you understand them.

While some poker games, especially home games, are played for a high/low split of the pot, Texas Hold'em is played for high hand only. The only time a Hold'em pot is split is when two (or more) players have finished the hand with identical hands, which occurs frequently since all players make use of at least three of the cards on the board in addition to their two hole or "pocket" cards. There are no wild cards in Hold'em. It is strictly the best five-card hand made from the seven cards comprised of a player's two pocket cards and the five cards on the board, called community cards.

Before the house dealer deals the hand, two things must happen. First, the dealer will place a "dealer button" in front of one player. This button, normally white in live games with the word "dealer" stamped on it, and plain black in Internet games, represents the player the dealer is dealing in place of, since the players can't actually deal themselves in either a cardroom or on the Internet.

The second thing that must happen is that two players, on a rotating basis, are required to put money into the pot as "seed" money, or money which is used to generate betting action on each hand. These two players are known as the small blind and the big blind. They are, in effect, putting money "blindly" into the pot before they see their cards. It also lends a bit of mystery to the hand, since these two players have money invested in the pot without seeing their hands. The other players who choose to play their cards do so with the knowledge of their two pocket cards.

The two blinds are always the first two players to the immediate left of the dealer button. The first player to the left of the dealer button is the small blind; the player to his left is the big blind. The amount of the blinds is dependent on the level of the tournament. The big blind must put in the equivalent of one full bet while the small blind puts in the equivalent of half a full bet. For example, a tournament may consist of ten-minute rounds. For the first ten minutes, the blinds might be fifteen chips and thirty chips. When the first round ends, the blinds increase to twenty-five and fifty chips, which is designated as 25-50. The next round, blinds will go to 50-100. The blind structure keeps going up for the whole tournament, sometimes reaching 10,000-20,000 in big tournaments that last a long time.

The dealer then deals the cards, starting with the player to the immediate left of the dealer button and gives every player two cards, face down. These are known as your pocket cards and you should keep anyone else from seeing these cards. The betting then begins with the player to the immediate left of the big blind for the first betting round. If the blinds are, for example, 50-100, then the first player to act, or bet, must bet at least one hundred chips (the minimum full bet), but he can bet anything over that he wants to, up to and including all of his chips. The next player to act must either fold, call for the same amount, raise by betting double whatever the current bet is, raise to a larger amount than the current bet, or go all in.

The opportunity to act (fold, call, raise, or go all in) continues around the table in clockwise fashion until all players have acted and the betting is completed. There are four betting rounds, assuming at least two players still have chips with which to bet. The first betting round takes place after the two pocket cards are dealt; the second, after the three-card flop; the third after the turn, or fourth community card is dealt; the last after the fifth and final community card is dealt face up, called the river.

The order of play is the same as in limit Hold'em. The first player to act for the first betting round is the player immediately to the left of the big blind. The players then act in clockwise fashion from there until all players have exercised their option of playing or not. When play comes back to the small and big blinds, they have the option of raising themselves if they so desire, because their initial bet was forced into the pot. When the action gets to the big blind, if no one has raised up to that point, the dealer will ask him, "Big enough?" This is the dealer's way of asking the person in the big blind position if their big blind bet is big enough or if he wants to raise it. When the betting round is complete, the dealer will deal three cards face up in the middle of the table, called the flop. Another betting round occurs, but this time it starts with the player to the immediate left of the dealer button. Play again proceeds in clockwise fashion until all players have had a chance to act. Once betting is complete, the dealer brings a fourth community card, called the turn (or fourth street). There is another round of betting, again starting with the player to the immediate left of the dealer button. Once all action is complete, the dealer will bring a final community card, called the river (or fifth street) and a final round of betting will take place. The showdown then occurs, where all players reveal their pocket cards and the dealer declares a winner. On the Internet, of course, all of these actions are done automatically once player betting has been completed in each round.

There are not structured betting requirements as in limit Hold'em with the following exceptions: the first bet has to be at least the amount of the big blind, any raise has to be at least equal to the current bet, and at any point any player can go all in, even if he doesn't have enough chips to actually double the previous bet.

Once all players have made their final bets, everyone's pocket cards are turned face up on the table for the showdown. If all five community cards have not yet been dealt, the dealer will do so, and at the end of the hand declare the winner. When the hand is finally over, the dealer will move the dealer button in clockwise fashion to the next player and deal the next hand. If a losing all-in player had less chips in the pot than the winning player, he's done, knocked out of the tournament unless it is a tournament that allows optional rebuys.

A rebuy is, essentially, a second chance in which a player can pay an additional fee and get another stack of chips, usually around one thousand. Some tournaments allow no rebuys, some allow one, and some allow multiple rebuys, usually within the first hour of the tournament whereupon they are ended. If a player loses all his chips after that first hour, he's done.

Some tournaments allow what is called an "add-on" buy-in which players can, at a designated time, purchase another stack of chips for a set price. Add-ons are not required, but optional. Most players who are low on chips at the time of the add-on period will purchase the add-on. Some players who did well in the first hour and accumulated a lot of chips will decline the add-on purchase. Rebuys and add-ons are both usually ended at the one-hour mark of the tournament, although a few have different times for concluding these options. Once all rebuys and add-ons have been purchased, the rebuy/add-on period is declared over and play proceeds.

Chapter 2

Pregame Preparation

Once you've decided that no-limit Hold'em is your game, the next question is where to go to find a game. If you have an Internet connection, you can play online, and finding a game is as easy as falling out of bed. There are now more than one thousand poker sites on the Internet where you can play no-limit Texas Hold'em. If you don't know the names of any of the sites, simply type in "poker" and do a search and you'll get the names of more sites than you can handle. Many of them now advertise on television, usually on ESPN, FOX, and other networks that have a lot of sports coverage.

To play online, you have to have an account with the poker site. You'll either transfer money into your poker account through a credit card such as VISA, MasterCard, Amex, Discover, etc., or by electronic funds transfer such as FirePay, NETeller, InstaCASH, Click2Pay, ePassporte, Moneybookers, 900Pay, or eWalletXPress. You may also be able to mail a money order to the site's physical address or use PrePaidATM. This usually takes several days to accomplish and each site will walk you through the account set-up process step by step.

The no-limit games you can find on the Internet vary from $1 buy-ins to $1,000 buy-ins, and sometimes higher. The games vary from one-table games called sit 'n' go tournaments that start whenever they get ten players signed up, to extremely large tournaments with several thousand players that begin at scheduled times. The sit 'n' gos can usually be played in an hour or less. The larger tournaments can often take four to eight hours to play.

One question I often get asked by novice players and many radio interviewers is whether or not the Internet games are on the up and up. They may seem quirky from time to time in the cards they deal, but then so do games in cardrooms. I don't know that I would play an Internet ring game with a $1,000 buy-in. There is the possibility of two or more players conspiring to get into the same game together and keeping in contact with each other via cell phone in order to fleece the others in the game for big money. But a tournament shouldn't be a problem. In essence, the problem you might run into in an Internet game would come from crooked players, not a crooked site.

Once you get hooked up with your desired Internet site or two (or three, or four!), you'll find regular no-limit tournaments you like to play in. I play exclusively on PokerRoom.com (only because they accept Macs where most other sites require PCs) under the name Ghost Duster, in case you want to play in a game or tournament with me. I particularly like their $20, $30, and $50 buy-in tournaments held several times a day. They tend to attract 600–1,000 players at peak times and 175–350 players at off-peak times (like 3 a.m.), and I've done well. They also have a wide selection of Turbo tournaments from $1 to $100.

Virtually all of the Internet sites also offer free poker, in effect giving you Monopoly-type money with which to play. The amount of play money they give you is usually limited to a certain amount per day, since, after all, they don't want you playing for free all day, they just want to get you hooked on the game so you'll come back with money. This is fine as far as it goes, as it gives you a chance to get used to playing online if you haven't. The problem with the play money sites is that many players, in fact the vast majority, tend not to play in the traditional manner. What do you learn about Hold'em when all ten players at the table tend to call or raise every hand? Nothing. If you've never played Hold'em before, or you've never played online before, use the play money side of the site until you get used to the game and/or the controls used in playing the game, then go to the real money side and play real poker, not fantasy poker.

One thing you'll appreciate about online play is the speed. In a live game, a dealer can deal about thirty to thirty-five hands per hour. In an online game, the rate is more like sixty to eighty hands an hour, and sometimes one hundred hands in a no-limit tournament. If you're going to play online, you'd better know your stuff, because if you make the same mistake over and over again, it's going to be much costlier in an online game than a live game.

Another problem with online poker is that occasionally your connection gets disrupted, which means you have to log on again, and invariably you'll find that you've lost a bit of money while you were off line due to the blinds having come and gone.

Certainly online poker has a place and an appeal; you can play twenty-four hours a day, seven days a week, in your bathrobe if you want to. It's quick and easy to get into a game and you can–like me–do other things at the same time if you want to, like watch a movie, paint your nails, or write a book on poker. Also, you don't have to be around a bunch of smokers if you don't want to. You can raid the fridge whenever you want, help your kids with their homework (yeah, right!), or fill out your 1040 form, making sure to include all your gambling winnings.

If your cup of tea is live play in a casino or cardroom, you'll find very few no-limit games outside of the big gambling meccas like Vegas, Atlantic City, and Los Angeles, or wherever the pros like to congregate. What you will find, however, in most casinos and cardrooms is daily/nightly tournaments. These are similar to the Internet tournaments in which you pay a relatively small entry fee, usually in the neighborhood of $25, and get a stack of chips, usually around one to two thousand. These regular cardroom tournaments represent 99 percent of the no-limit action you're going to find in person. Call your local cardroom or casino and find out their schedule for no-limit tournaments. Don't forget your local bowling alleys, as many of them now have cardrooms. Some hold them every morning at 9 a.m., attempting to attract the workers who've just gotten off the third shift at the local factory. Some hold them at 11 a.m., appealing to the retired crowd and housewives who've just gotten their kids off to school. Most, however, hold them in the evenings, usually starting around 6 to 8 p.m., appealing to the majority of folks who've just finished with their workdays. Some establishments only hold their tournaments once or twice a week. Many players have scoped out all the tournaments in their local area, and move from one tourney to the next as time allows, rarely playing in a ring game.

If you're new to the live play circuit (assuming your local area has numerous cardrooms/casinos from which to choose), you need to be aware of a few things. Your safest places to play are usually the larger facilities, particularly casinos, as they tend to have better security, lighting, and monitoring. Trust your instincts and use common sense. Gambling, because of the allure of money, tends to attract some unsavory characters. Would you rather walk around at night in a well-lit facility with a lot of cameras and security guards, or a small, dimly lit joint three blocks off the main drag with half a dozen customers, three of whom are related?

Another phenomenon that has sprung up is the home or private game. I hear more and more stories all the time about people renting out apartments and converting them to mini-cardrooms for regular poker games. Some of these illegal games are even frequented by the local police chief and city prosecutor, attesting to the popularity of poker and unpopularity of gambling laws. The attraction of these games, besides the poker itself, is that they are unregulated (as in, no taxes!), and usually a smaller rake/fee to play. If you're contemplating getting into one of these private games, be very, very careful. There are no legitimate police or security personnel on duty charged with your safety and the integrity of the games. If you don't personally know someone who frequents these games regularly and can vouch for their honesty and safety, don't go.

Once you've chosen your game, you need to get prepared. You mean, *"I don't just sit down and play?"* No. If I'm going to play live in a cardroom or casino (live as opposed to "online," not live as opposed to "dead"), I make sure that I take everything with me that I might need while away from home, including any medications I might be taking, eye drops (smokers!), nasal spray, Q-tips, dental floss, aspirin, throat lozenges, a small notebook and pen for taking poker-related notes, and my credit-card sized poker percentage charts that I keep in my wallet for handy reference in case I've had too many margaritas and my memory is a bit cloudy. I'll even take a change of shirt and keep it in my car. If I wear a sweater, I'll take a cool, short-sleeved shirt in case the room temperature inside the cardroom is warm. If I wear a T-shirt, I'll take a sweater in the car. Either way, I can change into what's comfortable once I get to the casino. If I know I'm going to a particularly smoky cardroom, I'll take a tiny battery-operated fan that I use to blow the smoke away from me. In short, you should take anything with you that you'd miss in case you get caught up in a long game or tournament.

You should also take the proper bankroll for whatever game you're going to play. If you know you're only going to be playing the no-limit tournament(s) of your choice for that evening, all you need is your entry fee and supper money. If, however, you're going to get into the 20-40 no-limit game at your local casino, you might need to take $1,000 with you if you don't have the ability to write a check or use an ATM card at the casino.

You should also take a proper mindset with you. Don't play if you're tired, angry at your wife, kids, or pet squirrel, hungry, distracted, or have been drinking heavily. Don't play with a chip on your shoulder, or to get even with anyone over a bad beat. Don't play as though you have anything to prove to anyone except yourself. If you can't play with a relaxed, positive attitude, stay home. Adhering to this principle will save you a lot of money in the long run.

Once you've arrived at your preferred establishment, if you'll be playing in their tournament, get signed up as soon as possible. A lot of no-limit tournaments have become so popular that they fill up early. Some establishments allow players to sign up days or weeks ahead for their tourneys.

Once you're in your game, remember to keep your eyes open and your mouth shut. If you want to become a winning Texas Hold'em player, your mind has to be like a sponge, and you can't absorb the playing habits and strategies of other players if you're gabbing to the guy next to you about the latest lemon soufflé recipe you've discovered. Even if you're not in a particular hand, watch the other players. Mentally file away their tendencies toward raising or folding, playing strong or weak hands, or any tell they may have that might give something away. You have two eyes and ears and only one mouth for a reason–to be a better poker player, so hold up your end of the bargain.

Chapter 3

Let the Game Begin

If you are playing in an online tournament, once you sign up, the poker site does everything for you automatically in terms of assigning seat position at the tables. If you're playing in a live tourney, you will most likely draw cards for table and seat position. You may have been given a receipt, which you'll give to the dealer once the tournament has been seated, and for which you'll receive your chips. All players get the same number of chips to begin the tourney (unless it's a freeroll tournament in which players are entered for free, based on some sort of points basis earned by playing in the casino for a certain number of hours over a certain period of time).

If you have experience playing in a casino's live limit games, then you'll notice that the no-limit tournaments usually progress much faster. This is because in a no-limit tournament many more players will fold their hands than in a ring game. And even if they do play, when someone goes all in, many opponents often fold right there. Also, the blinds in a ring game always stay the same, whereas in a no-limit tournament, they increase every so often, usually about every ten to fifteen minutes. If the blinds didn't increase in a no-limit tournament, many players would be tempted to toss almost all of the hands away until they caught a real good one. By escalating the blinds four to six times an hour, it forces players to play something at some point. It is much more common to see players "blinded out" in a no-limit tournament than in a ring game. It is because of the escalating blind nature of the no-limit tournament that players have to be cognizant of winning chips every so often, if for no other reason than to keep even with the game.

One thing I will do in a large Internet tournament (with five hundred or more players) is not play any hand in the early going except pocket Aces, Kings, or Queens, or Ace-King suited and unsuited, or Ace-Queen suited. Reason being is that many players fall by the wayside every minute. In a typical tournament with two thousand players, approximately ten to fifteen players are getting knocked out of the tournament every minute for the first two hours or so. If you pick and choose your spots to play, you can pick up some small wins during this time and make the top half of the tournament while hardly playing. It might be tough for some to do, but exercising this kind of patience will move you up the ladder just as surely as playing every other hand and going up and down, up and down, and put you at a lot less risk.

Generally speaking, in a no-limit tournament you should play tight and aggressive in the early rounds. This means playing only the better hands, and playing them aggressively when you do catch them.

When you get close to the money in a no-limit tournament, keep in mind that if you have a larger stack of chips, you can often "bully" the smaller stacks, making them fold to your big raise because they are trying to survive until they make the money. You should be careful, however, of players in the blind or those who have half or more of their chips in the pot, as they are hard to bully. These types of players will often call anything, so if you bet into them, you better have a good hand, because they won't go away.

If you get close to the money and have a small stack, you need to be more judicious about when you bet. Pick a good spot, if possible, because a short stack may only get one shot at winning more chips. Granted, it isn't always possible, mostly because the increasing blinds can be quite unforgiving when you have no choice in the matter. Once you're in the money, if you have a large stack, you should try and dominate the small stacks by bullying them so long as you are in proper position to do so, and I'll go into this in more depth in the situations. If you're in the money and have a small stack, do everything you can to hang on, because in most tournaments every rung you climb on the prize-money ladder means more money in your pocket.

Once play has begun, remember the rules of good poker etiquette and common sense:

- Be polite. Don't call other players names or comment on how badly they play. There are enough hammerheads at the table who will do this, particularly in online games, so don't be one of them.
- When you muck (discard) your hand, do it respectfully. Don't flick or toss your cards aggressively toward the dealer. Sometimes this will result in your cards accidentally hitting another player's cards, and if his hand is unprotected, he'll be forced to muck his hand, too, and he won't be very happy with you. Besides, the dealer doesn't need to be treated disrespectfully. The Golden Rule applies at the poker table, too.
- Don't expose your hole (pocket) cards when discarding your hand, either to the player next to you or the whole table. This is just plain bad sportsmanship.
- Keep burning cigarettes off the poker table, as the ashes soil the felt surface and get onto the cards.
- Keep food and drinks off the table for the same reasons.
- If you place in the prize money of a live tournament, be sure to tip the dealers. They all work for minimum wage and tips, and usually the no-limit tournaments are hosted by the establishment as a loss leader event. Without the dealers, there would be no games.
- Keep your profanities to yourself. No one wants to listen to a profanity-laced game.
- If you smoke, please be sure the smoke isn't drifting directly into anyone else's face.
- If you have to use the restroom or take a food break, try not to do it when you're in the blinds, because the dealer will take the necessary chips out of your stack and you'll lose them. It's not like a limit game in which the dealer gives you a "missed blind" button and you make it up when you get back or sit out until the blinds come to you again.
- Don't ever, ever, EVER turn over another player's discarded hand. I did this once the first time I ever played in a no-limit tournament, not realizing what a big no-no it was. When the other player mucked his hand, he carelessly flicked the cards with his finger. Instead of the cards traveling to the center of the table as he'd intended, they landed right in front of me. I took it to mean he was showing me his cards. Wrong! Boy, was he pissed.

- Don't abuse the dealers by swearing at them, calling them names, or belittling them. All they do is deal the cards, they don't tell lousy players to stay in until the river in order to hit a runner-runner suck out hand to beat you. These players do it themselves.
- Be honorable in your play. Don't use sneaky, underhanded tricks or tactics in order to win. Remember, there is such a thing as karma, and someone physically bigger than you is always in charge of it.
- Don't educate the competition at the table. It's not fair to all the other players. If you feel the need to take someone under your wing, do so away from the table, recommending to him that he buy this book if you're really serious about helping him.

Chapter 4

The Rules of Good Basic Strategy

There are almost as many strategies for playing no-limit Texas Hold'em as there are books about the game itself. One thing is clear, however: no-limit Hold'em is vastly different than limit Hold'em. While the two games have many similarities and share many of the same rules, no-limit strategy and limit strategy are two different buggers. In limit Hold'em, for example, you can make an occasional mistake and it might cost you an acre of corn. If you make a mistake in no-limit, it can cost you the whole farm!

In low level, low limit Hold'em there are, quite frankly, a lot of bad players, both on the Internet and in live games. In the no-limit game there are a lot of bad players, too, but they tend to be in the tournaments with the lowest buy-ins, like $5 and $10. I've noticed that as the entry fees go up, so does the caliber of play. Players tend to get nuts and go all in more often (and sooner) in the $5 tournaments than they do in the $50 tournaments, and I suppose this makes sense. That's one of the main reasons I play in the $20-$50 tournaments rather than the cheaper ones. Also, the prize money is much better in the tournaments with higher buy-ins. I guess a lot of it has to do with how much players think of a $5 bill as opposed to a $50 bill. The reasoning goes, I guess, *"It's only five bucks, so what's the big deal?"* So, beware of that tendency when you sign up for a tournament, especially an Internet one.

The first rule of good basic strategy is to play only good starting hands. (Pssstt! Chantaille! King-9 unsuited is NOT a good starting hand.) At the end of this chapter you'll find a chart titled Relative Win Rate. This chart ranks all 169 possible pocket hands by their *relative win rate, not their hand rank.* Most of the time I play only the top twenty-five to thirty hands on this chart, with occasional situational exceptions.

The second rule of good basic strategy is that the flop must hit your hand or you fold if someone bets. After the flop, more than 70 percent of the cards you're going to get in your hand have been dealt, and this will go a long ways toward determining whether or not you should play the hand further.

The third rule of good basic strategy is that if you play a drawing hand, such as a flush or straight draw, you need to hold at least four of the needed cards by the flop or you should probably get out unless you've made something else with the hand. Three hearts after the flop is not considered a legitimate flush draw because you need to hit a heart on both the turn and river to get there. Nor are three cards to a straight after the flop considered a straight draw. Again, having to hit runner-runner on the turn and river to make your hand is not considered a legitimate opportunity to make a straight. You should hold four cards to a flush or straight after the flop in order to properly try for them on the turn and river, and the four to a straight should preferably be in consecutive order, in other words, an open-ender rather than a gutshot. Also, it is generally preferable that you have *at least* three or four opponents when chasing a four flush or open-ender because usually you need that many players in order to get correct pot odds, which will be covered in more depth within the situations section.

The fourth rule of good basic strategy says that if you're not on a drawing hand, to continue after the flop, in most cases, you should hold at least top pair with a big kicker, or an overpair to the flop. An overpair is a pocket pair that is of higher rank than any card on the flop. This also assumes that the flop didn't come up three of one suit, a suit you don't hold, or three cards of consecutive rank that doesn't fit into your hand for a straight but might easily fit into someone else's hand.

The fifth rule of good basic strategy is to keep your eyes open for possible danger, and in no-limit Hold'em danger lurks EVERYWHERE! Get used to looking at the flop and figuring out what the highest possible hand is that could be out there. Then, try to estimate how likely it is that some could be holding just such a hand. This knack for looking for danger should be ever present, as every turn of a card changes the current situation. Get in the habit of reassessing the board every time another card is brought, and mentally flag the potential perils.

The sixth rule says when you have the best hand, and you know you have the best hand, make your opponents pay, and preferably dearly. No free cards when you hold the power.

The seventh rule of good poker strategy is that you should always fold your hand when it's obvious that you're beaten. Don't call a river bet just to see if the other player really had what he was projecting. Once you've played for a while, it will become easier to recognize when you're beaten. In no-limit, however, there is a greater tendency to bluff than there is in limit, so you have to be careful not to throw away a winning hand. It can be tough, I know, but it's a skill you have to acquire in order to play no-limit. The more and more experienced you get, the easier it will become to throw your cards away earlier in the hand, thereby minimizing your losses. This goes back to the second rule that says the flop must hit your hand or you get out. The money you win in Hold'em doesn't come just from your winning hands, but rather from the money you save by minimizing the losses of your losing hands.

The eighth rule of good basic strategy is that you must take your position into consideration when deciding whether or not to play a particular hand. For example, if you were dealt a pair of 3s in first position, you should fold. But if you caught that same pair of 3s in last position or in the small blind, with no one having raised before you, with four or more players in the pot ahead of you you'd play them and see the flop because of the pot odds.

Actual Odds vs. Pot Odds

The ninth rule of good basic strategy is to learn and understand the concept of actual odds and pot odds. "Actual odds" means the actual mathematical chance of something occurring. "Pot odds" means the ratio of the money in the pot to the amount you are being asked to bet in relationship to the actual odds of something occurring to give you that pot.

For example, let's consider that you and I were to engage in a quarter flipping contest. If I asked you to call the coin flip–heads or tails–you would understand that the actual odds of you guessing correctly would be 50 percent, or even. Put another way, the way we calculate poker hand probabilities, it would be 1-to-1.

Now, what if I said that every time you guessed right I would give you a dollar and every time you guessed wrong you would give me three dollars? Would you do it? Of course not, and rightfully so, because you understand the actual odds are 1-to-1, but the money odds against you are 3-to-1.

Put in poker terms, if you flopped four cards to an inside straight draw (as in your pocket cards were 9-10 and the flop came Queen-King-4, therefore you need a Jack on either the turn or river to complete your straight), your odds of hitting the Jack by the river are approximately 5-to-1 against you. So, if you are alone in the hand (heads up) with one other player, depending on how much money was put into the pot before the flop, it probably will not be correct (or worth your while) to keep calling the other player's bet to stay in the pot until the river as you'll only be getting 1-to-1 money on a proposition that is 5-to-1 against you from occurring. If you keep playing such hands, you'll go broke in short order. If, on the other hand, there were seven players in the pot, then it would be worth your while to try and hit the Jack since you'd be getting 6-to-1 money on a proposition that is 5-to-1 against you from occurring.

I will go into the pot odds formulas in more detail in the 150 Situations, but I will provide an example here of the type of mathematical calculations you'll have to learn how to perform if you want to be a winning Texas Hold'em player.

Let's say, for example, that you hold a pocket hand of Jack-10 of diamonds and the flop comes Queen-8-7, with two of them being diamonds. This means you have a shot at a diamond flush and a straight. To make the flush you need one more diamond, and to make your straight you need a 9 of any suit. Once the flop has come, you now can see five cards, the three on the flop and the two in your hand. This means that there are forty-seven unseen cards, any of which could contain your needed cards. Therefore, we have to figure out how many cards of the forty-seven will make either your flush or straight and how many will not. There are nine diamonds that could make your flush and four 9s that could make your straight for a total of thirteen cards, or "outs." But you have to deduct one from this because the 9 of diamonds was counted twice. That means you have twelve legitimate outs. You still may not win the hand with either your straight or flush because someone else may hold a higher hand, but that is irrelevant at this point; we're just calculating the probabilities.

Okay, of the forty-seven unseen cards, twelve will get us where we need to be, a straight or a flush. That means thirty-five cards will not. This ratio of bad cards to good cards is shown as 35-to-12, or just slightly less than 3-to-1 (2.92, actually). So, on one flip of the cards, we have a 3-to-1 chance of making one of our two desired hands. Therefore, if the pot contains more than three times what we are being asked to bet to make the call, it is appropriate to call. If not, then it isn't. But wait! If it's only after the flop, don't we have two more chances to hit our straight or flush? Correct. That means we can divide our 3-to-1 ratio in half, and it becomes only 1.5-to-1 odds *with two cards to go*. So after the flop, with this hand, we only need to have 1.5 times the amount of the bet we are being asked to make in the pot to make this an appropriate call. If we miss on the turn, then we calculate it again as forty-six unseen cards, thirty-four of which are bad, twelve of which are good; 34-to-12 reduces to 2.83-to-1, or about 3-to-1 odds. We must now have at least three times the amount of the bet we are being asked to make in the pot to make it an appropriate call. Clear as mud? Don't worry, it'll come easier with practice.

Most hands won't have this many outs, unfortunately. Let's say you hold pocket 9s and the flop came Ace-7-3 and you decided to play it. Let's also assume that at least one of your opponents holds an Ace for a pair of Aces. This means that for you to have an expectation of winning, you'll have to hit another 9 on the turn or river and your opponent can't hit another Ace. For the sake of ease, we'll assume he won't hit his third Ace. What are the odds of you hitting your third 9 by the river and overtaking him to win the pot? Let's figure it out.

After the flop there are five cards showing, the three-card flop and your two pocket cards. That means that there are forty-seven unseen cards, any of which could be your needed 9. This translates into 47 cards - 2 cards = 45 cards that are not your third 9 and two that are. So, 45 ÷ 2 = 22.5, or 22.5-to-1 odds of catching a third 9 on the next dealt card, which is the turn. Since you still have two cards to go, the odds of catching a third 9 by the river are 22.5-to-1 ÷ 2, or just a shade over 11-to-1. This means that after the flop, if you want to chase a third 9 to the river, you need to have at least 11 times the amount of the bet you're being asked to make already in the pot to make it mathematically correct to call. Put in money terms, if there's $40 (or 40 chips in a no-limit tournament) in the pot, and the betting level is $20 or 20 chips, then you are being asked to bet 2-to-1 money on an event (catching a third 9) that is only 11-to-1 likely to happen. Very poor betting proposition, and you should fold. If, however, there is $300 (or 300 chips) in the pot and you are being asked to bet $20 (or 20 chips) to make the same call, then yes, you make the call because the odds are 11-to-1 for a money return of 15-to-1. It all boils down to the same principle as the quarter-flip exercise. When the money odds of any particular mathematical proposition are in your favor, you make the call, and when they're not, you don't. Now, that is a bit of an oversimplification because there are other aspects that you have to take into consideration when being asked to make a particular bet. For example, would you make the above 11-to-1 call for 15-to-1 money early in the game when it will only cost you 20 chips? Yeah, most likely. Will you make the same call late in the tournament, one spot from making the money, with your last 20 chips? Uh-oh, maybe not. Maybe not is right, because the circumstances are different, and in no-limit Hold'em you have to take those other factors into consideration. In limit Hold'em, in the above situation you can just pull more money out of your pocket and buy more chips. In no-limit you can't.

While this aspect of no-limit Hold'em might seem a bit difficult right now, it will eventually become second nature to you as you mold yourself into a winning player. Now, let's get to the 150 Situations, the meat of this book.

Texas Hold'em Relative Win Rates for All 169 Pocket Hands

The following chart shows the win rate of each hand when randomly played against any other hand. This does not mean, for example, that a pair of pocket Aces wins 86.1 percent of the times played in a regular game, since in a normal game there is almost always more than one player in a hand and each player holding the Aces and the other hands will play them differently. This chart is only intended to give you, the reader, an idea of the relative strength of each starting hand as compared to all other hands.

These figures were calculated from a computer simulation of one million dealt hands.

(s = suited, un = unsuited)

#	Hand	Rate	#	Hand	Rate	#	Hand	Rate
1.	A-A pair	86.1%	17.	Q-J s	44.2%	33.	A-3 s	21.3%
2.	K-K pair	74.6%	18.	A-8 s	41.5%	34.	5-5 pair	20.7%
3.	A-K s	68.6%	19.	K-10 s	40.9%	35.	K-J un	20.5%
4.	Q-Q pair	68.5%	20.	A-9 s	40.5%	36.	A-2 s	20.0%
5.	A-K un	67.0%	21.	J-10 s	40.0%	37.	K-9 s	20.0%
6.	A-Q s	64.9%	22.	Q-10 s	39.4%	38.	Q-9 s	19.1%
7.	J-J pair	64.4%	23.	K-Q un	39.2%	39.	A-9 un	17.4%
8.	10-10 pair	60.8%	24.	10-9 s	38.3%	40.	Q-J un	16.8%
9.	A-Q un	60.5%	25.	A-10 un	34.4%	41.	A-7 un	10.2%
10.	A-J s	58.6%	26.	A-7 s	33.9%	42.	A-8 un	10.0%
11.	9-9 pair	55.4%	27.	A-4 s	30.6%	43.	A-6 un	9.9%
12.	K-Q s	54.6%	28.	A-5 s	29.7%	44.	9-8 s	9.8%
13.	8-8 pair	51.8%	29.	A-6 s	29.6%	45.	J-8 s	9.8%
14.	A-10 s	50.7%	30.	7-7 pair	28.6%	46.	A-4 un	9.6%
15.	A-J un	48.9%	31.	J-9 s	27.9%	47.	K-8 s	9.5%
16.	K-J s	45.3%	32.	6-6 pair	26.2%	48.	10-8 s	9.5%

49.	A-5 un	9.4%	94.	K-8 un	3.4%	139.	7-2 un	0.4%
50.	J-10 un	9.4%	95.	9-7 un	3.4%	140.	J-5 un	0.4%
51.	Q-10 un	9.3%	96.	J-4 s	3.3%	141.	J-3 un	0.4%
52.	K-10 un	9.1%	97.	8-4 s	3.3%	142.	10-4 un	0.4%
53.	Q-9 un	8.8%	98.	10-5 s	3.2%	143.	9-2 s	0.4%
54.	A-2 un	8.8%	99.	9-6 s	3.2%	144.	9-5 un	0.4%
55.	10-9 un	8.8%	100.	K-6 un	3.1%	145.	9-3 un	0.4%
56.	K-7 s	8.6%	101.	Q-2 s	3.1%	146.	8-3 s	0.4%
57.	A-3 un	8.5%	102.	J-6 s	3.1%	147.	8-3 un	0.4%
58.	K-6 s	8.4%	103.	Q-3 s	3.0%	148.	7-3 un	0.4%
59.	J-9 un	8.4%	104.	Q-4 s	3.0%	149.	5-4 un	0.4%
60.	10-7 s	8.4%	105.	K-7 un	2.8%	150.	4-2 un	0.4%
61.	4-4 pair	8.3%	106.	6-3 s	2.4%	151.	Q-2 un	0.3%
62.	K-9 un	8.2%	107.	7-3 s	2.1%	152.	10-6 un	0.3%
63.	8-7 s	8.0%	108.	K-2 un	1.6%	153.	9-3 s	0.3%
64.	7-6 s	7.2%	109.	Q-4 un	1.6%	154.	9-4 un	0.3%
65.	9-7 s	5.8%	110.	4-3 s	1.6%	155.	8-6 un	0.3%
66.	3-3 pair	4.5%	111.	K-4 un	1.5%	156.	8-2 un	0.3%
67.	Q-5 s	4.4%	112.	K-3 un	1.5%	157.	7-2 s	0.3%
68.	K-5 s	4.3%	113.	Q-6 un	1.5%	158.	7-5 un	0.3%
69.	Q-8 s	4.2%	114.	Q-7 un	1.4%	159.	6-2 s	0.3%
70.	6-5 s	4.2%	115.	Q-5 un	1.4%	160.	5-2 un	0.3%
71.	J-8 un	4.1%	116.	J-2 s	1.4%	161.	4-3 un	0.3%
72.	2-2 pair	4.0%	117.	K-5 un	1.3%	162.	10-2 un	0.3%
73.	K-3 s	4.0%	118.	10-4 s	1.3%	163.	8-2 s	0.3%
74.	10-6 s	3.9%	119.	10-3 s	1.3%	164.	6-5 un	0.3%
75.	K-4 s	3.9%	120.	3-2 s	0.7%	165.	5-3 un	0.3%
76.	10-8 un	3.9%	121.	9-4 s	0.7%	166.	3-2 un	0.3%
77.	8-5 s	3.9%	122.	7-6 un	0.7%	167.	6-4 un	0.2%
78.	7-4 s	3.9%	123.	5-2 s	0.6%	168.	6-3 un	0.2%
79.	9-5 s	3.8%	124.	10-2 s	0.5%	169.	6-2 un	0.2%
80.	Q-7 s	3.8%	125.	4-2 s	0.5%			
81.	J-7 s	3.8%	126.	J-6 un	0.5%			
82.	J-3 s	3.8%	127.	J-4 un	0.5%			
83.	9-8 un	3.8%	128.	J-2 un	0.5%			
84.	8-7 un	3.8%	129.	9-6 un	0.5%			
85.	5-3 s	3.7%	130.	8-5 un	0.5%			
86.	8-6 s	3.6%	131.	Q-3 un	0.4%			
87.	7-5 s	3.6%	132.	J-7 un	0.4%			
88.	6-4 s	3.6%	133.	10-7 un	0.4%			
89.	K-2 s	3.6%	134.	10-5 un	0.4%			
90.	5-4 s	3.6%	135.	10-3 un	0.4%			
91.	Q-8 un	3.5%	136.	9-2 un	0.4%			
92.	Q-6 s	3.5%	137.	8-4 un	0.4%			
93.	J-5 s	3.5%	138.	7-4 un	0.4%			

Texas Hold'em Odds Chart

The Odds of...	Are...
Catching a pocket pair	6%
Catching two cards of the same suit in your pocket	24%
Catching suited connectors in your pocket	4%
Catching pocket Aces or pocket Kings	0.9%
Catching Ace-King suited in your pocket	0.3%
Catching Ace-King unsuited in your pocket	1.2%
Catching one Ace in your pocket hand	16%
Catching pocket Aces, Kings, Queens, or Jacks	1.8%
Your pocket Kings facing pocket Aces in a heads up game	0.004%
Your Ace-King pocket hitting either an Ace or a King by the river	50%
Pocket Queens holding up against Ace-King through the river	56%
Both pocket cards being Jacks or higher	9%
Flopping four cards to a flush and making it by the river	39%
Flopping an open-ended straight flush and making either a straight or flush by the river	54%
Flopping an open-ended straight and making it by the river	34%
Flopping two pair and making a full house by the river	17%
Flopping three of a kind and making a full house or four of a kind by the river	37%
Flopping a set when holding a pocket pair	12%
Flopping a pair when holding cards of two different ranks	32%
Flopping two more of the same suit when holding two suited cards	11%

Flopping a pair and improving to two pair or three of a kind by the river 22%

Flopping a set after holding a pocket pair 9%

A gutshot straight draw improving to a straight by the river 17%

Making a flush by the river when flopping three cards to a flush (i.e.,
  making a backdoor flush, also known as runner-runner) 4%

Making a straight by the river when flopping three cards to a straight
  (i.e., making a backdoor straight, also known as runner-runner) 1.5%

Catching an Ace on the turn or river when holding one in your hand and
  missing on the flop 13%

Someone holding an Ace in their hand when one is on the board with...

5 players in on the hand 58%

4 players in on the hand 47%

3 players in on the hand 35%

2 players in on the hand 23%

Someone holding a set of two cards that are paired on the board with...

5 players in on the hand 43%

4 players in on the hand 34%

3 players in on the hand 26%

2 players in on the hand 17%

Texas Hold'em Hand Rank Chart

The following chart ranks the hands of poker from high to low and includes the exact odds of getting each hand in just five dealt cards.

Hand	Explanation	Odds
Royal Flush	A/K/Q/J/10, all of the same suit (e.g., all clubs or all hearts). It is not possible for two players to hold Royal Flushes in the same Hold'em hand.	649,739 to 1
Straight Flush	Five consecutively ranked cards of the same suit (e.g., the Q/J/10/9/8 of diamonds). If two players hold straight flushes on the same hand, the one with the highest card in his hand is the winner.	64,973 to 1
Four of a Kind	Four cards of the same rank, such as four Kings or four 10s. If two players each hold four of a kind, the one with the higher ranked cards is the winner.	4,164 to 1
Full House	Three cards of one rank and two of another rank (e.g., three Jacks and two 7s). If two players hold full houses on the same hand, the one holding the higher three-card group is the winner. If this is a tie, than the one holding the higher pair is the winner. If this is a tie as well, then the pot is split.	693 to 1
Flush	Five cards of the same suit, but not in consecutive order (e.g., all clubs or all spades). If two players hold flushes on the same hand, the one with the higher ranked card of the flush suit is the winner.	508 to 1

Hand	Explanation	Odds
Straight	Five cards in consecutive rank, but not in the same suit (e.g., J/10/9/8/7 of different suits). If two players each hold straights, the one with the higher ranked card in his straight hand is the winner.	254 to 1
Three of a Kind	Three cards of one rank and no other pairs (e.g., three Queens or three 6s). If two players each hold three-of-a-kind hands, the one with the higher ranked cards is the winner. If this is a tie, then the player with the highest card remaining in his hand is the winner. If this is also a tie, then the player with the next highest card is the winner. If this, too, is a tie, then the pot is split.	46 to 1
Two Pair	Two cards of one rank and two cards of another rank (e.g., two Aces and two 4s). If two players both have two pair, then the one with the highest pair is the winner. If this is a tie, then the one with the next highest pair is the winner. If this is also a tie, then whoever has the highest "kicker" (remaining card) is the winner. If this is also a tie, then the pot is split.	20 to 1
One Pair	Two cards of the same rank with no other pairs (e.g., two Kings or two 9s). If two players each hold one pair, the player holding the higher ranked pair is the winner. If this is a tie, then the player holding the next highest ranked card in their hand is the winner. If this is a tie, then whichever player holds the next highest "fourth" card is the winner. If this is also a tie, then whoever holds the highest "fifth" card in their hand is the winner. If this is also a tie, then the pot is split.	1.25 to 1
No Pair	Five cards of different ranks and not of the same suit or in consecutive order (e.g., K/Q/10/8/6 of mixed suits). If two players go to showdown and neither has a pair, then whichever player holds the highest card in their hole is the winner. If this is a tie, then whichever player holds the second highest card in the hole is the winner. If this is also a tie, then the pot is split.	1 to 1

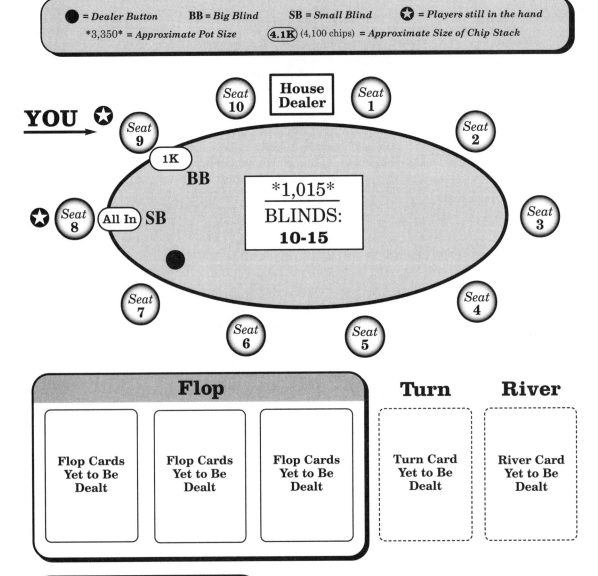

● = *Dealer Button*   BB = *Big Blind*   SB = *Small Blind*   ★ = *Players still in the hand*

3,350 = *Approximate Pot Size*   (4.1K) (4,100 chips) = *Approximate Size of Chip Stack*

YOU ★ → Seat 9   Seat 10   House Dealer   Seat 1   Seat 2

1K — BB

1,015
BLINDS:
10-15

★ Seat 8   All In — SB   Seat 3

Seat 7   Seat 6   Seat 5   Seat 4

Flop

| Flop Cards Yet to Be Dealt | Flop Cards Yet to Be Dealt | Flop Cards Yet to Be Dealt |

Turn

Turn Card Yet to Be Dealt

River

River Card Yet to Be Dealt

Pocket

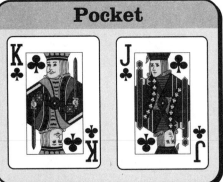

Situation 1:

You have been dealt King-Jack suited in your pocket while in the big blind position. It is the first hand of the tournament, a nightly affair that you play in regularly. Everyone folded except the small blind, a player nicknamed "All-In Allen" because of his tendency to go all in on the first hand of every tournament without looking at his cards, something he did here. Do you call or fold?

> Starting Hand (Pocket): **K♣J♣**
> This Pocket's Win Rate: **45.3%**
> Win Rate Rank: **16 of 169 possible**

Tournament Situation:

Paid Entries: **40 x $25**

Starting Chip Stack: **1,000**

Players Remaining: **40**

Places Paid: **5**

Your Current Standing: **Tied with everyone**

Time Left in Round: **12 minutes**

Rebuys Allowed: **No**

Next Blind Level: **15-30**

This Tournament's Prize Money:

1. **$450**
2. **$250**
3. **$150**
4. **$100**
5. **$50**

Total Prize Pool:

$1000

Answer 1:

Many times when playing in a Texas Hold'em tournament with a low buy-in such as this one, you will witness players such as All-in Allen exhibiting strange, even erratic behavior. Don't get flustered, as this can be the nature of Texas Hold'em. Obviously Allen has a quirk about him that lends to him making such a bet on the first hand of the tournament every time. Now, if the buy-in was $100 instead of just $25, he might not be making such a silly bet. You, however, have to deal with what you've been given by Allen.

Statistically, you have a hand that ranks sixteenth best of the 169 possible pocket hands in terms of relative win rate against a random hand, which is purely the case in this situation because Allen has gone all in without looking at his cards. If you call his all-in bet, you are making a sound call. If you fold and let Allen win your 15-chip blind, you'll certainly live to fight another day and he'll have gotten the silliness out of his system. Given that he is such an obviously poor player, he'll most likely get knocked out in the early stages of the tournament. Personally, I'd call the all-in bet, knowing that I have the odds solidly in my favor.

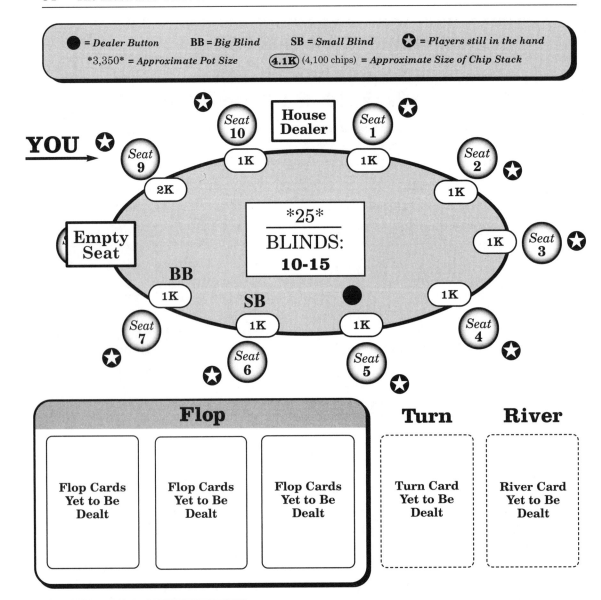

Pocket

Situation 2:

After you knocked out All-in Allen a few hands earlier, the play has proceeded briskly around the table with virtually no action. It is very early in the tourney and you are the chip leader. You are now first to act and received Jack-10 unsuited in the pocket. Do you fold, call the 15-chip big blind bet, or raise to an as yet undetermined level?

Starting Hand (Pocket): **J♥10♦**
This Pocket's Win Rate: **9.4%**
Win Rate Rank: **50 of 169 possible**

Tournament Situation:

Paid Entrys: **40 x $25**

Starting Chip Stack: **1,000**

Players Remaining: **39**

Places Paid: **5**

Your Current Standing: **1st place**
(chip leader)

Time Left in Round: **4 minutes**

Rebuys Allowed: **No**

Next Blind Level: **15-30**

This Tournament's Prize Money:

1. **$450**
2. **$250**
3. **$150**
4. **$100**
5. **$50**

———————

Total Prize Pool:

$1000

Answer 2:

Over the years, I would say, I have heard more players mention that they like Jack-10, suited or unsuited. Many even say it is their favorite hand. Statistically, however, it is not that good of a hand. While it may hold the illusion of possessing potential, especially for straights, it just doesn't perform that well when push comes to shove. The only pocket hand that should be your favorite is Ace-Ace, otherwise any other hand should be considered on its merits, especially when you are in first position, like with this hand.

When you are in first position, you have no information yet on what the other players may be holding. You don't know yet how many opponents you might be facing or the relative strength of their hands. To call this fairly weak hand in this position would be just plain foolish. You took the early chip lead when you knocked out All-in Allen earlier in the round. Although it is still early in the tournament, you are the chip leader, which means you more than any other player in the tournament can afford to wait for a good hand in a good position. Toss this hand away, and forget about favorite hands.

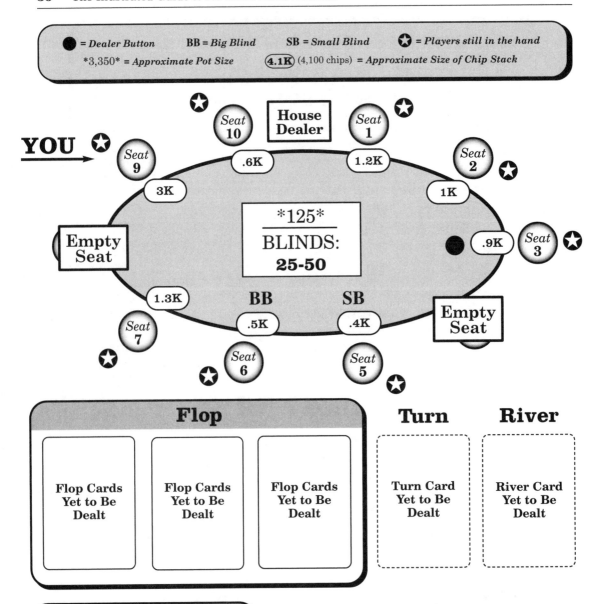

● = *Dealer Button*   **BB** = *Big Blind*   **SB** = *Small Blind*   ⭐ = *Players still in the hand*

3,350 = *Approximate Pot Size*   (**4.1K**) (4,100 chips) = *Approximate Size of Chip Stack*

YOU →

Seat 10   House Dealer   Seat 1

.6K   1.2K

Seat 9   Seat 2

3K   1K

Empty Seat

125

BLINDS: 25-50

.9K   Seat 3

1.3K   BB   SB   Empty Seat

Seat 7   .5K   .4K

Seat 6   Seat 5

Flop

| Flop Cards Yet to Be Dealt | Flop Cards Yet to Be Dealt | Flop Cards Yet to Be Dealt |

Turn

Turn Card Yet to Be Dealt

River

River Card Yet to Be Dealt

Pocket

A♦ A♦   7♣ 7♣

Situation 3:

Forty minutes into this tourney you've increased your chip stack to 3,000, the leader at your table and second overall. Seat 7 called the 50-chip big blind bet. With an Ace-7 unsuited, should you fold, call the bet, or make a large raise, thinking that four of the players at your table (Seats 3, 5, 6, and 10) all have less than 1,000 chips in their stacks and will likely fold to your big raise and stack?

> ## Starting Hand (Pocket): **A♦7♣**
> ## This Pocket's Win Rate: **10.2%**
> ## Win Rate Rank: **41 of 169 possible**

Tournament Situation:

Paid Entrys: **40 x $25**

Starting Chip Stack: **1,000**

Players Remaining: **35**

Places Paid: **5**

Your Current Standing: **2nd place overall, chip leader at your table**

Time Left in Round: **8 minutes**

Rebuys Allowed: **No**

Next Blind Level: **50-100**

This Tournament's Prize Money:

1. **$450**
2. **$250**
3. **$150**
4. **$100**
5. **$50**

Total Prize Pool:
$1000

Answer 3:

First of all, Ace-7 unsuited is not a good hand, as its 10.2 percent relative win rate suggests. Second, you've been dealt this hand in early position, another factor that works against you because you don't know yet what everyone acting after you is going to do. Third, to think that a large raise, say to 1,000 chips, is going to drive out the small stacks is misguided. It might just be that because their stacks are small and they caught a so-so hand (such as a pair of 2s, or suited connectors such as 10-9 of spades, or Ace-anything) that out of desperation they will call your large raise, effectively putting them all in.

Also, there are three stacks at the table who aren't under 1,000, and if you make a big raise now with a weak hand like this, you might bite into a real hand with a stack that will knock you down from chip leader at the table to second best. This hand is typically played by many beginning and low level Texas Hold'em players, which is one reason they don't do well in the long run. Ace-7 suited should not usually be played other than in a short-handed situation, like late in the tournament when there are few players left and the blinds are high. Fold this hand and wait for a better one.

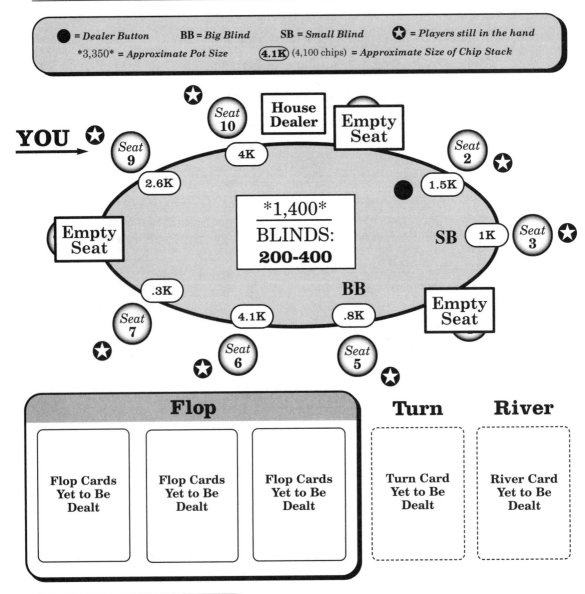

= Dealer Button   **BB** = *Big Blind*   **SB** = *Small Blind*   **= Players still in the hand**

3,350 = *Approximate Pot Size*   **4.1K** (4,100 chips) = *Approximate Size of Chip Stack*

YOU →

Seat 10   House Dealer   Empty Seat

Seat 9   4K   Seat 2

2.6K   1.5K

1,400
BLINDS:
200-400

Empty Seat

SB   1K   Seat 3

.3K   BB   Empty Seat

Seat 7   4.1K   .8K

Seat 6   Seat 5

Flop

| Flop Cards Yet to Be Dealt | Flop Cards Yet to Be Dealt | Flop Cards Yet to Be Dealt |

Turn

Turn Card Yet to Be Dealt

River

River Card Yet to Be Dealt

Pocket

4♦   4♠

Situation 4:

It's now well into the tourney (roughly half of the players have been knocked out) but your chip stack hasn't grown since your earlier success. You've received a pair of 4s in your pocket. Seats 6 and 7 both call the 400-chip big blind. Should you fold, call the bet, or raise to some unspecified level?

Starting Hand (Pocket): **4♦4♠**
This Pocket's Win Rate: **8.3%**
Win Rate Rank: **61 of 169 possible**

Tournament Situation:

Paid Entries: **40 x $25**

Starting Chip Stack: **1,000**

Players Remaining: **22**

Places Paid: **5**

Your Current Standing: **6th place overall, 3rd at your table**

Time Left in Round: **2 minutes**

Rebuys Allowed: **No**

Next Blind Level: **300-600**

This Tournament's Prize Money:

1. **$450**
2. **$250**
3. **$150**
4. **$100**
5. **$50**

Total Prize Pool:

$1000

Answer 4:

Technically, a pair of 4s is the eleventh ranked two-card hand that you could hold, but when you look at its relative win rate in the chart above against any other random hand, you'll notice that it only fares a meager sixty-first. What this should tell you is that your pocket pair of 4s is going to get steadily worse as the hand plays out. Your only realistic hope of winning this hand is to catch another 4 on the board, the odds of which are decidedly against you, and the blinds are high enough now that it's going to get expensive to chase another 4. And even if you do catch another 4, what good will it do you when one of the other four players already in the hand (or likely to be in the hand) hits their higher pair? Nothing. This hand in this situation is a classic setup for failure.

Yes, the blinds are starting to get to a painful level if you don't catch a hand, but a pair of 4s in this position is not a hand worth playing. Resist the temptation to play a small pair with this many opponents and in this position. Besides, the players in seats 10 and 2 could raise or go all in behind you, and then you'd be faced with the decision of going all in with a pair of 4s or losing your 400 chips. At this point, you still have time to catch a better hand.

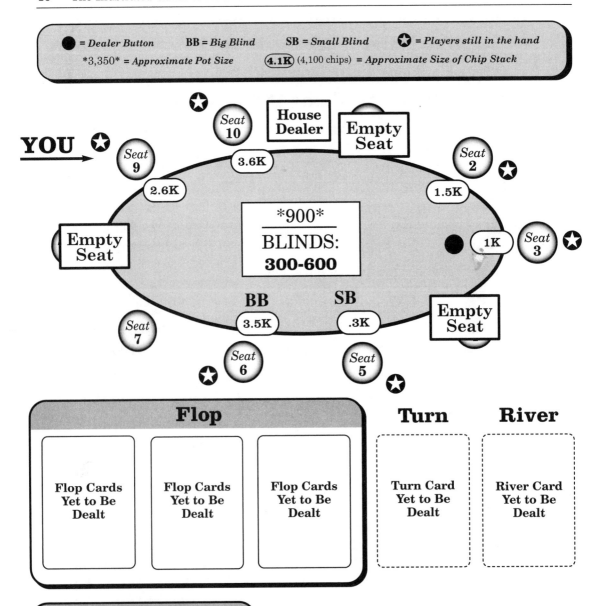

YOU →

Seat 10 — 3.6K

House Dealer

Empty Seat

Seat 2 — 1.5K

Seat 9 — 2.6K

Empty Seat

900
BLINDS:
300-600

1K — Seat 3

BB — 3.5K

SB — .3K

Empty Seat

Seat 7

Seat 6

Seat 5

Flop

| Flop Cards Yet to Be Dealt | Flop Cards Yet to Be Dealt | Flop Cards Yet to Be Dealt |

Turn

Turn Card Yet to Be Dealt

River

River Card Yet to Be Dealt

Pocket

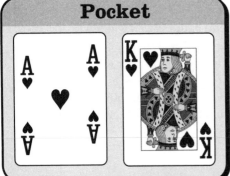

Situation 5:

On the very next hand after folding your pocket 4s you caught an Ace-King suited (see, I told you there was still time to catch a good hand!). Seat 7 folded and it's now your turn to act with five players yet to act after you. Should you fold, call the 600-chip big blind bet, raise to some unspecified level, or go all in?

Starting Hand (Pocket): **A♥K♥**

This Pocket's Win Rate: **68.6%**

Win Rate Rank: **3 of 169 possible**

Tournament Situation:

Paid Entrys: **40 x $25**

Starting Chip Stack: **1,000**

Players Remaining: **22**

Places Paid: **5**

Your Current Standing: **6th place overall, 3rd at your table**

Time Left in Round: **12 minutes**

Rebuys Allowed: **No**

Next Blind Level: **400-800**

This Tournament's Prize Money:

1. **$450**
2. **$250**
3. **$150**
4. **$100**
5. **$50**

Total Prize Pool:

$1000

Answer 5:

Ace-King suited is a very nice beginning, but you're not there yet, so in spite of how pretty your hand looks, you can't go crazy and go all in yet. You obviously are not going to fold this hand either, so it's a matter of what move you make that's between all in and folding. Ace-King suited means you have a shot at both an Ace-high flush and Ace-high straight. You also have a shot at top pair, whether it ends up being Aces or Kings, with a great kicker. The problem is, it doesn't always end up the way you want it, so the best move now would be to make a raise that will discourage the stupid hands from staying in (i.e., Ace-9 or lower, small pairs, mid-range suited connectors such as 9-8 of diamonds, etc.). If you don't hit your straight or flush, which will probably be the case, you're going to have to pair up your Ace or King in all likelihood. If you don't hit any of the hands possible for you, you're going to want to leave yourself an out in terms of chip stack, so a raise to 1,200 chips seems to be in order here. If no one raises you, then you can see the flop before committing any more chips. If you get raised in this situation, however, you'll be faced with having to fold and lose 1,200 chips, or calling, putting your tournament on the line with this hand.

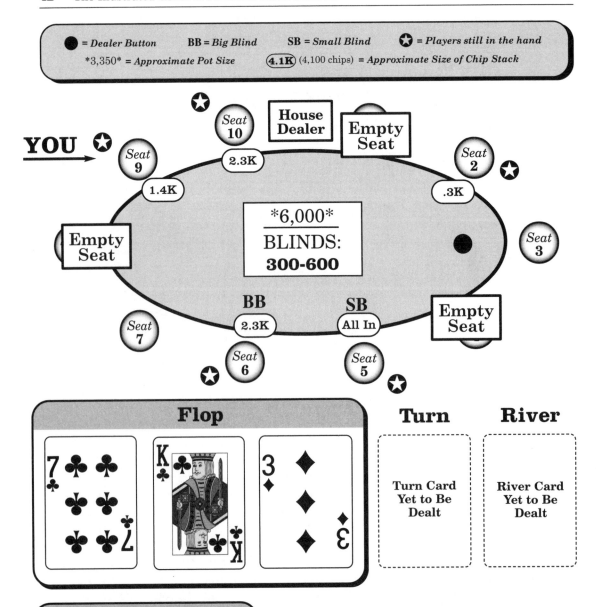

● = *Dealer Button*   **BB** = *Big Blind*   **SB** = *Small Blind*   ⭐ = *Players still in the hand*

3,350 = *Approximate Pot Size*   **4.1K** (4,100 chips) = *Approximate Size of Chip Stack*

YOU →

Seat 10   House Dealer   Empty Seat
2.3K

Seat 9   Seat 2
1.4K   .3K

Empty Seat

6,000
―――――――
BLINDS:
300-600

Seat 3

BB   SB   Empty Seat
2.3K   All In

Seat 7   Seat 6   Seat 5

Flop

7♣ K♣ 3♦

Turn

Turn Card Yet to Be Dealt

River

River Card Yet to Be Dealt

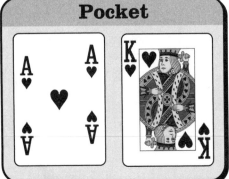

Pocket

A♥ K♥

Situation 6:

No one raised your 1,200-chip bet preflop, but you did get four callers. After the flop, Seat 5 checked (because he was all in) and Seat 6 bet 600 chips. It is now your turn to act with three players to act after you. Now facing the biggest pot of the tournament so far, should you fold, call the 600, raise to 1,200, or go all in?

Starting Hand (Pocket): **A♥K♥**
This Pocket's Win Rate: **68.6%**
Win Rate Rank: **3 of 169 possible**

Tournament Situation:

Paid Entrys: **40 x $25**

Starting Chip Stack: **1,000**

Players Remaining: **22**

Places Paid: **5**

Your Current Standing: **6th place overall, 3rd at your table**

Time Left in Round: **11 minutes**

Rebuys Allowed: **No**

Next Blind Level: **400-800**

This Tournament's Prize Money:

1. **$450**
2. **$250**
3. **$150**
4. **$100**
5. **$50**
_____

Total Prize Pool:
$1000

Answer 6:

Since this is the biggest pot of the tournament so far, your decision is critical. Okay, you've flopped top pair and you've got an Ace kicker. That's a nice hand. But what are you up against? A possible club flush draw, and that appears to be it, at least realistically. There's a remote chance that someone holds a pair of 3s, 7s, or Kings, but not too likely. Pocket Kings would have probably reraised you. Pocket 3s wouldn't have likely stayed in on your raise, if at all. Pocket 7s could be iffy, but not likely. Straight draws aren't there, unless someone was playing a 4-5 or 5-6, but again, not likely. No, it looks like this hand is going to come down to some combination of Kings and/or clubs.

If you just bet 600, it will leave you with only 800 chips, which will be eaten up by the two blinds in just a few hands. If you call, you could let a weak-kneed player limp in with one club who, if he catches another club on the turn, will get bolder.

As for me, I make my move right now and go all in with my remaining 1,400 chips and force the issue onto the other players. This is a significant pot and critical points (opportunities) like this one won't come along often in a tournament.

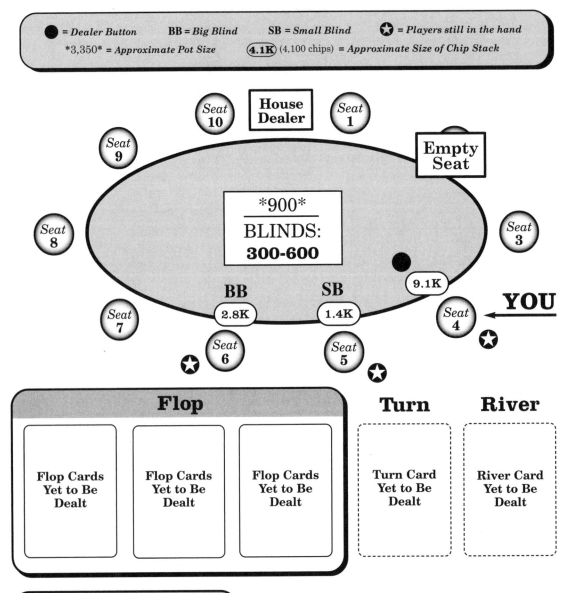

Seat 10   House Dealer   Seat 1

Seat 9   Empty Seat

900
———
BLINDS:
300-600

Seat 8   Seat 3

BB **2.8K**   SB **1.4K**   9.1K   **YOU**

Seat 7   Seat 6   Seat 5   Seat 4

Flop

| Flop Cards Yet to Be Dealt | Flop Cards Yet to Be Dealt | Flop Cards Yet to Be Dealt |

Turn

Turn Card Yet to Be Dealt

River

River Card Yet to Be Dealt

Pocket

Situation 7:

After winning the hand in Situation 6, you became the chip leader, then moved to a new table after the tournament condensed. Two hands later you received Queen-10 unsuited while on the button. Everyone folded to you. With only the blinds to act after you, should you fold, call the 600 big blind, raise to 1,200, or go all in, attempting to bully the blinds into folding with your much larger chip stack?

Starting Hand (Pocket): **Q♦10♠**
This Pocket's Win Rate: **9.3%**
Win Rate Rank: **51 of 169 possible**

Tournament Situation:
Paid Entrys: **40 x $25**
Starting Chip Stack: **1,000**
Players Remaining: **19**
Places Paid: **5**
Your Current Standing: **1st place**
   (chip leader)
Time Left in Round: **7 minutes**
Rebuys Allowed: **No**
Next Blind Level: **400-800**

This Tournament's Prize Money:

1. **$450**
2. **$250**
3. **$150**
4. **$100**
5. **$50**

_____

Total Prize Pool:
$1000

Answer 7:

This is one of those marginal plays in which your decision might come down to how well you know the other players still in the hand. With 9,100 chips, you have a heavy chip advantage over the two blinds, whose chip counts are 1,400 and 2,800. Part of playing a successful game of tournament Texas Hold'em is to push your opponents around (bully them) when you have a strong chip advantage. By betting more than their whole stack you force them to decide if they want to risk their entire tournament on a particular hand. If you know the players in the blinds are traditionally conservative, then a big raise by you will likely get them to fold. If you try this bullying ploy now with a weak hand like Queen-10 unsuited, the worst that will happen is you'll lose 3,400 chips if the big blind calls your all in bet and beats you. A sizeable number of chips, yes, but not the end of the world.

However, if you fold this hand, you'll remain the solid chip leader and maybe Seat 5 or Seat 6 will get knocked out on this hand and lower the remaining players to eighteen. Part of the reason for gaining a chip advantage is to use them to your advantage, such as in bullying. But it's also not prudent to risk nearly 40 percent of them on a weak hand. I would fold this hand.

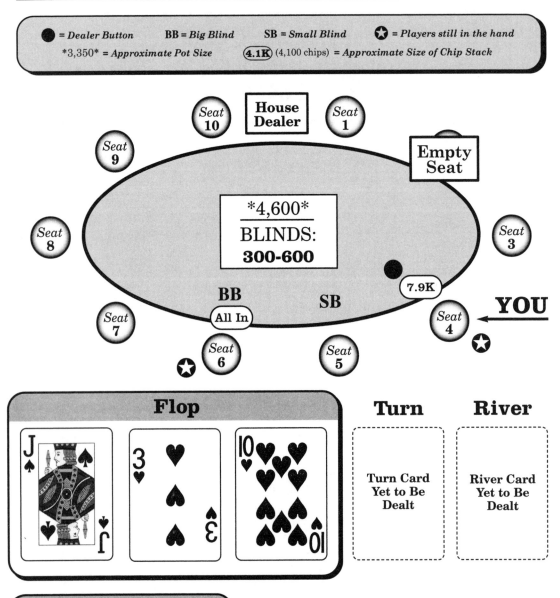

● = *Dealer Button*   BB = *Big Blind*   SB = *Small Blind*   ⭐ = *Players still in the hand*
3,350 = *Approximate Pot Size*   (**4.1K**) (4,100 chips) = *Approximate Size of Chip Stack*

Seat 10 | House Dealer | Seat 1

Empty Seat

Seat 9

4,600
BLINDS:
300-600

Seat 8

Seat 3

7.9K

YOU

BB   SB
All In   Seat 4 ⭐

Seat 7

Seat 6 ⭐   Seat 5

Flop

J♠ 3♥ 10♥

Turn

Turn Card Yet to Be Dealt

River

River Card Yet to Be Dealt

Pocket

Q♦ 10♠

Situation 8:

For some strange reason, you chose not to listen to me and fold the previous hand, nor did you choose to bully the blinds by going all in. Instead, you just called the 600-chip bet. After the flop, both Seats 5 and 6 checked, so you bet another 600. Seat 5 folded, but Seat 6 quickly went all in for 2,800. Now in a heads-up situation, and having been check-raised, should you fold or call the additional 2,200 chips?

Starting Hand (Pocket): **Q♦10♠**

This Pocket's Win Rate: **9.3%**

Win Rate Rank: **51 of 169 possible**

Tournament Situation:

Paid Entrys: **40 x $25**

Starting Chip Stack: **1,000**

Players Remaining: **19**

Places Paid: **5**

Your Current Standing: **1st place (chip leader)**

Time Left in Round: **7 minutes**

Rebuys Allowed: **No**

Next Blind Level: **400-800**

This Tournament's Prize Money:

1. **$450**
2. **$250**
3. **$150**
4. **$100**
5. **$50**

Total Prize Pool:

$1000

Answer 8:

Well, I must say, you got yourself into a sticky wicket by not folding this hand for free when you could have. Now you're in it 1,200 chips and facing a check-raise. So, what you have to do now is try and figure out what your opponent is check-raising on. Is it a total bluff on his part? Did he pair up his Jack? Did he pair up his 10 (just like you)? If so, how does your Queen kicker stand up against his kicker? Did he maybe flop a straight or flush draw? Maybe he holds an Ace-3 and paired up his 3s, and is now making a semibluff at you knowing that even if you have a pair of 10s or Jacks, he can catch an Ace on the turn or river and still beat you. Maybe he had pocket 3s and now has a set.

See what I mean by a sticky wicket? If only you'd have folded this hand when I told you to. Okay, let's deal with what we have. He went all in after the flop. I have to believe he either paired his Jack or his 10, holds two over-cards, like Ace-King/Queen, or King-Queen, or has a flush draw. He might even have an open-ended straight draw. If he hit a set of threes, he'd be laying a trap for you. Personally, I'd fold this hand and keep the 7,900 chips I still have and wait for a better hand/position to present itself. This hand is trouble.

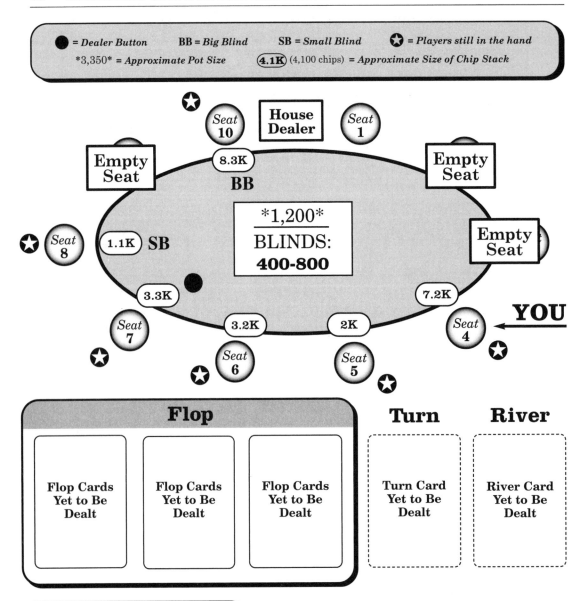

Situation 9:

You're deeper into the tournament now, with only fourteen players left (seven at each table). You received a King-4 suited in your pocket. Seat 1 was first to act and he folded. It is now your turn. Do you fold, call the 800-chip big blind bet, raise to some unspecified level, or go all in?

Starting Hand (Pocket): **K♦4♦**

This Pocket's Win Rate: **3.9%**

Win Rate Rank: **75 of 169 possible**

Tournament Situation:

Paid Entrys: **40 x $25**

Starting Chip Stack: **1,000**

Players Remaining: **14**

Places Paid: **5**

Your Current Standing: **2nd place overall, 2nd at your table**

Time Left in Round: **3 minutes**

Rebuys Allowed: **No**

Next Blind Level: **500-1,000**

This Tournament's Prize Money:

1. **$450**
2. **$250**
3. **$150**
4. **$100**
5. **$50**

Total Prize Pool:

$1000

Answer 9:

This should be a no-brainer, as the 3.9 percent relative win rate in the above chart suggests. But you would be surprised how many players will play a hand like this in an attempt to catch a flush. If you play a hand like this in this position, all I have to say is, *"Are you stuck on stupid?"* When you hold two cards of the same suit, like in this case, your odds of flopping two more of the same suit are about 11 percent. And you still need another diamond on either the turn or river to make your flush.

In reality, what you have here is a King with a lousy kicker. If you flop a King, then you have a pair of Kings with a lousy kicker which is easily beaten by many other King-something hands, or even Ace-something when an Ace comes on the board, and many players play Ace-anything in low-level tournaments like this.

The best thing you can do with this hand is fold it, and let the other guy play King-4 suited and put his tournament at risk.

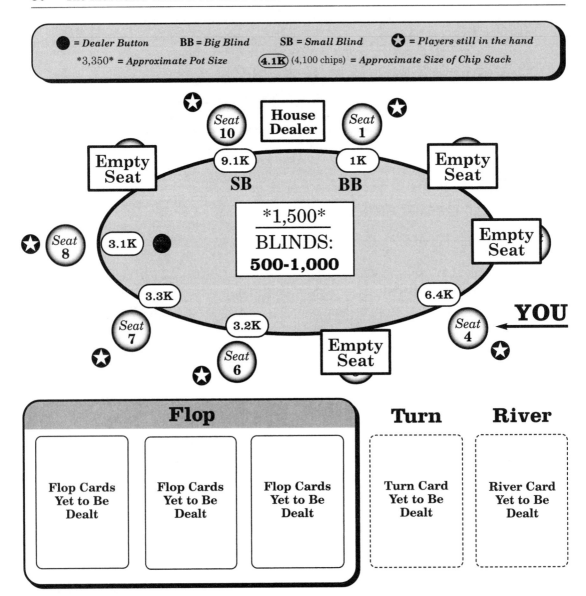

● = *Dealer Button*   **BB** = *Big Blind*   **SB** = *Small Blind*   ⭐ = *Players still in the hand*

3,350 = *Approximate Pot Size*   **4.1K** (4,100 chips) = *Approximate Size of Chip Stack*

House Dealer

Seat 10 — 9.1K — **SB**

Seat 1 — 1K — **BB**

Empty Seat

Empty Seat

Empty Seat

1,500
————
BLINDS:
500-1,000

Seat 8 — 3.1K

3.3K

3.2K

Seat 7

Seat 6

Empty Seat

6.4K

Seat 4 — **YOU**

Flop

| Flop Cards Yet to Be Dealt | Flop Cards Yet to Be Dealt | Flop Cards Yet to Be Dealt |

Turn

Turn Card Yet to Be Dealt

River

River Card Yet to Be Dealt

Pocket

Situation 10:

There are twelve players left in the tournament (six at each table). You received a pair of Jacks in your pocket and are first to act. Do you fold, call the 1,000-chip big blind bet, raise to some unspecified level, or go all in?

Starting Hand (Pocket): **J♠J♣**

This Pocket's Win Rate: **64.4%**

Win Rate Rank: **7 of 169 possible**

Tournament Situation:

Paid Entrys: **40 x $25**

Starting Chip Stack: **1,000**

Players Remaining: **12**

Places Paid: **5**

Your Current Standing: **3rd place overall, 2nd at your table**

Time Left in Round: **10 minutes**

Rebuys Allowed: **No**

Next Blind Level: **600-1,200**

This Tournament's Prize Money:

1. **$450**
2. **$250**
3. **$150**
4. **$100**
5. **$50**

Total Prize Pool:

$1000

Answer 10:

A pair of Jacks is the fourth highest pocket hand you could hold, but has only the seventh highest relative win rate, which means it starts strong, but gets knocked down a bit once the board play begins, since many players will play Aces, Kings, and Queens in various combinations.

Certainly you're not going to fold this hand, so what you have to decide is how aggressive to get. Unfortunately, you are in first position, so you have no information on what the other players are going to do. If you go all in now, Seats 6, 7, 8, and 1 will have to decide whether or not to risk their whole tournament on their hands. An all-in bet in first position indicates power—which you have—and they will likely fold unless they have a very good hand. The real problem for you is Seat 10, who has a larger chip stack. Whatever you can do, he can do better. Since you are starting to get fairly close to the money positions, I'd play this cautiously by either betting just 1,000 chips or raising only to 2,000. This gives you an out in case Seat 10 comes over the top of you and goes all in. At that point you can decide whether to fold and lose only 1,000 or 2,000 chips, or call his all-in bet.

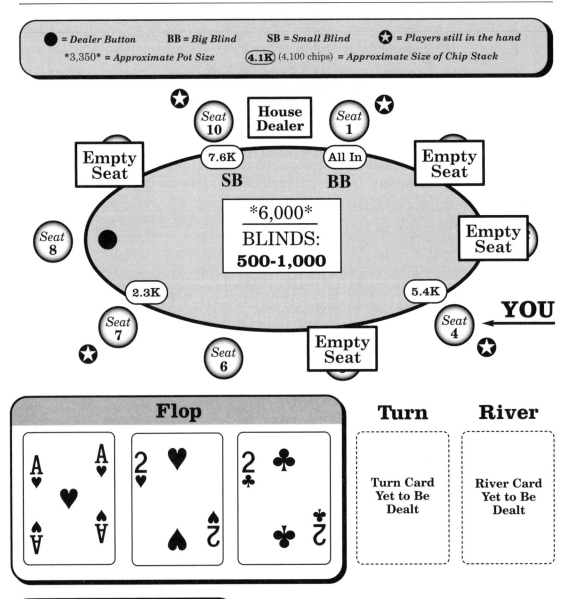

- = Dealer Button   BB = Big Blind   SB = Small Blind   ⭐ = Players still in the hand
- *3,350* = Approximate Pot Size   **4.1K** (4,100 chips) = Approximate Size of Chip Stack

Seat 10 — SB — 7.6K
House Dealer
Seat 1 — BB — All In
Empty Seat
Empty Seat

6,000
BLINDS:
500-1,000

Seat 8
Empty Seat
Seat 7 — 2.3K
Seat 6
Empty Seat
Seat 4 — 5.4K — **YOU**

Flop

A♥ 2♥ 2♣

Turn

Turn Card Yet to Be Dealt

River

River Card Yet to Be Dealt

Pocket

J♠ J♣

Situation 11:

You decided to bet just the minimum 1,000 and received three callers. After the flop, Seat 10 bet 1,000 and Seat 1 called, putting him all in. It is now your turn to act with only Seat 7 to act after you. Do you fold, call the 1,000-chip bet, raise to an unspecified level, or go all in?

Starting Hand (Pocket): **J♠J♣**
This Pocket's Win Rate: **64.4%**
Win Rate Rank: **7 of 169 possible**

Tournament Situation:

Paid Entrys: **40 x $25**

Starting Chip Stack: **1,000**

Players Remaining: **12**

Places Paid: **5**

Your Current Standing: **3rd place overall, 2nd at your table**

Time Left in Round: **8 minutes**

Rebuys Allowed: **No**

Next Blind Level: **600-1,200**

This Tournament's Prize Money:

1. **$450**
2. **$250**
3. **$150**
4. **$100**
5. **$50**

———

Total Prize Pool:

$1000

Answer 11:

This flop is a prime example of why a pair of Jacks falls in stature once the board play begins. You've got trouble facing you fourteen ways from Sunday after this flop. First, an Ace hit the board, the worst overcard you could have seen, and you have to believe at least one of your opponents holds an Ace, which means you're already beaten. Second, a pair of 2s arrived, and if anyone happened to stay in on Ace-2 suited, you can turn out the lights. Third, who knows what the big blind has, since he was forced to put in 1,000 chips and no one raised him out, so he could easily hold a 2 in his hand for a set. Fourth, two hearts hit the board, so a flush is a real possibility.

The Jacks were nice to see initially, but once the flop came they literally got destroyed. And if you don't believe it, what did Seats 10 and 1 bet on after this dangerous flop hit the board? You can bet it probably wasn't a pair of Jacks. They hit something workable, in all likelihood, and you didn't. Fold this hand now and limit your loss to the 1,000 chip preflop bet.

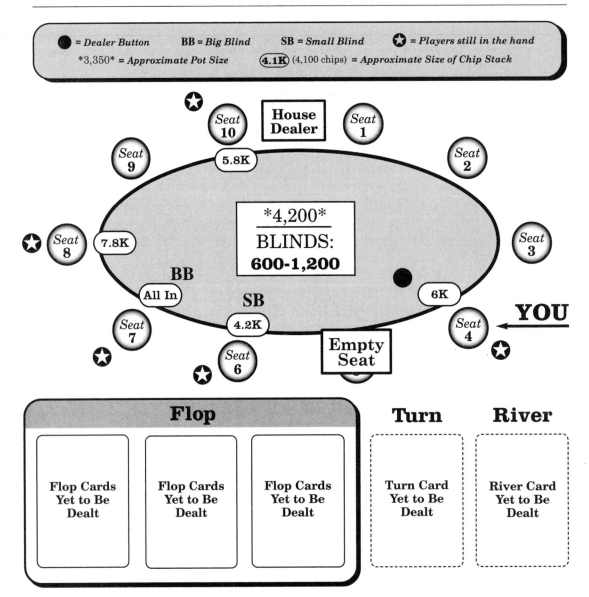

Pocket

Situation 12:

You are at the final table with only nine players left in the tournament. You are currently in third place in a closely contested game. You receive a pair of 8s in your pocket while in the button position. Seats 8 and 10 both called the 1,200 big blind bet, while Seats 9, 1, 2, and 3 all folded. It is now your turn to act. With only the two blinds to act after you, do you fold, call the 1,200, raise to an unspecified level, or go all in?

Starting Hand (Pocket): **8♠8♥**

This Pocket's Win Rate: **51.8%**

Win Rate Rank: **13 of 169 possible**

Tournament Situation:

Paid Entrys: **40 x $25**

Starting Chip Stack: **1,000**

Players Remaining: **9**

Places Paid: **5**

Your Current Standing: **3rd place overall; final table**

Time Left in Round: **4 minutes**

Rebuys Allowed: **No**

Next Blind Level: **800-1,600**

This Tournament's Prize Money:

1. **$450**
2. **$250**
3. **$150**
4. **$100**
5. **$50**

———

Total Prize Pool:

$1000

Answer 12:

At this point, you are solidly in the game, so you don't want to make any foolish mistakes that could lead to your suddenly being bounced from the tournament without any cash.

A pair of 8s is the seventh highest ranked hand, but only the thirteenth ranked hand in terms of relative win rate. This means that once the cards start coming on the board, a pair of 8s will diminish in value. There are already two callers in the hand and there will likely be two more (the two blinds) if you don't raise. If you were to go all in at this point, you might get the small blind to fold (the big blind is already all in), but the first two bettors, both of whom have projected strong hands, will likely call you. You are out of position for an all-in bet at this point, so the best course of action now would be to call the 1,200 and hope Seat 6 doesn't raise you, thereby letting you see the flop as cheaply as possible. With this many callers at this stage of the tournament and with this hand, it's best to play it safe.

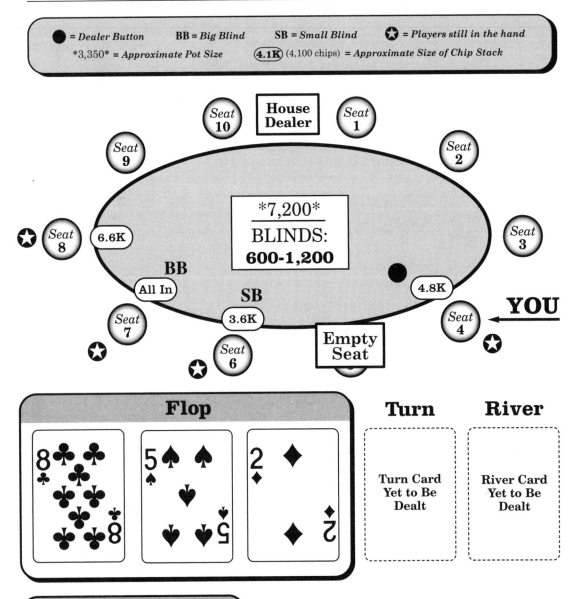

● = *Dealer Button*   **BB** = *Big Blind*   **SB** = *Small Blind*   ★ = *Players still in the hand*

3,350 = *Approximate Pot Size*   **4.1K** (4,100 chips) = *Approximate Size of Chip Stack*

Seat 10 | House Dealer | Seat 1

Seat 9

Seat 2

7,200
BLINDS:
600-1,200

★ Seat 8   6.6K

Seat 3

BB
All In

SB
3.6K

4.8K

YOU ←

Seat 7 ★

Seat 6 ★

Empty Seat

Seat 4 ★

Flop

8♣ 5♠ 2♦

Turn

Turn Card Yet to Be Dealt

River

River Card Yet to Be Dealt

Pocket

8♠ 8♥

Situation 13:

Before the flop, Seat 6 just called the 1,200 bet as well, making for five players in the hand. After the flop, Seat 6 checked, Seat 7 was already all in, Seat 8 bet 1,200 and Seat 10 folded. It is now your turn to act. With only Seat 6 to act behind you, do you fold, call the 1,200, raise to an unspecified level, or go all in?

Starting Hand (Pocket): **8♠8♥**
This Pocket's Win Rate: **51.8%**
Win Rate Rank: **13 of 169 possible**

Tournament Situation:
Paid Entrys: **40 x $25**
Starting Chip Stack: **1,000**
Players Remaining: **9**
Places Paid: **5**
Your Current Standing: **3rd place overall; final table**
Time Left in Round: **3 minutes**
Rebuys Allowed: **No**
Next Blind Level: **800-1,600**

This Tournament's Prize Money:

1. **$450**
2. **$250**
3. **$150**
4. **$100**
5. **$50**

Total Prize Pool:
$1000

Answer 13:

These are the rare situations you wait for in Texas Hold'em. You flopped the absolute nuts and you are on the button, meaning you get to act last following the flop, turn, and river. It doesn't matter what anyone else holds, with the flop that came, you have the best possible hand at this point. Now what you have to do is milk this hand for all it's worth. You also have to be mindful of turn and river cards that might make your hand second best. For example, if someone holds a pocket pair higher than your 8s and the turn or river brings them a third one, you're beat, although with the betting the way it was before the flop, there wasn't any real indication that one of the other callers held a powerful pair.

Given all this, I would just call Seat 8's bet of 1,200, hoping to keep Seat 6 in the hand. And, should Seat 6 raise you or go all in, you will be more than happy to oblige him by calling that bet.

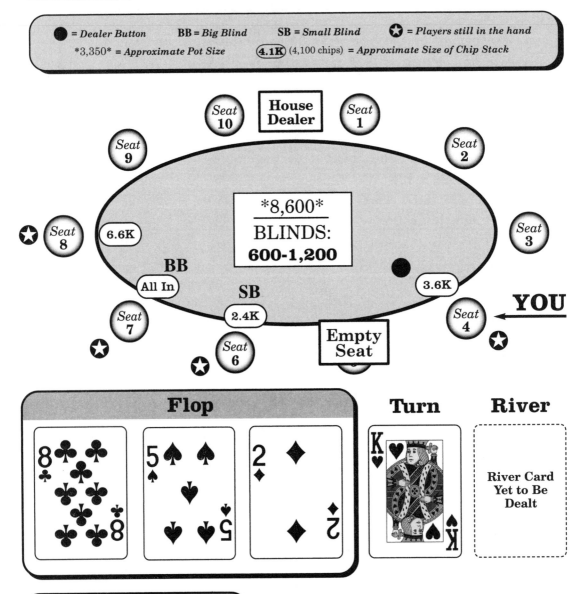

● = *Dealer Button*   **BB** = *Big Blind*   **SB** = *Small Blind*   ⭐ = *Players still in the hand*

3,350 = *Approximate Pot Size*   **4.1K** (4,100 chips) = *Approximate Size of Chip Stack*

Seat 10   House Dealer   Seat 1

Seat 9   Seat 2

Seat 8   6.6K   *8,600* BLINDS: 600-1,200   Seat 3

BB All In   SB 2.4K   3.6K   YOU

Seat 7   Empty Seat   Seat 4

Seat 6

Flop

8♣ 5♠ 2♦

Turn

K♥

River

River Card Yet to Be Dealt

Pocket

8♠ 8♥

Situation 14:

As you had hoped, Seat 6 called the previous bet and remained in the hand. After the King of hearts was dealt on the turn, Seat 6 checked, Seat 7 was still all in, and Seat 8 checked. It is now your turn to act with no one behind you. Should you check as well, raise to an unspecified level, or go all in?

Starting Hand (Pocket): **8♠8♥**
This Pocket's Win Rate: **51.8%**
Win Rate Rank: **13 of 169 possible**

Tournament Situation:
Paid Entrys: **40 x $25**
Starting Chip Stack: **1,000**
Players Remaining: **9**
Places Paid: **5**
Your Current Standing: **3rd place overall; final table**
Time Left in Round: **1 minute**
Rebuys Allowed: **No**
Next Blind Level: **800-1,600**

This Tournament's Prize Money:

1. **$450**
2. **$250**
3. **$150**
4. **$100**
5. **$50**

Total Prize Pool:
$1000

Answer 14:

When the King of hearts came on the turn, it eliminated the possibility of anyone making a flush on this hand, since all four suits have been exposed on the board. It also diminished the realistic possibility that anyone will make a straight on the river on this hand, since it would be hard to believe that someone played something like a 3-4, 6-7, or something similar before the flop that would make a straight out of this board.

Since both Seats 6 and 8 checked, either they have a King and are thinking about check-raising, or they don't have a King and it scared them. Right now, you hope that one or both of them do have a King with something besides an 8, 5, or 2 for two pair, or Ace-King, because if they do they're drawing dead, meaning that no matter what comes on the river they can't beat you. The only hand that can beat you at this point is pocket Kings, which no one has projected, and the only thing that can beat you on the river is a King if they hold two pair, Kings up. At this stage of the tournament, had someone held pocket Kings, they likely would have made a large bet or gone all in before or after the flop in order to keep someone else from potentially hitting a pair of Aces. So, just check and hope that either Seat 6 or 8 catches something on the river to help him out and which entices him to make a big bet, because if he does, you'll own him.

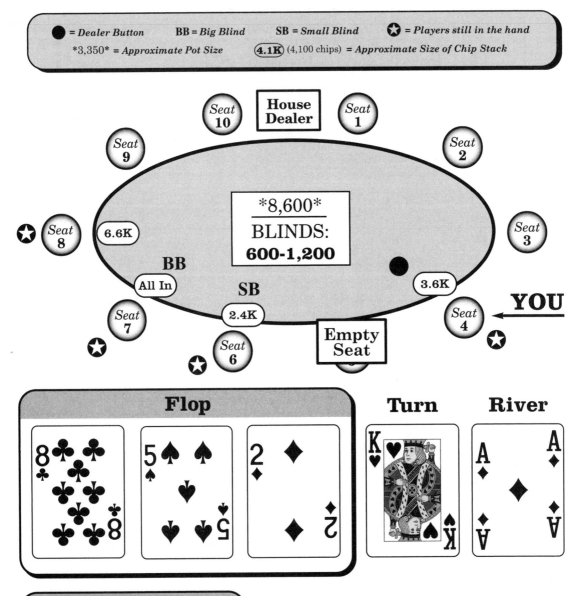

Situation 15:

After the Ace of diamonds came on the river, Seat 6 checked, Seat 7 was already all in, and Seat 8 checked. Do you check as well, being fearful of pocket Aces, raise to an unspecified level, or go all in?

Starting Hand (Pocket): **8♠8♥**

This Pocket's Win Rate: **51.8%**

Win Rate Rank: **13 of 169 possible**

Tournament Situation:

Paid Entrys: **40 x $25**

Starting Chip Stack: **1,000**

Players Remaining: **9**

Places Paid: **5**

Your Current Standing: **3rd place overall; final table**

Time Left in Round: **1 minute**

Rebuys Allowed: **No**

Next Blind Level: **800-1,600**

This Tournament's Prize Money:

1. **$450**
2. **$250**
3. **$150**
4. **$100**
5. **$50**

Total Prize Pool:

$1000

Answer 15:

It would be hard to imagine that someone held pocket Aces this long without betting them strong. Anyone holding pocket Aces should have been fearful of someone drawing out on them, especially at this stage of the tournament. And, when no Ace came on the flop or turn, it would have only heightened their anxiety that someone would draw out on them after being let in for little or no bets on the previous two rounds of betting.

Thus, it should be safe to assume that no one holds a set higher than your 8s. And, since there is no flush or straight possible with this five-card board, you likely hold the highest hand. Since everyone checked to you, the only way you are going to get any more money out of this hand is to bet something. If you go all in, you're likely to scare away both Seats 6 and 8. If you make a bet of 1,200, you might get one of them to call you if he had Ace-something in his hand, especially if he held a good kicker like a Queen or Jack. So, make the minimum bet of 1,200 and hope that you can entice at least one caller.

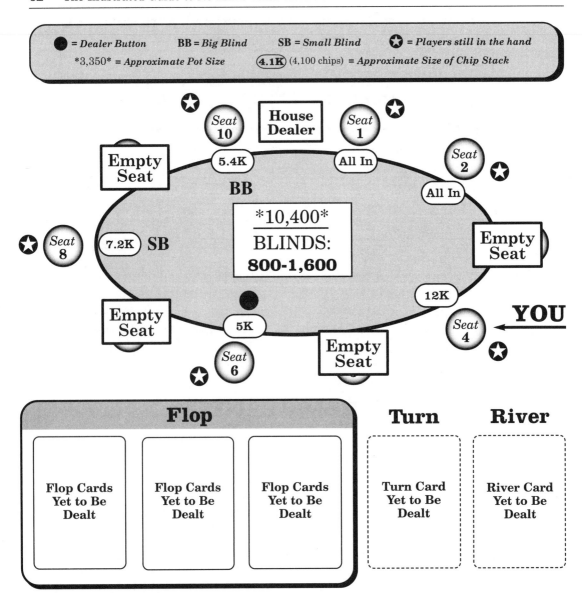

● = *Dealer Button*   BB = *Big Blind*   SB = *Small Blind*   ⭐ = *Players still in the hand*

3,350 = *Approximate Pot Size*   (**4.1K**) (4,100 chips) = *Approximate Size of Chip Stack*

House Dealer

Seat 10 — 5.4K

Seat 1 — All In

Seat 2 — All In

Empty Seat

BB

Empty Seat

10,400
BLINDS:
800-1,600

Seat 8 — 7.2K — SB

12K

YOU

Seat 4

Empty Seat

5K

Seat 6

Empty Seat

Flop

| Flop Cards Yet to Be Dealt | Flop Cards Yet to Be Dealt | Flop Cards Yet to Be Dealt |

Turn

Turn Card Yet to Be Dealt

River

River Card Yet to Be Dealt

Pocket

9♣ 9♥

Situation 16:

After a brisk turn around the table with little action, you, being the chip leader, catch a pair of 9s in your pocket. Seat 1 is first to bet and he goes all in for 3,000 chips. Seat 2 follows by going all in for 5,000 chips. It is now your turn to act. Do you fold your pocket 9s, call the 5,000-chip bet, raise to an unspecified level, or go all in as well?

Starting Hand (Pocket): **9♣9♥**

This Pocket's Win Rate: **55.4%**

Win Rate Rank: **11 of 169 possible**

Tournament Situation:

Paid Entrys: **40 x $25**

Starting Chip Stack: **1,000**

Players Remaining: **6**

Places Paid: **5**

Your Current Standing: **1st place**
   (chip leader)

Time Left in Round: **6 minutes**

Rebuys Allowed: **No**

Next Blind Level: **1,000-2,000**

This Tournament's Prize Money:

1. **$450**
2. **$250**
3. **$150**
4. **$100**
5. **$50**

———————

Total Prize Pool:
   $1000

Answer 16:

First of all, let's look at your hand. Your pocket 9s are the sixth highest ranked hand, but only the ninth highest in terms of their relative win rate. Again, this means that once the board cards start hitting, a pair of 9s will typically go down in value.

Now, let's consider what Seats 1 and 2 are doing. Seat 1 went all in for 3,000 chips. He may very well have a decent hand, but had he not played this hand he would have been facing losing almost all of his chips in the next two hands because of the blinds. This could just indicate that on this particular hand he has something only remotely decent, but something better than two as yet unseen blinds, and his all-in bet indicates he'd rather take his chances now rather than later. Seat 2, on the other hand, raised Seat 1 with an all-in bet of his own. It is much more likely that Seat 2 holds a better hand than Seat 1, a *real* hand, if you will. Certainly a pair of 9s is a good hand, but in lieu of two all-in bets in front of you, the fact that there are others to act behind you, and the fact that there are still six of you left in a game which will eventually pay only five places, I would fold this hand and let one or two of the other players take themselves out of the tourney on this hand, thereby clinching your position in the money.

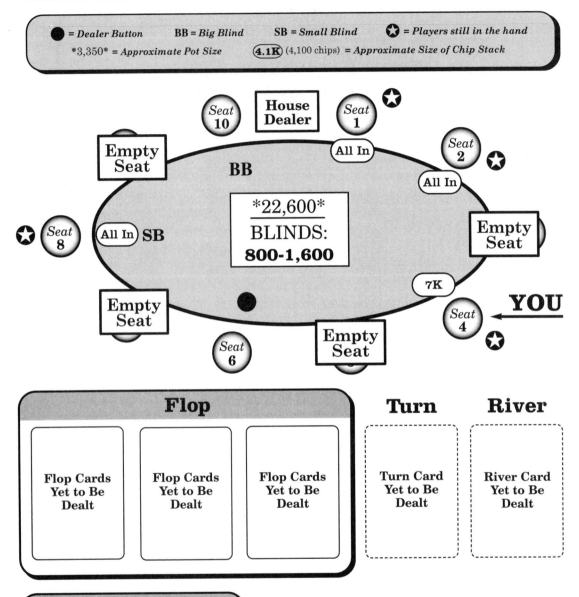

● = *Dealer Button*   BB = *Big Blind*   SB = *Small Blind*   ⭐ = *Players still in the hand*

3,350 = *Approximate Pot Size*   (4.1K) (4,100 chips) = *Approximate Size of Chip Stack*

22,600
BLINDS:
800-1,600

Flop

Flop Cards Yet to Be Dealt

Flop Cards Yet to Be Dealt

Flop Cards Yet to Be Dealt

Turn

Turn Card Yet to Be Dealt

River

River Card Yet to Be Dealt

Pocket

Situation 17:

In spite of my recommendation, you decided to call the 5,000 bet with your pair of 9s. Seat 6 folded, Seat 8 then went all in for 7,200 chips, and Seat 10 folded. Since Seats 1 and 2 were both already all in, it is now your turn to act again. Do you fold, forfeiting your initial 5,000-chip bet, or call the additional 2,200 chips?

Starting Hand (Pocket): **9♣9♥**
This Pocket's Win Rate: **55.4%**
Win Rate Rank: **11 of 169 possible**

Tournament Situation:
Paid Entrys: **40 x $25**
Starting Chip Stack: **1,000**
Players Remaining: **6**
Places Paid: **5**
Your Current Standing: **1st place
(chip leader)**
Time Left in Round: **5 minutes**
Rebuys Allowed: **No**
Next Blind Level: **1,000-2,000**

*This Tournament's
Prize Money:*

1. **$450**
2. **$250**
3. **$150**
4. **$100**
5. **$50**

Total Prize Pool:
$1000

Answer 17:

Well, there's no doubt about it, this is *the* critical hand of the tournament. Instead of sitting back and watching three or four other players cannibalize themselves, you chose to jump into the fray with your pair of 9s against three opponents. Now what you are faced with is the proposition of betting 2,200 chips in order to win more than 22,000 chips, more than half of all the chips in the tournament. You can't fold now because the pot odds are too good at 11-to-1 and the winner of this hand will have a stranglehold on the tournament. Go ahead and call the bet at this point because it's proper, even though you shouldn't have found yourself in this situation to begin with. I don't know about you, but I'm getting an uneasy feeling about this hand.

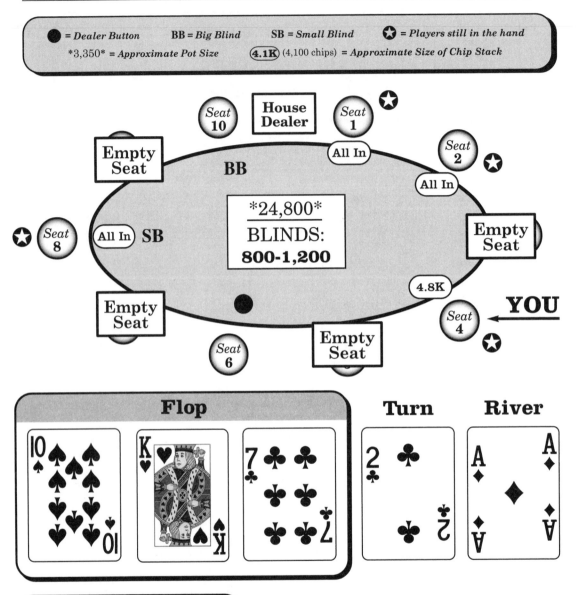

Situation 18:

Once you called the 2,200 raise dictated by Seat 8's all-in bet, the betting was completed for the rest of this hand because three of the four players contesting the pot were all in (Seats 8, 1, and 2).

Starting Hand (Pocket): **9♣9♥**
This Pocket's Win Rate: **55.4%**
Win Rate Rank: **11 of 169 possible**

Tournament Situation:
Paid Entrys: **40 x $25**
Starting Chip Stack: **1,000**
Players Remaining: **6**
Places Paid: **5**
Your Current Standing: **1st place**
   (chip leader)
Time Left in Round: **4 minutes**
Rebuys Allowed: **No**
Next Blind Level: **1,000-2,000**

This Tournament's Prize Money:

1. **$450**
2. **$250**
3. **$150**
4. **$100**
5. **$50**

_____

Total Prize Pool:
$1000

Answer 18:

Since all betting was completed for the remainder of the hand, all the dealer had to do was deal out the five board cards and declare the winner. In this case, which was drawn from an actual hand I was involved in, Seat 8 turned over big slick for two pair, Seat 2 turned over an Ace-Queen of clubs for a pair of Aces with a busted flush draw, and Seat 1—*remember Seat 1 in his desperation position?*—turned over a Queen-Jack unsuited for a straight to capture the hand, at least the portion he could with his 3,000-chip bet.

Seat 8 became the new chip leader at 12,800, with Seat 1 right on his heels at 12,000. Seats 10 and 6, neither of whom played the hand, are now third and fourth with 5,400 and 5,000 respectively. Seat 2 got knocked out leaving you in fifth place with 4,800 chips. Now how do you feel about playing a mid-level pair in the face of two raises before you?

Part of becoming a winning Texas Hold'em player is knowing when to get out of the way of others who are willing to fight it out when they're on the money bubble, which is what you all were before the hand: six players left with five money positions. You need to recognize those times when folding a hand, no matter how good it may be, is better than playing it. This was one of those cases.

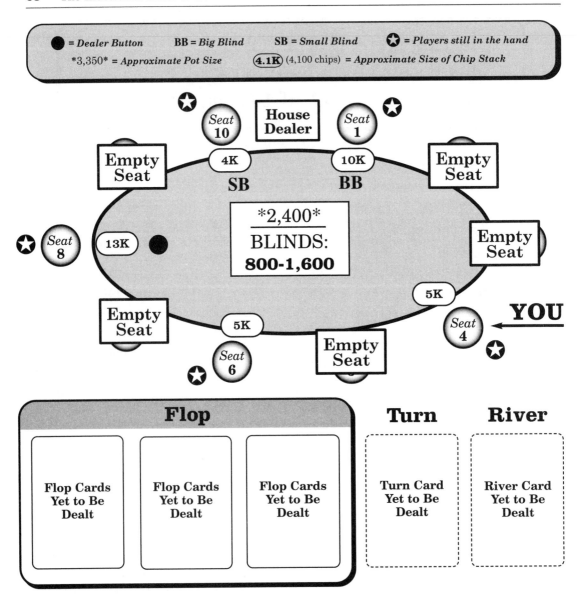

= *Dealer Button*   **BB** = *Big Blind*   **SB** = *Small Blind*   ⭐ = *Players still in the hand*

3,350 = *Approximate Pot Size*   **4.1K** (4,100 chips) = *Approximate Size of Chip Stack*

Seat 10

House Dealer

Seat 1

Empty Seat

4K

SB

10K

BB

Empty Seat

2,400
BLINDS:
800-1,600

Seat 8

13K

Empty Seat

5K

YOU

Empty Seat

5K

Seat 4

Seat 6

Empty Seat

Flop

| Flop Cards Yet to Be Dealt | Flop Cards Yet to Be Dealt | Flop Cards Yet to Be Dealt |

Turn

Turn Card Yet to Be Dealt

River

River Card Yet to Be Dealt

Pocket

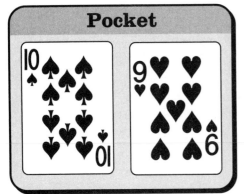

Situation 19:

You've made it into the money, despite the tough loss on the hand before. You have received a hand of 10-9 unsuited in the pocket and are first to act. You also have the smallest stack at the table with just 4,800 chips. Should you fold, call the 1,600 big blind bet, raise to some unspecified level, or go all in?

Starting Hand (Pocket): **10♠9♥**
This Pocket's Win Rate: **8.8%**
Win Rate Rank: **55 of 169 possible**

Tournament Situation:
Paid Entrys: **40 x $25**
Starting Chip Stack: **1,000**
Players Remaining: **5**
Places Paid: **5**
Your Current Standing: **5th place overall,**
 in the money
Time Left in Round: **2 minutes**
Rebuys Allowed: **No**
Next Blind Level: **1,000-2,000**

This Tournament's Prize Money:

1. **$450**
2. **$250**
3. **$150**
4. **$100**
5. **$50**

———

Total Prize Pool:
$1000

Answer 19:

Clearly you are in a tough position. You've got the smallest stack on the table and you caught a hand that is less than desirable. If you call the 1,600 bet, you'll be risking at least one-third of your chips on this hand, and if someone raises, you'll likely be making your tournament stand on these two cards. Your option is to fold and wait for the next hand in which case you will be the big blind.

Again, you are in a bad spot here. Even though a 10-9 unsuited has a chance of becoming a straight, I'd toss this one away and wait for the big blind, hoping to at least catch an Ace or King. Besides, you don't know what's going to happen after you, and in this case I wouldn't be putting my focus on what the other players would do behind me if I played this hand, I'd be focusing more on hoping that two of them lock horns and go all in and maybe one of them will knock out the other, thereby raising me one spot in the money without even playing. So, fold this hand, hope two players go after each other, and cross your fingers for something to fight with on the next hand.

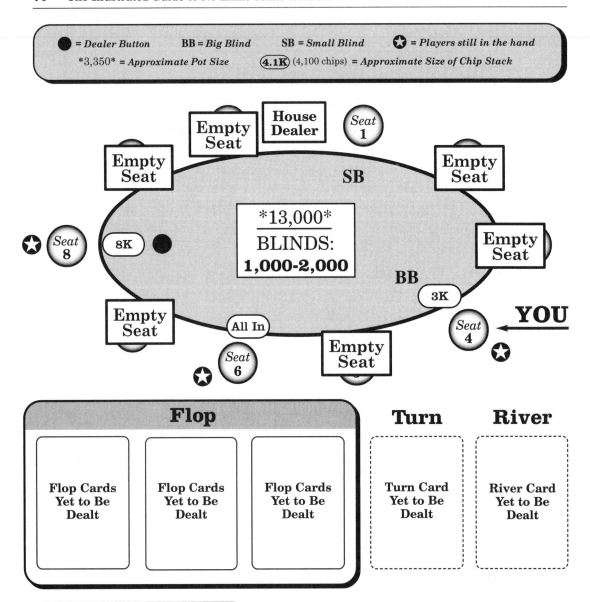

● = *Dealer Button*   **BB** = *Big Blind*   **SB** = *Small Blind*   ⭐ = *Players still in the hand*
3,350 = *Approximate Pot Size*   (**4.1K**) (4,100 chips) = *Approximate Size of Chip Stack*

House Dealer

Empty Seat

Empty Seat

Seat 1

Empty Seat

SB

Empty Seat

13,000
BLINDS:
1,000-2,000

Seat 8   8K   ●

Empty Seat

BB   3K

Empty Seat

All In

YOU

Seat 4

Empty Seat

Seat 6

Empty Seat

Flop

| Flop Cards Yet to Be Dealt | Flop Cards Yet to Be Dealt | Flop Cards Yet to Be Dealt |

Turn

Turn Card Yet to Be Dealt

River

River Card Yet to Be Dealt

Pocket

Situation 20:

As you had hoped, two players got into it on the hand before and Seat 10 was knocked out, thereby moving you up another notch in the money. You are now in the big blind position and have been dealt King-4 suited. Seat 6 was first to act and went all in for 5,000 chips. Seat 8 called and Seat 1 folded. It is now your turn to act. Do you fold or call the all-in bet with your remaining 3,000 chips?

Starting Hand (Pocket): **K♦4♦**
This Pocket's Win Rate: **3.9%**
Win Rate Rank: **75 of 169 possible**

Tournament Situation:
Paid Entrys: **40 x $25**
Starting Chip Stack: **1,000**
Players Remaining: **4**
Places Paid: **5**
Your Current Standing: **4th place overall,
in the money**
Time Left in Round: **10 minutes**
Rebuys Allowed: **No**
Next Blind Level: **1,500-3,000**

*This Tournament's
Prize Money:*

1. **$450**
2. **$250**
3. **$150**
4. **$100**
5. **$50**

———————

Total Prize Pool:
$1000

Answer 20:

Don't be deceived by the two diamonds in your hand. Your odds of flopping two more diamonds to give you a four-flush and at least a shot at a flush are 8-1. And then you still have to catch another diamond on either the turn or river.

Yes, 40 percent of your chips went into the pot already, but more important than your hand, however, is your position and what has happened in front of you. Seat 6, who had about the same number of chips you did, went all in and was called by Seat 8 who had enough to cover the bet. Seat 6 is facing the big blind on the next hand, so he might not have the best hand in the world to have gone all in on, figuring that this one was better than an unknown one. This means there is a realistic shot that Seat 8 has a better hand, which then means that Seat 8 could very well knock out Seat 6, and you'll move up another position in the money...without even playing! This is a crucial aspect of no-limit tournament play. If you can move up without playing, do so. Like my Grandma Gracie used to say, "If you can skin a cat without getting the room all bloody, why not do it that way?" Fold this hand and hope that, once again, one player takes out another, and improves your money situation.

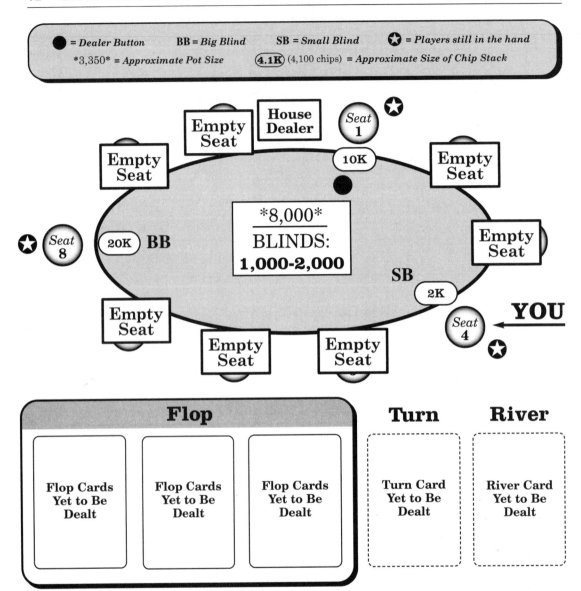

Situation 21:

Seat 6 got knocked out in the previous hand, moving you one rung higher on the payout ladder. With only three players left you are in the small blind position and are at a decided chip disadvantage to both Seats 1 and 8. You are dealt King-9 unsuited in your pocket. Seat 1 is first to act and bets 5,000 chips. Do you fold or go all in with your remaining 2,000 chips?

Starting Hand (Pocket): **K♣9♠**
This Pocket's Win Rate: **8.2%**
Win Rate Rank: **62 of 169 possible**

Tournament Situation:
Paid Entries: **40 x $25**
Starting Chip Stack: **1,000**
Players Remaining: **3**
Places Paid: **5**
Your Current Standing: **3rd place overall, in the money**
Time Left in Round: **8 minutes**
Rebuys Allowed: **No**
Next Blind Level: **1,500-3,000**

This Tournament's Prize Money:

1. **$450**
2. **$250**
3. **$150**
4. **$100**
5. **$50**

Total Prize Pool:
$1000

Answer 21:

King-9 unsuited is not the best hand in Texas Hold'em, to be sure, but in a short-handed game like this, it's not the worst hand you could have drawn. Also, you are almost out of chips and if you don't play this hand, then the big blind is coming in two hands and you'll play that one regardless, even if it's 7-2 unsuited.

So, considering the odds of the garbage you're likely to catch in the next two hands (one free one and then the big blind), take a deep breath and go all in with your remaining 2,000 chips and hope that the King can bail you out. With a 9 kicker, you even have a remote chance for a straight. Obviously this is not a hand you would play under normal circumstances, but the sand is nearly out of your tournament hourglass.

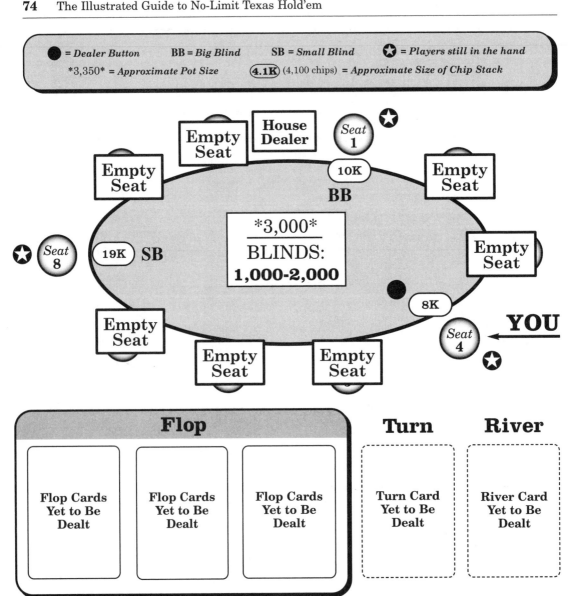

● = *Dealer Button*   BB = *Big Blind*   SB = *Small Blind*   ★ = *Players still in the hand*

3,350 = *Approximate Pot Size*   **4.1K** (4,100 chips) = *Approximate Size of Chip Stack*

Empty Seat · House Dealer · Seat 1 ★ · 10K · BB

Empty Seat · Empty Seat

Empty Seat · Empty Seat

Seat 8 ★ · 19K · SB

3,000 BLINDS: 1,000-2,000

Empty Seat · 8K · Seat 4 ★ · **YOU**

Empty Seat · Empty Seat · Empty Seat

Flop

| Flop Cards Yet to Be Dealt | Flop Cards Yet to Be Dealt | Flop Cards Yet to Be Dealt |

Turn

Turn Card Yet to Be Dealt

River

River Card Yet to Be Dealt

Pocket

Situation 22:

Seat 8 folded the previous hand to get out of the way and you prevailed when you paired a 9 after Seat 1 revealed big slick, which went unimproved. You are now back in the hunt and received a pair of Queens in your pocket while on the button. Do you fold, call the 2,000 big blind bet, raise to 4,000 chips, or go all in for 8,000 chips?

Starting Hand (Pocket): **Q♥Q♠**
This Pocket's Win Rate: **68.5%**
Win Rate Rank: **4 of 169 possible**

Tournament Situation:
Paid Entrys: **40 x $25**
Starting Chip Stack: **1,000**
Players Remaining: **3**
Places Paid: **5**
Your Current Standing: **3rd place overall,
    in the money**
Time Left in Round: **5 minutes**
Rebuys Allowed: **No**
Next Blind Level: **1,500-3,000**

*This Tournament's
Prize Money:*

1. **$450**
2. **$250**
3. **$150**
4. **$100**
5. **$50**

Total Prize Pool:
$1000

Answer 22:

Now is not the time to get cute with this powerful hand by calling the 2,000 bet in an attempt to slow play it. You could easily let a player in with Ace-something or King-something, or even a small pair if they are allowed to get in cheaply, which would allow them to hit a set or higher pair and beat you. If you're determined to play it conservatively and only put at risk the minimum number of chips, bet the 2,000 with the intent of folding if you get raised with an all-in bet. Right now, though, you have the *probable* best hand, so my advice would be to make your opponents pay and not give them the opportunity to draw out on you for a small bet. Go all in for your remaining 8,000 chips and make them pay to play. If they don't, you'll pick up 3,000 in blind money which you can use to ride out a few more hands.

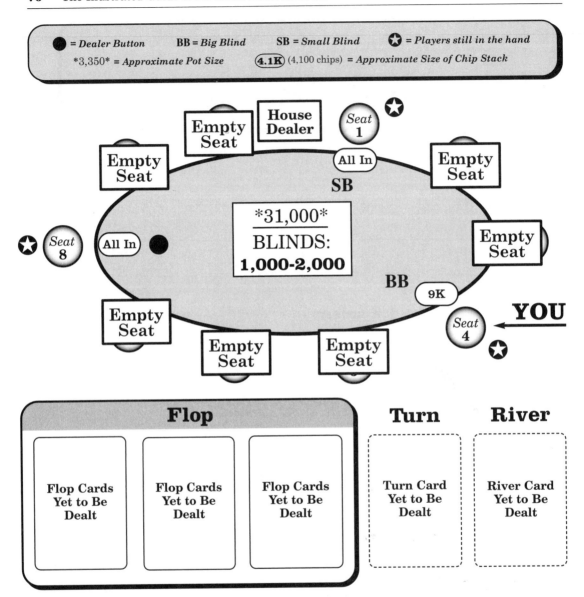

● = *Dealer Button*   **BB** = *Big Blind*   **SB** = *Small Blind*   ⭐ = *Players still in the hand*

3,350 = *Approximate Pot Size*   (**4.1K**) (4,100 chips) = *Approximate Size of Chip Stack*

31,000
BLINDS:
1,000-2,000

Flop

Flop Cards Yet to Be Dealt

Flop Cards Yet to Be Dealt

Flop Cards Yet to Be Dealt

Turn

Turn Card Yet to Be Dealt

River

River Card Yet to Be Dealt

Pocket

Situation 23:

Both of your opponents folded the previous hand and you picked up their blinds. Now in the big blind position, you have caught a pair of Kings. Seat 8 is first to act and goes all in for 19,000 chips. Seat 1 then calls with his 9,000 chips. Do you fold, forfeiting the 2,000 chips you placed in the big blind, or do you call by going all in as well?

Starting Hand (Pocket): **K♦K♥**
This Pocket's Win Rate: **74.6%**
Win Rate Rank: **2 of 169 possible**

Tournament Situation:
Paid Entrys: **40 x $25**
Starting Chip Stack: **1,000**
Players Remaining: **3**
Places Paid: **5**
Your Current Standing: **2nd place overall,**
   in the money
Time Left in Round: **4 minutes**
Rebuys Allowed: **No**
Next Blind Level: **1,500-3,000**

This Tournament's Prize Money:

1. **$450**
2. **$250**
3. **$150**
4. **$100**
5. **$50**

———

Total Prize Pool:
$1000

Answer 23:

For many of you, this might seem to be a no-brainer. A pair of Kings is the second best pocket hand possible in Texas Hold'em, and at this stage of a short-handed game you've got to call, right?

Not necessarily. Think about it. Seat 8 went all in and Seat 1 called. If you fold your pair of Kings, Seat 8 might take out Seat 1, thereby elevating you to a guaranteed finish of at least second place, another $100 bump in the prize money. On the other hand, if you jump in now and win, you'll take out one opponent and have a 3-to-1 chip advantage.

You should also consider that if you do play this hand, you'll have to beat two opponents, not one, and they both projected power in front of you. With two opponents instead of one, your odds of getting drawn out on double. It's likely that at least one if not both of your opponents holds an Ace, and if you don't catch a third King, a pair of Aces will knock you out. Granted, you can't run scared late in a tournament, but if you fold this hand now, you have a 50-50 shot of advancing in the money. Had only one player acted before you, then I would say you should jump in all the way, but since both went all in before you, I'd fold this hand.

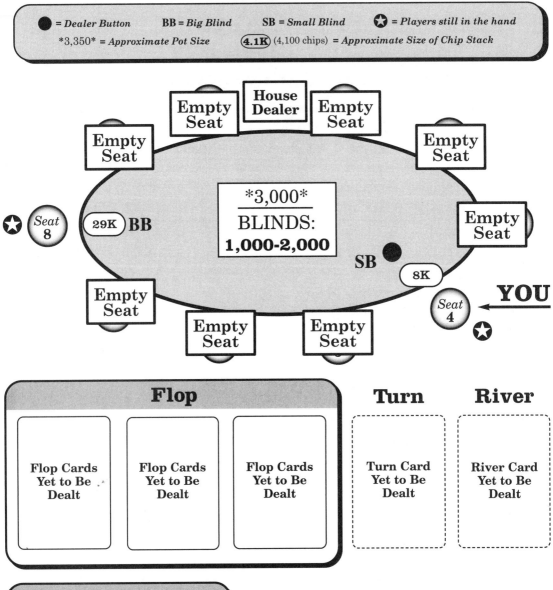

● = *Dealer Button*   BB = *Big Blind*   SB = *Small Blind*   ⭐ = *Players still in the hand*

3,350 = *Approximate Pot Size*   **4.1K** (4,100 chips) = *Approximate Size of Chip Stack*

House Dealer

Empty Seat

Empty Seat

Empty Seat

Empty Seat

Empty Seat

Empty Seat

Empty Seat

Empty Seat

Empty Seat

29K BB

⭐ *Seat 8*

3,000
———
BLINDS:
1,000-2,000

SB ●

8K

YOU ←

Seat 4 ⭐

Flop

| Flop Cards Yet to Be Dealt | Flop Cards Yet to Be Dealt | Flop Cards Yet to Be Dealt |

Turn

Turn Card Yet to Be Dealt

River

River Card Yet to Be Dealt

Pocket

| Pocket Cards Yet to Be Dealt | Pocket Cards Yet to Be Dealt |

Situation 24:

Seat 8 did indeed take out Seat 1 when he made a pair of Aces on the turn, and the tournament is now heads-up between you and Seat 8, and he holds about a 3-to-1 chip advantage. Before the hand is dealt, Seat 8 offers you a deal to split the pot $425- $275 if you agree to end the tournament now. Should you accept or respectfully decline his offer?

Starting Hand (Pocket): **X - X**
This Pocket's Win Rate: **----%**
Win Rate Rank: **X of 169 possible**

Tournament Situation:
Paid Entrys: **40 x $25**
Starting Chip Stack: **1,000**
Players Remaining: **2**
Places Paid: **5**
Your Current Standing: **2nd place overall, in the money**
Time Left in Round: **1 minute**
Rebuys Allowed: **No**
Next Blind Level: **1,500-3,000**

This Tournament's Prize Money:

1. **$450**
2. **$250**
3. **$150**
4. **$100**
5. **$50**

Total Prize Pool:
$1000

Answer 24:

Deals to split the pot between the final two players (and often between the final three or four players) are often made. The motivation for the offered deals can vary. Sometimes you run into a friendly chip leader who offers to make the deal so he can go home, join in a ring (live) game, because he's tired, etc. You should base your decision on accepting an offer upon your own realistic assessment of your chances as well as your own desires to end the tournament session. You could also counter with a $400-$300 split, he might accept it.

In this case, if you play it out, the winner will get $450 and the loser will get $250, a $200 difference. He does hold a chip advantage over you of slightly more than 3-to-1. While you might be inclined to accept this offer given his chip advantage, if you decided to play it out, you are only one all-in hand away from being basically even, so it wouldn't be a wrong decision either way. Again, assess your own reasons for accepting the deal or not and go from there. In small nightly tournaments such as this, I've found that there is limited space in the ring games that begin as players are knocked out of the tournament, and I might base my decision on whether or not I could immediately get into a ring game or if I'd have to wait. If I had to wait for a chair in a ring game, I wouldn't accept the deal, and if accepting the deal got me one of the last chairs available in a ring game, I might.

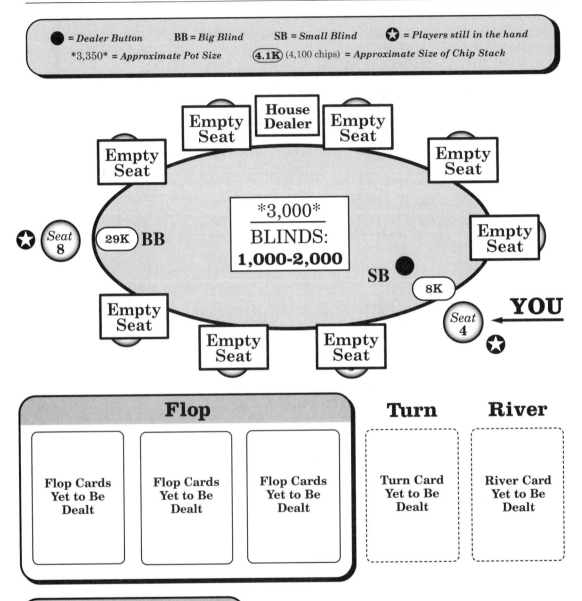

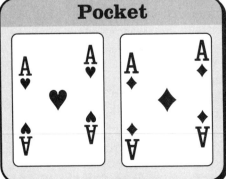

Situation 25:

You decided not to accept his offer, choosing rather to play on and were dealt pocket Aces, continuing your rush of powerful hands late in the tournament. You are first to act. Do you fold, call the 2,000 big blind bet by placing another 1,000 chips into the pot, raise to an unspecified level, or go all in for 8,000 more chips?

Starting Hand (Pocket): A♥A♦
This Pocket's Win Rate: **86.1%**
Win Rate Rank: **1 of 169 possible**

Tournament Situation:
Paid Entrys: **40 x $25**
Starting Chip Stack: **1,000**
Players Remaining: **2**
Places Paid: **5**
Your Current Standing: **2nd place overall, in the money**
Time Left in Round: **1 minute**
Rebuys Allowed: **No**
Next Blind Level: **1,500-3,000**

This Tournament's Prize Money:

1. **$450**
2. **$250**
3. **$150**
4. **$100**
5. **$50**

Total Prize Pool:
$1000

Answer 25:

Obviously you aren't going to fold this hand. The question is how to play it. If you just call and your opponent has a weak hand, you're giving him an opportunity to draw out on you. If you go all in, you might scare him out and all you'll win is his blind money. If you go halfway and raise to 4,000, he might stay in.

Personally, if I were in this position of a 3-to-1 chip disadvantage, I'd just call and try and trap him for more chips. If I held the chip lead, I'd go all in and make sure I forced his hand, and if I only won his blind it would be okay, in effect using my big stack to bully him.

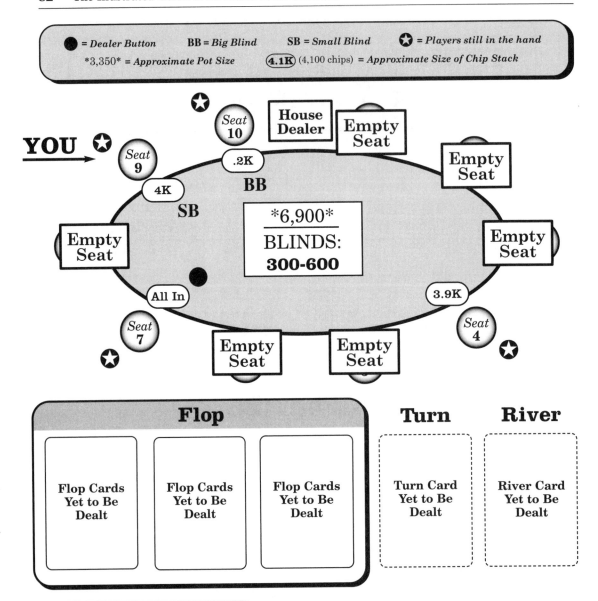

● = Dealer Button   BB = Big Blind   SB = Small Blind   ★ = Players still in the hand
3,350 = Approximate Pot Size   (4.1K) (4,100 chips) = Approximate Size of Chip Stack

YOU →

Seat 10   House Dealer   Empty Seat
Seat 9   Empty Seat
.2K   Empty Seat
4K   BB
SB
Empty Seat   *6,900* BLINDS: 300-600   Empty Seat
All In   3.9K
Seat 7   Empty Seat   Empty Seat   Seat 4

Flop

| Flop Cards Yet to Be Dealt | Flop Cards Yet to Be Dealt | Flop Cards Yet to Be Dealt |

Turn

Turn Card Yet to Be Dealt

River

River Card Yet to Be Dealt

Pocket

Situation 26:

You are now in the later stage of another tournament.

Seat 4, who is first to act, folds. Seat 7 goes all in for 6,000 chips. You, holding a pocket pair of 10s, have 300 chips invested in the small blind and it is now your turn to act with only the big blind to act behind you. Given the tournament situation presented above and on the opposite page, what do you do?

> ## Starting Hand (Pocket): **10♣10♦**
> ## This Pocket's Win Rate: **60.8%**
> ## Win Rate Rank: **8 of 169 possible**

Tournament Situation:
Tourney: **1-Table Sit 'n Go, Internet**
Paid Entrys: **10 x $30**
Starting Chip Stack: **1,500**
Players Remaining: **4**
Places Paid: **3**
Your Current Standing: **2nd place overall, in the money**
Time Left in Round: **5 minutes**
Rebuys Allowed: **No**
Next Blind Level: **400-800**

This Tournament's Prize Money:

1. **$150**
2. **$90**
3. **$60**

Total Prize Pool:
$1000

Answer 26:

A pair of 10s in the pocket is a very good hand indeed, but should you play it? In the situation given above, you see that you are involved in a single table sit 'n' go tournament. A sit 'n' go tournament is one in which as soon as the required number of participants have entered, the tournament begins. Usually this is one table, but occasionally it is two or three tables, sometimes more.

You'll notice that this sit 'n' go tourney pays three places out of the ten original entries, a very common format for sit 'n' go tourneys. There are still four players left, and only three will make the money. Seat 4 folded in first position, so he's out of the picture on this hand. Seat 7 went all in for 6,000 chips. If you call Seat 7, you can bet your last dollar that Seat 10 will fold, hoping that Seat 7 knocks you out of the tournament (he does have more chips than you) and putting him in the money by the skin of his teeth. If, on the other hand, you fold this strong hand, you can almost be assured that Seat 10 will toss in his remaining 200 chips and stands a good likelihood of being knocked out, thereby moving you into the money instead of him. Your main objective is to get to the money, and by folding you are almost guaranteed of making it. Even if Seat 10 folds, he only has 200 chips left and is the small blind on the very next hand and could be forced out of the money then.

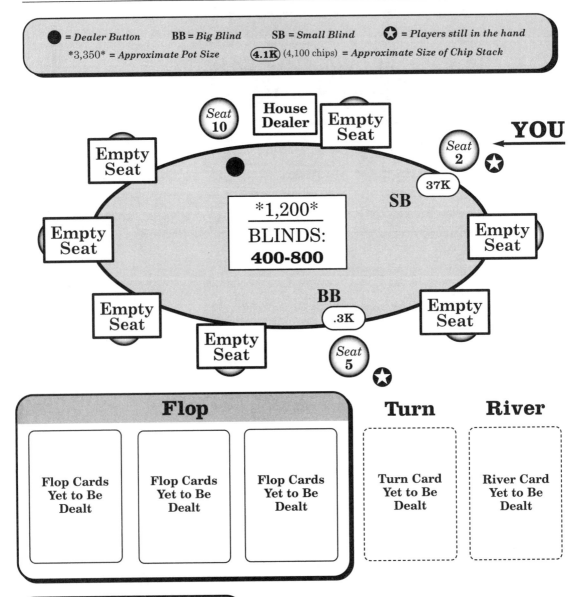

● = *Dealer Button*   BB = *Big Blind*   SB = *Small Blind*   ⭐ = *Players still in the hand*
3,350 = *Approximate Pot Size*   (4.1K) (4,100 chips) = *Approximate Size of Chip Stack*

Seat 10

House Dealer

Empty Seat

YOU

Seat 2   ⭐

37K

Empty Seat

SB

1,200
BLINDS:
400-800

Empty Seat

Empty Seat

Empty Seat

BB
.3K

Empty Seat

Empty Seat

Seat 5   ⭐

Flop

| Flop Cards Yet to Be Dealt | Flop Cards Yet to Be Dealt | Flop Cards Yet to Be Dealt |

Turn

Turn Card Yet to Be Dealt

River

River Card Yet to Be Dealt

Pocket

Situation 27:

You are now in the later stage of another tournament.

Seat 10, who has 51,000 chips and is first to act, folds. You, with 37,000 chips and a pocket hand of King-7 unsuited, are next to act. Only Seat 5, with 300 chips remaining, is left in the tournament and will act after you. Given the tournament situation presented above and on the opposite page, what do you do?

> ## Starting Hand (Pocket): K♣7♦
> ## This Pocket's Win Rate: 2.8%
> ## Win Rate Rank: 105 of 169 possible

Tournament Situation:
Tourney: **Multiple tables, card room**
Paid Entrys: **60 x $15**
Starting Chip Stack: **1,500**
Players Remaining: **3**
Places Paid: **7**
Your Current Standing: **2nd place overall,**
   guaranteed in the money
Time Left in Round: **9 minutes**
Rebuys Allowed: **No**
Next Blind Level: **500-1,000**

This Tournament's Prize Money:

1. **$350**
2. **$200**
3. **$100**
4. **$75**
5. **$65**
6. **$60**
7. **$50**
—————
Total Prize Pool:
$900

Answer 27:

You were dealt a King-7 unsuited in your pocket, not a very good hand to be sure. Normally you would fold this hand, but in this situation you would not only play it, but you would raise it enough to cover Seat 5's remaining 300 chips, in effect forcing him to go all in. The reason you would do this is because, statistically, he probably didn't catch a very good hand and you want to try and knock him out of the tournament. If you folded this relatively poor hand, Seat 5 would save his 800-chip big blind bet and get 400 of your chips.

With such a large chip stack as you have remaining (37,000), it is worth the risk of getting beat on this hand in order to try and knock him out. In fact, when the big blind has so few chips left, you should play almost any two cards in an effort to knock him out. As an example of this, I played in an 800-player Internet tournament one time and lost 1,460 of my 1,500 chips in the second hand of the tournament, yet I came back to win it, finishing with 1.2 million chips. Like Yogi Berra once said, "It ain't over till it's over," and it is always possible to come back, so when you get a chance to knock someone out for such a small risk, take it.

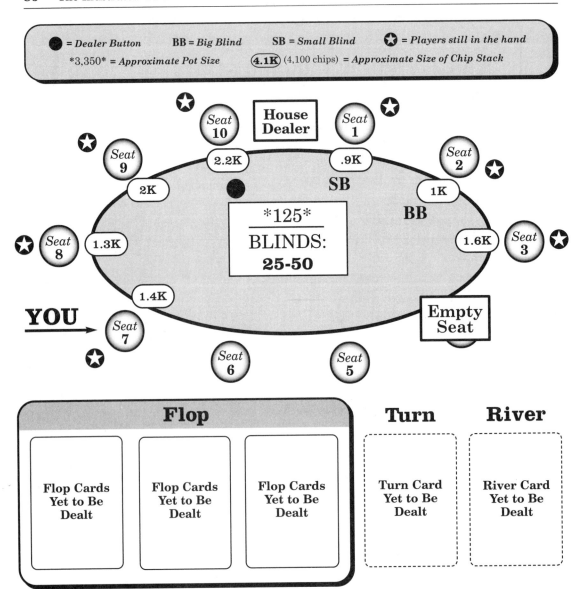

● = *Dealer Button*   BB = *Big Blind*   SB = *Small Blind*   ★ = *Players still in the hand*

3,350 = *Approximate Pot Size*   4.1K (4,100 chips) = *Approximate Size of Chip Stack*

Seat 10 — 2.2K
House Dealer
Seat 1 — .9K   SB
Seat 9 — 2K
Seat 2 — 1K   BB
Seat 8 — 1.3K
Seat 3 — 1.6K

125
—————
BLINDS:
25-50

YOU → Seat 7 — 1.4K

Empty Seat

Seat 6

Seat 5

Flop

| Flop Cards Yet to Be Dealt | Flop Cards Yet to Be Dealt | Flop Cards Yet to Be Dealt |

Turn

Turn Card Yet to Be Dealt

River

River Card Yet to Be Dealt

Pocket

Situation 28:

The next 33 situations deal with your progression through the same large Internet tournament.

Seat 3 was first to act and called the big blind bet of 50 chips. Seats 5 and 6 folded. You have been dealt a King-Queen unsuited in your pocket. Given the tournament situation presented above and on the opposite page, what do you do?

Starting Hand (Pocket): **K♣Q♦**
This Pocket's Win Rate: **39.2%**
Win Rate Rank: **23 of 169 possible**

Tournament Situation:

Tourney: **Multiple tables, Internet**

Paid Entrys: **622 x $30**

Starting Chip Stack: **1,500**

Players Remaining: **571**

Places Paid: **90**

Your Current Standing: **308th place overall,**
   4th at your table

Time Left in Round: **11 minutes**

Rebuys Allowed: **Yes, 1 in first hour**

Next Blind Level: **50-100**

This Tournament's Prize Money:

1. $3,000		11-20. $200
2. $1,800		21-40. $100
3. $1,400		41-70. $75
4. $1,200		71-90. $40
5. $1,000		
6. $900		
7. $700		
8. $600		
9. $550		
10. $440		

Total Prize Pool:
$18,660*

*and it will grow larger
as the rebuys take place

Answer 28:

King-Queen unsuited is a very decent starting hand, but it's not a power hand. Since it is early in the tournament (you've just started the third round), you don't want to get carried away with a big bet now, especially since you have five players yet to act after you. The proper bet under these circumstances is to call the bet of 50 chips (limp in, in other words), and see what happens behind you. This is not the sort of hand to risk a lot of chips on before you see the flop, which could make you or break you. It would be too easy for an Ace to come on the board, or a pair of 7s, or even three spades or hearts, none of which are a King or Queen. Take it easy until you see the flop, which in most cases you should try and do as cheaply as possible, because once you've seen the flop, you've seen just over 71 percent of your hand, thereby making your decisions regarding larger bets easier.

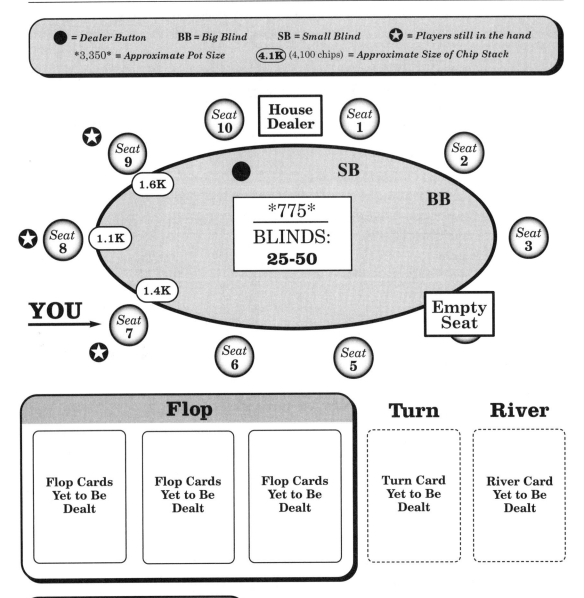

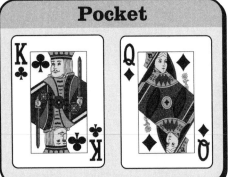

Situation 29:

After you limped in (called) for 50 chips, Seat 8 raised to 200 chips and Seat 9 reraised to 400 chips. All the other players folded to you. Given the tournament situation presented above and on the opposite page, what do you do?

Starting Hand (Pocket): **K♣Q♦**
This Pocket's Win Rate: **39.2%**
Win Rate Rank: **23 of 169 possible**

Tournament Situation:
Tourney: **Multiple tables, Internet**
Paid Entrys: **622 x $30**
Starting Chip Stack: **1,500**
Players Remaining: **571**
Places Paid: **90**
Your Current Standing: **308th place overall,**
    4th at your table
Time Left in Round: **11 minutes**
Rebuys Allowed: **Yes, 1 in first hour**
Next Blind Level: **50-100**

This Tournament's Prize Money:

1.	$3,000	11-20.	$200
2.	$1,800	21-40.	$100
3.	$1,400	41-70.	$75
4.	$1,200	71-90.	$40
5.	$1,000		
6.	$900		
7.	$700		
8.	$600		
9.	$550		
10.	$440		

Total Prize Pool:
$18,660*

*and it will grow larger
as the rebuys take place

Answer 29:

Although King-Queen unsuited is a decent starting hand, it's not a power hand, and this precisely the reason you limped in for 50 chips, so you could see what the other players would do after you. When Seat 8 raised to 200 chips, he was saying, in effect, "I have a power hand." When Seat 9 reraised, he was saying, "I don't care how powerful a hand you have, Seat 8, mine is better, so I'm going to reraise you."

The next four players all folded, as should you. In an Internet tournament like this, with over six hundred players, there is a long, long way to go. Pick a better hill to die on than King-Queen unsuited when facing two raises. After all, it would be very easy for something like an Ace to come on the board, or a pair of 7s, or three hearts or spades, none of which you hold in your hand. And even if you did decide to play this hand, you're in a bad position, since the other two players both act after you.

Big tourneys such as this require a lot of patience. What you were hoping to do was limp in as cheaply as possible with a decent starting hand and then make your decision regarding further betting based on the flop. Unfortunately, these two aggressive bettors aren't going to give you the chance.

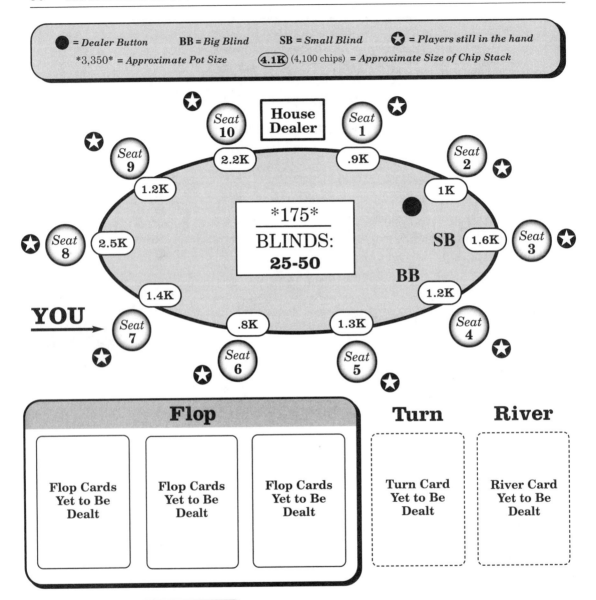

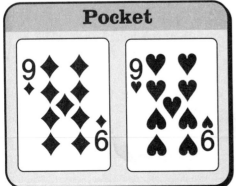

Situation 30:

A few minutes later in the same tournament, after your table had been filled with a tenth player, you were dealt a pair of 9s. Seats 5 and 6 both called the 50-chip big blind bet. It is now your turn to act with seven players yet to act after you. Given the tournament situation presented above and on the opposite page, what do you do?

Starting Hand (Pocket): **9♦9♥**

This Pocket's Win Rate: **55.4%**

Win Rate Rank: **11 of 169 possible**

Tournament Situation:

Tourney: **Multiple tables, Internet**

Paid Entrys: **622 x $30**

Starting Chip Stack: **1,500**

Players Remaining: **540**

Places Paid: **90**

Your Current Standing: **325th place overall,**
4th at your table

Time Left in Round: **8 minutes**

Rebuys Allowed: **Yes, 1 in first hour**

Next Blind Level: **50-100**

This Tournament's Prize Money:

1.	$3,000	11-20.	$200
2.	$1,800	21-40.	$100
3.	$1,400	41-70.	$75
4.	$1,200	71-90.	$40
5.	$1,000		
6.	$900		
7.	$700		
8.	$600		
9.	$550		
10.	$440		

Total Prize Pool:

$18,660*

*and it will grow larger as the rebuys take place

Answer 30:

A pair of 9s is a good starting hand, as the chart at the top of this page shows, but it is also quite vulnerable, especially with seven players yet to act after you. The first two bettors, Seats 5 and 6, limped in for one bet, indicating no real power unless they are slow playing their hands. Since you have a good but vulnerable hand, it would be appropriate in this position to try to "thin the herd" by raising.

The key here is to raise enough to get some of the folks on the fence to fold, yet not raise so much that if one of the remaining seven players comes over the top of you with a big raise you can't afford to fold it. So, in this case I would raise to 150 chips, or three times the big blind, primarily to thin the herd and secondarily for information, i.e., to see what the other players behind you do.

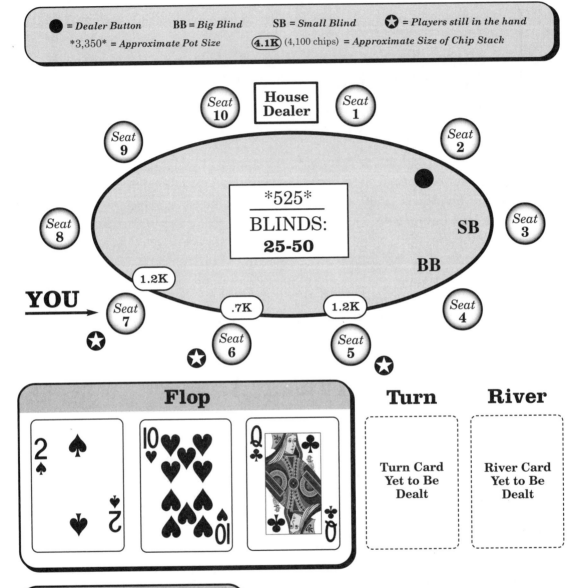

● = *Dealer Button*   BB = *Big Blind*   SB = *Small Blind*   ★ = *Players still in the hand*
3,350 = *Approximate Pot Size*   (4.1K) (4,100 chips) = *Approximate Size of Chip Stack*

Seat 10 — House Dealer — Seat 1
Seat 9 — Seat 2
525
BLINDS: 25-50
Seat 8 — SB — Seat 3
BB
YOU → Seat 7   .7K   1.2K   Seat 4
1.2K
Seat 6 — Seat 5

Flop

Turn

Turn Card Yet to Be Dealt

River

River Card Yet to Be Dealt

Pocket

Situation 31:

After your raise, everyone folded except Seats 5 and 6, both of whom called your raise. After the flop, both of your opponents checked to you. Should you check as well, bet the 50-chip minimum, raise to an unspecified level, or go all in?

Starting Hand (Pocket): **9♦9♥**

This Pocket's Win Rate: **55.4%**

Win Rate Rank: **11 of 169 possible**

Tournament Situation:

Tourney: **Multiple tables, Internet**

Paid Entries: **622 x $30**

Starting Chip Stack: **1,500**

Players Remaining: **540**

Places Paid: **90**

Your Current Standing: **323th place overall, 4th at your table**

Time Left in Round: **7 minutes**

Rebuys Allowed: **Yes, 1 in first hour**

Next Blind Level: **50-100**

This Tournament's Prize Money:

1.	$3,000	11-20.	$200
2.	$1,800	21-40.	$100
3.	$1,400	41-70.	$75
4.	$1,200	71-90.	$40
5.	$1,000		
6.	$900		
7.	$700		
8.	$600		
9.	$550		
10.	$440		

Total Prize Pool:
$18,660*

*and it will grow larger as the rebuys take place

Answer 31:

This is where no-limit Texas Hold'em can get nerve-wracking. Since both your opponents limped in to begin with, and since they both just called your raise, you don't have a good indication of what they think of their hands other than that both are worth calling with. The two problems you have now is that the flop missed your hand, and beyond that it brought two overcards, the Queen and 10, which means if either of your opponent holds either of these cards, you're already beat.

On the other hand, they don't know they have you beat, if in fact they do. It would be easy, safe, and probably proper to just check at this point and see what the turn card brings. However, depending on how well you know your opponents, if you made a strong bet at this point, say 150 chips again, you might get both of them to fold now. If they fold, then fine, you have a nice win. If one of them is slow playing you, however, and he check-raises you, you'll have an indication that either the flop helped him, or didn't hurt him, something you can't say. If one or both call you, though, you'll likely have to hit another 9 to win this hand, as they would be indicating they hold a hand that appears to work with the flop, possibly even an open-ended straight draw. Since there is a long way to go, you don't want to burn up chips with a raise here unless you're pretty sure you can get them both to fold.

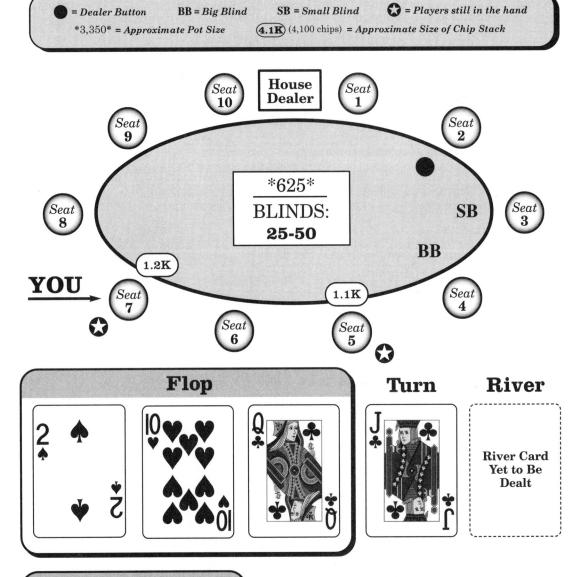

Flop

Turn

River

River Card
Yet to Be
Dealt

Pocket

Situation 32:

You decided to play if safe and check as well after the flop. After the turn card brought the Jack of clubs, Seat 5 bet—what appeared to you to be almost reluctantly—100 chips, the minimum, and Seat 6 folded. Should you fold, call the 100-chip bet, raise to an unspecified level, or go all in?

Starting Hand (Pocket): **9♦9♥**

This Pocket's Win Rate: **55.4%**

Win Rate Rank: **11 of 169 possible**

Tournament Situation:

Tourney: **Multiple tables, Internet**

Paid Entrys: **622 x $30**

Starting Chip Stack: **1,500**

Players Remaining: **540**

Places Paid: **90**

Your Current Standing: **323th place overall,**
   4th at your table

Time Left in Round: **7 minutes**

Rebuys Allowed: **Yes, 1 in first hour**

Next Blind Level: **50-100**

This Tournament's Prize Money:

1.	$3,000	11-20.	$200
2.	$1,800	21-40.	$100
3.	$1,400	41-70.	$75
4.	$1,200	71-90.	$40
5.	$1,000		
6.	$900		
7.	$700		
8.	$600		
9.	$550		
10.	$440		

Total Prize Pool:
$18,660*

*and it will grow larger as the rebuys take place

Answer 32:

Unless you've played with Seat 5 long enough to know his habits well, don't believe his reluctant-appearing bet for a minute. If he was truly reluctant to bet, especially considering he was in first position and had no idea what you and Seat 6 were going to do, he wouldn't have bet to begin with. He'd have waited for one or both of you to act.

Irrespective of Seat 5's antics, you still have to look at the merits of your hand, because you can't always be certain that your pickup of another player's tell (such as Seat 5's feigning reluctance) is accurate. The turn brought you a third overcard, which hurts you. It did, however, give you an open-ended straight draw, which is good. Sort of. You need an 8 or a King for a straight, but if you hit the King, your last remaining opponent may hold an Ace for a higher straight, which essentially makes any King a "dead" out for you. Which is not good. You'd probably be okay if you miraculously hit the 8 on the river, but in a heads-up situation, it's not even worth trying because of the poor pot odds you'd be getting trying to hit it.

Your hand began well, but after these four board cards, you're still not there, your opponent is betting into you, you've only got one card to go, and the odds of you actually hitting a winning hand are poor. Fold it now, and pick a better situation to tussle over.

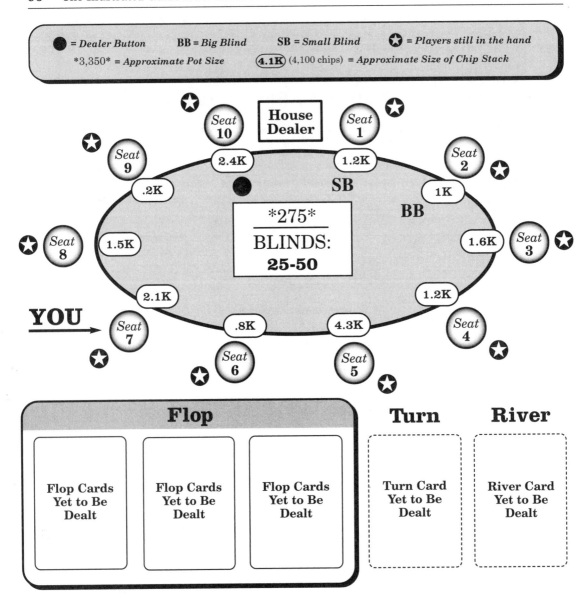

● = *Dealer Button*   **BB** = *Big Blind*   **SB** = *Small Blind*   ⭐ = *Players still in the hand*

3,350 = *Approximate Pot Size*   **4.1K** (4,100 chips) = *Approximate Size of Chip Stack*

House Dealer

Seat 10 — 2.4K
Seat 1 — 1.2K
Seat 9 — .2K
Seat 2 — 1K
Seat 8 — 1.5K
Seat 3 — 1.6K
Seat 7 — 2.1K
Seat 4 — 1.2K
Seat 6 — .8K
Seat 5 — 4.3K

SB
BB

275
BLINDS:
25-50

YOU →

Flop

| Flop Cards Yet to Be Dealt | Flop Cards Yet to Be Dealt | Flop Cards Yet to Be Dealt |

Turn

Turn Card Yet to Be Dealt

River

River Card Yet to Be Dealt

Pocket

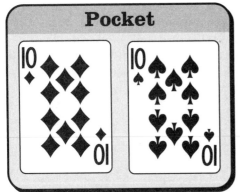

Situation 33:

You received a pair of 10s in your pocket. Seat 3 was the first to act and called the big blind bet of 50 chips. Seats 4, 5, and 6 then all called the bet as well. It is now your turn to act. Given the tournament situation presented above and on the opposite page, do you fold, call as well, raise to an unspecified level, or go all in?

> ## Starting Hand (Pocket): **10♦10♠**
> ## This Pocket's Win Rate: **60.8%**
> ## Win Rate Rank: **8 of 169 possible**

Tournament Situation:

Tourney: **Multiple tables, Internet**

Paid Entrys: **622 x $30**

Starting Chip Stack: **1,500**

Players Remaining: **519**

Places Paid: **90**

Your Current Standing: **298th place overall,**
   3rd at your table

Time Left in Round: **2 minutes**

Rebuys Allowed: **Yes, 1 in first hour**

Next Blind Level: **50-100**

This Tournament's Prize Money:

1. $3,000		11-20. $200
2. $1,800		21-40. $100
3. $1,400		41-70. $75
4. $1,200		71-90. $40
5. $1,000		
6. $900		
7. $700		
8. $600		
9. $550		
10. $440		

Total Prize Pool:
$18,660*

**and it will grow larger as the rebuys take place*

Answer 33:

You received a very nice starting hand, as its nearly 61 percent relative win rate shows in the above chart. You will clearly not fold this hand, so the question is what to do. If you go all in, you are not only facing four potential players already, but you have five seats to act after you, and you don't have any idea yet of their hands' relative strength. You also have to be concerned about the two players who will then act after you with larger stacks, in effect putting you at risk of being knocked out of the tournament. This is something you might feel like risking with pocket Aces or Kings, but not 10s. Even something like an Ace-Jack unsuited will knock you out if they catch a pair on the board and you don't hit a set.

If you raise, say to 200 chips, you will likely force some of those to act after you to fold, but with three players already in the pot in front of you, you have to believe they hold something worth playing, since they jumped into the pot in early position. A large raise, say to 1,000 chips will likely force out all those with marginal hands, but you don't know yet what those first three players called with, or if one of them might be slow playing a big pair, waiting for more money to get thrown into the pot before pouncing.

Right now, I would just call the 50-chip bet and see what happens. If someone goes all in, especially a player with a larger stack than yours, you can fold your hand cheaply.

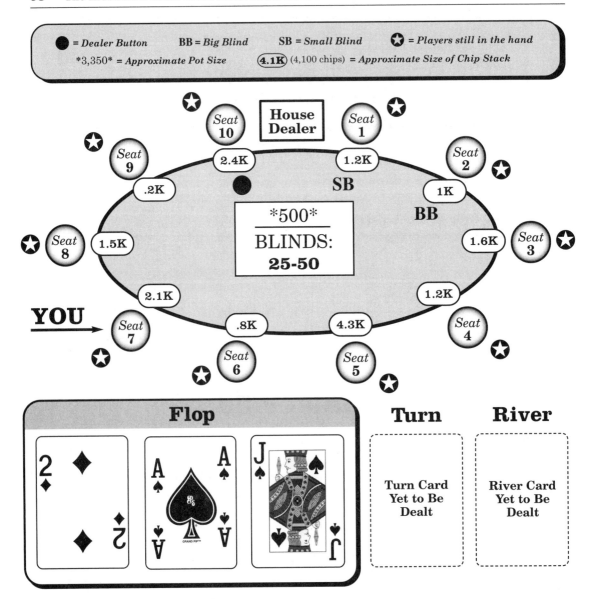

● = *Dealer Button*   **BB** = *Big Blind*   **SB** = *Small Blind*   ★ = *Players still in the hand*
3,350 = *Approximate Pot Size*   **4.1K** (4,100 chips) = *Approximate Size of Chip Stack*

House Dealer

500
BLINDS: 25-50

SB

BB

YOU → Seat 7

Flop

2♦   A♠   J♠

Turn

Turn Card Yet to Be Dealt

River

River Card Yet to Be Dealt

Pocket

10♦   10♠

Situation 34:

After you called, the five players to act after you all called as well, making this a true "family" pot with all ten players at the table in on the hand. After receiving the above flop, the first six players all checked to you. Do you check as well, raise to an unspecified level, or go all in?

> ## Starting Hand (Pocket): **10♦10♠**
> ## This Pocket's Win Rate: **60.8%**
> ## Win Rate Rank: **8 of 169 possible**

Tournament Situation:

Tourney: **Multiple tables, Internet**

Paid Entrys: **622 x $30**

Starting Chip Stack: **1,500**

Players Remaining: **519**

Places Paid: **90**

Your Current Standing: **298th place overall,**
   3rd at your table

Time Left in Round: **1 minute**

Rebuys Allowed: **Yes, 1 in first hour**

Next Blind Level: **50-100**

This Tournament's Prize Money:

1.	$3,000	11-20.	$200
2.	$1,800	21-40.	$100
3.	$1,400	41-70.	$75
4.	$1,200	71-90.	$40
5.	$1,000		
6.	$900		
7.	$700		
8.	$600		
9.	$550		
10.	$440		

Total Prize Pool:
$18,660*

*and it will grow larger as the rebuys take place

Answer 34:

Wow. Ten players in on a hand. Unusual, but it does happen, particularly at the lower betting levels. It would be hard to believe that the Ace and/or the Jack didn't help somebody, even some of the six players in front of you who all called. So what's going on here? Well, maybe the two spades on the flop has everyone scared of a flush. And the fact that they're two big spades might have contributed to everyone's willingness to check, too. Maybe they're all holding small or medium pairs, or hands like King-Queen of diamonds, clubs, or hearts. Or, even more diabolical, maybe the flop hit someone huge, such as a player holding pocket Jacks, or Ace-Jack, or Ace-2 suited for two pair.

In any event, it's time to gain some information here, and narrow the field as well. It's time you made a bet for information, or a "probe" bet. If I were in this position, I would bet something like 150 chips just to see what the other players do. You'll likely get at least half the players at the table to fold. The question will be whether or not anyone comes over top of you with a big raise, and which player it will be, if any. If someone does goes in for a big raise, or all in, you can always fold your hand and not be out too many chips, but right now this is a dangerous situation for you to be in with so many callers. It's time to make this hand "put up or shut up."

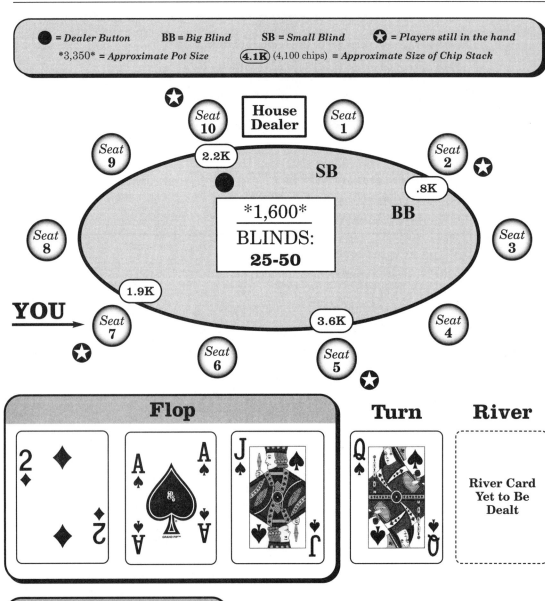

● = *Dealer Button*   **BB** = *Big Blind*   **SB** = *Small Blind*   ★ = *Players still in the hand*
3,350 = *Approximate Pot Size*   (**4.1K**) (4,100 chips) = *Approximate Size of Chip Stack*

Flop   **Turn**   **River**

River Card Yet to Be Dealt

Pocket

Situation 35:

After your bet of 150 chips, six of your opponents folded and three called, but no one reraised you. After the turn card was dealt, Seat 2 checked, but Seat 5, the chip leader at your table, made a bet of 500 chips. With Seats 10 and 2 to act after you, do you fold, call the bet, raise to 1,000 chips, or go all in with your remaining 1,900 chips?

Starting Hand (Pocket): **10♥10♠**

This Pocket's Win Rate: **60.8%**

Win Rate Rank: **8 of 169 possible**

Tournament Situation:

Tourney: **Multiple tables, Internet**

Paid Entrys: **622 x $30**

Starting Chip Stack: **1,500**

Players Remaining: **519**

Places Paid: **90**

Your Current Standing: **298th place overall,**
   3rd at your table

Time Left in Round: **Zero**

Rebuys Allowed: **Yes, 1 in first hour**

Next Blind Level: **50-100**

This Tournament's Prize Money:

1.	$3,000	11-20.	$200
2.	$1,800	21-40.	$100
3.	$1,400	41-70.	$75
4.	$1,200	71-90.	$40
5.	$1,000		
6.	$900		
7.	$700		
8.	$600		
9.	$550		
10.	$440		

Total Prize Pool:

$18,660*

*and it will grow larger
as the rebuys take place

Answer 35:

Finally, a situation that'll get your blood flowing! Someone makes a big bet and you've got fourth-best pair. But is that all you got? No. There are now three spades on the board and you hold one in your hand, the 10, for a four-flush with one card to go. You also hold a gut-shot straight draw, needing only a King for the straight. And if you don't believe the bettor (or anyone else) holds a straight or flush already, you might be able to win this hand if another 10 comes on the river. That's a lot of outs: 9 spades, 4 Kings, and two 10s, although if you catch a 10 on the river, you will lose if anyone holds a King.

As for Seat 5, I can't believe he holds a King-high flush, because if he did he'd have the nuts and would sit back and wait for more money to be placed into the pot before running over everyone with a big bet. He might hold a small flush and be afraid of another spade coming on the river, giving someone a higher flush, therefore he's trying to bully everyone out with his larger stack. He might hold an Ace or two pair, and be trying to bully out someone on straight/flush draws. In any event, the pot holds 1,600 chips. With forty-six remaining cards, fifteen of which could give you the winning hand, that means the pot odds are slightly better than 3-to-1 (1,600 chips for a 500-chip bet) for a hand that is only about 2-to-1 against hitting (31 misses to 15 outs). Make the call and hold your breath.

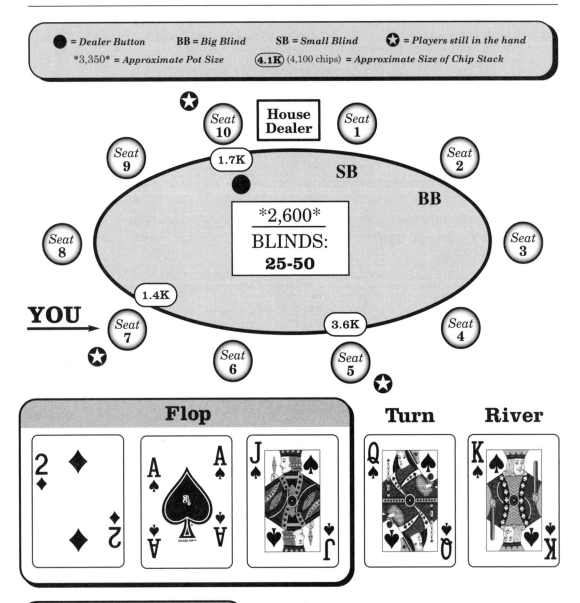

Situation 36:

After your call of the 500-chip bet placed by Seat 5, Seat 10 called as well and Seat 2 folded. After the river card was dealt, Seat 5 checked. It is now your turn to act. Do you check as well, raise to an unspecified level, or go all in?

Starting Hand (Pocket): **10♥10♠**
This Pocket's Win Rate: **60.8%**
Win Rate Rank: **8 of 169 possible**

Tournament Situation:

Tourney: **Multiple tables, Internet**

Paid Entrys: **622 x $30**

Starting Chip Stack: **1,500**

Players Remaining: **519**

Places Paid: **90**

Your Current Standing: **298th place overall,
3rd at your table**

Time Left in Round: **Zero**

Rebuys Allowed: **Yes, 1 in first hour**

Next Blind Level: **50-100**

*This Tournament's
Prize Money:*

1.	$3,000	11-20.	$200
2.	$1,800	21-40.	$100
3.	$1,400	41-70.	$75
4.	$1,200	71-90.	$40
5.	$1,000		
6.	$900		
7.	$700		
8.	$600		
9.	$550		
10.	$440		

Total Prize Pool:
$18,660*

*and it will grow larger
as the rebuys take place

Answer 36:

The first question I have to ask is, "Did you keep your poker face on when you hit your Royal Flush or did you give it away?" As strange as it may sound, I've been in games where the player who hit a Royal Flush out and out told the other players he hit it. Now why do that? You're supposed to be trying to win the other guys' chips, not broadcast your good fortune. Along the same lines, I've been in hands in which a player who hit the nuts, such as the best full house possible on a board, also told his opponents he had the nuts and that they should save their bets. Of course the player could be lying, but I've just seen it happen so many times that it makes me wonder about them.

Anyway, after Seat 5 checked, you obviously held the highest hand possible. If you were to go all in, both players would likely fold, unless they could be convinced you're trying to bully them out with a lesser hand, such as a 7-high flush instead of your 10-high. If, on the other hand, you checked, you might get Seat 10 to make a bet that you will later gobble up. You might also consider making a small bet, say 100 or 200 chips, projecting it more like a probe bet, in an effort to get one or both of the other players to call, making them think you don't have the nuts (even though you do); heck, maybe they'll even raise you.

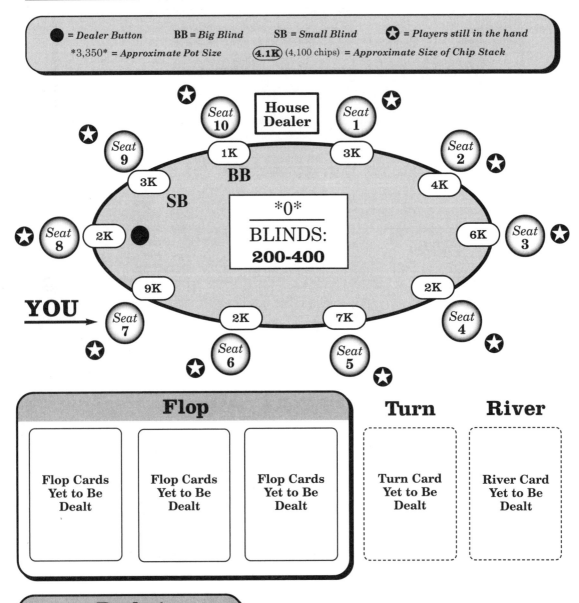

● = *Dealer Button*   **BB** = *Big Blind*   **SB** = *Small Blind*   ★ = *Players still in the hand*

3,350 = *Approximate Pot Size*   **4.1K** (4,100 chips) = *Approximate Size of Chip Stack*

House Dealer

Seat 10
Seat 1
Seat 9
Seat 2
Seat 8
Seat 3
Seat 7
Seat 4
Seat 6
Seat 5

1K
3K
3K
4K
2K
6K
9K
2K
2K
7K

BB
SB

0
BLINDS:
200-400

YOU →

Flop

| Flop Cards Yet to Be Dealt | Flop Cards Yet to Be Dealt | Flop Cards Yet to Be Dealt |

Turn

Turn Card Yet to Be Dealt

River

River Card Yet to Be Dealt

Pocket

| Pocket Cards Yet to Be Dealt | Pocket Cards Yet to Be Dealt |

Situation 37:

The tournament's fifth twelve-minute round has just ended and all players are now being offered the option of purchasing 2,000 additional chips, called an "add-on," for an additional $20 before the tournament continues. Seven of the other players at your table have opted to take the add on, while two declined. Should you take this option or not?

Starting Hand (Pocket): **X - X**

This Pocket's Win Rate: **----%**

Win Rate Rank: **X of 169 possible**

Tournament Situation:

Tourney: **Multiple tables, Internet**

Paid Entrys: **622 x $30**

Starting Chip Stack: **1,500**

Players Remaining: **335**

Places Paid: **90**

Your Current Standing: **147th place overall, 1st at your table**

Time Left in Round: **12 minutes**

Rebuys Allowed: **Rebuy period over**

Next Blind Level: **300-600**

This Tournament's Prize Money:

1.	$3,000	11-20.	$200
2.	$1,800	21-40.	$100
3.	$1,400	41-70.	$75
4.	$1,200	71-90.	$40
5.	$1,000		
6.	$900		
7.	$700		
8.	$600		
9.	$550		
10.	$440		

Total Prize Pool:

$18,660*

*and it will grow larger as the rebuys take place

Answer 37:

Some tournaments feature rebuys and add-ons while others do not. A rebuy is a chance to purchase a designated amount of chips (usually 1,000-2,000) for an additional price when you've either lost all your chips or fallen below a certain chip level, such as 300 chips when the starting chip stacks were 1,500. Rebuys can vary from, for example, just one in the tournament's first hour to unlimited rebuys within the first hour. I once played in a tournament that featured a $110 buy-in with unlimited $20 rebuys through the end of the fourth round. I watched as one player at my table actually purchased seventeen rebuys. It seemed ludicrous to most of us as we watched him go all in every few hands, but he actually ended up winning the tournament. How, I don't know.

Add-ons are similar to rebuys, but you only get one, and the opportunity is extended to everyone at the table, regardless of the size of their chip stack. Occasionally I pass on the add-ons when I've done particularly well in the first hour. If I've amassed 20,000 chips, for example, and am far ahead of most players, I don't feel an additional 1,500 chips is necessary. In the case of this tournament, however, I would purchase the add-on, if for no other reason than to keep my status as the chip leader at my table.

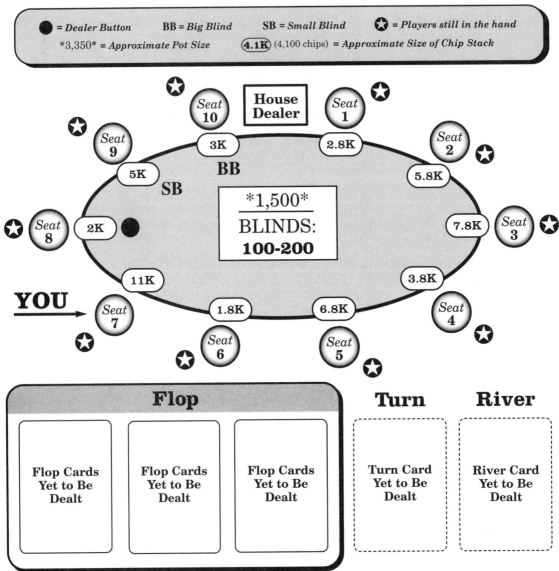

Situation 38:

The rebuy and add-on periods are now over and play is resuming with the start of the sixth round. You were dealt 7-5 unsuited in your pocket. Seat 1 bet 200 chips and the next five players to act in front of you all called the bet. Should you fold, call the 200, raise to an unspecified level, or go all in?

Starting Hand (Pocket): **7♣5♥**

This Pocket's Win Rate: **0.3%**

Win Rate Rank: **158 of 169 possible**

Tournament Situation:

Tourney: **Multiple tables, Internet**

Paid Entrys: **622 x $30**

Starting Chip Stack: **1,500**

Players Remaining: **335**

Places Paid: **90**

Your Current Standing: **147th place overall, 1st at your table**

Time Left in Round: **12 minutes**

Rebuys Allowed: **Rebuy period over**

Next Blind Level: **200-400**

This Tournament's Prize Money:

1.	$4,600	11-20.	$260
2.	$2,900	21-40.	$145
3.	$2,250	41-70.	$100
4.	$1,900	71-90.	$65
5.	$1,650		
6.	$1,300		
7.	$1,100		
8.	$940		
9.	$860		
10.	$740		

Total Prize Pool:
$28,040*

Larger now due to the rebuys and add ons.

Answer 38:

To be sure, 7-5 unsuited is not a very good hand, as its 0.3 percent relative win rate suggests. You certainly wouldn't go all in with this hand because you already have a gaggle of opponents who all think, or represent, that they have a hand worth playing. The only realistic shot you have is to flop a straight—or at least an open-ended straight draw—or two pair or three of a kind, long odds all. However, if the other players keep calling and making the pot bigger and bigger, it does get tempting to make this call.

My advice would be to toss this hand away now so you won't be tempted to play some half-breed hand after the flop that will entice you, ensnare you, and then embalm you. However, if you were to call this bet for 200— you do have a strong chip lead at your table, after all—because the pot is large and getting larger by the moment, it wouldn't be the worst call in the world IF you did so with the firm commitment that if someone behind you raised the bet even to 400, or if you didn't hit an EXTREMELY strong flop, you would fold, essentially accepting the risk of 200 chips towards a really handsome return while you currently enjoy a large chip advantage. An extremely strong flop to me would be a straight or three of a kind. Anything less, or if there's a raise, I fold.

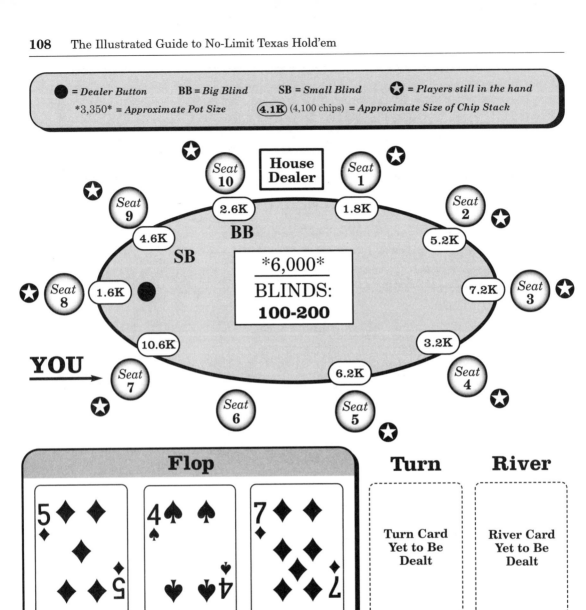

Situation 39:

You decided to call the 200-chip bet. Seats 8 and 9 did as well, but the big blind raised to 400 chips. Seats 1 to 6 all called, as did you. Seats 8 and 9 then called, making for a family pot at 400 chips each. After the flop, Seats 9 and 10 both checked, Seat 1 bet 400 and Seats 2 through 5 all called. After Seat 6 folded, it is your turn to act. Do you fold, call the 400, raise to an unspecified level, or go all in?

Starting Hand (Pocket): **7♣5♥**

This Pocket's Win Rate: **0.3%**

Win Rate Rank: **158 of 169 possible**

Tournament Situation:

Tourney: **Multiple tables, Internet**

Paid Entrys: **622 x $30**

Starting Chip Stack: **1,500**

Players Remaining: **335**

Places Paid: **90**

Your Current Standing: **147th place overall, 1st at your table**

Time Left in Round: **11 minutes**

Rebuys Allowed: **Rebuy period over**

Next Blind Level: **200-400**

This Tournament's Prize Money:

1. $4,600	11-20. $260
2. $2,900	21-40. $145
3. $2,250	41-70. $100
4. $1,900	71-90. $65
5. $1,650	
6. $1,300	
7. $1,100	
8. $940	
9. $860	
10. $740	

Total Prize Pool:
$28,040*

Larger now due to the rebuys and add ons.

Answer 39:

Well, you went and did it, didn't you? After getting raised before the flop you decided to call instead of fold like I suggested. Now you've hit two pair, and *top* two pair, no less. Now what to do...Okay, let's take a look at this budding mess. Your hand, as it sits now, is probably quite good, maybe even the best. The troubling aspect to this is that you have at least five players in front of you still hanging around and who knows how many behind you since there are still three to act. It's pretty tough to get out now after that flop, but you do have some hazards. First, there are two diamonds, so a flush is a real possibility. Second, anyone holding a 6 in their hands now has an open-ended straight draw. It's hard to imagine anyone holds three of a kind, but it certainly wouldn't be out of the realm of possibility. Perhaps if you had a feel for all your opponents, you might be able to gauge whether or not a big raise now would get all or most of them to fold. Again, though, the trouble you have is too many opponents. Now you have to decide whether to bet big in an effort to drive them out, possibly going all in, or bet the minimum 400 chips and see what the turn brings as cheaply as possible, assuming none of the three players behind you decides to raise. Personally, I'd opt for trying to drive out as many of my opponents as possible right now, giving them no chance to hit their card on the turn or river. 2,000 chips should suffice.

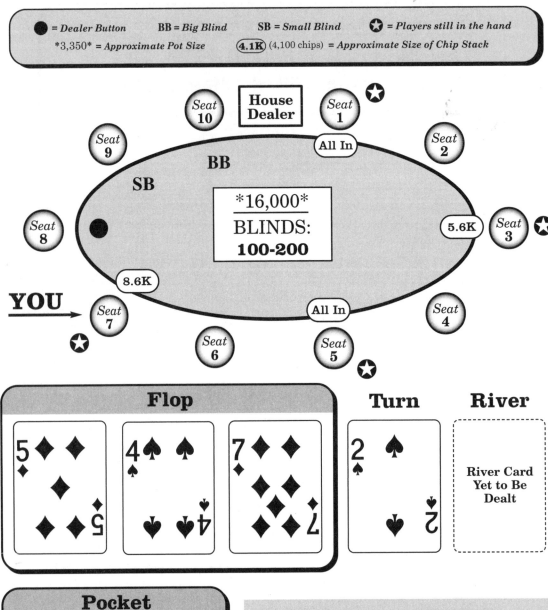

- = *Dealer Button*   **BB** = *Big Blind*   **SB** = *Small Blind*   ★ = *Players still in the hand*
- *3,350* = *Approximate Pot Size*   **4.1K** (4,100 chips) = *Approximate Size of Chip Stack*

House Dealer

Seat 10
Seat 1 — All In
Seat 9
Seat 2
BB
SB
Seat 8
16,000
BLINDS:
100-200
5.6K Seat 3 ★
8.6K
YOU → Seat 7 ★
Seat 6
Seat 5 — All In ★
Seat 4

Flop

5♦   4♠   7♦

Turn

2♠

River

River Card Yet to Be Dealt

Pocket

7♣   5♥

Situation 40:

You decided to raise to 2,000 chips. After your large raise, six players folded and three called. When the turn card was dealt, Seats 1 and 3 checked, but Seat 5 went all in for his remaining 4,600 chips. Do you now fold, call the 4,600, or go all in for your remaining 8,600 chips?

Starting Hand (Pocket): **7♣5♥**

This Pocket's Win Rate: **0.3%**

Win Rate Rank: **158 of 169 possible**

Tournament Situation:

Tourney: **Multiple tables, Internet**

Paid Entrys: **622 x $30**

Starting Chip Stack: **1,500**

Players Remaining: **335**

Places Paid: **90**

Your Current Standing: **147th place overall, 1st at your table**

Time Left in Round: **10 minutes**

Rebuys Allowed: **Rebuy period over**

Next Blind Level: **200-400**

This Tournament's Prize Money:

1. $4,600	11-20. $260
2. $2,900	21-40. $145
3. $2,250	41-70. $100
4. $1,900	71-90. $65
5. $1,650	
6. $1,300	
7. $1,100	
8. $940	
9. $860	
10. $740	

Total Prize Pool:
$28,040*

Larger now due to the rebuys and add ons.

Answer 40:

It would be hard to imagine that the 2 on the turn hurt you as much as Seat 5's bet seems to indicate. What could he hold? Well, he doesn't have a flush yet, so he's only betting on a flush draw if that's his hand. As for a straight, he'd had to have been playing a 3-6, 6-8, or Ace-3 before the flop. The first two possibilities seem hard to imagine, but the Ace-3, especially suited, is all too possible. Could he have been playing a pair of deuces all this way, and now hold three of a kind? Was he slow playing a pair of 4s, 5s, or 7s, and now is deciding to bust loose because of the straight and flush draws on the board?

You see, you should have listened to me way back in the beginning when I told you to fold your hand if someone raised preflop, but oh no, you just had to jump in because the pot was so big, a common mistake many players make.

Okay, we have to deal with what we have now, because the situations change, almost with every flip of a card. It's tough to fold the top two pair, so we'll play it. If you just call for 4,600, it might entice Seat 3 to call as well, since he might want to hold onto 1,000 chips in case all goes badly. If you bet at least 5,600, you'll force him to fold or go all in. Since it's only 1,000 more chips to you, I'd raise to 5,600 and try and drive him out.

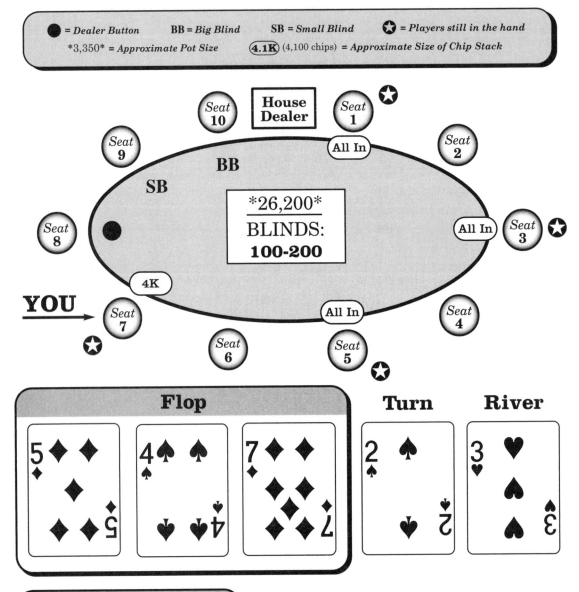

Situation 41:

You decided to bet just the 4,600 chips and Seat 3 called, leaving him with 1,000 chips and you with 4,000. After the river card was dealt, Seat 3 bet his remaining 1,000 chips. Seat 5 was already all in, so do you fold or call the bet?

Starting Hand (Pocket): **7♣5♥**
This Pocket's Win Rate: **0.3%**
Win Rate Rank: **158 of 169 possible**

Tournament Situation:
Tourney: **Multiple tables, Internet**
Paid Entrys: **622 x $30**
Starting Chip Stack: **1,500**
Players Remaining: **335**
Places Paid: **90**
Your Current Standing: **147th place overall,**
   1st at your table
Time Left in Round: **9 minutes**
Rebuys Allowed: **Rebuy period over**
Next Blind Level: **200-400**

This Tournament's Prize Money:

1.	$4,600	11-20.	$260
2.	$2,900	21-40.	$145
3.	$2,250	41-70.	$100
4.	$1,900	71-90.	$65
5.	$1,650		
6.	$1,300		
7.	$1,100		
8.	$940		
9.	$860		
10.	$740		

Total Prize Pool:
$28,040*
*Larger now due to the rebuys and add ons.

Answer 41:

Well, with 26,200 chips in the pot, you've got to take a shot at it for only 1,000 chips, but if you're like me, you've got a sinking feeling about this hand. This was an actual hand I encountered in a tournament a few years ago, back when I was undisciplined to the point where I played the hand to begin with, and then got trapped into playing it the whole way. The first mistake I made was playing the hand to begin with. There is a reason 7-5 unsuited has a relative win rate of only 0.3 percent, and that's against just one other random hand. When you play a hand like this against a lot of players, your odds are even worse. The second mistake I made was not folding before the flop after there was a raise, even when I told myself I would. The size of the pot made me rethink my commitment. By then I was trapped because I flopped the top two pair. But I just never got my full house.

At the showdown, Seat 5 turned over pocket 7s for the set he was slow playing, which came back to haunt him, and Seat 3 turned over his Ace-King of spades. He apparently stayed in because of his two big overcards to the flop and when he hit a fourth spade on the turn, he, too was trapped with his spade draw and the large pot. When the 3 hit the river, he hit a back-door straight, surprising even him, but he was the one who raked in 26,200 chips, not me with my 7-5 unsuited that shouldn't have been played in the first place.

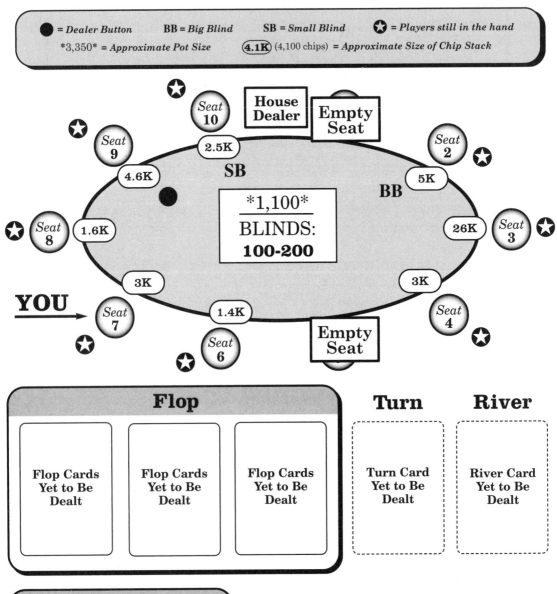

● = *Dealer Button*   BB = *Big Blind*   SB = *Small Blind*   ★ = *Players still in the hand*
3,350 = *Approximate Pot Size*   **4.1K** (4,100 chips) = *Approximate Size of Chip Stack*

Seat 10 — 2.5K
Seat 9 — 4.6K
Seat 8 — 1.6K
Seat 7 — 3K
Seat 6 — 1.4K
Seat 2 — 5K
Seat 3 — 26K
Seat 4 — 3K

House Dealer

Empty Seat

Empty Seat

SB

BB

1,100
BLINDS:
100-200

YOU →

Flop

| Flop Cards Yet to Be Dealt | Flop Cards Yet to Be Dealt | Flop Cards Yet to Be Dealt |

Turn

Turn Card Yet to Be Dealt

River

River Card Yet to Be Dealt

Pocket

Situation 42:

After losing 8,000 of your 11,000 chips on the previous hand, you received Queen-Jack suited in your pocket. Seat 3 was first to act and bet 200, which was called by Seat 4. Seat 6 raised to 400 chips and now it is your turn to act. With four players still to act after you, do you fold, call the 400, raise to an unspecified level, or go all in for your remaining 3,000 chips since you're upset over the last hand and almost in last place anyway?

Starting Hand (Pocket): **Q♥J♥**
This Pocket's Win Rate: **44.2%**
Win Rate Rank: **17 of 169 possible**

Tournament Situation:

Tourney: **Multiple tables, Internet**

Paid Entrys: **622 x $30**

Starting Chip Stack: **1,500**

Players Remaining: **321**

Places Paid: **90**

Your Current Standing: **278th place overall,**
   5th at your table

Time Left in Round: **7 minutes**

Rebuys Allowed: **Rebuy period over**

Next Blind Level: **200-400**

This Tournament's Prize Money:

1.	$4,600	11-20.	$260
2.	$2,900	21-40.	$145
3.	$2,250	41-70.	$100
4.	$1,900	71-90.	$65
5.	$1,650		
6.	$1,300		
7.	$1,100		
8.	$940		
9.	$860		
10.	$740		

Total Prize Pool:
$28,040*

Larger now due to the rebuys and add ons.

Answer 42:

Many players, after suffering a huge loss like you suffered on the previous hand, will become so upset they rashly push in all their chips on the next hand, acting out of anger instead of wisdom. This is called going on "tilt." The Texas Hold'em form of poker by its very nature is a game filled with potentially huge emotional swings, either because you were so close to hitting a hand that never came, or because an opponent can catch a miracle card at the end to dash your expectations. The thing to remember about a Texas Hold'em tournament is that it is a marathon, not a sprint, and as long as you have chips, you have life. Don't forget what I mentioned earlier in this book about the tournament I won after losing 1,460 of my 1,500 chips in the second hand of the tournament. I came back from absolute last place to beat a field of more than eight hundred opponents when it would have been so easy to throw in the towel. So, don't let despair over one large hand cause you to go on tilt.

As for this hand, you have a legitimate contender, unless someone were to go all in and force you to do the same. Call the 400-chip bet and help build this pot up to where the pot odds will be favorable for you take a shot at a drawing hand like this one, in which you have a chance for both a straight and a flush besides holding two big cards.

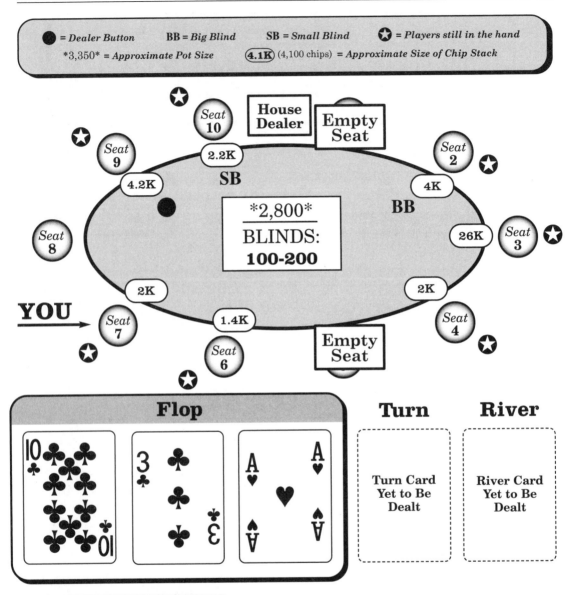

Situation 43:

After you called the bet to 400 chips, five other players called as well, and one folded. After the flop, the five players to act in front of you all checked. Do you check as well, bet the 200-chip minimum, raise to an unspecified level, or go all in?

Starting Hand (Pocket): **Q♥J♥**
This Pocket's Win Rate: **44.2%**
Win Rate Rank: **17 of 169 possible**

Tournament Situation:

Tourney: **Multiple tables, Internet**

Paid Entries: **622 x $30**

Starting Chip Stack: **1,500**

Players Remaining: **321**

Places Paid: **90**

Your Current Standing: **278th place overall,**
   5th at your table

Time Left in Round: **7 minutes**

Rebuys Allowed: **Rebuy period over**

Next Blind Level: **200-400**

This Tournament's Prize Money:

1. $4,600	11-20. $260
2. $2,900	21-40. $145
3. $2,250	41-70. $100
4. $1,900	71-90. $65
5. $1,650	
6. $1,300	
7. $1,100	
8. $940	
9. $860	
10. $740	

Total Prize Pool:
$28,040*
*Larger now due to the rebuys and add ons.

Answer 43:

This has suddenly turned into a very interesting situation. As you had hoped, you got one of the two draws possible, a straight. Unfortunately it's a gut-shot straight, meaning you need the King in the middle of your straight draw to finish it out. Also, you got hurt a bit when no hearts came on the flop, meaning you can't make a flush. Further, someone holding one or two clubs in their hand now has a shot at a club flush, which will beat your straight if you happen to hit it.

Now to the five players who checked in front of you. Are they afraid of the Ace? Are they afraid of the two clubs? Are they slow playing a monster hand? Every once in a while, a flop like this comes and misses everyone. You could certainly check along with the others and see what Seat 9—the last player to act—does with six checks in front of him. Or, you might think about making a bet right now, something in the neighborhood of 200-400 chips. Besides gaining information of what the others think of their hands, you will probably get some of your opponents to fold, which isn't a bad thing since you haven't got a made hand any way. Further still, a bet by you now, assuming no one really caught a good hand, might make the remaining players in the hand all check to you after the turn, in which case you could check, too, if you miss your King, thereby gaining you a free river card.

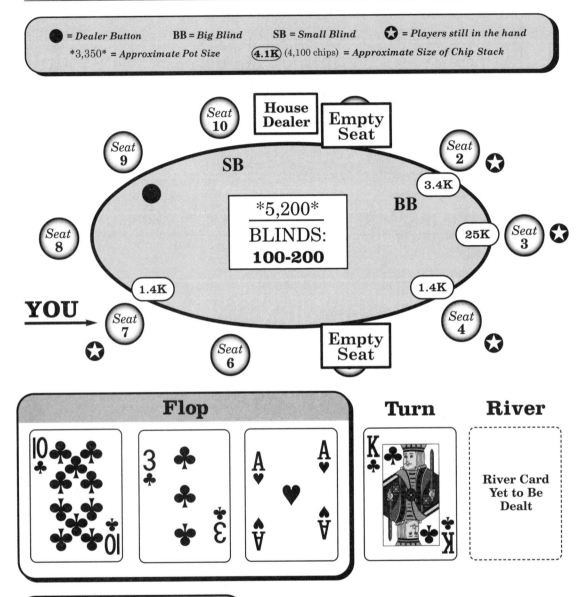

● = *Dealer Button*   BB = *Big Blind*   SB = *Small Blind*   ⭐ = *Players still in the hand*

3,350 = *Approximate Pot Size*   **4.1K** (4,100 chips) = *Approximate Size of Chip Stack*

Pocket

Situation 44:

You decided to get more aggressive on this hand and bet 600 chips. Three players folded and three players called. After the turn card was dealt, your three opponents all checked to you. Should you check as well, bet the minimum of 400 chips, raise to an unspecified level, or go all in?

Starting Hand (Pocket): **Q♥J♥**
This Pocket's Win Rate: **44.2%**
Win Rate Rank: **17 of 169 possible**

Tournament Situation:

Tourney: **Multiple tables, Internet**

Paid Entries: **622 x $30**

Starting Chip Stack: **1,500**

Players Remaining: **321**

Places Paid: **90**

Your Current Standing: **278th place overall,**
　5th at your table

Time Left in Round: **7 minutes**

Rebuys Allowed: **Rebuy period over**

Next Blind Level: **200-400**

This Tournament's Prize Money:

1.	$4,600	11-20.	$260
2.	$2,900	21-40.	$145
3.	$2,250	41-70.	$100
4.	$1,900	71-90.	$65
5.	$1,650		
6.	$1,300		
7.	$1,100		
8.	$940		
9.	$860		
10.	$740		

Total Prize Pool:
$28,040*

*Larger now due to the rebuys and add ons.

Answer 44:

The good news is you hit your straight. The potential bad news is that there are now three clubs on the board and anyone holding two clubs has made a flush. Those holding four clubs still have another card coming on the river and could still make their flushes. So, what to do? Other than Seat 6's early raise, no one has gotten aggressive on this hand except you, and Seat 6 is no longer in the hand. Because you only have 1,400 chips left, you need to be careful, but you also have to consider some sort of a bet in order to convince a potential flush drawer that he shouldn't stay in the hand. However, maybe he's already hit his flush and is slow playing the rest of you, waiting for someone to bet so he can check-raise them. Don't you just *love* this game?

If you go all in, you might force everyone to fold if they don't hold a flush. On the other hand, 1,400 chips is not exactly a bully stack, especially to Seat 3 who's still in the hand and has 25,000 chips, plenty to call you with. Also, if you go all in, it will look like you're trying to drive everyone out, which will tip off that you don't have the nuts. A small bet might look like a trap, indicating to them you hold a flush. Decisions, decisions. As for me, because my tournament would be on the line with an all-in bet, I'll check or bet the minimum 400 chips and hope another club doesn't come on the river.

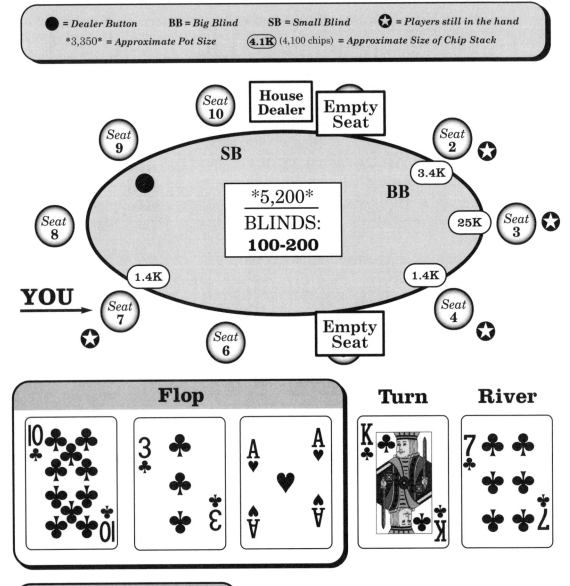

● = *Dealer Button*   **BB** = *Big Blind*   **SB** = *Small Blind*   ⭐ = *Players still in the hand*
3,350 = *Approximate Pot Size*   **4.1K** (4,100 chips) = *Approximate Size of Chip Stack*

Seat 10

House Dealer

Empty Seat

SB

Seat 9

Seat 2 ⭐

3.4K

BB

5,200
BLINDS:
100-200

Seat 8

25K Seat 3 ⭐

1.4K

1.4K

YOU → Seat 7
⭐

Seat 6

Empty Seat

Seat 4 ⭐

Flop   **Turn**   **River**

10♣   3♣   A♥ A♥   K♣   7♣

Pocket

Q♥   J♥

Situation 45:

You decided to check along with everyone else, opting to see the river for free. When the river card was dealt, your three opponents all checked to you again. Do you check as well, bet the 400-chip minimum, raise to an unspecified level, or go all in?

Starting Hand (Pocket): **Q♥J♥**
This Pocket's Win Rate: **44.2%**
Win Rate Rank: **17 of 169 possible**

Tournament Situation:

Tourney: **Multiple tables, Internet**

Paid Entrys: **622 x $30**

Starting Chip Stack: **1,500**

Players Remaining: **321**

Places Paid: **90**

Your Current Standing: **278th place overall,**
   5th at your table

Time Left in Round: **6 minutes**

Rebuys Allowed: **Rebuy period over**

Next Blind Level: **200-400**

*This Tournament's
Prize Money:*

1. $4,600	11-20. $260
2. $2,900	21-40. $145
3. $2,250	41-70. $100
4. $1,900	71-90. $65
5. $1,650	
6. $1,300	
7. $1,100	
8. $940	
9. $860	
10. $740	

Total Prize Pool:
$28,040*

*Larger now due to the
rebuys and add ons.*

Answer 45:

Now isn't that river card just flippin' Texas Hold'em typical?! This is one of those times that makes you say to yourself, "Well, boogers!" Now with four clubs on the board you just have to believe that someone holds a club. After all, there are six cards out there in the three hands, and one out of every four cards (statistically) is a club. But is this really true in this case? No, because four of them are already on the board. If you want to calculate the odds, there are forty-six unseen cards, and only nine of them are clubs. That makes it 37-to-9, or just under 20 percent, or one in five. Still, it only takes one club to beat you, even the deuce. If you make an all-in bet now, however, maybe the others will be convinced you have a club in your hand, the question for them being its rank. If either Seat 2 or Seat 4 hold the deuce or the 4 of clubs, they might be induced to fold. Seat 3, however, will probably call any bet you make since he has a huge chip stack.

Because the odds are that at least one club is out there somewhere, and because my entire tournament would be at risk with an all-in bet, as much as I'm chomping at the bit to go all in, I can only check as well, and hope that no one holds a flush, because if there isn't, then my straight will be the nuts.

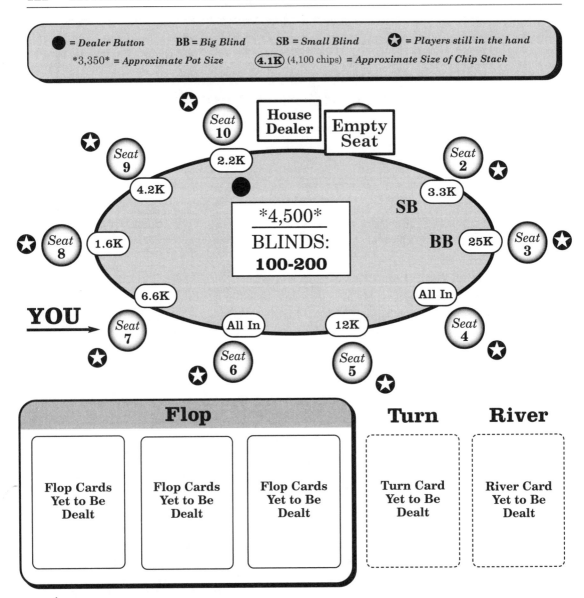

● = *Dealer Button*   **BB** = *Big Blind*   **SB** = *Small Blind*   ⭐ = *Players still in the hand*
3,350 = *Approximate Pot Size*   (4.1K) (4,100 chips) = *Approximate Size of Chip Stack*

Seat 10 — 2.2K
House Dealer
Empty Seat
Seat 9 — 4.2K
Seat 2 — 3.3K   **SB**
4,500
BLINDS: 100-200
Seat 8 — 1.6K
BB   25K — Seat 3
6.6K
All In
YOU →   Seat 7
All In   12K   Seat 4
Seat 6   Seat 5

Flop

| Flop Cards Yet to Be Dealt | Flop Cards Yet to Be Dealt | Flop Cards Yet to Be Dealt |

Turn

Turn Card Yet to Be Dealt

River

River Card Yet to Be Dealt

Pocket

Situation 46

Your straight held up on the last hand and you've replenished your chip stack to 6,600. One new player was seated at your table. On the next hand you were dealt King-10 suited in your pocket. Seat 4, the first to act, went all in for 1,400 chips and was called by Seat 5. Seat 6, who also had 1,400 chips, called the bet. It is now your turn. Do you fold, call the 1,400-chip bet, raise to an unspecified level, or go all in?

Starting Hand (Pocket): **K♦10♦**

This Pocket's Win Rate: **40.9%**

Win Rate Rank: **19 of 169 possible**

Tournament Situation:

Tourney: **Multiple tables, Internet**

Paid Entrys: **622 x $30**

Starting Chip Stack: **1,500**

Players Remaining: **292**

Places Paid: **90**

Your Current Standing: **181st place overall,**
 3rd at your table

Time Left in Round: **6 minutes**

Rebuys Allowed: **Rebuy period over**

Next Blind Level: **200-400**

This Tournament's Prize Money:

1. $4,600	11-20. $260
2. $2,900	21-40. $145
3. $2,250	41-70. $100
4. $1,900	71-90. $65
5. $1,650	
6. $1,300	
7. $1,100	
8. $940	
9. $860	
10. $740	

Total Prize Pool:
$28,040*

*Larger now due to the rebuys and add ons.

Answer 46:

You received another good starting hand with its decent relative win rate as shown in the chart above. The concern here is that the first three players are all projecting they have strong hands. Or are they? Two of the three players who bet in front of you were down to their last 1,400 chips and are facing the blinds in the next few hands, which might very well increase by then, depending on how slow the hands are played out. This means that Seats 4 and 6 might not have a strong hand, only a decent hand, and are playing it as opposed to something forced on them in a few hands. And Seat 5, with a large chip stack, only chose to call. Given these indications, I wouldn't necessarily put the three of them on tremendously powerful hands. So, I'd make a call of the 1,400 chips since I have a shot again at a straight or a flush, and if an Ace doesn't hit, my King might be good enough by the time the hand is over if I can catch one on the board. Raising or going all in is out of the question at this point because you don't have a made hand, and besides, with a drawing hand like this one, you want to encourage as many initial opponents as possible to help build the pot odds up to a level that will make it appropriate for you to play this hand further if the flop is right for you.

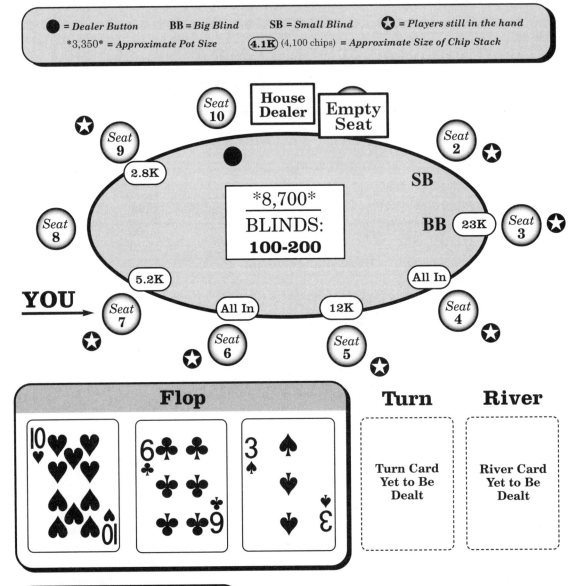

● = *Dealer Button*   **BB** = *Big Blind*   **SB** = *Small Blind*   ⭐ = *Players still in the hand*

3,350 = *Approximate Pot Size*   (4.1K) (4,100 chips) = *Approximate Size of Chip Stack*

Seat 10

House Dealer

Empty Seat

Seat 9   2.8K

Seat 2   SB

8,700

BLINDS: 100-200

Seat 8

BB   23K   Seat 3

5.2K   All In

YOU →   Seat 7   All In   12K   Seat 4

Seat 6   Seat 5

Flop
10♥   6♣   3♠

Turn
Turn Card Yet to Be Dealt

River
River Card Yet to Be Dealt

Pocket
K♦   10♦

Situation 47:

After you called the 1,400-chip bet, three of the remaining players folded while two of them called as well. After the flop, Seats 3 and 5 both checked, while Seats 4 and 6 were both already all in. Should you check as well, bet the minimum of 400 chips, raise to an unspecified level, or go all in?

Starting Hand (Pocket): **K♦10♦**
This Pocket's Win Rate: **40.9%**
Win Rate Rank: **19 of 169 possible**

Tournament Situation:

Tourney: **Multiple tables, Internet**

Paid Entrys: **622 x $30**

Starting Chip Stack: **1,500**

Players Remaining: **292**

Places Paid: **90**

Your Current Standing: **181st place overall,**
   3rd at your table

Time Left in Round: **5 minutes**

Rebuys Allowed: **Rebuy period over**

Next Blind Level: **200-400**

This Tournament's Prize Money:

1. $4,600	11-20.	$260
2. $2,900	21-40.	$145
3. $2,250	41-70.	$100
4. $1,900	71-90.	$65
5. $1,650		
6. $1,300		
7. $1,100		
8. $940		
9. $860		
10. $740		

Total Prize Pool:
$28,040*

*Larger now due to the rebuys and add ons.

Answer 47:

This was actually a pretty good flop for you as you made top pair and have a King kicker. No matter what Seats 4 and 6 hold, they can't hurt you any more than 1,400 chips because they're both all in. Seat 9, next to act, has about half of your chips, so unless he has something pretty good, he'll likely fold to a raise from you. Seats 3 and 5, on the other hand, have large chip stacks, so you won't intimidate them. A healthy raise by you will, however, get them to fold unless they have something fairly strong, as in a pair higher than 10s because they will probably put you on a pair of 10s if you raise after this flop.

There are, realistically, no straight or flush draws on the board. Seats 3, 5, and 9 didn't bet before the flop like they had pocket Aces, Kings, or Queens, so I wouldn't figure any of them for those hands. Seats 4 and 6 may have had such a hand, but it doesn't matter from here on out because they are all in. What you need to do, though, is make sure you win some chips in case either of the all ins do have a higher pocket pair than your 10s, leaving you second high at the showdown. I would make a healthy bet here, hoping to drive out Seat 9 and get no more than a call from Seats 3 and 5. Something like 2,200 chips should do it, and if either Seat 3 or 5 come back with a check-raise that forces you all in, then you might have to think about folding; 3,000 chips is enough to start again if need be.

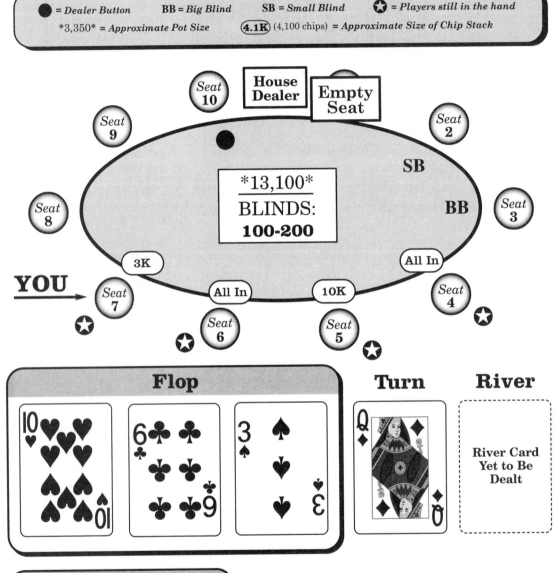

● = *Dealer Button*   **BB** = *Big Blind*   **SB** = *Small Blind*   ⭐ = *Players still in the hand*

3,350 = *Approximate Pot Size*   **4.1K** (4,100 chips) = *Approximate Size of Chip Stack*

Situation 48:

Seats 9 and 3 both folded to your raise while Seat 5 called. After the turn card was dealt, Seat 5 checked, while Seats 4 and 6 were both still already all in. Should you check as well, bet the minimum of 400 chips, raise to an unspecified level, or go all in for your remaining 3,000 chips?

Starting Hand (Pocket): **K♦10♦**

This Pocket's Win Rate: **40.9%**

Win Rate Rank: **19 of 169 possible**

Tournament Situation:

Tourney: **Multiple tables, Internet**

Paid Entrys: **622 x $30**

Starting Chip Stack: **1,500**

Players Remaining: **292**

Places Paid: **90**

Your Current Standing: **181st place overall, 3rd at your table**

Time Left in Round: **5 minutes**

Rebuys Allowed: **Rebuy period over**

Next Blind Level: **200-400**

This Tournament's Prize Money:

1.	$4,600	11-20.	$260
2.	$2,900	21-40.	$145
3.	$2,250	41-70.	$100
4.	$1,900	71-90.	$65
5.	$1,650		
6.	$1,300		
7.	$1,100		
8.	$940		
9.	$860		
10.	$740		

Total Prize Pool:
$28,040*

Larger now due to the rebuys and add ons.

Answer 48:

At this point it would probably do you no good to bet since the Queen on the turn did not improve your hand. In fact, you need to be aware of the possibility that Seat 5 has a Queen in his hand and is slow playing you, hoping to accomplish a check-raise and take all your chips.

There is no longer any possibility of a flush hitting the board, and no one can hold a straight yet, but a straight draw is possible. Right now I would just check and take the free card on the river and go from there. When the Queen hit the board, it put a crimp in your hand, so there's no point in getting stupid here and risking your whole tournament on second pair.

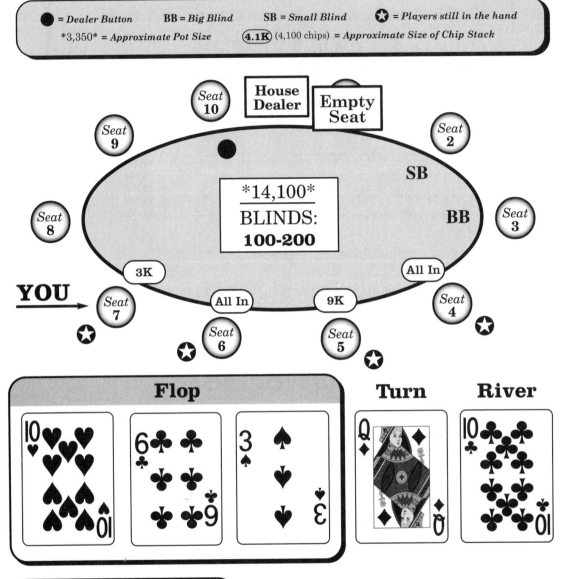

Situation 49:

After both you and Seat 5 checked following the turn, the river card was dealt. Seat 5 pumped the bet to 1,000 chips. It is now your turn to act. Do you fold, call the 1,000-chip bet, raise to 2,000 chips, or go all in for your remaining 3,000 chips?

Starting Hand (Pocket): **K♦10♦**

This Pocket's Win Rate: **40.9%**

Win Rate Rank: **19 of 169 possible**

Tournament Situation:

Tourney: **Multiple tables, Internet**

Paid Entrys: **622 x $30**

Starting Chip Stack: **1,500**

Players Remaining: **292**

Places Paid: **90**

Your Current Standing: **181st place overall,**
   3rd at your table

Time Left in Round: **5 minutes**

Rebuys Allowed: **Rebuy period over**

Next Blind Level: **200-400**

This Tournament's Prize Money:

1.	$4,600	11-20.	$260
2.	$2,900	21-40.	$145
3.	$2,250	41-70.	$100
4.	$1,900	71-90.	$65
5.	$1,650		
6.	$1,300		
7.	$1,100		
8.	$940		
9.	$860		
10.	$740		

Total Prize Pool:
$28,040*

Larger now due to the rebuys and add ons.

Answer 49:

During every tournament there comes a number of times when you just have to let it all out and take your chances. This is one of those times. Does your opponent have a flush? No. A straight? No. A full house? Possibly, but highly doubtful. That brings us to three of a kind. Could he hold three 10s, just like you? Yep, but even if he does you have a solid kicker with your King. He might hold Ace-10, in which case you're dead, but odds are he doesn't. I would rather suspect by the way he was betting he holds either two pair, or something like Ace-King or Ace-Jack, or was slow playing Ace-Queen after the turn and was hoping you'd bet, and then got a bit scared when the 10 hit the river.

In any event, you know what you've got, and it's a pretty darn good hand. Since I have to believe I've got him beat on this hand, I'm going to go all in for my remaining 3,000 chips and force his hand. If he's totally bluffing, like with Ace-King or Ace-Jack, he might fold, but since he's come this far and has a bigger chip stack, he's likely going to call you.

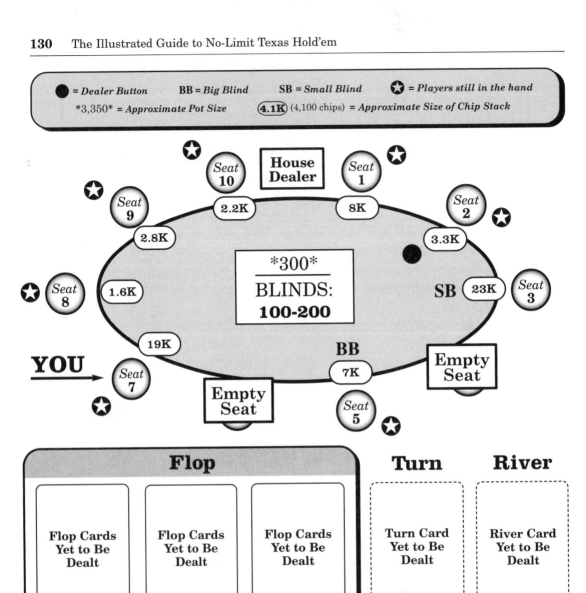

= Dealer Button   BB = Big Blind   SB = Small Blind   = Players still in the hand

3,350 = Approximate Pot Size   4.1K (4,100 chips) = Approximate Size of Chip Stack

Seat 10 — 2.2K
House Dealer
Seat 1 — 8K
Seat 9 — 2.8K
Seat 2 — 3.3K
Seat 8 — 1.6K

300
___
BLINDS:
100-200

SB — 23K — Seat 3
19K
BB — 7K
YOU → Seat 7
Empty Seat
Empty Seat
Seat 5

Flop

| Flop Cards Yet to Be Dealt | Flop Cards Yet to Be Dealt | Flop Cards Yet to Be Dealt |

Turn

Turn Card Yet to Be Dealt

River

River Card Yet to Be Dealt

Pocket

Situation 50:

After winning the previous hand (your opponent had Ace-Queen for two pair), you vaulted all the way from 181st place to 39th. Another player was seated at your table while two were knocked out on the previous hand. After receiving 10-9 suited in your pocket, you are first to act. Do you fold, call the 200-chip big blind bet, raise to an unspecified level since you now have plenty of chips to play with, or go all in?

Starting Hand (Pocket): **10♠ 9♠**

This Pocket's Win Rate: **38.3%**

Win Rate Rank: **24 of 169 possible**

Tournament Situation:

Tourney: **Multiple tables, Internet**

Paid Entrys: **622 x $30**

Starting Chip Stack: **1,500**

Players Remaining: **277**

Places Paid: **90**

Your Current Standing: **39th place overall,**
    1st at your table

Time Left in Round: **4 minutes**

Rebuys Allowed: **Rebuy period over**

Next Blind Level: **200-400**

This Tournament's
Prize Money:

1.	$4,600	11-20.	$260
2.	$2,900	21-40.	$145
3.	$2,250	41-70.	$100
4.	$1,900	71-90.	$65
5.	$1,650		
6.	$1,300		
7.	$1,100		
8.	$940		
9.	$860		
10.	$740		

Total Prize Pool:
$28,040*
*Larger now due to the
rebuys and add ons.*

Answer 50:

A pocket hand of 10-9 suited is a decent starting hand as its 38.3 percent relative win rate suggests. But not in this case, primarily because of your poor position for such a hand. This is purely a drawing hand, as you're trying to make a flush or a straight. To make the pot odds favorable, you need a lot of callers and hopefully no raisers. Right now you don't know whether you'll have either of these aspects working for you by the time the dust settles after the round of betting.

As for raising with this hand because you now have a lot of chips to play with, that's just plain silly, but a lot of players do approach their tournament play that way. When they have a lot of chips, they tend to be freer with them, when actually what they should be doing is guarding against the reckless play of their chips. You can and should alter your play a bit when you have a lot of chips, but what that means is using your large stack to bully the small stacks when you are in a position to do so. The proper move with this hand in this position is to fold it and stay out of trouble and not squander your chips because the blinds are getting higher and higher as you proceed through the tournament, and you're going to squander enough chips on the blinds before you're done.

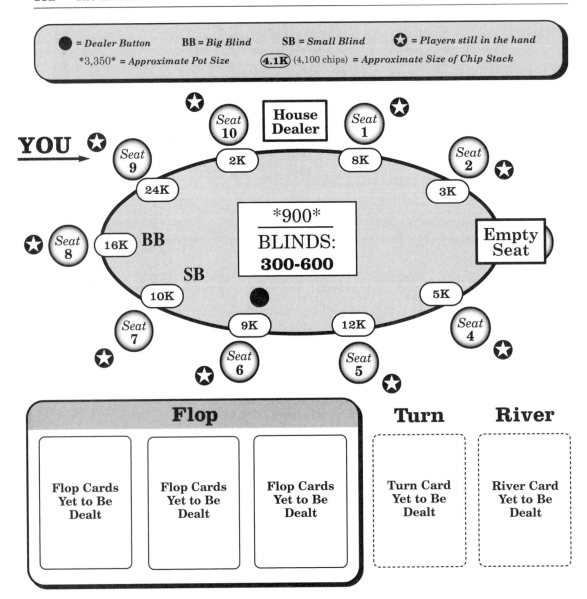

● = *Dealer Button*   **BB** = *Big Blind*   **SB** = *Small Blind*   ★ = *Players still in the hand*

3,350 = *Approximate Pot Size*   **4.1K** (4,100 chips) = *Approximate Size of Chip Stack*

Seat 10 — 2K
House Dealer
Seat 1 — 8K
Seat 2 — 3K
YOU → Seat 9 — 24K
Seat 8 — 16K **BB**
SB
Seat 7 — 10K
Seat 6 — 9K
Seat 5 — 12K
Seat 4 — 5K
Empty Seat

900
BLINDS: 300-600

Flop

| Flop Cards Yet to Be Dealt | Flop Cards Yet to Be Dealt | Flop Cards Yet to Be Dealt |

Turn

Turn Card Yet to Be Dealt

River

River Card Yet to Be Dealt

Pocket

A♣ A♣ | K♠

Situation 51:

It's now much deeper into the tournament with only 155 players remaining. After receiving Ace-King unsuited in your pocket, you are first to act. Given the tournament situation presented above and on the opposite page, should you fold, call the 600-chip big blind bet, raise to an unspecified level, or go all in?

Starting Hand (Pocket): **A♣K♠**
This Pocket's Win Rate: **67.0%**
Win Rate Rank: **5 of 169 possible**

Tournament Situation:
Tourney: **Multiple tables, Internet**
Paid Entrys: **622 x $30**
Starting Chip Stack: **1,500**
Players Remaining: **155**
Places Paid: **90**
Your Current Standing: **34th place overall,**
   1st at your table
Time Left in Round: **9 minutes**
Rebuys Allowed: **Rebuy period over**
Next Blind Level: **400-800**

*This Tournament's
Prize Money:*

1. $4,600	11-20. $260
2. $2,900	21-40. $145
3. $2,250	41-70. $100
4. $1,900	71-90. $65
5. $1,650	
6. $1,300	
7. $1,100	
8. $940	
9. $860	
10. $740	

Total Prize Pool:
$28,040*
*Larger now due to the
rebuys and add ons.*

Answer 51:

Ace-King unsuited is a strong hand, but if you don't catch anything on the flop it gets weak in a hurry. You're obviously going to play the hand and not fold, but you're not going to get silly here and go all in, so you're looking for the happy middle ground that suits your needs at this particular time.

If you just call the hand for 600 chips, you'll keep your hand disguised, but you'll also make it easier for your opponents to call with marginal hands. If I were in this position with this hand, and because I'm the chip leader at my table, I would raise to 2,000 chips, about three times the big blind. You've got a big stack and it's time to start using its intimidating power. If everyone folds, you still pick up a nice 900-chip profit, just in time to put it back in for your next two blinds.

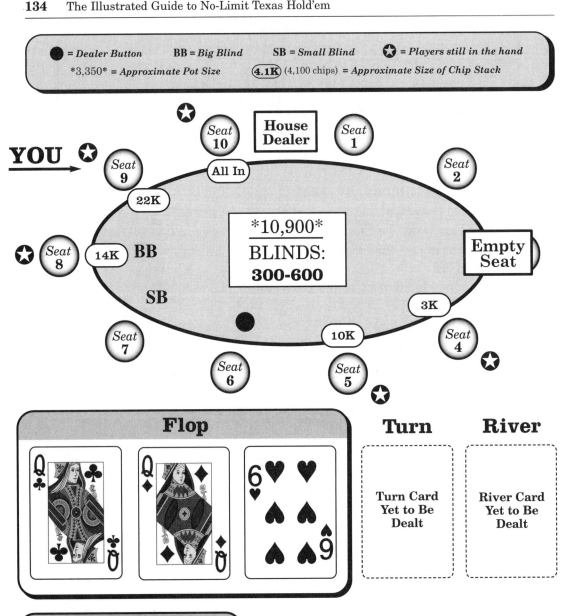

= Dealer Button   **BB** = *Big Blind*   **SB** = *Small Blind*   ⭐ = *Players still in the hand*
3,350 = *Approximate Pot Size*   (4.1K) (4,100 chips) = *Approximate Size of Chip Stack*

YOU →

Seat 10   House Dealer   Seat 1

Seat 9   All In   Seat 2

22K

10,900
BLINDS:
300-600

Seat 8   14K   BB

Empty Seat

SB

3K

Seat 7   10K   Seat 4

Seat 6   Seat 5

Flop

Q♣ Q♦ 6♥

Turn
Turn Card Yet to Be Dealt

River
River Card Yet to Be Dealt

Pocket

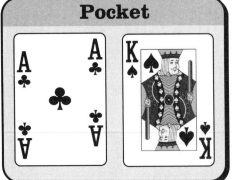

A♣ K♠

Situation 52:

You received four callers on your bet of 2,000 chips. After the flop, Seat 8 was first to act and he checked. Do you check as well, bet the minimum of 600 chips, raise to an unspecified level, or go all in?

Starting Hand (Pocket): **A♣K♠**
This Pocket's Win Rate: **67.0%**
Win Rate Rank: **5 of 169 possible**

Tournament Situation:

Tourney: **Multiple tables, Internet**

Paid Entrys: **622 x $30**

Starting Chip Stack: **1,500**

Players Remaining: **155**

Places Paid: **90**

Your Current Standing: **34th place overall,
    1st at your table**

Time Left in Round: **9 minutes**

Rebuys Allowed: **Rebuy period over**

Next Blind Level: **400-800**

*This Tournament's
Prize Money:*

1. $4,600	11-20. $260	
2. $2,900	21-40. $145	
3. $2,250	41-70. $100	
4. $1,900	71-90. $65	
5. $1,650		
6. $1,300		
7. $1,100		
8. $940		
9. $860		
10. $740		

Total Prize Pool:
$28,040*

*Larger now due to the
rebuys and add ons.

Answer 52:

You caught nothing on the flop other than a remote chance for an Ace-high straight. The only saving grace is that your two cards are overcards to the entire board, but that is little consolation with a pair of Queens showing. You could take a gamble here and make a bet in the 1,000-chip range in an effort to get everyone to fold, but that will only work if no one holds a Queen, and besides it would probably look like a probe bet to some or all of your opponents, signifying weakness on your part.

Unfortunately, about the only thing you can do here is check and hope everyone else does the same. Even if everyone checks, however, that does-n't mean someone couldn't be slow playing three Queens. You should recognize that in spite of your two big cards, you are on dangerous ground right now and probably will be through the completion of the hand because of the two Queens on the board. The only thing that would change that is if you hit either two Kings or two Aces on the turn and river.

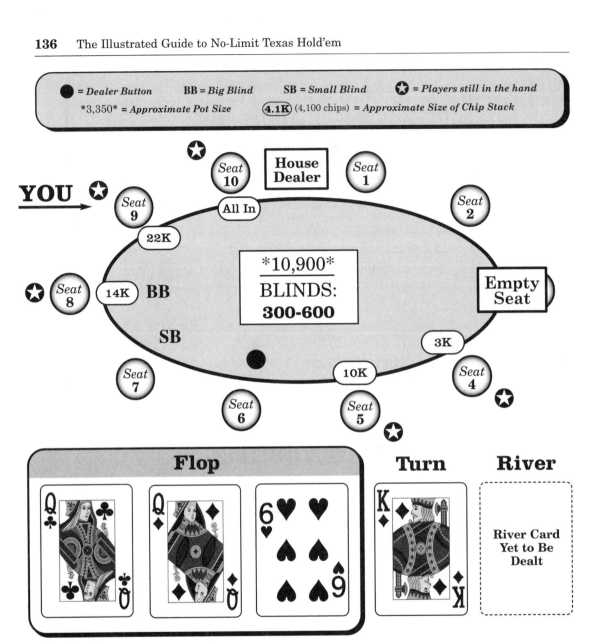

YOU →

Seat 10   House Dealer   Seat 1

All In

Seat 9   22K

Seat 2

10,900
BLINDS:
300-600

Seat 8   14K   BB

Empty Seat

SB

3K

Seat 7   10K   Seat 4

Seat 6   Seat 5

Flop

Q♣ Q♦ 6♥ 9♠

Turn

K♦

River

River Card Yet to Be Dealt

Pocket

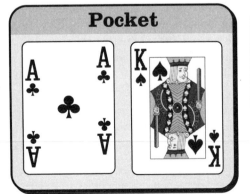

A♣ K♠

Situation 53:

You decided to check following the flop, and all your opponents followed by checking as well. After the turn card was dealt, Seat 8 checked. It is now your turn to act. Do you check as well, bet the minimum of 600 chips, raise to an unspecified level, or go all in?

Starting Hand (Pocket): **A♣K♠**
This Pocket's Win Rate: **67.0%**
Win Rate Rank: **5 of 169 possible**

Tournament Situation:
Tourney: **Multiple tables, Internet**
Paid Entrys: **622 x $30**
Starting Chip Stack: **1,500**
Players Remaining: **155**
Places Paid: **90**
Your Current Standing: **34th place overall,**
   1st at your table
Time Left in Round: **8 minutes**
Rebuys Allowed: **Rebuy period over**
Next Blind Level: **400-800**

*This Tournament's
Prize Money:*

1. $4,600	11-20. $260
2. $2,900	21-40. $145
3. $2,250	41-70. $100
4. $1,900	71-90. $65
5. $1,650	
6. $1,300	
7. $1,100	
8. $940	
9. $860	
10. $740	

Total Prize Pool:
$28,040*
**Larger now due to the
rebuys and add ons.*

Answer 53:

The King on the turn was definitely a sight for sore eyes, but don't get too excited yet. If there's a Queen running around out there in someone's hand, they still have you beat. And if some does hold a Queen and was slow playing it after the flop, the time has come for them to stop slow playing it for two reasons. First, if they don't start betting, they'll be wasting a very powerful hand, because they're running out of time to make something on it. Second, an overcard just hit the board on the turn, and now someone could take them down if they hold pocket Kings or hold one King (like you) and catch a third King on the river. This will be the round that anyone holding a Queen will likely bet it.

Therefore, I would just check again and see what develops. If someone makes a huge bet, or goes all in, you'll have to decide if they're betting three Queens and hoping to drive out anyone holding a King, or if they hold a King and are trying to drive out anyone with a better kicker. With this board I would seriously doubt anyone will be making a large bet with a pure bluff, say with pocket 7s, or Ace-Jack suited, or other hands like that. If someone bets now, you have to assume they have some part of this board. But then, so do you, and depending on how big the bet is, you can play or fold.

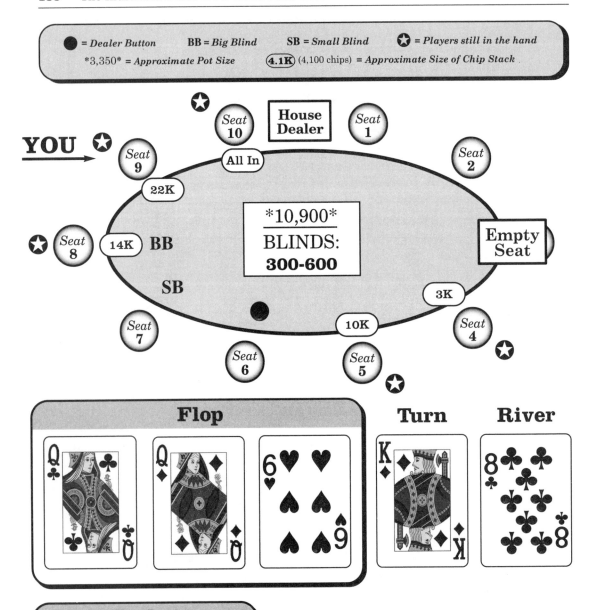

Pocket

Situation 54:

Once again, everyone checked. After the river card was dealt, Seat 8 again checked. It is now your turn to act. With three players still to act after you, should you check as well, bet the minimum of 600 chips, raise to an unspecified level, or go all in?

> ## Starting Hand (Pocket): A♣K♠
> ## This Pocket's Win Rate: 67.0%
> ## Win Rate Rank: 5 of 169 possible

Tournament Situation:

Tourney: **Multiple tables, Internet**

Paid Entrys: **622 x $30**

Starting Chip Stack: **1,500**

Players Remaining: **155**

Places Paid: **90**

Your Current Standing: **34th place overall,**
    1st at your table

Time Left in Round: **8 minutes**

Rebuys Allowed: **Rebuy period over**

Next Blind Level: **400-800**

This Tournament's Prize Money:

1. $4,600	11-20. $260
2. $2,900	21-40. $145
3. $2,250	41-70. $100
4. $1,900	71-90. $65
5. $1,650	
6. $1,300	
7. $1,100	
8. $940	
9. $860	
10. $740	

Total Prize Pool:
$28,040*

*Larger now due to the rebuys and add ons.

Answer 54:

It's starting to feel now like no one holds a Queen. Since there are no straights or flushes possible with this board, it's going to boil down to either three of a kind or two pair. If it's two pair, you are the likely winner, unless someone was refusing to bet their pocket Aces because of the two Queens on the flop. Had someone held pocket 6s, they would have bet them before now. If someone holds pocket 8s, however, and were allowed to stay in to the river because of all the checking that was going on, they just got a Christmas present. The only way you're going to find out, and to keep your opponents from controlling the action, is to bet now. It doesn't have to be a large bet, but anyone who missed entirely will fold. Anyone holding a piece of this board will likely call a small bet of 600 chips, which should become part of your stack after the showdown, barring the unexpected pocket 8s.

After your bet of 600 chips, anyone holding any kind of power will probably raise you. Depending on their raise, you can decide whether to fold, call, or reraise.

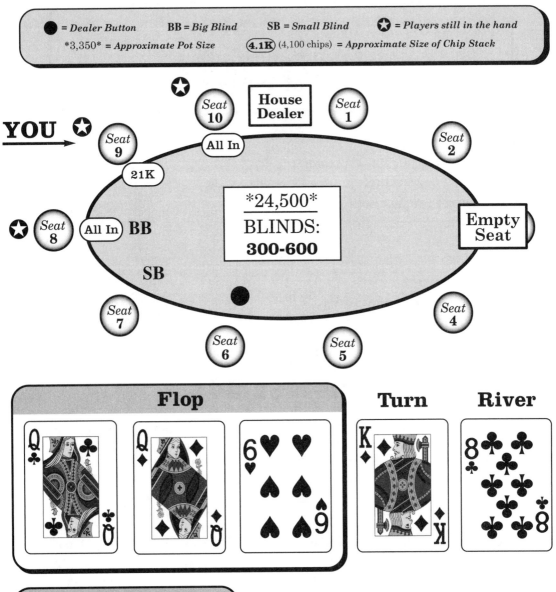

Situation 55:

Your 600-chip bet induced two players to fold. Seat 8, however, said, "Finally!" and went all in for 14,000 chips. Do you fold or place an additional 13,400 chips into the pot to call his raise?

> Starting Hand (Pocket): **A♣K♠**
> This Pocket's Win Rate: **67.0%**
> Win Rate Rank: **5 of 169 possible**

Tournament Situation:

Tourney: **Multiple tables, Internet**

Paid Entrys: **622 x $30**

Starting Chip Stack: **1,500**

Players Remaining: **155**

Places Paid: **90**

Your Current Standing: **34th place overall,**
    1st at your table

Time Left in Round: **8 minutes**

Rebuys Allowed: **Rebuy period over**

Next Blind Level: **400-800**

This Tournament's Prize Money:

1.	$4,600	11-20.	$260
2.	$2,900	21-40.	$145
3.	$2,250	41-70.	$100
4.	$1,900	71-90.	$65
5.	$1,650		
6.	$1,300		
7.	$1,100		
8.	$940		
9.	$860		
10.	$740		

Total Prize Pool:
$28,040*
Larger now due to the rebuys and add ons.

Answer 55:

Wow. Okay, what's this hammerhead doing? And what did he mean when he said, "Finally!"? Did he mean, "Finally, I caught the card I needed"? Or did he mean, "Finally, someone bet something that I can take away from them after slow playing my three Queens"? Or is just bluffing? Does he hold King-8? Or Queen-something? Or the dreaded pocket 8s? At this point it's hard to tell. Now what you have to decide is if your two pair are enough, and are they enough to risk another 13,400 chips? If you call this bet and lose, you'll be down to around 7,000 chips and face a long uphill battle to get back. On the other hand, if you call this bet and win, you'll vault to nearly 46,000 chips and become the tournament leader. This another one of those gut-check times in Texas Hold'em. Because it's getting to the late stages of the tournament, I'd probably fold this hand now and wait for a time when I was in better control of the hand. This one just doesn't feel right to me.

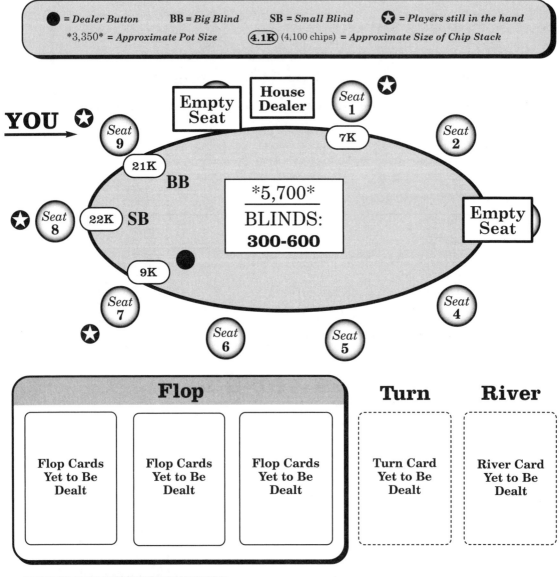

● = *Dealer Button*   BB = *Big Blind*   SB = *Small Blind*   ⭐ = *Players still in the hand*

3,350 = *Approximate Pot Size*   (**4.1K**) (4,100 chips) = *Approximate Size of Chip Stack*

YOU ⭐ →

Seat 9 — 21K

Empty Seat

House Dealer

Seat 1 — 7K ⭐

Seat 2

BB

5,700
BLINDS:
300-600

Seat 8 — 22K ⭐ SB

Empty Seat

9K

Seat 7 ⭐

Seat 6

Seat 5

Seat 4

Flop

| Flop Cards Yet to Be Dealt | Flop Cards Yet to Be Dealt | Flop Cards Yet to Be Dealt |

Turn

Turn Card Yet to Be Dealt

River

River Card Yet to Be Dealt

Pocket

7♣ 7♦

Situation 56:

After folding your previous hand to Seat 8's all-in wager, he showed two pair, Queens and 6s. You threw away a winner. You received two 7s in your pocket while in the big blind. Seat 1 raised to 1,200 and Seat 7 called. Seat 8 raised to 2,400. Do you fold, call the 2,400, raise to an unspecified level, or go all in, attempting to take some of the chips you lost to the idiot in Seat 8 on the previous hand?

> ## Starting Hand (Pocket): 7♣7♦
> ## This Pocket's Win Rate: 28.6%
> ## Win Rate Rank: 30 of 169 possible

Tournament Situation:

Tourney: **Multiple tables, Internet**

Paid Entrys: **622 x $30**

Starting Chip Stack: **1,500**

Players Remaining: **149**

Places Paid: **90**

Your Current Standing: **38th place overall, 2nd at your table**

Time Left in Round: **8 minutes**

Rebuys Allowed: **Rebuy period over**

Next Blind Level: **400-800**

This Tournament's Prize Money:

1.	$4,600	11-20.	$260
2.	$2,900	21-40.	$145
3.	$2,250	41-70.	$100
4.	$1,900	71-90.	$65
5.	$1,650		
6.	$1,300		
7.	$1,100		
8.	$940		
9.	$860		
10.	$740		

Total Prize Pool:
$28,040*

*Larger now due to the rebuys and add ons.

Answer 56:

A pair of 7s is a borderline decent hand if played in the right position. You were in the right position until Seat 1 raised and Seat 8 reraised. Those two raises projected power—power that you don't possess.

As for going all in in an attempt to get back at Seat 8 for bold play on the hand before, you need to forget about it. Bluffing and semi-bluffing is part of poker. What you need to keep in mind is that you made the best decision at the time, and that's all you can ever do in your pursuit of poker excellence. Make the best move every time, based on the information you have given the situation you are presented with. In this instance, a pair of 7s with two raises in front of you is not that good of a hand. For all practical purposes, you're probably going to have to at least catch a third 7 to win this hand, and maybe more.

No, if you have your heart set on getting even with Seat 8, you want to wait for the ideal situation. This isn't it. Play smart, not angry, and fold this hand now before you get in too deep.

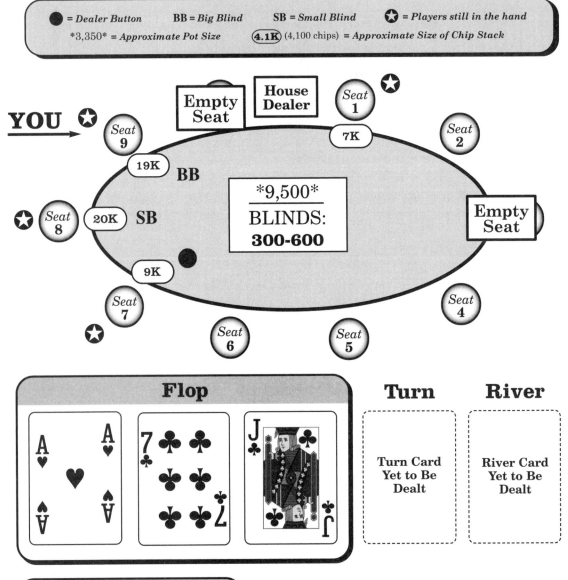

● = *Dealer Button*   BB = *Big Blind*   SB = *Small Blind*   ★ = *Players still in the hand*
3,350* = *Approximate Pot Size*   (4.1K) (4,100 chips) = *Approximate Size of Chip Stack

YOU ★ →

Seat 9 — 19K — BB

Seat 8 ★ — 20K — SB

9K

Seat 7 ★

Seat 6

Seat 5

Empty Seat

House Dealer

Seat 1 ★

7K

Seat 2

Empty Seat

Seat 4

9,500
BLINDS:
300-600

Flop

A♥ A♥   7♣ 7♣   J♣ J♣

Turn

Turn Card Yet to Be Dealt

River

River Card Yet to Be Dealt

Pocket

7♣ 7♣   7♦ 7♦

Situation 57:

You decided to call Seat 8's raise with your pair of 7s rather than fold. After the flop, Seat 8 was first to act and he bet 2,000 chips. With Seats 1 and 7 yet to act behind you, do you fold, call the 2,000 chips, raise to an unspecified level, or go all in?

Starting Hand (Pocket): **7♣7♦**

This Pocket's Win Rate: **28.6%**

Win Rate Rank: **30 of 169 possible**

Tournament Situation:

Tourney: **Multiple tables, Internet**

Paid Entrys: **622 x $30**

Starting Chip Stack: **1,500**

Players Remaining: **149**

Places Paid: **90**

Your Current Standing: **38th place overall, 2nd at your table**

Time Left in Round: **8 minutes**

Rebuys Allowed: **Rebuy period over**

Next Blind Level: **400-800**

This Tournament's Prize Money:

1.	$4,600	11-20.	$260
2.	$2,900	21-40.	$145
3.	$2,250	41-70.	$100
4.	$1,900	71-90.	$65
5.	$1,650		
6.	$1,300		
7.	$1,100		
8.	$940		
9.	$860		
10.	$740		

Total Prize Pool:
$28,040*

*Larger now due to the rebuys and add ons.

Answer 57:

Well, you might have made the proverbial silk purse out of the sow's ear on this hand. The 7 on the flop gave you a set, which is likely the highest hand out there, so long as no one holds pocket Aces or Jacks. Even if you do currently hold the best hand at the table, there is still danger lurking. With two clubs on the board, a flush is a real possibility. Also, the Ace-Jack combo on the flop means there's a realistic possibility of a straight. And don't forget the Jack-7 combo; it, too, could end up as a straight, although it's not as likely.

The pot is already large enough to pursue aggressively, so I would recommend a large raise, something in the neighborhood of 5,000 chips, in an effort to drive everyone out who doesn't have a serious hand. Your opponents will probably think you're raising because of the Ace, and the only reason they MIGHT call you would be if they had a flush draw or an Ace with a King kicker.

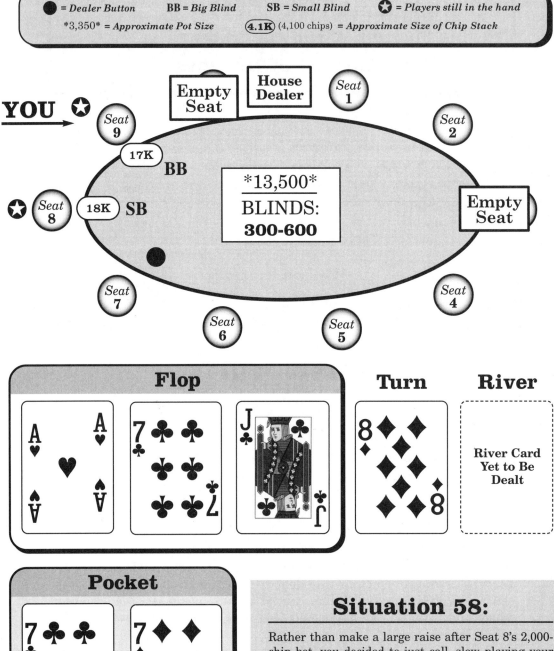

YOU ★

Empty Seat

House Dealer

Seat 1

Seat 9

Seat 2

17K BB

13,500
BLINDS:
300-600

Empty Seat

★ Seat 8   18K SB

Seat 7

Seat 4

Seat 6

Seat 5

Flop

A♥ A♥

7♣ 7♣

J♣ J♣

Turn

8♦ 8♦

River

River Card Yet to Be Dealt

Pocket

7♣ 7♣

7♦ 7♦

Situation 58:

Rather than make a large raise after Seat 8's 2,000-chip bet, you decided to just call, slow playing your set in order to trap your opponents, especially Seat 8, and extract as many chips as possible. After your call, Seats 1 and 7 folded, leaving you heads up with the idiot in Seat 8 who burned you earlier. After the turn, Seat 8 again bet 2,000 chips. Do you fold, call the 2,000, raise to an unspecified level, or go all in?

Starting Hand (Pocket): **7♣7♦**
This Pocket's Win Rate: **28.6%**
Win Rate Rank: **30 of 169 possible**

Tournament Situation:

Tourney: **Multiple tables, Internet**

Paid Entrys: **622 x $30**

Starting Chip Stack: **1,500**

Players Remaining: **149**

Places Paid: **90**

Your Current Standing: **38th place overall,**
  2nd at your table

Time Left in Round: **8 minutes**

Rebuys Allowed: **Rebuy period over**

Next Blind Level: **400-800**

This Tournament's Prize Money:

1. $4,600	11-20. $260
2. $2,900	21-40. $145
3. $2,250	41-70. $100
4. $1,900	71-90. $65
5. $1,650	
6. $1,300	
7. $1,100	
8. $940	
9. $860	
10. $740	

Total Prize Pool:
$28,040*
Larger now due to the rebuys and add ons.

Answer 58:

Even though you decided not to raise before the turn, Seat 8's bet of 2,000 was large enough to induce both Seat 1 and Seat 7 to fold, so a large raise by you would have driven them out for sure. What you don't know now is whether or not Seat 8 would have folded to your large raise. You are now in a heads-up situation with Seat 8, the "idiot" you are chomping at the bit to get even with. Based on your last hand against him, when he played two underpair to the river, you should now be convinced that he is willing to play lesser cards in the face of overcards. In this case it could mean he's playing some combination of Ace-anything (which could be two pair, leaving him with a possible full house on the river), or he could be playing a flush draw. Who knows—he's an idiot, right?

The only thing that's going to make him slow down and think is a large raise by you, which will force him to seriously assess his hand, and if he doesn't have any real power yet, your large raise will make him decide if he wants to pursue his current betting strategy or fold while it's still relatively inexpensive for him. Consider a raise here to at least 5,000 chips, and possibly going all in. You have real power, and if you pair the board you'll have a full house, and he hasn't projected real power yet. Every card you let him draw could get him closer to what he needs.

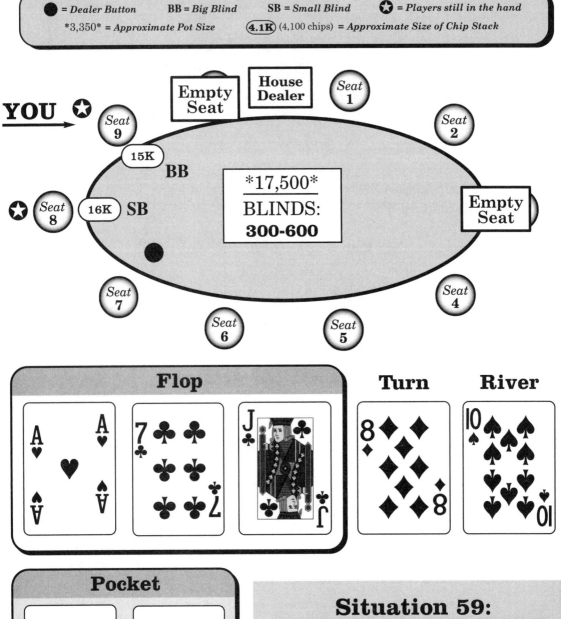

● = *Dealer Button*   BB = *Big Blind*   SB = *Small Blind*   ★ = *Players still in the hand*

3,350 = *Approximate Pot Size*   (4.1K) (4,100 chips) = *Approximate Size of Chip Stack*

YOU ★ →

Empty Seat   House Dealer   Seat 1   Seat 2

Seat 9

15K   BB

17,500
BLINDS:
300-600

Empty Seat

★ Seat 8   16K   SB

Seat 7   Seat 6   Seat 5   Seat 4

Flop

A♥ A♥

7♣ 7♣

J♣

Turn

8♦

River

10♠

Pocket

7♣ 7♣

7♦ 7♦

Situation 59:

Once again, you chose not to make the big raise, opting instead to call Seat 8's 2,000-chip bet after the turn in an effort to trap him for as many chips as possible. After the river card was dealt, Seat 8 seemed to hesitate a bit, then once again bet 2,000 chips. Do you now fold, call the 2,000, raise to an unspecified level, or go all in?

Starting Hand (Pocket): **7♣7♦**

This Pocket's Win Rate: **28.6%**

Win Rate Rank: **30 of 169 possible**

Tournament Situation:

Tourney: **Multiple tables, Internet**

Paid Entrys: **622 x $30**

Starting Chip Stack: **1,500**

Players Remaining: **149**

Places Paid: **90**

Your Current Standing: **38th place overall,**
2nd at your table

Time Left in Round: **7 minutes**

Rebuys Allowed: **Rebuy period over**

Next Blind Level: **400-800**

This Tournament's Prize Money:

1.	$4,600	11-20.	$260
2.	$2,900	21-40.	$145
3.	$2,250	41-70.	$100
4.	$1,900	71-90.	$65
5.	$1,650		
6.	$1,300		
7.	$1,100		
8.	$940		
9.	$860		
10.	$740		

Total Prize Pool:
$28,040*

*Larger now due to the rebuys and add ons.

Answer 59:

Well, you didn't catch the full house you were hoping for to put him away. What can you read into Seat 8's hesitation? I would interpret it in one of two ways. Either he missed and was momentarily unsure of how to bet, or he hit something really good, and was also unsure of how to bet. Big help, huh? That's why I personally don't put a lot of store in a player's poker tells, other than a few obvious ones, because sometimes you can misinterpret them with costly results.

The 10 on the river made three things possible: an Ace-high straight, a Jack-high straight, and a set of 10s, all of which beat your three 7s. The club flush, however, has now been eliminated. The pot is too large for you to fold now, and three 7s is nothing to sniffle about. I would call the 2,000-chip bet now rather than raise because of all the possibilities that now exist for you to lose on this hand.

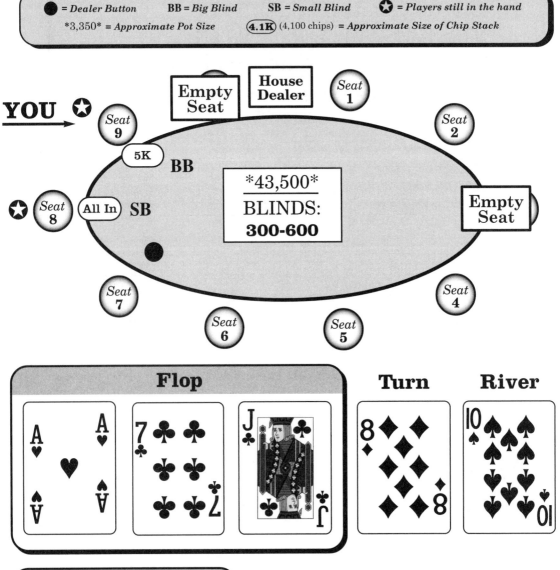

Flop

Turn   ### River

Pocket

Situation 60:

Rather than call Seat 8's bet of 2,000 chips after the river card came, you decided to raise big, pushing in 10,000 chips, feeling your set of 7s was the best hand. Seat 8 hesitated a long time and then went all in for 16,000 chips. Do you fold, preserving your remaining 5,000 chips and go off to a corner and lick your wounds, or call his raise and put your entire tournament on the line?

Starting Hand (Pocket): **7♣7♦**

This Pocket's Win Rate: **28.6%**

Win Rate Rank: **30 of 169 possible**

Tournament Situation:

Tourney: **Multiple tables, Internet**

Paid Entrys: **622 x $30**

Starting Chip Stack: **1,500**

Players Remaining: **149**

Places Paid: **90**

Your Current Standing: **38th place overall,**
   2nd at your table

Time Left in Round: **7 minutes**

Rebuys Allowed: **Rebuy period over**

Next Blind Level: **400-800**

This Tournament's Prize Money:

1. $4,600	11-20. $260
2. $2,900	21-40. $145
3. $2,250	41-70. $100
4. $1,900	71-90. $65
5. $1,650	
6. $1,300	
7. $1,100	
8. $940	
9. $860	
10. $740	

Total Prize Pool:
$28,040*

*Larger now due to the rebuys and add ons.

Answer 60:

It's too late to get out now, you've got to call. You put it all on the line way back in the beginning when you decided to play a pair of 7s in the face of two raises, when you should have folded. You kept putting it all on the line with this hand when you decided to slow play it. This is the kind of quagmire you can find yourself in when you play marginal hands such as this. I don't want to say, "I told you so," but *"I told you so!"* With a pot this large, it would be foolish to fold, so I would make the call, but I wouldn't feel good about it.

And, just for the record, at showdown, Seat 8 turned over a pair of red 9s for a straight. Had you made a large bet after the flop, when the board held an Ace and a Jack as well as two clubs, he likely would have folded and you'd still be in this tournament instead of leaving the table, convinced that you were knocked out by an idiot.

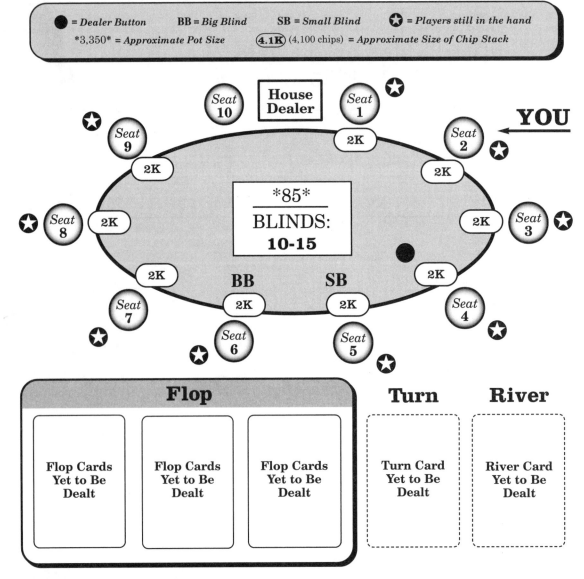

● = *Dealer Button*   BB = *Big Blind*   SB = *Small Blind*   ✪ = *Players still in the hand*

3,350 = *Approximate Pot Size*   (4.1K) (4,100 chips) = *Approximate Size of Chip Stack*

House Dealer

Seat 10 · Seat 1 · Seat 2 · Seat 3 · Seat 4 · Seat 5 · Seat 6 · Seat 7 · Seat 8 · Seat 9

YOU

85

BLINDS: 10-15

2K

BB   SB

Flop

| Flop Cards Yet to Be Dealt | Flop Cards Yet to Be Dealt | Flop Cards Yet to Be Dealt |

Turn

Turn Card Yet to Be Dealt

River

River Card Yet to Be Dealt

Pocket

Situation 61:

On the first hand of this single-table tournament hosted by a cardroom that uses it to get its daily action going, you were dealt King-Queen suited in your pocket. Four players called the 15-chip bet and one folded before you. It is now your turn to act. Given the tournament situation presented above and on the opposite page, should you fold, call, raise to an unspecified level, or go all in for your entire 2,000 chips?

Starting Hand (Pocket): **K♠Q♠**
This Pocket's Win Rate: **54.6%**
Win Rate Rank: **12 of 169 possible**

Tournament Situation:
Tourney: **1-table Sit 'n Go, Cardroom**
Paid Entrys: **10 x $10**
Starting Chip Stack: **2,000**
Players Remaining: **10**
Places Paid: **3**
Your Current Standing: **Even with everyone,
    first hand of the tourney**
Time Left in Round: **10 minutes**
Rebuys Allowed: **No**
Next Blind Level: **15-30**

*This Tournament's
Prize Money:*

1. **$50**
2. **$30**
3. **$20**

Total Prize Pool:
$100

Answer 61:

At this point you have a very nice starting hand with a lot of potential, but that's about it. It's worth playing, but not worth raising. This is the perfect type of hand in which you should want to see the flop as cheaply as possible because, let's face it, you need for at least two spades to come on the board, a King or a Queen, and no Ace. If someone behind you makes a large raise, you have to consider throwing this hand away.

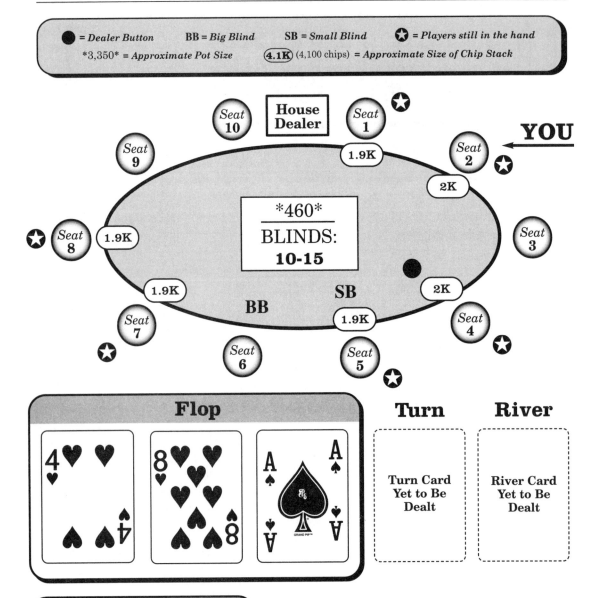

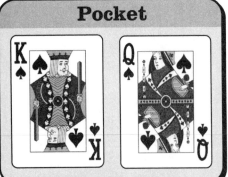

Situation 62:

After you called, Seat 3 folded and Seats 4, 5, and 6 all called, making eight players in the pot. After the flop, Seat 5 bet 85 chips and got three callers before the action got to you. It is now your turn to act. Do you fold, call the 85-chip bet, raise to an unspecified level, or go all in?

Starting Hand (Pocket): **K♠Q♠**
This Pocket's Win Rate: **54.6%**
Win Rate Rank: **12 of 169 possible**

Tournament Situation:
Tourney: **1-table Sit 'n Go, Cardroom**
Paid Entrys: **10 x $10**
Starting Chip Stack: **2,000**
Players Remaining: **10**
Places Paid: **3**
Your Current Standing: **Even with everyone, first hand of the tourney**
Time Left in Round: **10 minutes**
Rebuys Allowed: **No**
Next Blind Level: **15-30**

This Tournament's Prize Money:

1. **$50**
2. **$30**
3. **$20**

Total Prize Pool:
$100

Answer 62:

You got no help whatsoever on the board, other than remote chances for both an Ace-high straight and an Ace-high flush, which you would be foolish to try for since it would require you to hit runner-runner on the turn and river to make either of them. Even then, your straight could still be beaten if someone ends up making a heart flush since two of them are already on the board.

Seat 5 was willing to make a raise in light of the Ace and two hearts on the board, so the flop didn't scare him off. And with three other callers, you have to believe there are at least two Aces in your opponents' hands, and maybe one or two heart flush draws.

Let's assume for argument's sake there are no heart flush draws facing you, just consider the Ace. If even one player holds an Ace, and it's a strong possibility because of the way the betting progressed, that means you would have to hit either two Kings or two Queens on the turn and river in order to beat their pair of Aces, and that assumes they won't hit a third Ace. What are the odds of that occurring? About 1.35 percent of the time, or approximately 54-to-1. Is there at least 54 times the money you're being asked to bet already in the pot (around 4,500 chips)? No. Therefore, the current pot odds (about 4-to-1) are not even close to being correct for you to make this call. Toss this hand away now.

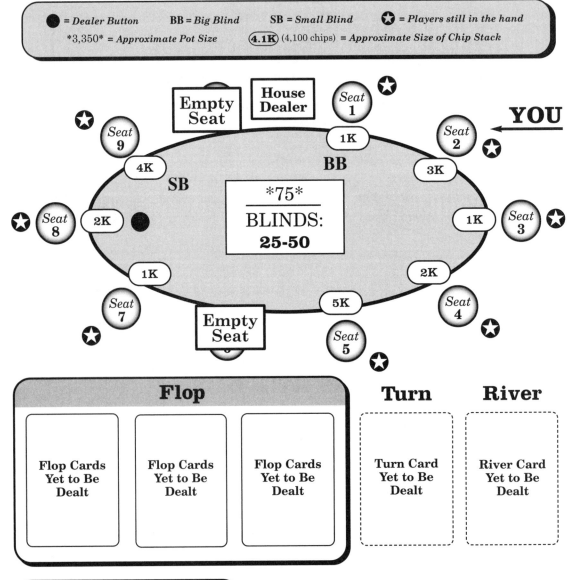

Situation 63:

It's now twenty-six minutes into this single-table sit 'n' go tournament and two players have been eliminated. You have received pocket Kings and are first to act. With seven players yet to act after you, do you fold, call the 50-chip big blind bet, raise to an unspecified level, or go all in with your 3,000 chips?

Starting Hand (Pocket): **K♠K♦**

This Pocket's Win Rate: **74.6%**

Win Rate Rank: **2 of 169 possible**

Tournament Situation:

Tourney: **1-table Sit 'n Go, Cardroom**

Paid Entrys: **10 x $10**

Starting Chip Stack: **2,000**

Players Remaining: **8**

Places Paid: **3**

Your Current Standing: **3rd place**

Time Left in Round: **4 minutes**

Rebuys Allowed: **No**

Next Blind Level: **50-100**

This Tournament's Prize Money:

1. **$50**
2. **$30**
3. **$20**

Total Prize Pool:

$100

Answer 63:

You received a great hand, the kind you sometimes wait all day for. Unfortunately for you, you caught them in first position, so you don't know what everyone else behind you is going to do yet, and secondly, if you bet this hand the way you should—strongly—most if not all of your opponents are going to fold, leaving you with little to show for this powerful hand.

Still, you must bet this hand strong in order to force out the stupid hands like Ace-7 unsuited and small pairs like 2s, 3s, and 4s, all of which could come back to haunt you if you let them in cheaply. I would make a bet of at least 400 chips, and if everyone folds, I'd be content to win the 75 chips in the blinds. If someone calls, that's fine, too, as statistically I know I've got them beat. If someone comes back with a raise of their own, or goes all in, I'd still call and keep my fingers crossed that they don't have pocket Aces. I wouldn't even consider a fold if I'm raised, because after all, if you're not going to play pocket Kings before the flop for all the marbles, what are you going to play? Especially since it's just a $10 buy-in tournament.

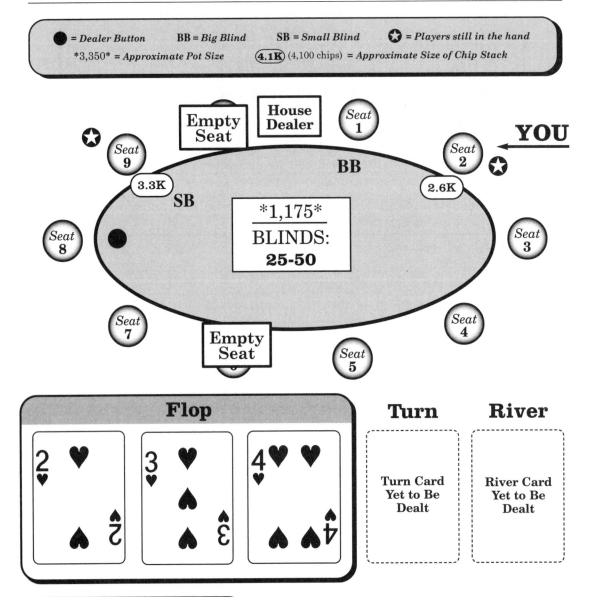

● = *Dealer Button*　　　BB = *Big Blind*　　　SB = *Small Blind*　　★ = *Players still in the hand*

3,350 = *Approximate Pot Size*　　(4.1K) (4,100 chips) = *Approximate Size of Chip Stack*

Empty Seat

House Dealer

Seat 1

YOU

★ Seat 9

Seat 2 ★

BB

3.3K

2.6K

SB

1,175
BLINDS:
25-50

Seat 8

Seat 3

Seat 7

Seat 4

Empty Seat

Seat 5

Flop

2♥ 3♥ 4♥

Turn

Turn Card Yet to Be Dealt

River

River Card Yet to Be Dealt

Pocket

K♠ K♦

Situation 64:

After you bet 400 chips before the flop in first position, everyone folded except Seat 9, who called your bet. After the flop, Seat 9 was first to act and bet 300 chips. It is now your turn to act. Do you fold in the face of his strong bet, call, raise to an unspecified level, or go all in with your remaining 2,600 chips?

Starting Hand (Pocket): **K♠K♦**

This Pocket's Win Rate: **74.6%**

Win Rate Rank: **2 of 169 possible**

Tournament Situation:

Tourney: **1-table Sit 'n Go, Cardroom**

Paid Entrys: **10 x $10**

Starting Chip Stack: **2,000**

Players Remaining: **8**

Places Paid: **3**

Your Current Standing: **3rd place**

Time Left in Round: **4 minutes**

Rebuys Allowed: **No**

Next Blind Level: **50-100**

This Tournament's Prize Money:

1. **$50**
2. **$30**
3. **$20**

_____

Total Prize Pool:

$100

Answer 64:

Your bet of 400 chips had both the desired and expected effect when everyone but one folded. You are now isolated against Seat 9 in a heads-up situation. You also have the advantage of position on him, acting last.

His large bet, though, must give you cause for pause. A lot of possibilities arose with this flop, and unfortunately none of them are good for you. But how bad is it? A heart flush is probably your worst fear at this point, because there are three on the board while you hold a big fat zero hearts in your hand. A straight draw is a very real possibility for your opponent as well, because he could easily hold an Ace, and a 5 will give him a straight. But do you think he actually holds a straight yet? I don't. Does he actually hold a flush yet? I don't think so, either, and I'll tell you why. If he flopped a heart flush, he would be eager to conceal that fact, hoping to get more chips from you. By making such a strong bet in first position, he's trying to force you to do something, which in this case is fold. I would tend to think that such a bet in first position implies weakness, such as being on a heart draw or he's afraid of you being on a heart flush. Either way, I'd feel safe making at least one more call for 300 chips and seeing what the turn card brings. Call the bet.

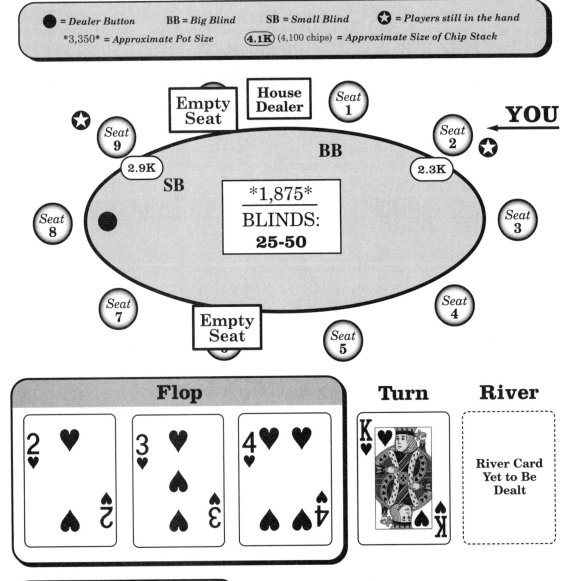

● = *Dealer Button*   BB = *Big Blind*   SB = *Small Blind*   ⭐ = *Players still in the hand*

3,350 = *Approximate Pot Size*   (4.1K) (4,100 chips) = *Approximate Size of Chip Stack*

Flop

Turn   **River**

River Card
Yet to Be
Dealt

Pocket

Situation 65:

After calling Seat 9's bet after the flop for 300 chips, the turn card was dealt. Seat 9 was first to act and bet 400 chips. It is now your turn to act. Do you fold, call his bet, raise to an unspecified level, or go all in for your remaining 2,300 chips?

Starting Hand (Pocket): **K♠K♦**
This Pocket's Win Rate: **74.6%**
Win Rate Rank: **2 of 169 possible**

Tournament Situation:
Tourney: **1-table Sit 'n Go, Cardroom**
Paid Entrys: **10 x $10**
Starting Chip Stack: **2,000**
Players Remaining: **8**
Places Paid: **3**
Your Current Standing: **3rd place**
Time Left in Round: **4 minutes**
Rebuys Allowed: **No**
Next Blind Level: **50-100**

This Tournament's Prize Money:

1. **$50**
2. **$30**
3. **$20**

Total Prize Pool:
$100

Answer 65:

So, did things get better for you, or did they get worse? What a turn card, huh? This is one of the reasons I have no hair on the top of my head; cards like this make me tear it out. Okay, let's take a look at it. The good news is you hit a third King, so now you have a shot at a full house or four of a kind. The bad news is he made a heart flush, assuming he's holding one in his hand. But again, if he made his flush, why is he betting so large? If he wanted to keep you in the hand, he should be betting smaller, like the 50-chip minimum. Larger bets like this will tend to make opponents fold unless they have a strong hand, too.

So let's take a look at the pot odds for this hand and see if it makes sense to call his 400-chip bet. Assuming he has a flush, we're going to need to hit a full house or four of a kind to beat him. With forty-six unseen cards, there are ten possibilities for us to make a full house or four of a kind (three 2s, three 3s, three 4s, and one King). That means our odds of getting one of these cards is 36-to-10, or about 3 1/2-to-1. We're being asked to make a 400-chip bet. Is there at least 400 x 3.5 (1,400 chips) in the pot? Since the pot contains 1,875 chips, then yes, the pot odds are sufficient for us to make this call. Had Seat 9 made a larger bet, say 1,500 to 3,300 chips, then the pot odds would not have been correct to call because it would have required a disproportionate amount of your chips to call. Make the call.

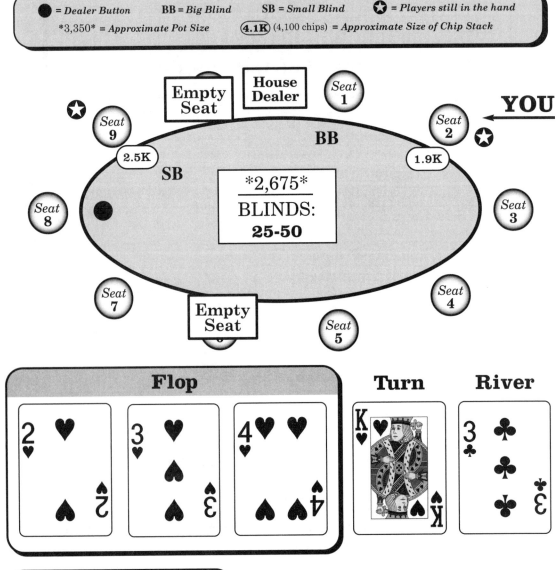

● = *Dealer Button*   BB = *Big Blind*   SB = *Small Blind*   ⭐ = *Players still in the hand*

3,350 = *Approximate Pot Size*   (4.1K) (4,100 chips) = *Approximate Size of Chip Stack*

Flop

2♥ 3♥ 4♥

Turn

K♥

River

3♣

Pocket

K♠ K♦

Situation 66:

After you called Seat 9's 400-chip bet following the turn, the river card was dealt. Seat 9 again bet 400 chips. Should you fold, call the 400, raise to an unspecified level, or go all in?

Starting Hand (Pocket): **K♠K♦**
This Pocket's Win Rate: **74.6%**
Win Rate Rank: **2 of 169 possible**

Tournament Situation:
Tourney: **1-table Sit 'n Go, Cardroom**
Paid Entrys: **10 x $10**
Starting Chip Stack: **2,000**
Players Remaining: **8**
Places Paid: **3**
Your Current Standing: **3rd place**
Time Left in Round: **4 minutes**
Rebuys Allowed: **No**
Next Blind Level: **50-100**

This Tournament's Prize Money:

1. **$50**
2. **$30**
3. **$20**

Total Prize Pool:
$100

Answer 66:

Unless Seat 9 somehow accidentally exposed his cards and revealed pocket 3s, you should go all in, because that's the only thing that's going to beat you. You have the best hand possible except for quad 3s, so make him pay. If he folds, fine. If he calls, even better. As for the realistic possibility that he holds pocket 3s, go back to the beginning of the hand. He called your bet of 400 chips before the flop. Would he have done so on pocket 3s? Possibly, since this is a low-level tournament and players in such tournaments often are beginners who will often play such hands, but statistically he doesn't have pocket 3s. Raise all in, relying on the knowledge that you have better than a 95 percent chance of winning this hand.

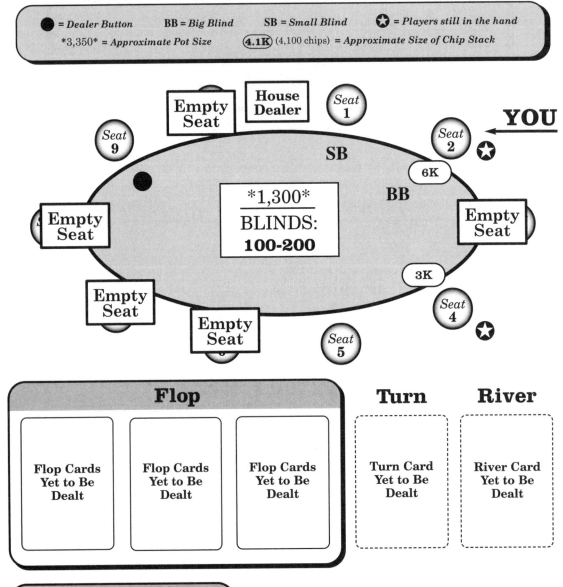

Situation 67:

It's now several more rounds into the tournament and there are just five players left of the ten who started. You are the chip leader and in the big blind position when you catch pocket Aces. Seat 4 acts first and bets 1,000 chips. Seats 5, 9, and 1 all fold. It is now your turn to act. Do you fold, call the 1,000-chip bet, raise to 2,000, or bet 3,800 and force him to go all in to call you?

Starting Hand (Pocket): **A♥A♦**
This Pocket's Win Rate: **86.1%**
Win Rate Rank: **1 of 169 possible**

Tournament Situation:
Tourney: **1-table Sit 'n Go, Cardroom**
Paid Entrys: **10 x $10**
Starting Chip Stack: **2,000**
Players Remaining: **5**
Places Paid: **3**
Your Current Standing: **1st place**
Time Left in Round: **7 minutes**
Rebuys Allowed: **No**
Next Blind Level: **200-400**

This Tournament's Prize Money:

1. **$50**
2. **$30**
3. **$20**

Total Prize Pool:
$100

Answer 67:

Seat 4 indicated real power with his strong bet in first position. You, of course, have the ultimate in power, at least for a pocket hand, so you don't have to fear him at this point. If you want to play it more conservatively, you could just call him and see what the flop brings, and then if it's something really stupid, like three spades or clubs without an Ace, you could still fold if he bets big again. If you want to play it more aggressively, go ahead and bet the 3,800 and force him to either fold or go all in by calling you. If you are afraid he might fold if you bet the 3,800, then just raise him to 2,000. I doubt he'd fold a hand for 1,000 that he's already into for 1,000, especially since he was first to act, unless it was a total bluff on his part. Besides, a bet of 2,000 will look to him like you have some power, but he probably won't put you on pocket Aces with a bet like that.

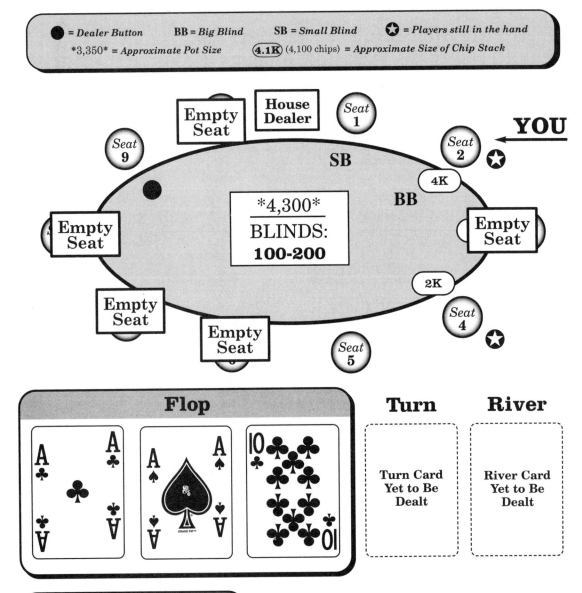

Flop

Turn

Turn Card
Yet to Be
Dealt

River

River Card
Yet to Be
Dealt

Pocket

Situation 68:

You decided to raise him to 2,000 chips, and he called. After the flop, you are first to act. Do you check, bet the minimum of 200 chips, bet to a higher unspecified level, or bet 2,000 chips, forcing Seat 4 to go all in to call you?

Starting Hand (Pocket): A♥A♦
This Pocket's Win Rate: **86.1%**
Win Rate Rank: **1 of 169 possible**

Tournament Situation:
Tourney: **1-table Sit 'n Go, Cardroom**
Paid Entrys: **10 x $10**
Starting Chip Stack: **2,000**
Players Remaining: **5**
Places Paid: **3**
Your Current Standing: **1st place**
Time Left in Round: **7 minutes**
Rebuys Allowed: **No**
Next Blind Level: **200-400**

This Tournament's Prize Money:

1. **$50**
2. **$30**
3. **$20**

Total Prize Pool:
$100

Answer 68:

After that flop, two things should come to mind: milk and nuts. You've got the nuts, so you should milk this hand for all it's worth. Obviously, a flop with two Aces is going to make almost every Hold'em player in the world check if they don't hold one in their hands. But anyone holding an Ace (or two, like you) will be checking as well, and almost every Hold'em player in the world knows that as well. So, you should do something different.

If you check, so will he. If you bet large, he'll probably fold, and you'll make no more money on this hand. So make a small bet, something that looks like a probe. In this case I'd try something like 100 chips. If he has anything at all, such as a club draw, or King-10, giving him two pair, he might call one more time to see what the turn brings if you let him in cheaply enough.

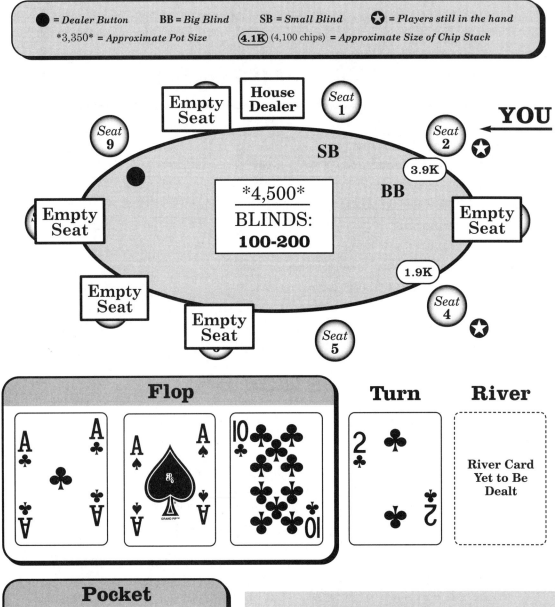

● = *Dealer Button*   BB = *Big Blind*   SB = *Small Blind*   ⭐ = *Players still in the hand*

3,350 = *Approximate Pot Size*   (4.1K) (4,100 chips) = *Approximate Size of Chip Stack*

Empty Seat

House Dealer

Seat 1

YOU

Seat 9

Seat 2 ⭐

SB

3.9K

4,500
BLINDS:
100-200

BB

Empty Seat

Empty Seat

1.9K

Empty Seat

Seat 4 ⭐

Empty Seat

Empty Seat

Seat 5

Flop

A♣ A♠ 10♣

Turn

2♣

River

River Card Yet to Be Dealt

Pocket

A♥ A♦

Situation 69:

After you made your 100-chip bet following the flop, Seat 4 called. After the turn card came, you are first to act. Do you check, make another small bet, make a larger bet, or go right to 1,900 chips, forcing him all in?

Starting Hand (Pocket): **A♥A♦**
This Pocket's Win Rate: **86.1%**
Win Rate Rank: **1 of 169 possible**

Tournament Situation:
Tourney: **1-table Sit 'n Go, Cardroom**
Paid Entries: **10 x $10**
Starting Chip Stack: **2,000**
Players Remaining: **5**
Places Paid: **3**
Your Current Standing: **1st place**
Time Left in Round: **7 minutes**
Rebuys Allowed: **No**
Next Blind Level: **200-400**

This Tournament's Prize Money:

1. **$50**
2. **$30**
3. **$20**

Total Prize Pool:
$100

Answer 69:

If your opponent was on a club flush draw, this was a great card for you. Keeping with the theme of milking this hand, you should not make a large bet at this point, because if he was on something other than a club draw, he'll fold and you'll get no more chips from him. If you make a small bet, and he was on a club flush draw, he'll either call you or raise. You might also consider a bit of acting here. When the third club hit the board, you could stare stone-faced at it and slightly shake your head in apparent displeasure. You could also softly whisper a profanity just loud enough for Seat 4 to hear, and then follow this up by checking, giving every indication that the club on the turn hurt you. If he bets big, then come over top of him and bring him all in and send him home. If he bets small to moderate, take a lot of time and then just call him and save your big bet for the river, milking every last chip out of him.

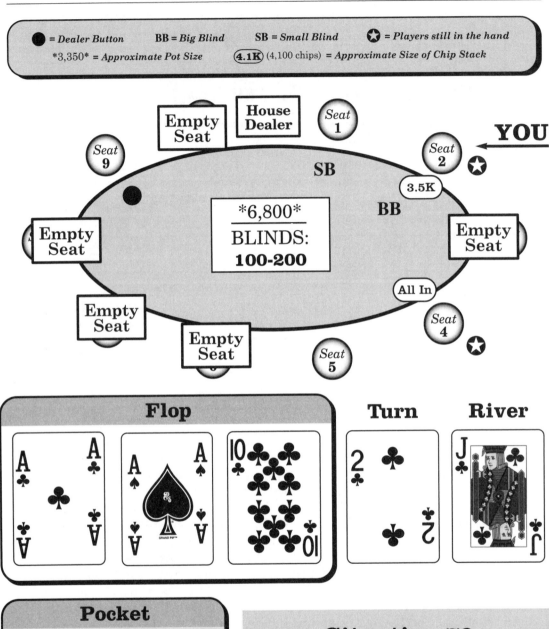

Flop | Turn | River

Pocket

Situation 70:

After you checked following the turn, Seat 4 bet 200 chips and you called. After the river card was dealt, you were first to act and bet 200 chips. Your opponent quickly went all in for his remaining 1,700 chips. While you are deciding what to do, he smiles broadly and says, "Since you're a nice guy, I'll show you one of my cards," and then turns over the King of clubs. Do you fold or call the additional 1,500 chips?

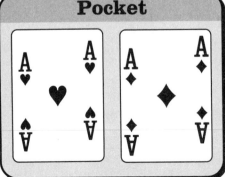

Starting Hand (Pocket): **A♥A♦**
This Pocket's Win Rate: **86.1%**
Win Rate Rank: **1 of 169 possible**

Tournament Situation:
Tourney: **1-table Sit 'n Go, Cardroom**
Paid Entrys: **10 x $10**
Starting Chip Stack: **2,000**
Players Remaining: **5**
Places Paid: **3**
Your Current Standing: **1st place**
Time Left in Round: **6 minutes**
Rebuys Allowed: **No**
Next Blind Level: **200-400**

This Tournament's Prize Money:

1. **$50**
2. **$30**
3. **$20**

_____

Total Prize Pool:
$100

Answer 70:

As Scooby-Doo would say, "Rut-ro!" What have we got ourselves into here?! What looked like the most sure thing since Stephanie Whatshername following the homecoming dance in 1971 has now turned into a nightmare. Could he really be holding the Queen of clubs for a royal flush? Ugh.

Well, let's think back a bit. When the hand started, he was first to act and he bet 1,000 chips in a fairly shorthanded game of only five players. Would he have really done this with a King-Queen suited in first position? It seems highly unlikely to me that he'd make such a strong bet with that kind of a hand. Then what, with the King of clubs, could have induced him to have bet so strongly in first position before the flop? Not Ace-King of clubs because the Ace is on the board. If not Ace-King of clubs, or King-Queen of clubs, then what? Ah, what about pocket Kings? That would induce a bet of 1,000 chips in first position, and properly so. So, my money (and yours) will go with pocket Kings, giving him the nut flush, which in this case, ain't good enough. Call the 1,500 chips.

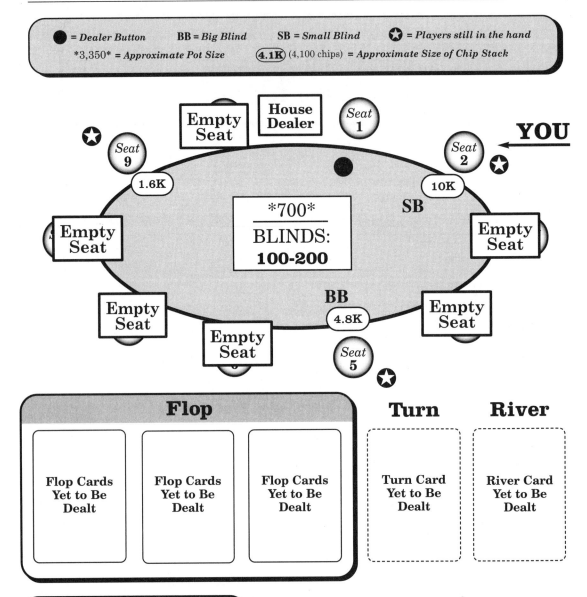

● = *Dealer Button*   **BB** = *Big Blind*   **SB** = *Small Blind*   ★ = *Players still in the hand*

3,350 = *Approximate Pot Size*   **4.1K** (4,100 chips) = *Approximate Size of Chip Stack*

Empty Seat

House Dealer

Seat 1

★ Seat 9

YOU ←

Seat 2 ★

1.6K

10K

SB

700
―――――
BLINDS:
100-200

Empty Seat

Empty Seat

BB

4.8K

Empty Seat

Empty Seat

Empty Seat

Seat 5 ★

Flop

| Flop Cards Yet to Be Dealt | Flop Cards Yet to Be Dealt | Flop Cards Yet to Be Dealt |

Turn

Turn Card Yet to Be Dealt

River

River Card Yet to Be Dealt

Pocket

Situation 71:

After knocking out Seat 4 on the previous hand (he did have pocket Kings, just like you thought), you received Jack-9 suited in your pocket while in the small blind position. Seat 9 was first to act and bet 400 chips. Seat 1 folded and now it is your turn. Do you fold, call the additional 300 chips, raise to an unspecified level, or go all in for 10,000 chips, attempting to bully your opponents into folding with your larger stack?

Starting Hand (Pocket): **J♣9♣**
This Pocket's Win Rate: **27.9%**
Win Rate Rank: **31 of 169 possible**

Tournament Situation:
Tourney: **1-table Sit 'n Go, Cardroom**
Paid Entrys: **10 x $10**
Starting Chip Stack: **2,000**
Players Remaining: **4**
Places Paid: **3**
Your Current Standing: **1st place**
Time Left in Round: **6 minutes**
Rebuys Allowed: **No**
Next Blind Level: **200-400**

This Tournament's Prize Money:

1. **$50**
2. **$30**
3. **$20**

_____

Total Prize Pool:
$100

Answer 71:

You have major control of this tournament right now, so the last thing you want to do is squander your chips. While Jack-9 suited is a decent starting hand, it needs to be played under the proper circumstances and in the proper position, and neither factor is present here. If you call this bet, Seat 5 could fold and you'd be in a heads up situation with a Jack-9. Seat 5 could go all in for 4,800 chips and then you'd be faced with either calling with half of your chips on a Jack-9, or folding and losing 400 chips instead of 100.

Pick a better hill to die on, because this ain't it. You have the largest chip stack and can ride out the increasing blinds much better than any of your opponents right now. Time is on your side and against your opponents.

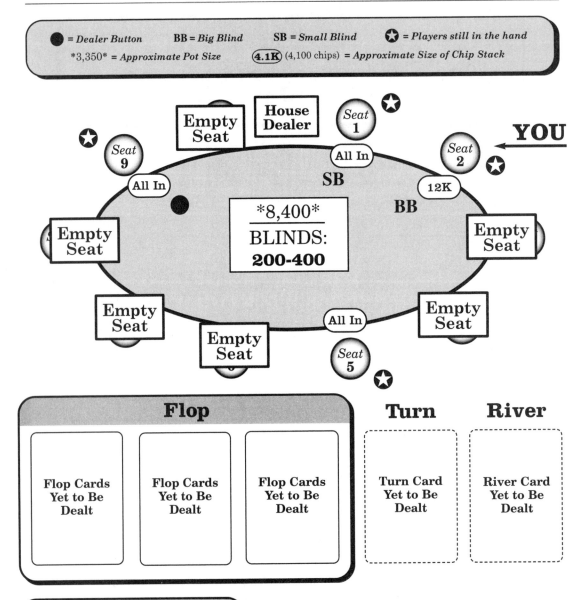

= Dealer Button   **BB** = *Big Blind*   **SB** = *Small Blind*   ⭐ = *Players still in the hand*

3,350 = *Approximate Pot Size*   **4.1K** (4,100 chips) = *Approximate Size of Chip Stack*

Empty Seat

House Dealer

Seat 1

⭐

YOU ⟵

Seat 9   ⭐

Seat 2

All In

All In

SB

12K

8,400
——————
BLINDS:
200-400

BB

Empty Seat

Empty Seat

Empty Seat

All In

Empty Seat

Empty Seat

Seat 5   ⭐

Flop

| Flop Cards Yet to Be Dealt | Flop Cards Yet to Be Dealt | Flop Cards Yet to Be Dealt |

Turn

Turn Card Yet to Be Dealt

River

River Card Yet to Be Dealt

Pocket

6♥   6♣

Situation 72:

It's now deeper into the tournament and you still have control of the game. You received pocket 6s while in the big blind position. Seat 5 goes all in for 3,000 chips and is called by Seat 9 who has the same size stack. Seat 1 then tosses his 2,000 chips into the pot, making all three of your opponents all in. Do you fold or put in 3,000 chips as well and make it a family pot, knowing you could end the tournament right now with a win?

Starting Hand (Pocket): **6♥6♣**

This Pocket's Win Rate: **26.2%**

Win Rate Rank: **32 of 169 possible**

Tournament Situation:

Tourney: **1-table Sit 'n Go, Cardroom**

Paid Entrys: **10 x $10**

Starting Chip Stack: **2,000**

Players Remaining: **4**

Places Paid: **3**

Your Current Standing: **1st place**

Time Left in Round: **6 minutes**

Rebuys Allowed: **No**

Next Blind Level: **300-600**

This Tournament's Prize Money:

1. **$50**
2. **$30**
3. **$20**

Total Prize Pool:

$100

Answer 72:

It would be nice to end it all right here and take home the top prize, but fighting it out with a pair of 6s just doesn't make sense. Had you been allowed to see the flop for free, and a 6 came, then you could fight it out with a set of 6s, sure, but not a pair.

You also need to keep in mind that fortunes can change rapidly in Texas Hold'em by virtue of the power of doubling up. If you get careless and put a few thousand of your chips into play loosely, they can turn into a lot of chips in a hurry for an opponent who uses them to double up his chip stack two or three hands in a row.

On this hand, with all three of your opponents contesting the pot already, fold your hand and maybe when the dust clears only one of them will be left standing, and you'll go from a position of probably going to make the money, to being assured of second place at the very least—without even playing.

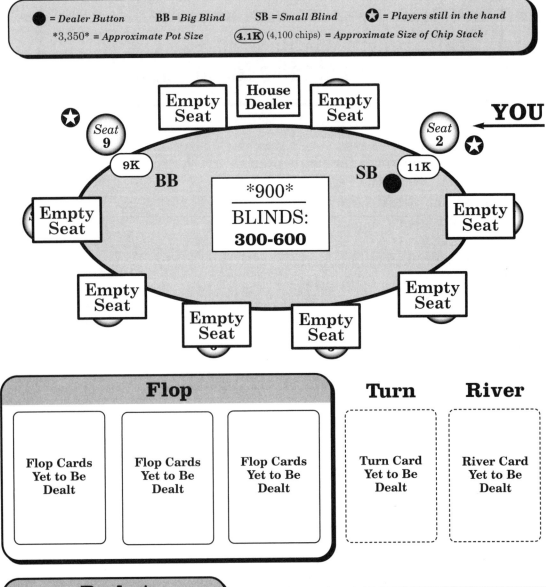

● = *Dealer Button*   **BB** = *Big Blind*   **SB** = *Small Blind*   ★ = *Players still in the hand*

3,350 = *Approximate Pot Size*   (**4.1K**) (4,100 chips) = *Approximate Size of Chip Stack*

Empty Seat   House Dealer   Empty Seat   **YOU**

★   Seat 9   9K   **BB**

Seat 2   11K   **SB** ●

900 / BLINDS: **300-600**

Empty Seat   Empty Seat

Empty Seat   Empty Seat

Empty Seat   Empty Seat

Flop

Flop Cards Yet to Be Dealt | Flop Cards Yet to Be Dealt | Flop Cards Yet to Be Dealt

Turn
Turn Card Yet to Be Dealt

River
River Card Yet to Be Dealt

Pocket

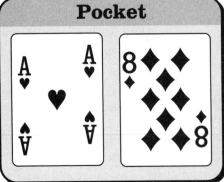

Situation 73:

It's now late in the tournament and you are heads up with Seat 9. You are in the small blind position and catch an Ace-8 unsuited in your pocket. Do you fold, call the additional 300 chips, raise to an unspecified level, or go all in?

Starting Hand (Pocket): **A♥8♦**
This Pocket's Win Rate: **10.0%**
Win Rate Rank: **42 of 169 possible**

Tournament Situation:
Tourney: **1-table Sit 'n Go, Cardroom**
Paid Entries: **10 x $10**
Starting Chip Stack: **2,000**
Players Remaining: **2**
Places Paid: **3**
Your Current Standing: **1st place**
Time Left in Round: **10 minutes**
Rebuys Allowed: **No**
Next Blind Level: **400-800**

This Tournament's Prize Money:

1. **$50**
2. **$30**
3. **$20**

_____

Total Prize Pool:
$100

Answer 73:

Normally this is a no-brainer, at least for good players. You throw it away. But in situations like this, where it's heads up, a hand like Ace-8 unsuited becomes a better hand. As the chart above shows, Ace-8 unsuited ranks 42 out of the 169 possible pocket hands in terms of relative win rate. Not great, but not stinky, either. Statistically, your opponent doesn't hold an Ace, and in a heads-up game, almost any Ace becomes valuable.

This would be a good time to try and steal his blind, so make a small raise, say to 1,200 or 1,800 chips (2x or 3x the big blind). He might perceive this as a blind stealing move on your part because of the small raise, but if he doesn't have a hand, so what? If he does have a strong hand, he'll either call or raise, and if he calls, he gives you a chance to catch up. If he raises strong, you can always fold and wait for the next opportunity. Right now, though, you have to take advantage of your Ace because there's no telling how long it will be before you see another one.

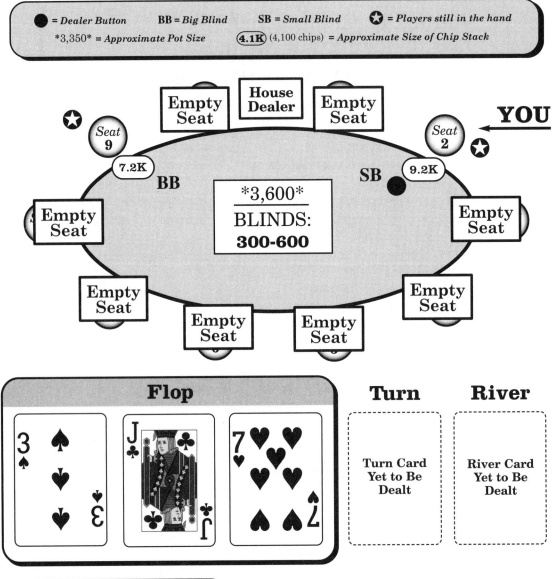

Situation 74:

After you raised to 1,800 chips, Seat 9 called. After the flop, Seat 9 was first to act and checked. Do you check as well, bet the minimum of 600 chips, raise to an unspecified level, or go all in for your remaining 9,200 chips?

Starting Hand (Pocket): **A♥8♦**

This Pocket's Win Rate: **10.0%**

Win Rate Rank: **42 of 169 possible**

Tournament Situation:

Tourney: **1-table Sit 'n Go, Cardroom**

Paid Entries: **10 x $10**

Starting Chip Stack: **2,000**

Players Remaining: **2**

Places Paid: **3**

Your Current Standing: **1st place**

Time Left in Round: **10 minutes**

Rebuys Allowed: **No**

Next Blind Level: **400-800**

This Tournament's Prize Money:

1. **$50**
2. **$30**
3. **$20**

Total Prize Pool:

$100

Answer 74:

What a mess. You started off with basically an Ace and the hope that you could somehow improve on your hand. This flop missed your hand about as far as it could be missed. You could make a bet anyway, hoping that he missed as badly as you did, but remember, you raised before the flop and he called you. Let's emphasize this: he called you after you raised, which means he probably has a pretty decent hand, maybe even better than yours, especially now after the flop.

This isn't a hand you can get cute with. You should just check here, if for no other reason than to keep him from check-raising you.

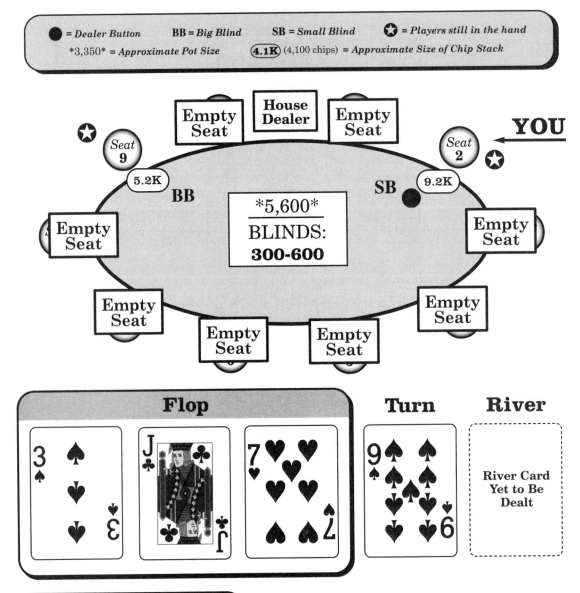

Situation 75:

After you checked following the flop, the turn card was dealt. Seat 9 bet first, pushing 2,000 chips into the pot. Do you fold, call his bet, raise to an unspecified level, or go all in?

Starting Hand (Pocket): **A♥8♦**
This Pocket's Win Rate: **10.0%**
Win Rate Rank: **42 of 169 possible**

Tournament Situation:
Tourney: **1-table Sit 'n Go, Cardroom**
Paid Entrys: **10 x $10**
Starting Chip Stack: **2,000**
Players Remaining: **2**
Places Paid: **3**
Your Current Standing: **1st place**
Time Left in Round: **10 minutes**
Rebuys Allowed: **No**
Next Blind Level: **400-800**

This Tournament's Prize Money:

1. **$50**
2. **$30**
3. **$20**

Total Prize Pool:
$100

Answer 75:

You started off with slop, flopped a mess, and turned a longshot. It's time to get rid of this hand. Your efforts to make him fold in the beginning didn't work and so far you've got nothing to work with on this board except a gutshot straight draw. But do you really want to risk a large amount of your chips on a 10 coming on the river? I know I don't. Fold this hand now and try again on the next one.

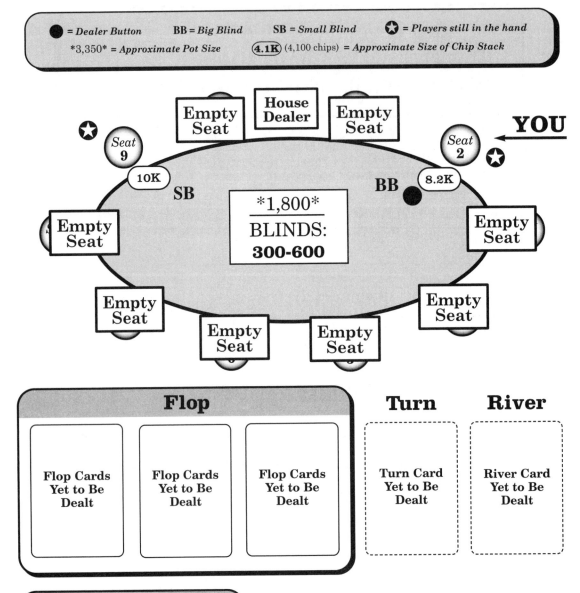

● = *Dealer Button*   BB = *Big Blind*   SB = *Small Blind*   ★ = *Players still in the hand*
3,350 = *Approximate Pot Size*   (4.1K) (4,100 chips) = *Approximate Size of Chip Stack*

Empty Seat · House Dealer · Empty Seat · YOU

★ Seat 9 — 10K — SB

Seat 2 ★ — 8.2K — BB

Empty Seat

1,800
BLINDS:
300-600

Empty Seat

Empty Seat · Empty Seat · Empty Seat · Empty Seat

Flop

| Flop Cards Yet to Be Dealt | Flop Cards Yet to Be Dealt | Flop Cards Yet to Be Dealt |

Turn

Turn Card Yet to Be Dealt

River

River Card Yet to Be Dealt

Pocket

Situation 76

After jockeying back and forth for about ten hands, you are in the big blind position and catch a 10-9 suited in your pocket. Seat 9 raises to 1,200 chips. Do you fold, call, raise to an unspecified level, or go all in?

Starting Hand (Pocket): **10♦9♦**

This Pocket's Win Rate: **38.3%**

Win Rate Rank: **24 of 169 possible**

Tournament Situation:

Tourney: **1-table Sit 'n Go, Cardroom**

Paid Entrys: **10 x $10**

Starting Chip Stack: **2,000**

Players Remaining: **2**

Places Paid: **3**

Your Current Standing: **1st place**

Time Left in Round: **3 minutes**

Rebuys Allowed: **No**

Next Blind Level: **400-800**

This Tournament's Prize Money:

1. **$50**
2. **$30**
3. **$20**

_____

Total Prize Pool:

$100

Answer 76:

Normally this isn't that great of a hand in a heads up game. In this case I would play it, however, for a number of reasons. First, you have both a straight and flush draw. Second, there's not that much difference between the first and second place prize money in this tiny one-table tournament. Third, since this tournament is taking place in a cardroom as a preliminary event to get the action going at the live tables, I'd be wanting to play in a full game where I could make more money than the $20 difference between first and second place in this tournament. If I were playing this tournament on one of the Internet sites, I wouldn't be so easily persuaded to end this thing sooner rather than later because I could jump to another Internet tournament, sit 'n' go, or a ring game immediately.

While I would play this hand, I wouldn't get crazy and go all in like a lot of bored players might. Just make the call and see what the flop brings. With three more cards to look at, it should make it easier to decide what to do after that. And if the jockeying continues for much longer, I'd make an offer to my opponent to just split the pot, $40 each and go on to a live game. He probably wants to get in a game with more action just as much as you.

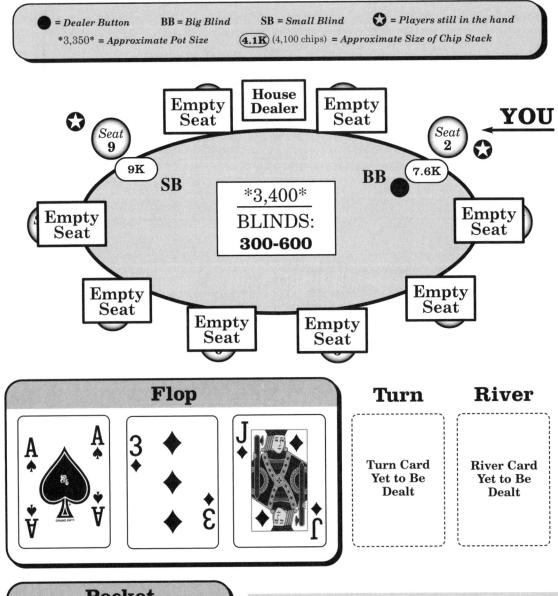

● = *Dealer Button*   BB = *Big Blind*   SB = *Small Blind*   ★ = *Players still in the hand*

3,350 = *Approximate Pot Size*   **4.1K** (4,100 chips) = *Approximate Size of Chip Stack*

House Dealer

Empty Seat

Empty Seat

★ Seat 9 9K SB

Seat 2 ★ YOU

7.6K BB

3,400
BLINDS:
300-600

Empty Seat

Empty Seat

Empty Seat

Empty Seat

Empty Seat

Empty Seat

Flop

A♠ 3♦ J♦

Turn

Turn Card Yet to Be Dealt

River

River Card Yet to Be Dealt

Pocket

10♦ 9♦

Situation 77:

After the flop, your opponent bets 1,000 chips. It is now your turn to act. Do you fold, call his 1,000-chip bet, raise to an unspecified level, or go all in?

Starting Hand (Pocket): **10♦9♦**

This Pocket's Win Rate: **38.3%**

Win Rate Rank: **24 of 169 possible**

Tournament Situation:
Tourney: **1-table Sit 'n Go, Cardroom**
Paid Entrys: **10 x $10**
Starting Chip Stack: **2,000**
Players Remaining: **2**
Places Paid: **3**
Your Current Standing: **1st place**
Time Left in Round: **3 minutes**
Rebuys Allowed: **No**
Next Blind Level: **400-800**

This Tournament's Prize Money:

1. **$50**
2. **$30**
3. **$20**

———

Total Prize Pool:
$100

Answer 77:

It was a decent flop for you, bringing two more diamonds. Now the question is, what did your opponent like about the flop, if anything, to induce him to bet 1,000 chips? He did, after all, raise preflop, so maybe the flop didn't help him. If it didn't, however, then you have to believe the Ace either hurt him or potentially hurt him.

In any event, let's assume we can win this hand with a diamond flush. Are the pot odds correct for making this call? We're being asked to make a 1,000-chip bet in order to win 3,400 chips, giving us pot odds of exactly 3.4-to-1. The odds of hitting a flush by the river after flopping four of the same suit are about 2-to-1 (forty-seven unseen cards minus nine diamonds equals thirty-eight non-diamonds ÷ nine diamonds = 4.22-to-1. Since we have two shots at hitting a diamond, we have to divide 4.22-to-1 by 2, which gives us our 2.11-to-1 ratio.). Therefore, the pot odds are more than correct to make this call for 1,000 chips.

You might also consider a raise to 2,000 chips, then, if you miss your diamond on the turn, he might well check to you, thereby giving you a free river card.

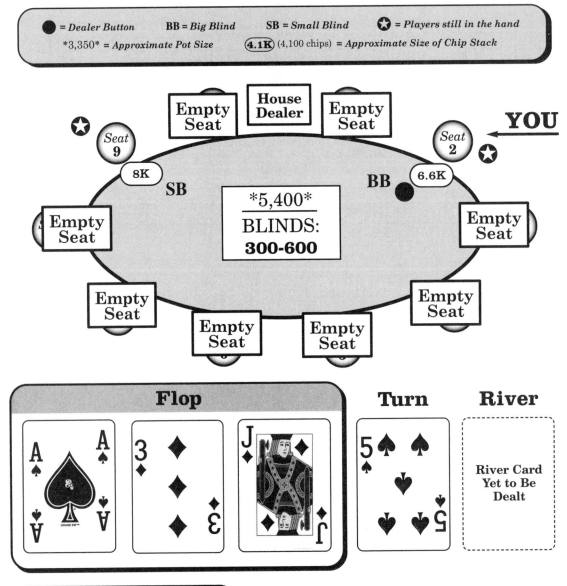

● = *Dealer Button*   BB = *Big Blind*   SB = *Small Blind*   ★ = *Players still in the hand*

3,350 = *Approximate Pot Size*   **4.1K** (4,100 chips) = *Approximate Size of Chip Stack*

House Dealer

Empty Seat

Empty Seat

YOU

★ Seat 9   8K   SB

Seat 2   6.6K   ★

BB ●

5,400
————
BLINDS:
300-600

Empty Seat

Empty Seat

Empty Seat

Empty Seat

Empty Seat

Empty Seat

Flop

A♠ 3♦ J♦

Turn

5♠

River

River Card Yet to Be Dealt

Pocket

10♦ 9♦

Situation 78:

After the turn card was dealt, Seat 9 again bet 1,000 chips. Do you fold, call the 1,000, raise to an unspecified level, or go all in?

Starting Hand (Pocket): **10♦9♦**
This Pocket's Win Rate: **38.3%**
Win Rate Rank: **24 of 169 possible**

Tournament Situation:
Tourney: **1-table Sit 'n Go, Cardroom**
Paid Entrys: **10 x $10**
Starting Chip Stack: **2,000**
Players Remaining: **2**
Places Paid: **3**
Your Current Standing: **1st place**
Time Left in Round: **3 minutes**
Rebuys Allowed: **No**
Next Blind Level: **400-800**

This Tournament's Prize Money:

1. **$50**
2. **$30**
3. **$20**

_____

Total Prize Pool:
$100

Answer 78:

Not much changed with the 5 on the turn unless your opponent holds a hand of 4-2, which isn't likely given he raised from the beginning. So, if we assume we still need to hit a diamond flush to win this hand, is it still correct to make this call? Let's figure it out.

There are now forty-six unseen cards of which nine are diamonds, but we now have only one chance to hit the flush. We calculate the odds thusly:

46 unseen cards - 9 diamonds = 37 non-diamonds

37 non-diamonds ÷ 9 diamonds = 4.11, or about 4.1-to-1 actual odds

Chips in the pot compared to the bet we're being asked to make is:

4,400-to-1,000, or 4.4-to-1

Therefore, it is still correct to make this call. Don't forget, however, that even if we hit our flush, we may not win because our opponent may hold two diamonds as well, one of which is higher than our 10. We're just operating under the assumption that a flush will give us the win.

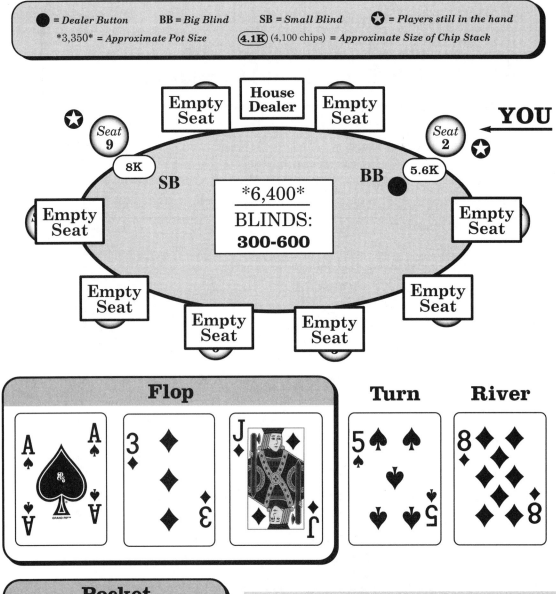

YOU

Seat 9

Seat 2

8K

SB   *6,400*   BB   5.6K
BLINDS:
300-600

Flop   **Turn**   **River**

Pocket

Situation 79:

After the river card was dealt, Seat 9 again bet 1,000 chips. Do you fold, call the 1,000, raise to an unspecified level, or go all in?

Starting Hand (Pocket): **10♦9♦**

This Pocket's Win Rate: **38.3%**

Win Rate Rank: **24 of 169 possible**

Tournament Situation:

Tourney: **1-table Sit 'n Go, Cardroom**

Paid Entrys: **10 x $10**

Starting Chip Stack: **2,000**

Players Remaining: **2**

Places Paid: **3**

Your Current Standing: **1st place**

Time Left in Round: **2 minutes**

Rebuys Allowed: **No**

Next Blind Level: **400-800**

This Tournament's Prize Money:

1. **$50**
2. **$30**
3. **$20**

Total Prize Pool:

$100

Answer 79:

Okay, you got your flush. Now what? Seat 9 never deviated from his betting pattern of around 1,000 chips each time while he was in first position, including before the flop when there were no diamonds yet on the board. This would lead me to believe he doesn't hold two diamonds in his pocket. Given the low money return on this tournament, i.e., the small difference between first and second place prize money, I'd go all in and force the issue.

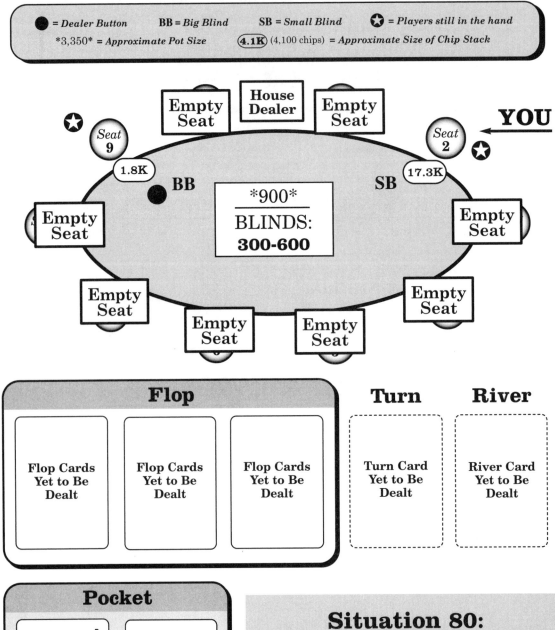

Situation 80:

After your all-in bet on the previous hand was called by Seat 9, you took him down and now have a huge chip lead. You received a pocket hand of Ace-6 unsuited and are first to act. Do you fold, call the 600-chip big blind bet, raise to an unspecified level, or raise to 2,400 chips, forcing your opponent to fold or go all in?

Starting Hand (Pocket): **A♠6♦**
This Pocket's Win Rate: **9.9%**
Win Rate Rank: **43 of 169 possible**

Tournament Situation:
Tourney: **1-table Sit 'n Go, Cardroom**
Paid Entrys: **10 x $10**
Starting Chip Stack: **2,000**
Players Remaining: **2**
Places Paid: **3**
Your Current Standing: **1st place**
Time Left in Round: **2 minutes**
Rebuys Allowed: **No**
Next Blind Level: **400-800**

This Tournament's Prize Money:

1. **$50**
2. **$30**
3. **$20**

Total Prize Pool:
$100

Answer 80:

Once again, you've caught a hand that you shouldn't normally play, but in a heads up situation, Ace-anything becomes playable, especially when you have a huge chip lead like you do currently. This is the proper time to use your big stack to bully the small stack(s). Any pair 4s or higher, Ace-anything, two suited connectors 8 and above, two unsuited connectors 10 and above, and essentially anything that can be made into something good or has at least one big card such as an Ace, King, or Queen.

If your opponent has caught a lousy hand, which will be the case at least 70 percent of the time, he could very easily fold, losing his 600 chips, hoping for a better hand the next time. Becoming a bully doesn't mean, however, becoming stupid. Just because you have a large stack doesn't mean you should try to push through hands like 9-4 unsuited, 2-3 suited, etc. Be smart with your bullying. If you have to fold a few hands in a row, don't sweat it because you have the big stack, not your opponent. And in less than two minutes the blinds are going up to 400-800, another factor working against his small stack.

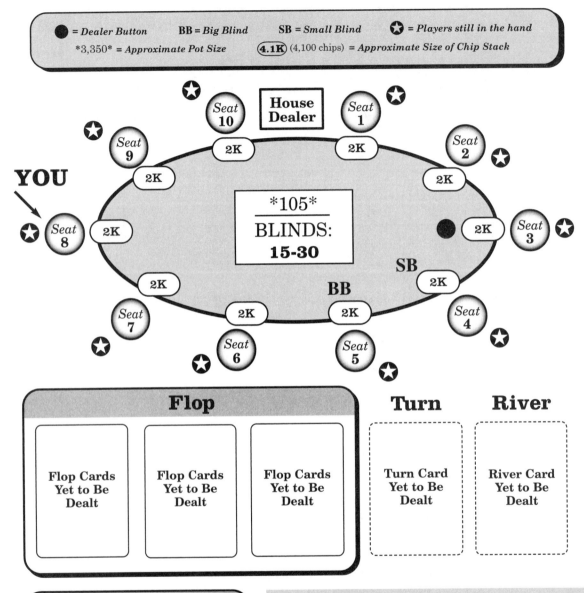

● = *Dealer Button*   **BB** = *Big Blind*   **SB** = *Small Blind*   ★ = *Players still in the hand*

3,350 = *Approximate Pot Size*   **4.1K** (4,100 chips) = *Approximate Size of Chip Stack*

YOU

Seat 10   House Dealer   Seat 1   Seat 2

Seat 9   Seat 8

Seat 3

105
BLINDS:
15-30

SB

BB

Seat 7   Seat 6   Seat 5   Seat 4

Flop

Flop Cards Yet to Be Dealt

Flop Cards Yet to Be Dealt

Flop Cards Yet to Be Dealt

Turn

Turn Card Yet to Be Dealt

River

River Card Yet to Be Dealt

Pocket

Situation 81:

The next 70 situations deal with your progression through the same tournament.

After winning the single-table sit 'n' go tourney in your local cardroom, you decided to go home and play in a large Internet tournament which awards fully paid entries into the World Series of Poker in Las Vegas. On the first hand you received a pocket of King-Jack unsuited. Seats 6 and 7 called the 30-chip big blind bet. It is now your turn to act. Do you fold, call the bet, raise to an unspecified level, or go all in?

Starting Hand (Pocket): **K♠J♣**

This Pocket's Win Rate: **20.5%**

Win Rate Rank: **35 of 169 possible**

Tournament Situation:

Tourney: **Internet Qualifier**

Paid Entrys: **2,400 x $50**

Starting Chip Stack: **2,000**

Players Remaining: **2,400**

Places Paid: **15 (See chart)**

Your Current Standing: **Tied with everyone else, just starting**

Time Left in Round: **15 minutes**

Rebuys Allowed: **No**

Next Blind Level: **25-50**

This Tournament's Prize Money:

**1st-10th:
Paid entry to
World Series of
Poker Main Event
(worth $10,000)**
11th: $7,500
12th: $5,000
13th: $4,000
14th: $2,500
15th: $1,000

Total Prize Pool:
$120,000

Answer 81:

Before you make a move in this tournament, you need to get your head straight about a few things. First, with twenty-four hundred entries and fifteen-minute rounds, this will be a long, long tournament to the final table, probably somewhere in the neighborhood of four to eight hours. You need to think about outside distractions and/or commitments that might interfere with keeping your mind on a tournament like this. While the investment ($50) isn't that much, the potential reward (a seat in the World Series of Poker in Las Vegas with its first-place prize of between $5-10 million) is tremendous, so you want to be able to tend to business in this tournament.

Second, with twenty-four hundred entries, players will seemingly drop like flies (three to ten per minute), thus you need to be patient. If you don't play a hand for fifteen minutes, losing only a couple of cheap early blinds, you'll likely find there are one hundred fewer competitors in that span. Also, with no rebuys allowed, you have to make sure that the hill you pick to die on is worth it. Don't go all in until you've either got the nuts or have little alternative. Even a few chips can come back to life in short order by doubling up.

As for this hand, it's not as good as it first appears. If you do decide to play, just call with the firm commitment that if raised, you'll fold in this early position.

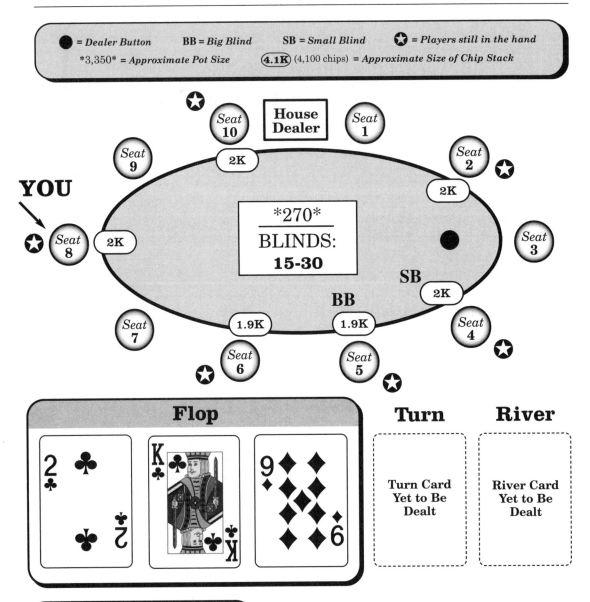

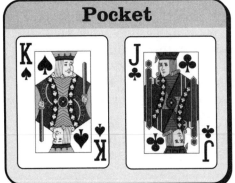

Situation 82:

After you called, four other players did as well, leaving seven of you to contest the pot. When the flop hit the board, Seat 4 checked, Seat 5 bet 30 chips and was called by Seat 6. Seat 7 folded and now it is your turn. With three players to act after you, do you fold, call the 30-chip bet, raise to an unspecified level, or go all in?

> ## Starting Hand (Pocket): K♠J♣
> ## This Pocket's Win Rate: 20.5%
> ## Win Rate Rank: 35 of 169 possible

Tournament Situation:

Tourney: **Internet Qualifier**

Paid Entrys: **2,400 x $50**

Starting Chip Stack: **2,000**

Players Remaining: **2,400**

Places Paid: **15 (See chart)**

Your Current Standing: **Tied with everyone else, just starting**

Time Left in Round: **15 minutes**

Rebuys Allowed: **No**

Next Blind Level: **25-50**

This Tournament's Prize Money:

1st-10th:
Paid entry to World Series of Poker Main Event (worth $10,000)
11th: $7,500
12th: $5,000
13th: $4,000
14th: $2,500
15th: $1,000

Total Prize Pool:

$120,000

Answer 82:

The King was nice to see, but with two clubs on the board you have to be careful. At this point, just call the bet and see what happens behind you. You've got top pair, so it's worth playing, but the clubs, potential Aces out there, players yet to act, and a kicker (Jack) that's a bit lower than ideal all require that you proceed cautiously with this hand.

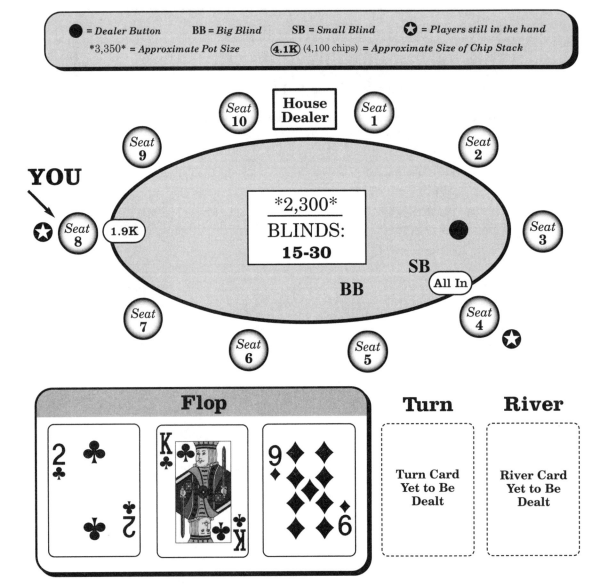

● = *Dealer Button*   **BB** = *Big Blind*   **SB** = *Small Blind*   ⭐ = *Players still in the hand*

3,350 = *Approximate Pot Size*   (**4.1K**) (4,100 chips) = *Approximate Size of Chip Stack*

Seat 10   House Dealer   Seat 1

Seat 9

YOU

Seat 8   1.9K

2,300
BLINDS:
15-30

SB
All In

BB

Seat 7

Seat 6   Seat 5

Seat 2

Seat 3

Seat 4   ⭐

Flop

2♣   K♣   9♦

Turn

Turn Card
Yet to Be
Dealt

River

River Card
Yet to Be
Dealt

Pocket

K♠   J♣

Situation 83:

After you called, Seats 10 and 2 both folded. Seat 4, who had checked earlier, now goes all in for 1,970 chips. Seats 5 and 6 then fold. It is now your turn to act. Do you fold as well or call the all in with your remaining 1,940 chips?

Starting Hand (Pocket): **K♠J♣**

This Pocket's Win Rate: **20.5%**

Win Rate Rank: **35 of 169 possible**

Tournament Situation:

Tourney: **Internet Qualifier**

Paid Entrys: **2,400 x $50**

Starting Chip Stack: **2,000**

Players Remaining: **2,400**

Places Paid: **15 (See chart)**

Your Current Standing: **Tied with everyone else, just starting**

Time Left in Round: **15 minutes**

Rebuys Allowed: **No**

Next Blind Level: **25-50**

This Tournament's Prize Money:

1st-10th:
Paid entry to World Series of Poker Main Event (worth $10,000)
11th: $7,500
12th: $5,000
13th: $4,000
14th: $2,500
15th: $1,000

Total Prize Pool:
$120,000

Answer 83:

An unusual move, to say the least, to see a player go all in on the first hand of a tournament like this. Nevertheless, you have to deal with what you've got. You hold top pair with a Jack kicker. Since this is an Internet tournament, you can't check out his facial expressions or body language. It's not likely that you've ever played against him/her before, so you don't have any idea of what kind of a player you're dealing with.

Did he go all in on a club draw as a semi-bluff? Or does he hold a King with a better kicker than you? Maybe he holds a medium pair like 10s or Jacks and is taking a chance that no one holds a higher pair, especially Kings since one came on the flop.

The underlying principle here is this: do you want to risk your whole tournament right now on top pair with a Jack kicker and two more cards to come? Even though you might have him beat, at this stage of the game I'd fold this hand and wait for a time when I felt in better control of the hand. Had he made a smaller bet, say 100-200 chips, then you could have called that, but not his all in which puts your tournament at risk. Fold it.

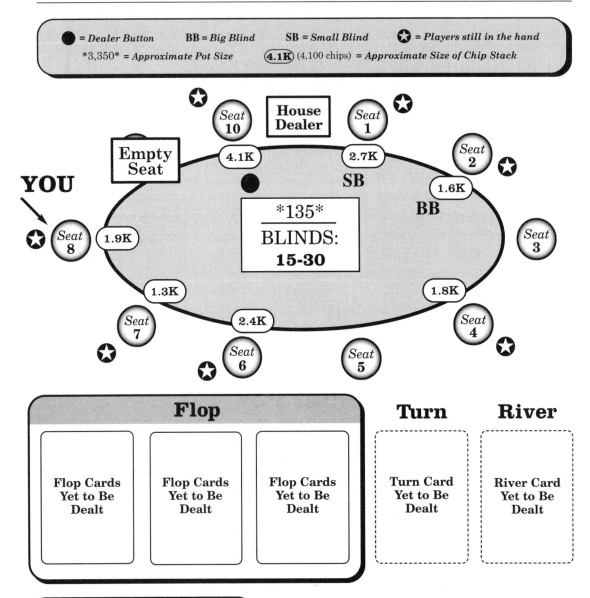

Situation 84:

It's now halfway through the first round and you have been dealt pocket 5s. One player at your table has been knocked out. Of the five players to act in front of you, three of them called the 30-chip big blind bet and two folded. It is now your turn to act. With three players yet to act after you, do you fold, call as well, raise to an unspecified level, or go all in?

Starting Hand (Pocket): **5♣5♥**

This Pocket's Win Rate: **20.7%**

Win Rate Rank: **34 of 169 possible**

Tournament Situation:

Tourney: **Internet Qualifier**

Paid Entrys: **2,400 x $50**

Starting Chip Stack: **2,000**

Players Remaining: **2,351**

Places Paid: **15 (See chart)**

Your Current Standing: **1,394th overall, 5th at your table**

Time Left in Round: **7 minutes**

Rebuys Allowed: **No**

Next Blind Level: **25-50**

This Tournament's Prize Money:

1st-10th:
Paid entry to World Series of Poker Main Event (worth $10,000)
11th: **$7,500**
12th: **$5,000**
13th: **$4,000**
14th: **$2,500**
15th: **$1,000**

Total Prize Pool:
$120,000

Answer 84:

You should fold. Yes, I know, I know, you've got a pair, but you can't be playing hands like this in middle position. Look, three players in early position have already called the bet. Maybe they're not projecting power, but they must have something worth calling with. And you still have three players to act behind you. What are you going to do if someone goes all in? Call with a pair of 5s? Of course not.

Technically a pair of 5s beats Ace-King, but what if you don't catch another 5 on the board and the player holding Ace-King catches either of his overcards to your 5s? Then he takes all your money and you get to go find another tournament. And it doesn't have to be Ace-King that your opponent holds. He could hold King-Queen, or Queen-Jack, or any two connected cards higher than 5. You also can't forget about players holding a pair of 6s, 7s, 8s...well, you get the idea. Any pair higher than 5s, which MOST pairs will be.

Fold this hand now before you get yourself into trouble you can't get out of, at least inexpensively. One sign of a mature Texas Hold'em player is when he can throw away seemingly good hands when in the wrong position.

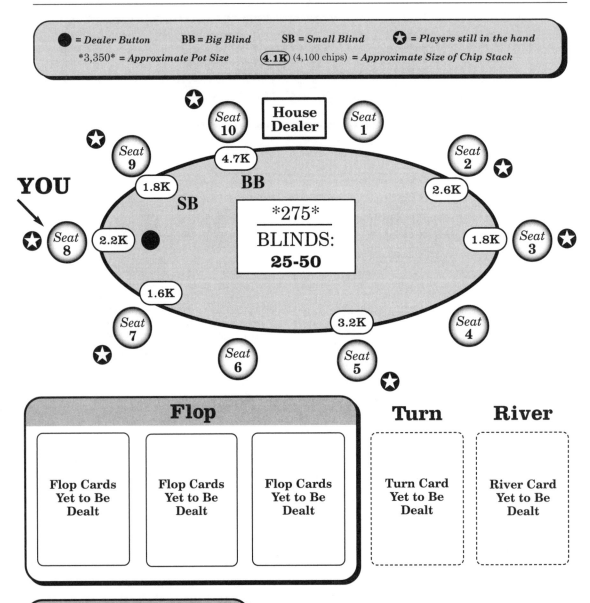

= Dealer Button   **BB = Big Blind**   **SB = Small Blind**   ⭐ = *Players still in the hand*

3,350 = *Approximate Pot Size*   **4.1K** (4,100 chips) = *Approximate Size of Chip Stack*

House Dealer

Seat 10 — 4.7K
Seat 1
Seat 9 — 1.8K
Seat 2 — 2.6K

BB

SB

275
—
BLINDS:
25-50

YOU

Seat 8 — 2.2K
Seat 3 — 1.8K
Seat 7 — 1.6K
Seat 4
Seat 5 — 3.2K
Seat 6

Flop

| Flop Cards Yet to Be Dealt | Flop Cards Yet to Be Dealt | Flop Cards Yet to Be Dealt |

Turn

Turn Card Yet to Be Dealt

River

River Card Yet to Be Dealt

Pocket

5♣ 5♥

Situation 85:

It's now early in the second round and your table has been filled with another player. You are in the button position and have been dealt a pair of 5s in your pocket. There were four callers of the 50-chip big blind bet in front of you while three players folded. It is now your turn to act with only the two blinds to act after you. Do you fold, call as well, raise to an unspecified level, or go all in with your 2,200 chips?

Starting Hand (Pocket): **5♣5♥**
This Pocket's Win Rate: **20.7%**
Win Rate Rank: **34 of 169 possible**

Tournament Situation:
Tourney: **Internet Qualifier**
Paid Entrys: **2,400 x $50**
Starting Chip Stack: **2,000**
Players Remaining: **2,298**
Places Paid: **15 (See chart)**
Your Current Standing: **1,366th overall,
    5th at your table**
Time Left in Round: **14 minutes**
Rebuys Allowed: **No**
Next Blind Level: **50-100**

*This Tournament's
Prize Money:*

**1st-10th:
Paid entry to
World Series of
Poker Main Event
(worth $10,000)**
11th: $7,500
12th: $5,000
13th: $4,000
14th: $2,500
15th: $1,000

Total Prize Pool:
$120,000

Answer 85:

You should call this bet. Huh? Just a while ago I told you to fold pocket 5s, you say? That's right, because you were out of position with that hand. This time you are in a good position. What's better about this time? Well, you already have the knowledge of what seven of the players in front of you are going to do; they called or folded, and no one raised. Now, with only the two blinds yet to act, the odds are good that they won't raise, because statistically they didn't catch a good hand. And even if they did, with five callers already in the pot in front of them, they will have to be careful about raising anything but a very, very strong hand, because someone's going to call them if they do about anything but go all in, and even then they may get a caller.

This is the ideal time to play a small pocket pair, when you can get in cheaply and garner last betting position on the next three rounds of the hand. See the flop cheaply and see what happens. As for the expectations of a win, with a pair of 5s you are realistically going to need at least a third 5. Your odds of flopping a third 5 are about 8-to-1. Your odds of catching a third 5 by the river are about 5-to-1. So, with six or seven players in the pot right now, the pot odds are already correct to make this call.

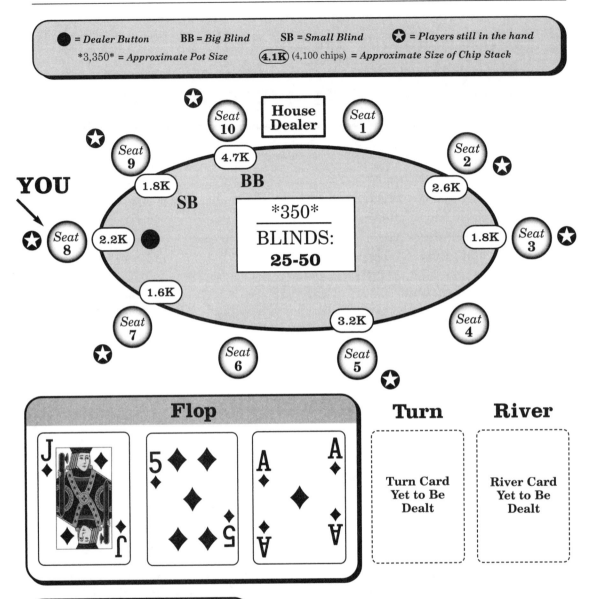

Seat 10
House Dealer
Seat 1

4.7K

Seat 9

BB

Seat 2

1.8K

2.6K

YOU

SB

350

BLINDS:

25-50

Seat 8

2.2K

1.8K

Seat 3

1.6K

Seat 7

3.2K

Seat 4

Seat 6

Seat 5

Flop

J♦ 5♦ A♦

Turn

Turn Card Yet to Be Dealt

River

River Card Yet to Be Dealt

Pocket

5♣ 5♥

Situation 86:

After you called, the small blind called and the big blind checked, leaving seven of you in the hand. Following the flop, all six players in front of you checked. Do you check as well, opting for a free card on the turn, bet the minimum of 50 chips, raise to an unspecified level, or go all in?

Starting Hand (Pocket): **5♣5♥**
This Pocket's Win Rate: **20.7%**
Win Rate Rank: **34 of 169 possible**

Tournament Situation:
Tourney: **Internet Qualifier**
Paid Entrys: **2,400 x $50**
Starting Chip Stack: **2,000**
Players Remaining: **2,298**
Places Paid: **15 (See chart)**
Your Current Standing: **1,366th overall,
5th at your table**
Time Left in Round: **14 minutes**
Rebuys Allowed: **No**
Next Blind Level: **50-100**

*This Tournament's
Prize Money:*

1st-10th:
**Paid entry to
World Series of
Poker Main Event
(worth $10,000)**
11th: **$7,500**
12th: **$5,000**
13th: **$4,000**
14th: **$2,500**
15th: **$1,000**

Total Prize Pool:
$120,000

Answer 86:

Well, dang it, anyway. The 5 was terrific, but the three diamonds are painful to look at. You have some options here. If you check, you'll get to see the turn card for free, but then so will everyone else. Was everyone else scared of the three diamonds that hit the board, or is someone slow playing a flush or flush draw? If you check now, you won't know.

On the other hand, if you make a bet now, say in the 200-chip range, you'll likely get some players—and maybe all of them—to fold. And anyone who calls your bet and hangs in there with you will likely check in front of you after the turn no matter what card comes, even if they hit a flush, because maybe they'll be intent on check-raising you. The advantage for you in betting something now is that if the turn card doesn't bring you a full house or four of a kind, and everyone checks to you again, you can choose to get a free river card, which could be valuable to you if your set of 5s is chasing someone else's flush.

So, go ahead and make a bet now, but make it substantial enough that lollygaggers, wishers, and hopers will fold, leaving only the real hands in the game.

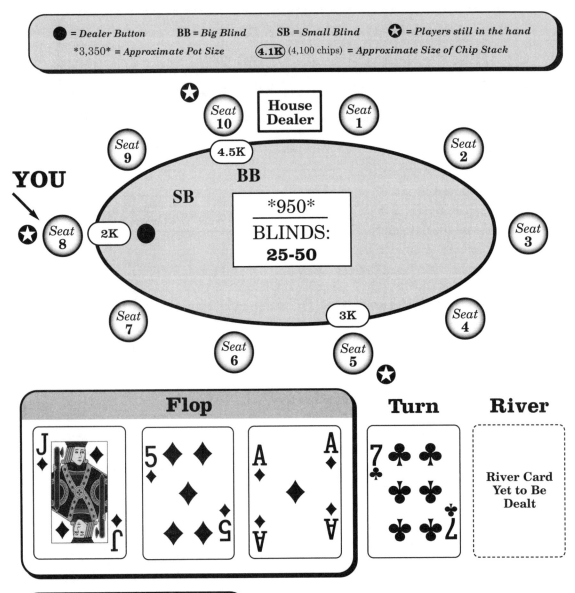

Situation 87:

After you bet 200 chips following the flop, two players called and four folded. After the turn card was dealt, both Seats 10 and 5 checked to you. It is now your turn to act with no one to act after you. Do you check, too, or do you bet the minimum of 50 chips, raise to an unspecified level, or go all in?

Starting Hand (Pocket): **5♣5♥**
This Pocket's Win Rate: **20.7%**
Win Rate Rank: **34 of 169 possible**

Tournament Situation:
Tourney: **Internet Qualifier**
Paid Entrys: **2,400 x $50**
Starting Chip Stack: **2,000**
Players Remaining: **2,298**
Places Paid: **15 (See chart)**
Your Current Standing: **1,366th overall,**
  5th at your table
Time Left in Round: **13 minutes**
Rebuys Allowed: **No**
Next Blind Level: **50-100**

This Tournament's Prize Money:

1st-10th:
Paid entry to
World Series of
Poker Main Event
(worth $10,000)
11th: $7,500
12th: $5,000
13th: $4,000
14th: $2,500
15th: $1,000

Total Prize Pool:

$120,000

Answer 87:

Well, that was a big fat nothin' card, which for you is probably okay. Both of your opponents checked again, so I'm starting to get the feel that neither of them already holds a flush. I would tend to think that the two of them hold some combination of a diamond draw or an Ace-something. Hopefully it's not an Ace-7/Jack that gets paired on the river.

Go ahead and make another modest bet, 'cause if they're going to sit there and try and draw out on you, at least make them pay for the privilege of watching you play poker.

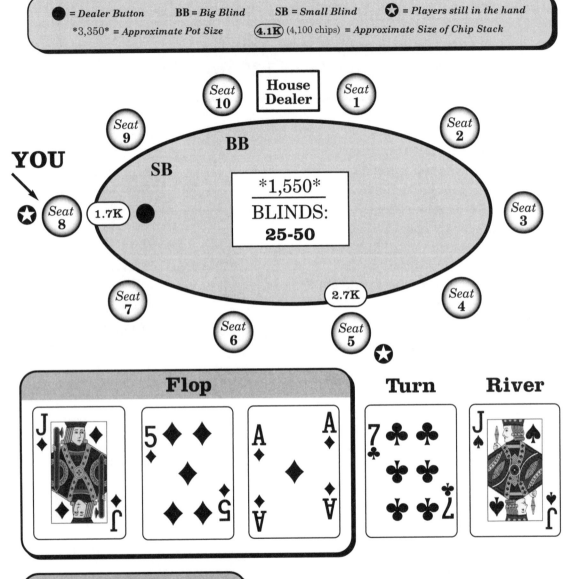

= Dealer Button   **BB** = Big Blind   **SB** = Small Blind   = Players still in the hand
3,350 = Approximate Pot Size   **4.1K** (4,100 chips) = Approximate Size of Chip Stack

YOU

Seat 10 | House Dealer | Seat 1
Seat 9
Seat 2
BB
SB
Seat 8   1.7K
1,550
BLINDS:
25-50
Seat 3
Seat 7
2.7K
Seat 4
Seat 6   Seat 5

Flop — J♦ 5♦ A♦

Turn — 7♣

River — J♠

Pocket — 5♣ 5♥

Situation 88:

You decided to bet 300 chips after the turn and received one caller, bringing the hand into a heads up situation between you and Seat 5. After the river card was dealt, Seat 5 checked. It is now your turn to act. Do you check as well, bet the minimum of 50 chips, raise to an unspecified level, or go all in?

Starting Hand (Pocket): **5♣5♥**
This Pocket's Win Rate: **20.7%**
Win Rate Rank: **34 of 169 possible**

Tournament Situation:
Tourney: **Internet Qualifier**
Paid Entrys: **2,400 x $50**
Starting Chip Stack: **2,000**
Players Remaining: **2,298**
Places Paid: **15 (See chart)**
Your Current Standing: **1,366th overall,**
   5th at your table
Time Left in Round: **13 minutes**
Rebuys Allowed: **No**
Next Blind Level: **50-100**

This Tournament's Prize Money:

1st-10th:
Paid entry to
World Series of
Poker Main Event
(worth $10,000)
11th: $7,500
12th: $5,000
13th: $4,000
14th: $2,500
15th: $1,000

Total Prize Pool:
$120,000

Answer 88:

The river brought you a full house, but not the nuts. If your opponent was playing Ace-Jack, he now holds a full house as well, and a higher one than yours. If for some reason he played a Jack-7 or Jack-5, he also holds a higher full house. It would be hard to imagine he played either of the last two hands, especially since he had to keep calling your bets with an Ace on the board. As for having an Ace-Jack, it's also hard to imagine he didn't do some kind of betting along the way other than calling, although the three diamonds on the flop could have been a legitimate reason for just checking and calling. He may have been slow playing a diamond flush the whole time because his diamonds are lower in rank.

I would go under the assumption that he's got something worth playing but that you've got him beat, so make a bet in the 200-400 chip range and maybe he'll call and you'll pick up some more chips.

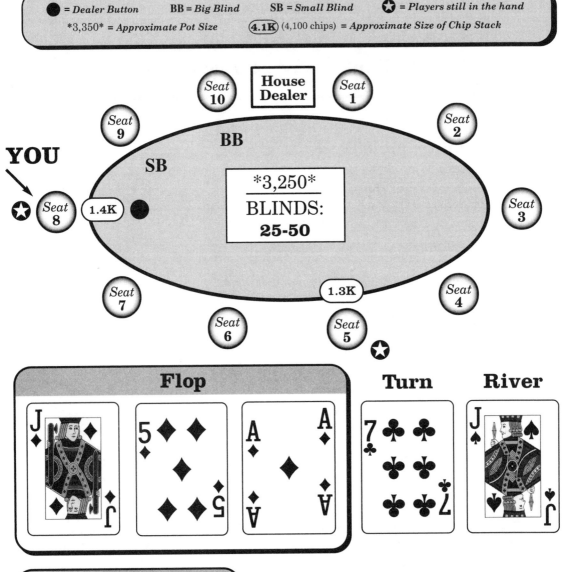

= Dealer Button   BB = Big Blind   SB = Small Blind   ⭐ = Players still in the hand

3,350 = Approximate Pot Size   (4.1K) (4,100 chips) = Approximate Size of Chip Stack

House Dealer

Seat 10 Seat 1 Seat 9 Seat 2 Seat 8 Seat 3 Seat 7 Seat 4 Seat 6 Seat 5

BB SB YOU

1.4K   1.3K

3,250
BLINDS:
25-50

Flop

Turn   River

Pocket

Situation 89:

When the river card came and Seat 5 checked, you decided to bet 300 chips. He check-raised you another 1,400 chips, forcing you to go all in if you decide to call him. Do you fold or call the bet with your remaining 1,400 chips?

Starting Hand (Pocket): **5♣5♥**
This Pocket's Win Rate: **20.7%**
Win Rate Rank: **34 of 169 possible**

Tournament Situation:

Tourney: **Internet Qualifier**

Paid Entrys: **2,400 x $50**

Starting Chip Stack: **2,000**

Players Remaining: **2,298**

Places Paid: **15 (See chart)**

Your Current Standing: **1,366th overall, 5th at your table**

Time Left in Round: **13 minutes**

Rebuys Allowed: **No**

Next Blind Level: **50-100**

This Tournament's Prize Money:

1st-10th:
Paid entry to
World Series of
Poker Main Event
(worth $10,000)
11th: $7,500
12th: $5,000
13th: $4,000
14th: $2,500
15th: $1,000

Total Prize Pool:

$120,000

Answer 89:

Okay, it's no-limit Texas Hold'em gut check time. Seat 5's check-raise means one of three things: 1) he flopped a flush but his cards were lower than he liked and he was waiting to make sure four diamonds didn't hit the board, thereby giving anyone holding one high diamond in their hand a higher flush; 2) the Jack on the river somehow helped him, either giving him three Jacks or a full house; 3) he's totally bluffing and trying to buy this pot.

Personally, in this kind of a tournament with a $50 buy-in, I don't think he's trying to pull a total bluff here. I think he caught something on the river, but exactly what he caught remains to be seen. I've just felt all along on this hand that he wasn't holding a flush, small or large. By slow playing a flopped flush, he would be allowing anyone else to catch up and hit, for example, a full house, the possibility (and reality in your case) of which occurred on the river. No, I'd tend to think that the Jack on the river somehow helped him. I also don't think he hit a full house of his own. Call his all in bet and hold your breath. After all, if you're not going to fight with a full house, what are you going to fight with?

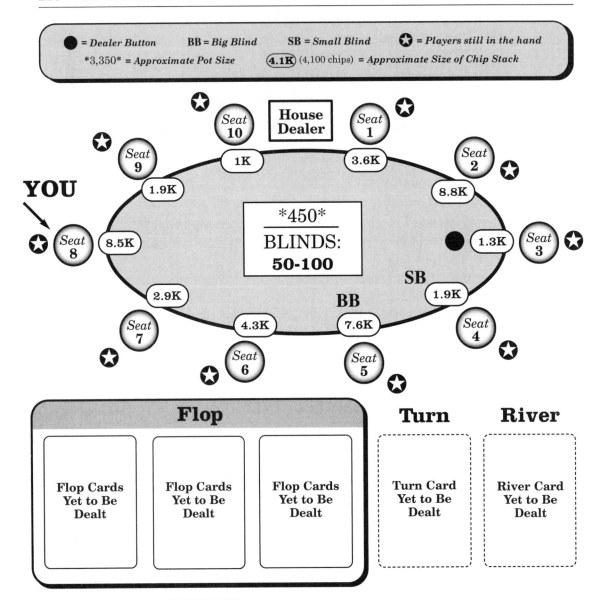

● = *Dealer Button*　　**BB** = *Big Blind*　　**SB** = *Small Blind*　　⭐ = *Players still in the hand*

3,350 = *Approximate Pot Size*　　(4.1K) (4,100 chips) = *Approximate Size of Chip Stack*

House Dealer

Seat 10 — 1K
Seat 1 — 3.6K
Seat 2 — 8.8K
Seat 3 — 1.3K
Seat 4 — 1.9K
Seat 5 — 7.6K (BB)
Seat 6 — 4.3K
Seat 7 — 2.9K
Seat 8 — 8.5K (YOU)
Seat 9 — 1.9K

450
BLINDS: 50-100

SB

Flop

Flop Cards Yet to Be Dealt

Flop Cards Yet to Be Dealt

Flop Cards Yet to Be Dealt

Turn

Turn Card Yet to Be Dealt

River

River Card Yet to Be Dealt

Pocket

Situation 90:

Your full house stood up on the previous situation and it's now late in the third round of the tournament. You have been dealt Ace-Queen unsuited in your pocket. Seat 6 was first to act and called the 100-chip big blind bet. Seat 7 raised to 200 chips. Do you fold, call the 200, raise to an unspecified level, or go all in?

Starting Hand (Pocket): **A♠Q♦**
This Pocket's Win Rate: **60.5%**
Win Rate Rank: **9 of 169 possible**

Tournament Situation:

Tourney: **Internet Qualifier**

Paid Entrys: **2,400 x $50**

Starting Chip Stack: **2,000**

Players Remaining: **2,118**

Places Paid: **15 (See chart)**

Your Current Standing: **302nd overall,
2nd at your table**

Time Left in Round: **2 minutes**

Rebuys Allowed: **No**

Next Blind Level: **100-200**

*This Tournament's
Prize Money:*

1st-10th:
**Paid entry to
World Series of
Poker Main Event
(worth $10,000)**
11th: **$7,500**
12th: **$5,000**
13th: **$4,000**
14th: **$2,500**
15th: **$1,000**

Total Prize Pool:

$120,000

Answer 90:

Ace-Queen unsuited is a very promising power hand, as the chart above shows with its overall relative win rate rank of ninth place. From my own experience, however, Ace-Queen unsuited is long on promise and short on power. I've probably been burned (i.e., disappointed) on Ace-Queen unsuited more than any other big hand. And I suppose the reasons should be obvious: you still need four more of either suit to make a flush; you need three more exact cards (King, Jack, and 10) to make a straight; if you pair up your Queen, someone will invariably hit a pair of Kings.

My whining notwithstanding, you should just call this raise from Seat 7 and see what the flop brings. The flop usually makes or breaks most hands, and this one will likely be no exception.

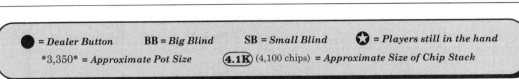

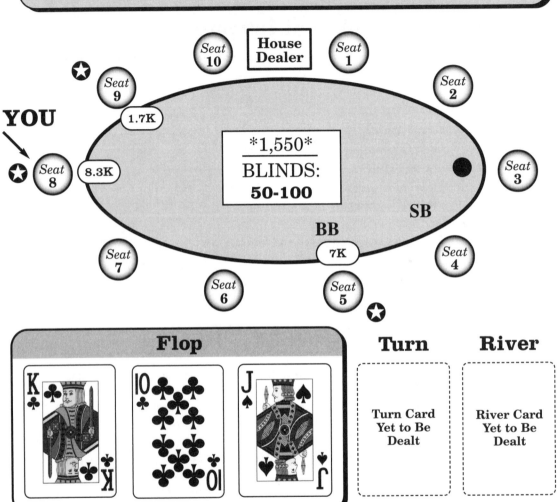

Seat 10 — House Dealer — Seat 1

Seat 9   Seat 2

⭐ YOU

1.7K

1,550
BLINDS:
50-100

Seat 8   8.3K   Seat 3

7K   BB   SB

Seat 7   Seat 6   Seat 5   Seat 4

⭐

Flop

Turn

Turn Card Yet to Be Dealt

River

River Card Yet to Be Dealt

Pocket

Situation 91:

After you called Seat 7's raise, three other players called as well and five players folded. Following the flop, Seat 5 bet 500 and Seats 6 and 7 folded. With only Seat 9 to act after you, should you fold, call the 500-chip bet, raise to an unspecified level, or go all in?

Starting Hand (Pocket): **A♠Q♦**
This Pocket's Win Rate: **60.5%**
Win Rate Rank: **9 of 169 possible**

Tournament Situation:
Tourney: **Internet Qualifier**
Paid Entrys: **2,400 x $50**
Starting Chip Stack: **2,000**
Players Remaining: **2,118**
Places Paid: **15 (See chart)**
Your Current Standing: **302nd overall,
    2nd at your table**
Time Left in Round: **2 minutes**
Rebuys Allowed: **No**
Next Blind Level: **100-200**

*This Tournament's
Prize Money:*

**1st-10th:
Paid entry to
World Series of
Poker Main Event
(worth $10,000)**
11th: $7,500
12th: $5,000
13th: $4,000
14th: $2,500
15th: $1,000

Total Prize Pool:
$120,000

Answer 91:

For some reason, I seem to flop this straight a fair amount of the time. Right now you've got the nuts. The only problem on the horizon at this point is the possible club draw. It doesn't matter what Seat 5 raised with, you've got him beat or tied (tied only if he holds an Ace-Queen like you).

Currently you are in the middle betting position. It would be nice to rid yourself of Seat 9 so that you can be last to act. Since you've got the nuts, but need to be mindful of the club draw, I'd push 1,700 chips into the pot and force Seat 9 to go all in or fold. Either way is of benefit to you: if he calls, you'll likely own his chips; if he folds, then he's out of the betting picture and you get to act last the rest of the way with your main threat, the guy in Seat 5.

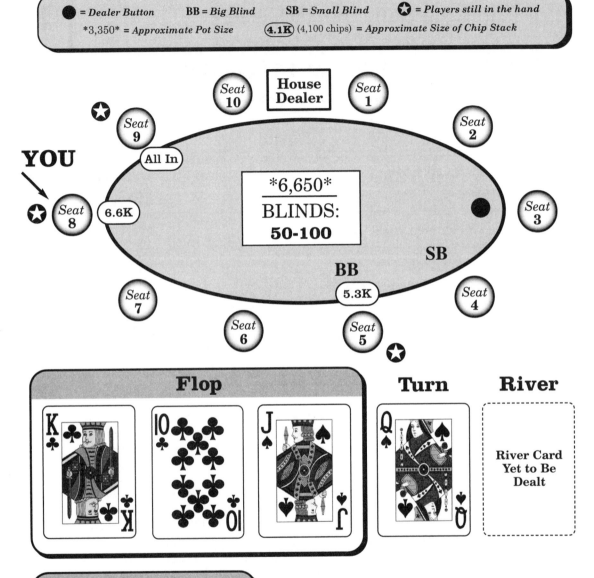

● = *Dealer Button*   **BB** = *Big Blind*   **SB** = *Small Blind*   ★ = *Players still in the hand*

3,350 = *Approximate Pot Size*   (**4.1K**) (4,100 chips) = *Approximate Size of Chip Stack*

YOU

All In

Seat 9   6.6K

★ **Seat 8**

6,650

BLINDS:

50-100

Seat 10   House Dealer   Seat 1

Seat 2

Seat 3   ●

SB

BB   5.3K

Seat 4

Seat 7

Seat 6   Seat 5   ★

Flop

Turn

River

River Card Yet to Be Dealt

Pocket

Situation 92:

After you bet 1,700 chips following the flop, Seat 9 called with his remaining 1,700 chips and Seat 5 called as well. After the turn card was dealt, Seat 5 was first to act and he checked. It is now your turn to act with no one behind you (Seat 9 is all in). Do you check as well, bet the minimum of 200 chips, bet a higher unspecified amount, or go all in?

Starting Hand (Pocket): **A♠Q♦**

This Pocket's Win Rate: **60.5%**

Win Rate Rank: **9 of 169 possible**

Tournament Situation:

Tourney: **Internet Qualifier**

Paid Entrys: **2,400 x $50**

Starting Chip Stack: **2,000**

Players Remaining: **2,118**

Places Paid: **15 (See chart)**

Your Current Standing: **302nd overall, 2nd at your table**

Time Left in Round: **2 minutes**

Rebuys Allowed: **No**

Next Blind Level: **100-200**

This Tournament's Prize Money:

1st-10th:
Paid entry to World Series of Poker Main Event (worth $10,000)
11th: **$7,500**
12th: **$5,000**
13th: **$4,000**
14th: **$2,500**
15th: **$1,000**

Total Prize Pool:

$120,000

Answer 92:

That was a lousy turn card for you, because now if either or both of your opponents hold an Ace, they're going to split the pot with you. And after you went to all that trouble to flop it. Okay, aside from begrudging your opponents their split pot, it could actually get worse, as in...*you could still lose this pot!* How? If either opponent holds two spades or two clubs, and another card of their suit comes on the river, voila...you're dead.

Some experts might disagree with what I'm about to tell you, but I would go all in right now. Why? First, because Seat 9 can't hurt you no matter what you do because he's already all in. Second, because if Seat 5 is only on a flush draw, he'll be forced to risk his entire tournament on hitting his suit, and the odds are roughly 3-to-1 against him. Third, if Seat 5 happens NOT to hold an Ace for a split pot, he'll have to put you on an Ace given the current board. Fourth, if he holds a pair of Kings, Queens, Jacks, or 10s, you can't allow him to draw for a full house, at least not without paying for it, and paying dearly if he misses.

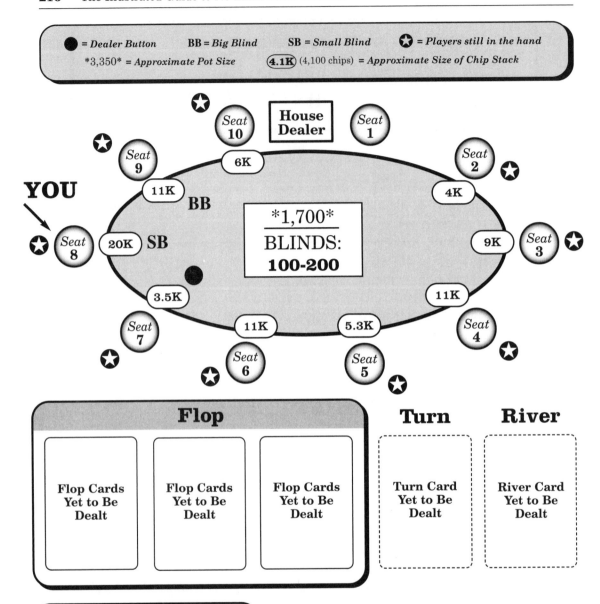

= Dealer Button   **BB = Big Blind**   **SB = Small Blind**   **= Players still in the hand**

3,350 = Approximate Pot Size   **4.1K (4,100 chips) = Approximate Size of Chip Stack**

House Dealer

Seat 10 — 6K
Seat 1
Seat 9 — 11K
Seat 2 — 4K
YOU — Seat 8 — 20K — SB
Seat 3 — 9K
3.5K
11K — Seat 4
Seat 7
11K — Seat 6
5.3K — Seat 5

BB

1,700
BLINDS:
100-200

Flop

| Flop Cards Yet to Be Dealt | Flop Cards Yet to Be Dealt | Flop Cards Yet to Be Dealt |

Turn

Turn Card Yet to Be Dealt

River

River Card Yet to Be Dealt

Pocket

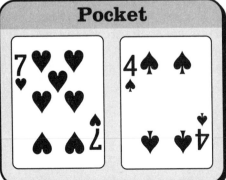

Situation 93:

Your straight held up and you knocked out both Seat 9 and Seat 5, who showed three Jacks. It's now the middle of the fourth round and you have received 7-4 unsuited in your pocket while in the small blind position. Seven of the eight players before you called the 200-chip big blind bet. Do you fold, call because it's only another 100 chips and because the pot potential has grown so large, raise to an unspecified level, or go all in?

Starting Hand (Pocket): **7♥4♠**
This Pocket's Win Rate: **0.4%**
Win Rate Rank: **138 of 169 possible**

Tournament Situation:
Tourney: **Internet Qualifier**
Paid Entrys: **2,400 x $50**
Starting Chip Stack: **2,000**
Players Remaining: **1,783**
Places Paid: **15 (See chart)**
Your Current Standing: **52nd overall,
    1st at your table**
Time Left in Round: **8 minutes**
Rebuys Allowed: **No**
Next Blind Level: **200-400**

*This Tournament's
Prize Money:*

1st-10th:
**Paid entry to
World Series of
Poker Main Event
(worth $10,000)**
11th: **$7,500**
12th: **$5,000**
13th: **$4,000**
14th: **$2,500**
15th: **$1,000**

Total Prize Pool:
$120,000

Answer 93:

First of all, you should never make a call just because it's relatively cheap compared to your stack. If you're going to make the call, there should be some reason behind the decision. In this case, if you were to say, "I'm going to call this for 100 chips because I have a huge chip stack and can afford it, and if I don't hit something really terrific on the flop, I'm going to fold," okay, I'll buy that.

Personally, I could go either way on this one, assuming you truly do throw the hand away if you don't hit something like three 7s, three 4s, or flop a straight. Based on experience, however, whenever I've played something like this, I end up flopping something like two pair or four hearts, one of which never seems to hold up and the other of which never seems to get there, and when the flush does get there, my 7 will invariably not be enough.

So in the final analysis, I would still throw the hand away now and save the 100 chips. You never know how handy they may come in later. If you do decide to play, you better be firm about your commitment to throw it away if you don't flop something very strong.

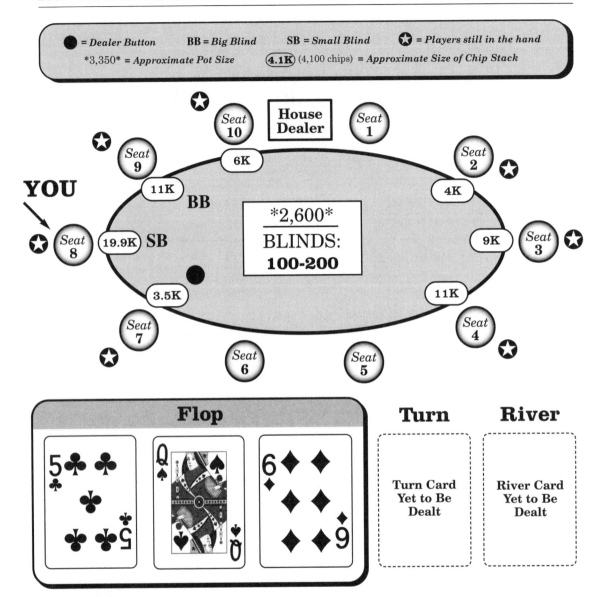

Situation 94:

You decided to play the hand since you have a strong chip lead and it only cost you another 100 chips. After the flop, Seat 2 was the first to bet and bet the minimum 200 chips. He was called by three of the next five players. It is now your turn to act. With Seats 9 and 10 to act after you, do you fold, call the bet of 200, raise to an unspecified level, or go all in?

Starting Hand (Pocket): **7♥4♠**
This Pocket's Win Rate: **0.4%**
Win Rate Rank: **138 of 169 possible**

Tournament Situation:

Tourney: **Internet Qualifier**

Paid Entrys: **2,400 x $50**

Starting Chip Stack: **2,000**

Players Remaining: **1,783**

Places Paid: **15 (See chart)**

Your Current Standing: **52nd overall,**
  1st at your table

Time Left in Round: **8 minutes**

Rebuys Allowed: **No**

Next Blind Level: **200-400**

This Tournament's
Prize Money:

1st-10th:
Paid entry to
World Series of
Poker Main Event
(worth $10,000)
11th: $7,500
12th: $5,000
13th: $4,000
14th: $2,500
15th: $1,000

Total Prize Pool:

$120,000

Answer 94:

You flopped an open-ended straight draw, and the fact that it was a rainbow (three different suits) helped. The situation that presents itself at this point is one of pot odds. Are the pot odds correct to call? Let's calculate them and see.

If we assume that we will win this hand by making our straight, that means there are exactly eight cards that will do it for us, the four 3s and the four 8s. Thus:

47 unseen cards minus the 8 cards that makes our straight translates to:

$39 \div 8 = 4.88$, or 4.88-to-1

Since we have two chances to catch one of our desired cards, we translate this to:

$4.88 \div 2 = 2.44$, or 2.44-to-1

This means the odds of hitting our open-ended straight draw by the river are about 2½-to-1 by the river. With a 13-to-1 ratio of chips in the pot (2,600) to the amount we are being asked to bet (200), this is an easy decision with a very profitable long-range expectation, i.e., if you get this situation with this kind of pot odds over and over again, you'll hit enough of them to make a living at this game! Make the call.

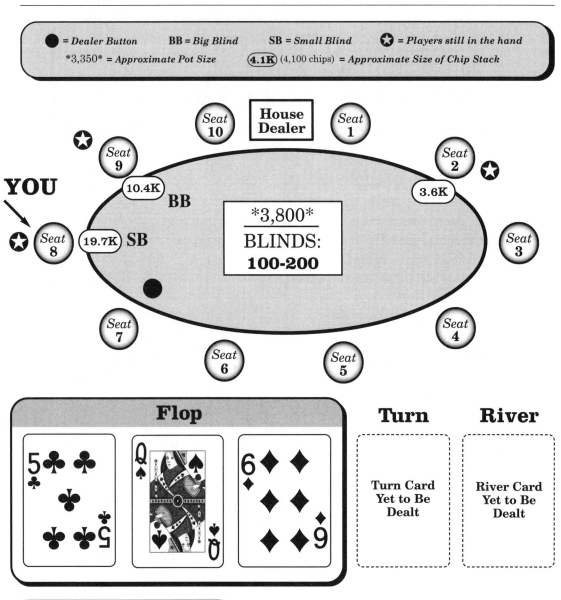

● = *Dealer Button*   **BB** = *Big Blind*   **SB** = *Small Blind*   ✪ = *Players still in the hand*
3,350 = *Approximate Pot Size*   **4.1K** (4,100 chips) = *Approximate Size of Chip Stack*

Seat 10   House Dealer   Seat 1

Seat 9

YOU

10.4K   **BB**

3,800
BLINDS:
100-200

Seat 2   3.6K

Seat 8   19.7K   **SB**

Seat 3

Seat 7

Seat 4

Seat 6   Seat 5

Flop

5♣   Q♠   6♦

Turn

Turn Card
Yet to Be
Dealt

River

River Card
Yet to Be
Dealt

Pocket

7♥   4♠

Situation 95:

After you called, Seat 9 raised to 600 chips and Seat 10 folded. Seat 2 called and Seats 3, 4, and 7 all folded. With no one to act after you, do you now fold, call the additional 400 chips, raise to an unspecified level, or go all in?

Starting Hand (Pocket): **7♥4♠**

This Pocket's Win Rate: **0.4%**

Win Rate Rank: **138 of 169 possible**

Tournament Situation:

Tourney: **Internet Qualifier**

Paid Entrys: **2,400 x $50**

Starting Chip Stack: **2,000**

Players Remaining: **1,783**

Places Paid: **15 (See chart)**

Your Current Standing: **52nd overall,
    1st at your table**

Time Left in Round: **8 minutes**

Rebuys Allowed: **No**

Next Blind Level: **200-400**

*This Tournament's
Prize Money:*

**1st-10th:
Paid entry to
World Series of
Poker Main Event
(worth $10,000)**
11th: $7,500
12th: $5,000
13th: $4,000
14th: $2,500
15th: $1,000

Total Prize Pool:

$120,000

Answer 95:

Now we finally have a player trying to break out after the flop. Seat 9's raise to 600 chips succeeded in driving out four players. This is generally not good news to someone holding a hand like yours, because you typically need a lot of callers to make a drawing hand pay off. Seat 9 apparently liked the Queen that came on the flop. Good, because we liked both the 5 and 6 that came. Now, as to whether or not we continue to call this hand, we just need to calculate our pot odds again. The odds of hitting the straight by the river (2.44-to-1) haven't changed because no new cards have been dealt yet. Only the pot odds have changed because of the money added and the new amount we're asked to bet.

Since the pot now contains 3,800 chips, and we're being asked to bet another 400 to play, that translates into 9.5-to-1 (3,800 ÷ 400 = 9.5). Not as good as before, but still plenty good enough to make this a worthy call.

Something else to consider in tournament play: just because the pot odds are correct in a particular situation doesn't mean you should always call. Reason? Because a few misses—which will come—could deplete your chip stack, whereas in live play it's not an issue because you can always buy more chips.

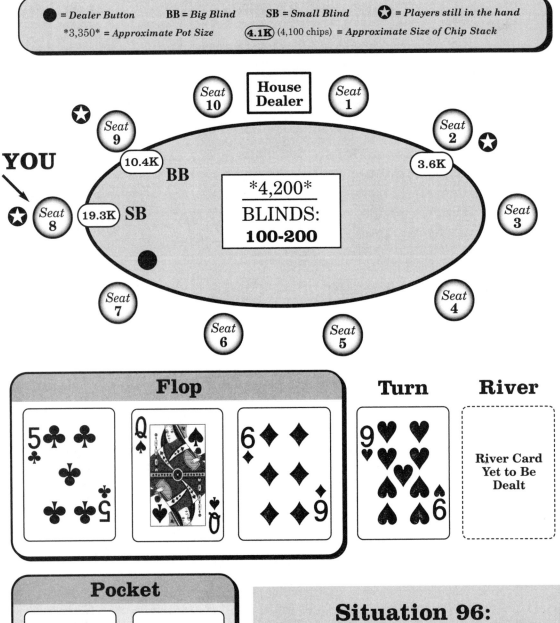

Situation 96:

After the turn card was dealt, Seat 2 checked. With only Seat 9 to act after you, do you check as well, bet the minimum of 200 chips, raise to an unspecified level, or go all in?

Starting Hand (Pocket): **7♥4♠**

This Pocket's Win Rate: **0.4%**

Win Rate Rank: **138 of 169 possible**

Tournament Situation:

Tourney: **Internet Qualifier**

Paid Entrys: **2,400 x $50**

Starting Chip Stack: **2,000**

Players Remaining: **1,783**

Places Paid: **15 (See chart)**

Your Current Standing: **52nd overall,**
   1st at your table

Time Left in Round: **8 minutes**

Rebuys Allowed: **No**

Next Blind Level: **200-400**

This Tournament's Prize Money:

1st-10th:
Paid entry to
World Series of
Poker Main Event
(worth $10,000)
11th: $7,500
12th: $5,000
13th: $4,000
14th: $2,500
15th: $1,000

Total Prize Pool:

$120,000

Answer 96:

It would be pretty hard to bet anything at all at this point since you don't have a made hand yet. It's also fairly obvious that Seat 9 is going to bet something as it's hard to believe the 9 on the river did him any damage. Just check at this point and hope it doesn't cost too much to go to the river. One thing to be aware of, too, is that the 9 on the river made a straight for anyone holding a 7-8 in their pocket. Not too likely that's the case, but you need to be cognizant of it. Also, anyone holding a pair of 9s (a real possibility) now has a set, and if the next card pairs the board they'll make a full house, although that's almost irrelevant to your situation because you'll be folding unless you hit your straight.

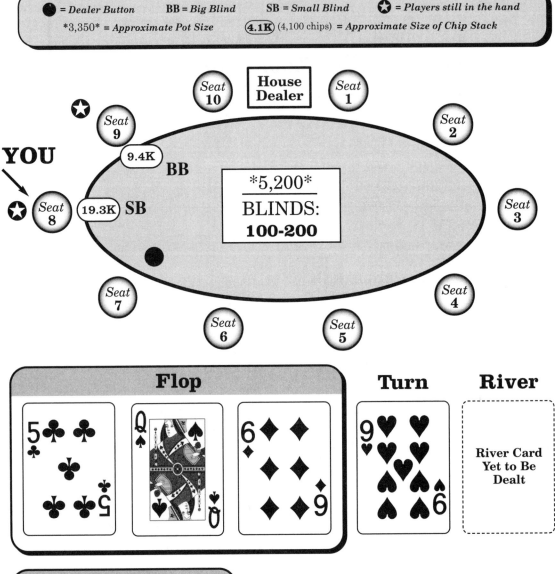

YOU

Situation 97:

After you followed Seat 2's check with a check of your own, Seat 9 bet 1,000 chips and Seat 2 folded. Do you fold as well, call the 1,000-chip bet, raise to an unspecified level, or go all in, projecting a check-raise in hopes of bullying (bluffing) Seat 9 into folding since your chip stack is twice as large as his?

Starting Hand (Pocket): **7♥4♠**
This Pocket's Win Rate: **0.4%**
Win Rate Rank: **138 of 169 possible**

Tournament Situation:

Tourney: **Internet Qualifier**

Paid Entrys: **2,400 x $50**

Starting Chip Stack: **2,000**

Players Remaining: **1,783**

Places Paid: **15 (See chart)**

Your Current Standing: **52nd overall,
  1st at your table**

Time Left in Round: **8 minutes**

Rebuys Allowed: **No**

Next Blind Level: **200-400**

*This Tournament's
Prize Money:*

1st-10th:
**Paid entry to
World Series of
Poker Main Event
(worth $10,000)**
11th: $7,500
12th: $5,000
13th: $4,000
14th: $2,500
15th: $1,000

Total Prize Pool:

$120,000

Answer 97:

Well, you can forget about bullying/bluffing Seat 9 into folding. If you project a check-raise type of situation to him, the first thing he's going to do is look at the board, look at the turn card, and then try to figure out what you're doing given the turn card that came. What he'll see is that you would have to be holding a 7-8 for a straight, a Queen-9 for two pair, or pocket 9s for a set. He'll probably surmise that the first two hands aren't too likely, and if he can beat the set of 9s, he's going to call you. I doubt he'll put you on a stone-cold bluff, but who cares, you can't win with your hand anyway.

The thing you need to do—again—is figure out what the pot odds are for the situation you are presented with. With forty-six unseen cards now, we still have eight cards that will make our straight. That means: 46 - 8 = 38, and 38 ÷ 8 = 4.75, so the odds of us hitting our straight are 4.75-to-1. If there isn't at least 4.75 x 1,000 chips (4,750) in the pot, then the correct move would be to fold. Since there are 5,200 chips in the pot, the correct move would be to call, although it's now a lot less desirable proposition at 5.2-to-1 pot odds.

Keep in mind, too, that even if your 8 comes, if your opponent holds a Jack-10, you're dead. While I would still call because of your large chip advantage, a fold in this situation wouldn't necessarily be the wrong move either.

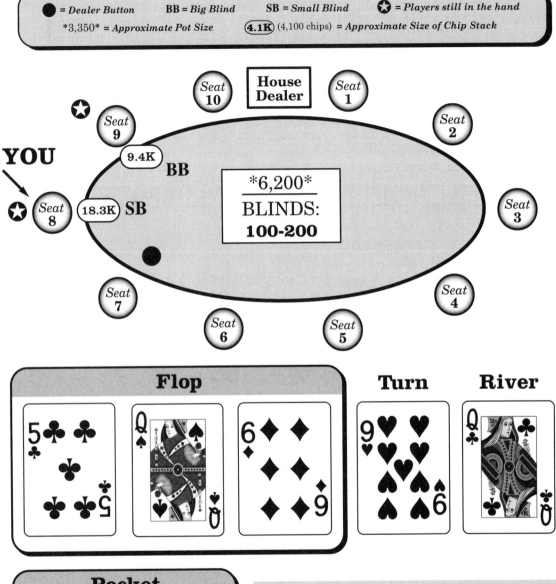

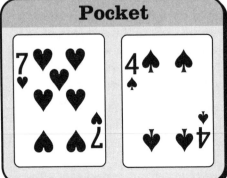

Situation 98:

After the river card was dealt, you are first to act. Do you check, bet the minimum of 200 chips, raise to an unspecified level, or go all in?

Starting Hand (Pocket): **7♥4♠**
This Pocket's Win Rate: **0.4%**
Win Rate Rank: **138 of 169 possible**

Tournament Situation:

Tourney: **Internet Qualifier**

Paid Entrys: **2,400 x $50**

Starting Chip Stack: **2,000**

Players Remaining: **1,783**

Places Paid: **15 (See chart)**

Your Current Standing: **52nd overall,**
  1st at your table

Time Left in Round: **7 minutes**

Rebuys Allowed: **No**

Next Blind Level: **200-400**

This Tournament's Prize Money:

1st-10th:
Paid entry to World Series of Poker Main Event (worth $10,000)
11th: $7,500
12th: $5,000
13th: $4,000
14th: $2,500
15th: $1,000

Total Prize Pool:
$120,000

Answer 98:

Now do you see why I said way back in the beginning that you shouldn't play hands like 7-4 unsuited, even if they're in your small blind? You've just lost 1,700 chips trying to hit this hand after being seduced by the flop.

Anyway, there isn't any way of making a silk purse out of a sow's ear on this hand. Or is there? For the record, I would say that you should check this hand. But, consider this. If you think that maybe Seat 9 wasn't playing the Queen, maybe he has pocket Aces or Kings, or somehow has two pair, a huge all-in bluff might work. Again, for the record, I would suggest that you check this hand, but if you somehow got the feeling he was playing something other than the Queen, an all in bluff now would certainly make him think. Your stack is twice as large as his, and if he miscalculates, he's out of the tournament. Again, I'm not recommending it, but it's something to think about, because every once in a while, especially at the later stages of a big tournament, you're going to have to bluff a hand here and there.

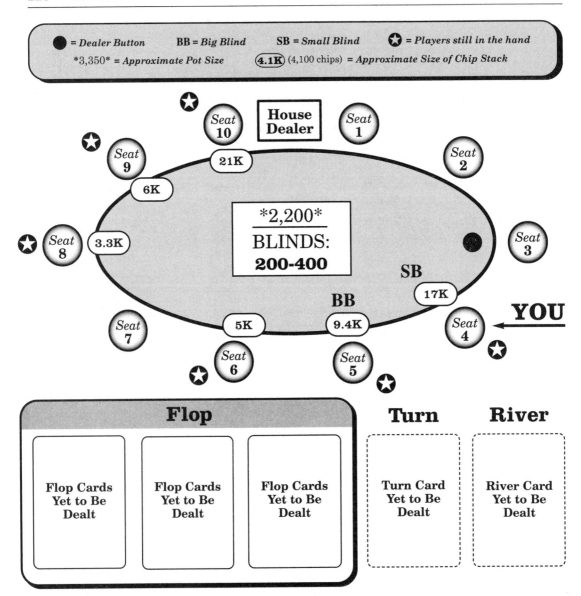

● = Dealer Button   **BB** = Big Blind   **SB** = Small Blind   ★ = Players still in the hand

3,350 = Approximate Pot Size   **4.1K** (4,100 chips) = Approximate Size of Chip Stack

House Dealer

Seat 10 — 21K
Seat 9 — 6K
Seat 8 — 3.3K
Seat 7 — 5K (BB)
Seat 6
Seat 5 — 9.4K (BB...)
Seat 1
Seat 2
Seat 3
Seat 4 — 17K (SB) **YOU**

2,200
BLINDS:
200-400

Flop

| Flop Cards Yet to Be Dealt | Flop Cards Yet to Be Dealt | Flop Cards Yet to Be Dealt |

Turn

Turn Card Yet to Be Dealt

River

River Card Yet to Be Dealt

Pocket

Situation 99:

It's now another round deeper into the tournament and your table was broken up and the players were sent to other tables as the tournament condensed. While in the small blind position, you caught a pocket hand of Jack-8 suited. Four players in front of you called the 400-chip big blind bet and four players folded. With only the big blind to act after you, do you fold, call the additional 200 chips, raise to an unspecified level, or go all in?

Starting Hand (Pocket): **J♦8♦**

This Pocket's Win Rate: **9.8%**

Win Rate Rank: **45 of 169 possible**

Tournament Situation:

Tourney: **Internet Qualifier**

Paid Entrys: **2,400 x $50**

Starting Chip Stack: **2,000**

Players Remaining: **1,502**

Places Paid: **15 (See chart)**

Your Current Standing: **68th overall, 2nd at your table**

Time Left in Round: **1 minute**

Rebuys Allowed: **No**

Next Blind Level: **300-600**

This Tournament's Prize Money:

**1st-10th:
Paid entry to
World Series of
Poker Main Event
(worth $10,000)**
11th: $7,500
12th: $5,000
13th: $4,000
14th: $2,500
15th: $1,000

Total Prize Pool:

$120,000

Answer 99:

Jack-8 suited isn't the greatest hand in the world, obviously, but in this position with four callers and no raisers in front of you, it's a good call, especially when it's only 200 chips because you were already in for 200 because of the small blind requirement. More than likely the big blind won't raise because statistically he didn't catch a good hand. And, even if he did, most players in the big blind like to disguise their hands, so he most likely won't be raising your call.

With a Jack-8 suited you have the potential for a flush and a straight, and even a straight flush. Since none of the first four bettors indicated any real strength by raising, you can comfortably make this call. The current pot odds are also nice, at 11-to-1.

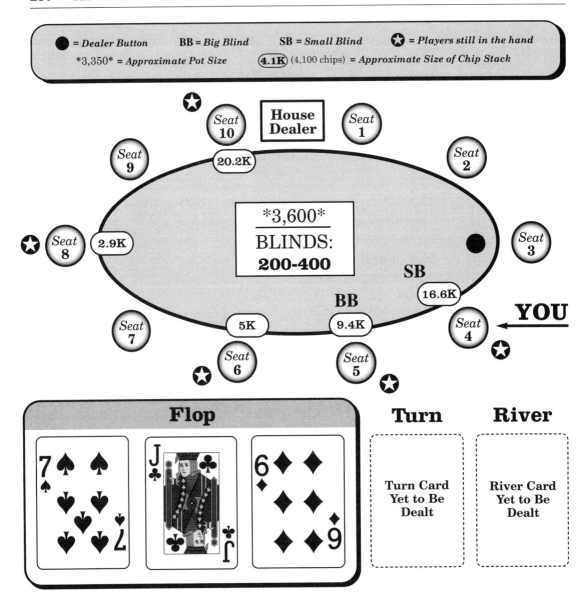

● = *Dealer Button*   **BB** = *Big Blind*   **SB** = *Small Blind*   ★ = *Players still in the hand*
3,350 = *Approximate Pot Size*   (**4.1K**) (4,100 chips) = *Approximate Size of Chip Stack*

Seat 10 — 20.2K
House Dealer
Seat 1
Seat 9
Seat 2
3,600 / BLINDS: 200-400
Seat 8 — 2.9K
Seat 3
SB — 16.6K
BB — 9.4K
YOU
Seat 4
Seat 7 — 5K
Seat 6
Seat 5

Flop

7♠ J♣ 6♦

Turn

Turn Card Yet to Be Dealt

River

River Card Yet to Be Dealt

Pocket

J♦ 8♦

Situation 100:

Seat 5 announced "Big enough," after your call, meaning that he wasn't going to raise his big blind bet of 400 chips, even though he had the option of doing so. After the flop, Seat 8 bet 400 chips and Seat 10 raised to 800. It is now your turn to act. With Seats 5 and 6 to act after you, do you fold, call the 800, raise to an unspecified level, or go all in?

Starting Hand (Pocket): **J♦8♦**
This Pocket's Win Rate: **9.8%**
Win Rate Rank: **45 of 169 possible**

Tournament Situation:

Tourney: **Internet Qualifier**

Paid Entrys: **2,400 x $50**

Starting Chip Stack: **2,000**

Players Remaining: **1,502**

Places Paid: **15 (See chart)**

Your Current Standing: **68th overall,
   2nd at your table**

Time Left in Round: **1 minute**

Rebuys Allowed: **No**

Next Blind Level: **300-600**

*This Tournament's
Prize Money:*

**1st-10th:
Paid entry to
World Series of
Poker Main Event
(worth $10,000)**
11th: $7,500
12th: $5,000
13th: $4,000
14th: $2,500
15th: $1,000

Total Prize Pool:

$120,000

Answer 100:

This isn't a situation to get real excited about, but you do have a bit of potential here, although you're going to have to go some to get there. You flopped top pair, that's good. Your kicker stinks, though. You also flopped three to a straight and three to a flush, both relative longshots, but possible. Had Seat 10 gone all in or made a fairly large bet, I probably would fold, but for 800 chips I'd call this hand and see if you couldn't catch a Jack, 8, 5, 9, or a diamond, any of which would substantially improve your hand. That's a total of a whopping twenty-three cards that can improve your hand.

Also, you've still got over 16,000 chips at your disposal and the average stack of those still left in the tournament is about 3,200, so this is the type of situation made for putting those 800 chips to use.

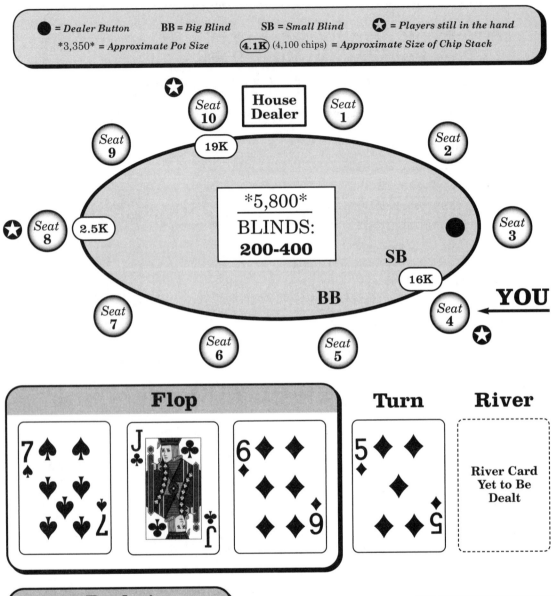

Situation 101:

After your call of 800 chips, Seats 5 and 6 folded and Seat 8 called. Following the deal of the turn card, Seat 8 was first to act and checked. Seat 10 bet 1,000 chips. It is now your turn to act. With Seat 8 to act behind you, do you fold, call the 1,000-chip bet, raise to an unspecified level, or go all in?

Starting Hand (Pocket): **J♦8♦**
This Pocket's Win Rate: **9.8%**
Win Rate Rank: **45 of 169 possible**

Tournament Situation:

Tourney: **Internet Qualifier**

Paid Entrys: **2,400 x $50**

Starting Chip Stack: **2,000**

Players Remaining: **1,502**

Places Paid: **15 (See chart)**

Your Current Standing: **68th overall, 2nd at your table**

Time Left in Round: **Expired**

Rebuys Allowed: **No**

Next Blind Level: **300-600**

This Tournament's Prize Money:

1st-10th:
Paid entry to World Series of Poker Main Event (worth $10,000)
11th: $7,500
12th: $5,000
13th: $4,000
14th: $2,500
15th: $1,000

Total Prize Pool:

$120,000

Answer 101:

This is a pretty straightforward hand with a potentially tricky result. Let's start with figuring how many outs you have to make potential winning hands, then calculate your pot odds, and then decide if it's a good play to continue in the hand.

To make a straight you need either a 4 or a 9, of which there are four of each still available. To make a flush you need another diamond, of which there are nine available. Together this makes seventeen outs, but you have to deduct one of the 4s and one of the 9s because they're diamonds. That leaves you with fifteen outs, or cards that will make your flush or straight. Keep in mind, however, that if, for example, the 4♣ comes, any opponent holding 9-8 will hold a higher straight. And if your flush comes on the river, someone could hold two diamonds, one of which is higher than a Jack.

Now the calculation. There are forty-six unseen cards, fifteen of which will make your straight or flush. That means 46 - 15 = 31. The ratio of 31-to-15 is about 2-to-1. There are 5,800 chips in the pot, and you're being asked to wager 1,000. The ratio of 5,800-to-1,000 is 5.8-to-1. Odds of 2-to-1 for a money return of 5.8-to-1 is a great betting proposition. Make the call.

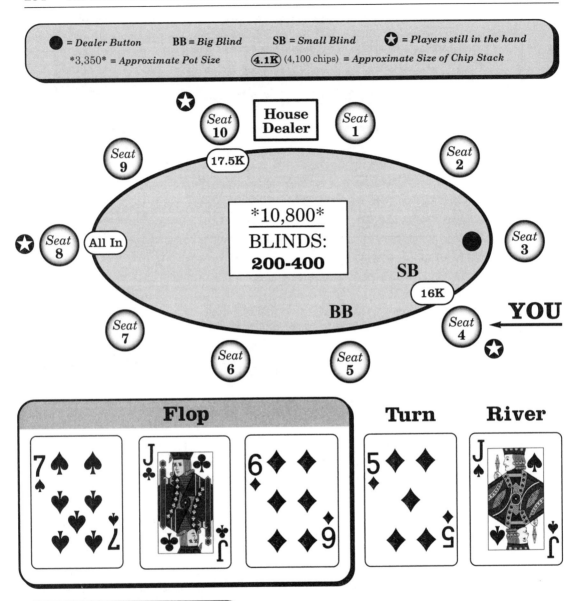

Situation 102:

Seat 8 called after the turn as well, leaving you with three players still in the hand. After the river card came, Seat 8 went all in for his remaining 1,500 chips and Seat 10 called. It is now your turn to act. Do you fold, call the 1,500 as well, raise to some unspecified level, or go all in?

Starting Hand (Pocket): **J♦8♦**

This Pocket's Win Rate: **9.8%**

Win Rate Rank: **45 of 169 possible**

Tournament Situation:

Tourney: **Internet Qualifier**

Paid Entrys: **2,400 x $50**

Starting Chip Stack: **2,000**

Players Remaining: **1,502**

Places Paid: **15 (See chart)**

Your Current Standing: **68th overall,
    2nd at your table**

Time Left in Round: **Expired**

Rebuys Allowed: **No**

Next Blind Level: **300-600**

*This Tournament's
Prize Money:*

**1st-10th:
Paid entry to
World Series of
Poker Main Event
(worth $10,000)**
11th: $7,500
12th: $5,000
13th: $4,000
14th: $2,500
15th: $1,000

Total Prize Pool:

$120,000

Answer 102:

Now THAT was an interesting river card. We didn't even figure that one in as one of our outs after the turn. What's also interesting is that Seat 8 now decided to jump in and initiate the betting, although he only had 1,500 chips left. What's also interesting is that Seat 10 now decided to just call instead of forcing the action on you. What could all this mean?

I'm not quite sure what it means for Seat 8. He could have gone all in just because his stack was dwindling. The Jack on the river may have helped him. If he's trying a bluff or semi-bluff, he hasn't got enough chips to pull it off. Seat 10, on the other hand, seems not to have liked the Jack on the river. If that's the case, it means he's afraid of a set of Jacks, which you hold. It could also be that he liked the Jack and is intent on check-raising you if you raise the bet, but I tend to think that's not the case here.

So, what I would do is raise the bet by about 5,000 chips, just in case Seat 8 has you both beat, and hope Seat 10 calls you, because that might be all the chips you win on this hand.

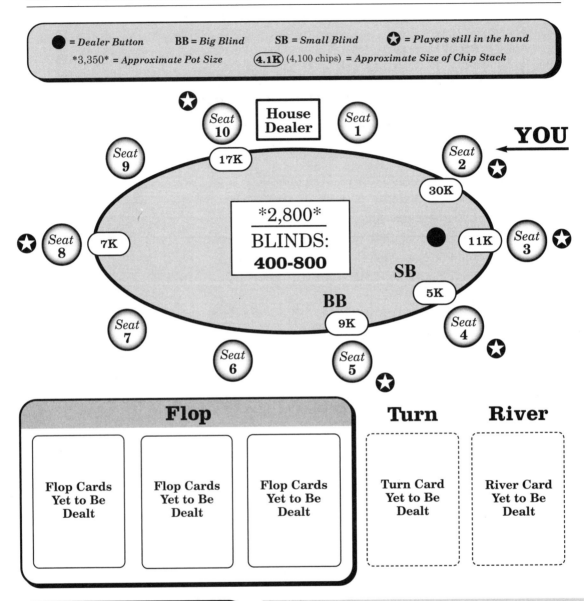

Situation 103:

You beat both of your opponents on the previous hand when they showed pocket Queens and Aces at the showdown. It is now several more rounds into the tournament and you've been moved to another table again as the tournament condensed, receiving a pair of 2s in your pocket. Four players in front of you folded and two called the 800-chip big blind bet. With three players yet to act after you, do you fold, call, raise to an unspecified level, or go all in?

Starting Hand (Pocket): **2♠2♥**

This Pocket's Win Rate: **4.0%**

Win Rate Rank: **72 of 169 possible**

Tournament Situation:

Tourney: **Internet Qualifier**

Paid Entrys: **2,400 x $50**

Starting Chip Stack: **2,000**

Players Remaining: **1,177**

Places Paid: **15 (See chart)**

Your Current Standing: **46th overall,
    1st at your table**

Time Left in Round: **4 minutes**

Rebuys Allowed: **No**

Next Blind Level: **500-1,000**

*This Tournament's
Prize Money:*

**1st-10th:
Paid entry to
World Series of
Poker Main Event
(worth $10,000)
11th: $7,500
12th: $5,000
13th: $4,000
14th: $2,500
15th: $1,000**

**Total Prize Pool:
$120,000**

Answer 103:

How good is a pair of 2s, really? Just look at the chart above. The relative win rate is 4.0 percent, or once every twenty-five hands against one other random hand. And you'd better believe that when played against multiple *select* hands, the percentage drops like a rock. Technically, a pair of twos is the thirteenth highest pocket hand, but look again at the chart and its relative win rate rank: seventy-two. The drop from thirteen to seventy-two is indicative of what happens to this hand once the cards start hitting the board. For all practical purposes, your only outs with a pair of 2s are the other two 2s.

Another problem with 2s (or any small pair) is that they can be counterfeited. What this means is that let's say the board comes 8-8-4. You have two pair. But if another 4 comes on the turn or river, your pair of 2s disappears because the pair of 4s now outrank your twos, and you're left playing the board. There are rare occasions when you would play a pair of 2s, but this isn't one of them.

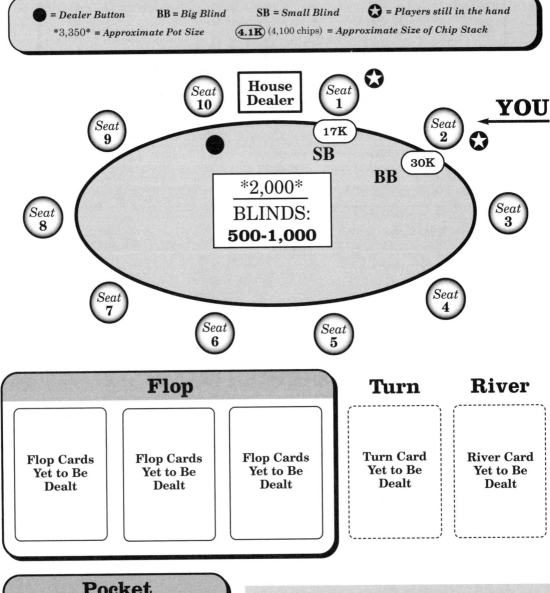

Situation 104:

It's now the next round of the tournament and you have received a pocket hand of Jack-10 unsuited while in the big blind position. Everyone folded to the small blind who then called the 1,000-chip big blind bet. It is now your turn to act with no one behind you. Do you announce, "Big enough," indicating a check, raise to an unspecified level, or go all in?

Starting Hand (Pocket): **J♠10♦**
This Pocket's Win Rate: **9.4%**
Win Rate Rank: **50 of 169 possible**

Tournament Situation:
Tourney: **Internet Qualifier**
Paid Entrys: **2,400 x $50**
Starting Chip Stack: **2,000**
Players Remaining: **1,177**
Places Paid: **15 (See chart)**
Your Current Standing: **46th overall,
    1st at your table**
Time Left in Round: **4 minutes**
Rebuys Allowed: **No**
Next Blind Level: **600-1,200**

*This Tournament's
Prize Money:*

**1st-10th:
Paid entry to
World Series of
Poker Main Event
(worth $10,000)**
11th: $7,500
12th: $5,000
13th: $4,000
14th: $2,500
15th: $1,000

Total Prize Pool:
$120,000

Answer 104:

To begin with, Jack-10 suited is not that good of a hand. The only reason you're still in this hand is because you're the big blind and your 1,000 chips were required to be placed in the pot. Of course you will continue in the hand, but you shouldn't raise for two reasons. First, you don't have much. Second, when the small blind called, he indicated he had some sort of hand worth playing, and probably a better hand than if he raised, because a raise in that situation could merely have been an effort to steal your blind, hoping that you caught a poor pocket hand. By calling, Seat 1 is letting you know he thinks the pot is worth fighting over in a heads up situation so long as it's not too expensive. Just tell the dealer your bet is big enough and proceed to the flop, where much more will be revealed.

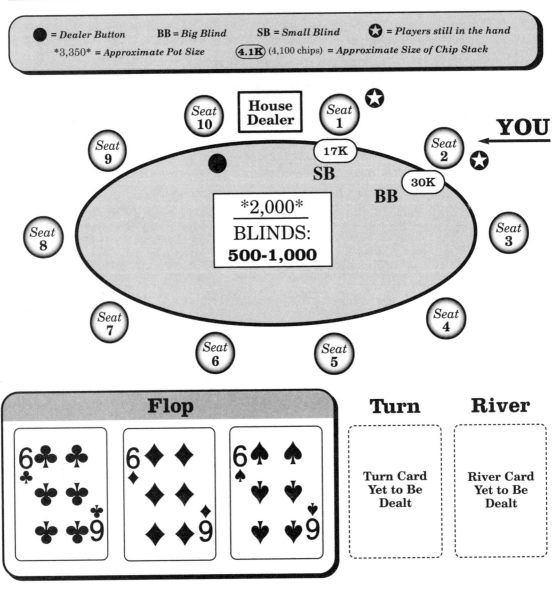

● = *Dealer Button*   BB = *Big Blind*   SB = *Small Blind*   ⭐ = *Players still in the hand*

3,350 = *Approximate Pot Size*   (4.1K) (4,100 chips) = *Approximate Size of Chip Stack*

Flop

Turn

Turn Card
Yet to Be
Dealt

River

River Card
Yet to Be
Dealt

Pocket

Situation 105:

After the flop, Seat 1 checked. It is now your turn to act. Do you check as well, raise to an unspecified level, or go all in?

Starting Hand (Pocket): **J♠10♦**

This Pocket's Win Rate: **9.4%**

Win Rate Rank: **50 of 169 possible**

Tournament Situation:

Tourney: **Internet Qualifier**

Paid Entries: **2,400 x $50**

Starting Chip Stack: **2,000**

Players Remaining: **1,177**

Places Paid: **15 (See chart)**

Your Current Standing: **46th overall, 1st at your table**

Time Left in Round: **4 minutes**

Rebuys Allowed: **No**

Next Blind Level: **600-1,200**

This Tournament's Prize Money:

1st-10th: Paid entry to World Series of Poker Main Event (worth $10,000)
11th: $7,500
12th: $5,000
13th: $4,000
14th: $2,500
15th: $1,000

Total Prize Pool:

$120,000

Answer 105:

Now THAT was a devilish flop. Sorry, couldn't resist it. It is understandable why Seat 1 checked. If he holds a 6 and bets, he's going to scare you off unless you hold a large pocket pair, in which case he's hoping you bet so he can call or raise you. You can either check or bet something. If you bet a small amount, you could be playing right into his hands. Remember, he had something worth betting on before the flop, you're just hanging around because you were already in. If you make a large bet, you'll force him out unless he truly has something, and it better be a pocket pair or at least an Ace-something, or he'll go away.

Given your current good standing in the tournament (see chart above), there is no sense in wasting chips making a bet at this time. Check and see what the turn brings. One advantage you have is your position. Had you checked first, and he held a good hand, he probably would have bet and you'd have folded. Once again, you can see how important position is; sometimes it's more important than your cards.

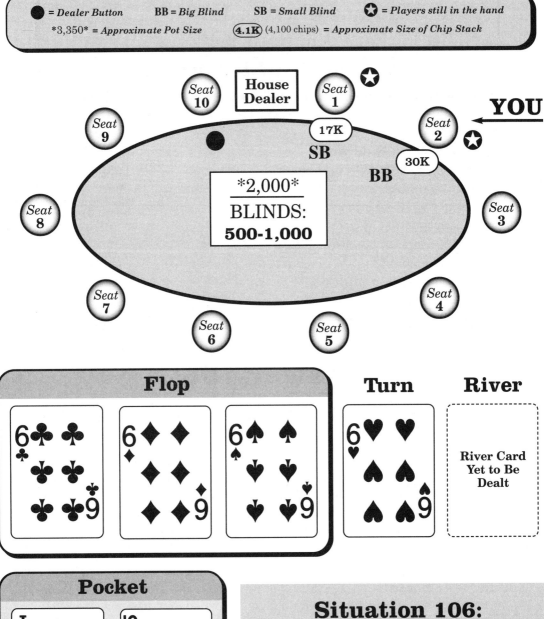

YOU

2,000
———
BLINDS:
500-1,000

Flop

Turn

River

River Card
Yet to Be
Dealt

Pocket

Situation 106:

After the turn card was dealt, Seat 1 checked. It is now your turn to act. Do you check as well, raise to an unspecified level, or go all in?

Starting Hand (Pocket): **J♠10♦**
This Pocket's Win Rate: **9.4%**
Win Rate Rank: **50 of 169 possible**

Tournament Situation:
Tourney: **Internet Qualifier**
Paid Entrys: **2,400 x $50**
Starting Chip Stack: **2,000**
Players Remaining: **1,177**
Places Paid: **15 (See chart)**
Your Current Standing: **46th overall,
    1st at your table**
Time Left in Round: **4 minutes**
Rebuys Allowed: **No**
Next Blind Level: **600-1,200**

*This Tournament's
Prize Money:*

**1st-10th:
Paid entry to
World Series of
Poker Main Event
(worth $10,000)**
11th: $7,500
12th: $5,000
13th: $4,000
14th: $2,500
15th: $1,000

Total Prize Pool:
$120,000

Answer 106:

Is this spooky, or what? Okay, he checked again. What's going on here? Is he trying to trap you? Does he hold a small or medium pair? This hand is clearly going to come down to the best kicker. For you, right now, it's your Jack. You can't bet now, because if he's holding an Ace, he's either going to come back over top of you or just call and try to string it out, either way costing you chips you don't need to spend. Just check this strange hand and take it to the river.

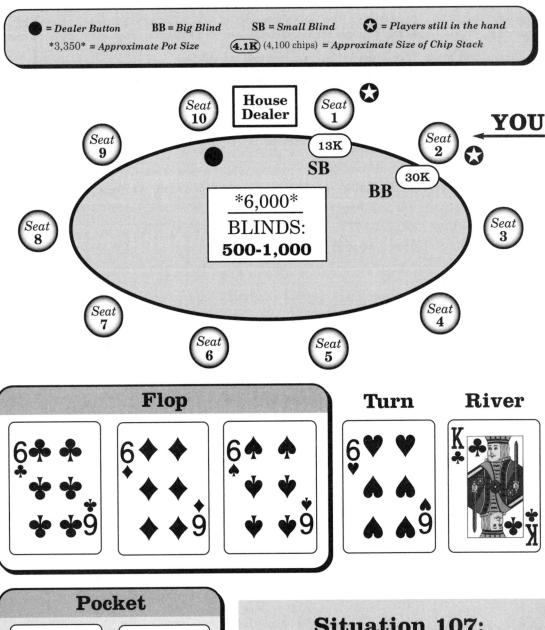

Flop

Turn

River

Pocket

Situation 107:

After the river card was dealt, Seat 1 bet 4,000 chips. It is now your turn to act. Do you fold, call the 4,000, raise to an unspecified level, or go all in?

Starting Hand (Pocket): **J♠10♦**
This Pocket's Win Rate: **9.4%**
Win Rate Rank: **50 of 169 possible**

Tournament Situation:
Tourney: **Internet Qualifier**
Paid Entrys: **2,400 x $50**
Starting Chip Stack: **2,000**
Players Remaining: **1,177**
Places Paid: **15 (See chart)**
Your Current Standing: **46th overall,**
   1st at your table
Time Left in Round: **4 minutes**
Rebuys Allowed: **No**
Next Blind Level: **600-1,200**

*This Tournament's
Prize Money:*

1st-10th:
Paid entry to
World Series of
Poker Main Event
(worth $10,000)
11th: $7,500
12th: $5,000
13th: $4,000
14th: $2,500
15th: $1,000

Total Prize Pool:

$120,000

Answer 107:

Well, it's time for the rubber to hit the road with this hand. No more checking. When the King came on the board it gave you—and your opponent—both quad 6s with a King kicker. UNLESS he holds an Ace in his hand. You, of course, do not hold an Ace, so you'll be playing the five cards on the board. What it boils down to now is whether or not you believe he holds an Ace. If he does, he beats you. If he doesn't, it's a split pot, but only if you call. Is it worth calling? Don't forget, he called before the flop, so he had something worth playing, and a lot of times that means Ace-something when you're limping in like he did.

As for me, I'd fold this hand. You only have 1,000 chips in this pot, that coming from your big blind bet. You're in great shape in this tournament and if you call and lose it'll set you back a bit. The goal is to get a little fatter and go up the ladder, and I just don't see it happening on this hand.

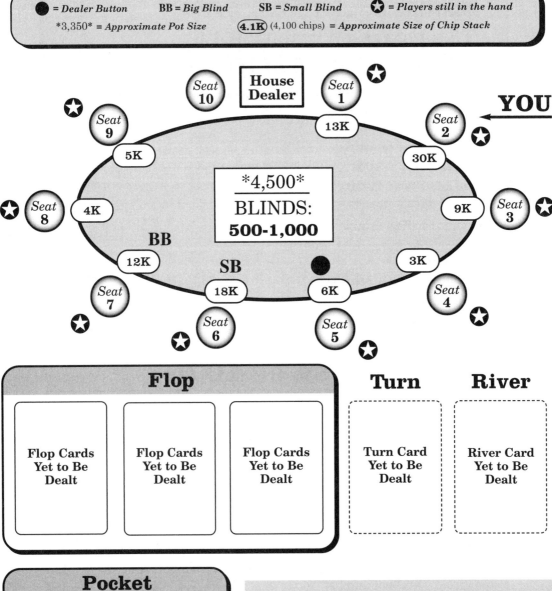

● = *Dealer Button*   **BB** = *Big Blind*   **SB** = *Small Blind*   ★ = *Players still in the hand*

3,350 = *Approximate Pot Size*   (**4.1K**) (4,100 chips) = *Approximate Size of Chip Stack*

Seat 10 · House Dealer · Seat 1 · **YOU** · Seat 2 · Seat 3 · Seat 4 · Seat 5 · Seat 6 · Seat 7 · Seat 8 · Seat 9

13K · 5K · 4K · 12K · 18K · 6K · 3K · 9K · 30K

4,500
BLINDS:
500-1,000

BB · SB

Flop

| Flop Cards Yet to Be Dealt | Flop Cards Yet to Be Dealt | Flop Cards Yet to Be Dealt |

Turn

Turn Card Yet to Be Dealt

River

River Card Yet to Be Dealt

Pocket

Q♦ J♦

Situation 108:

It's a short while later and you're playing the last hand of the current round and you catch a Queen-Jack suited in your pocket. Three players call the 1,000-chip big blind bet and one folds in front of you. It is now your turn to act. With five players to act after you, do you fold, call as well, raise to an unspecified level, or go all in?

Starting Hand (Pocket): **Q♦J♦**
This Pocket's Win Rate: **44.2%**
Win Rate Rank: **17 of 169 possible**

Tournament Situation:
Tourney: **Internet Qualifier**
Paid Entrys: **2,400 x $50**
Starting Chip Stack: **2,000**
Players Remaining: **1,120**
Places Paid: **15 (See chart)**
Your Current Standing: **49th overall,**
  1st at your table
Time Left in Round: **Expired**
Rebuys Allowed: **No**
Next Blind Level: **600-1,200**

This Tournament's Prize Money:

1st-10th:
**Paid entry to
World Series of
Poker Main Event
(worth $10,000)**
11th: **$7,500**
12th: **$5,000**
13th: **$4,000**
14th: **$2,500**
15th: **$1,000**

Total Prize Pool:

$120,000

Answer 108:

Generally speaking, only the top twenty to thirty hands are worth playing in most instances in Texas Hold'em, so long as the circumstances and your position are appropriate. As you can see in the chart above, Queen-Jack suited certainly qualifies as one such hand with its strong relative win rate of over 44 percent and a win rate rank of 17 out of the 169 possible two-card pockets. As for your position, it could be better, but middle position isn't the worst spot at the table. You've also received three callers so far and no raisers. Were this just a bit better hand you could help yourself gain a better position by raising in an attempt to drive out some of the players behind you, but for now it's appropriate just to call. Calling rather than raising will likely induce more callers, which will ultimately help your pot odds, something you need when you're playing a drawing hand like this one as you go for the straight or the flush.

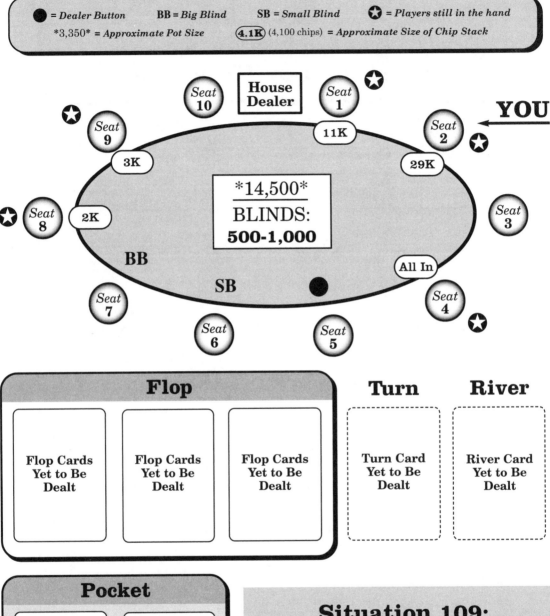

● = *Dealer Button*   BB = *Big Blind*   SB = *Small Blind*   ⭐ = *Players still in the hand*

3,350 = *Approximate Pot Size*   (**4.1K**) (4,100 chips) = *Approximate Size of Chip Stack*

Seat 10

House Dealer

Seat 1 ⭐

YOU

Seat 9 ⭐

Seat 2 ⭐

11K

3K

29K

14,500
BLINDS:
500-1,000

Seat 8 ⭐   2K

Seat 3

BB

All In

SB

●

Seat 4

Seat 7

Seat 6

Seat 5

⭐

Flop

| Flop Cards Yet to Be Dealt | Flop Cards Yet to Be Dealt | Flop Cards Yet to Be Dealt |

Turn

Turn Card Yet to Be Dealt

River

River Card Yet to Be Dealt

Pocket

Q♦   J♦

Situation 109:

After you called, Seat 3 folded and Seat 4 went all in for 3,000 chips. Seats 5, 6, and 7 all folded. Seats 8, 9, and 1 all called, bringing the action back to you. With no one to act after you, do you fold, call the additional 2,000 chips, raise to an unspecified level, or go all in?

Starting Hand (Pocket): **Q♦J♦**

This Pocket's Win Rate: **44.2%**

Win Rate Rank: **17 of 169 possible**

Tournament Situation:

Tourney: **Internet Qualifier**

Paid Entrys: **2,400 x $50**

Starting Chip Stack: **2,000**

Players Remaining: **1,120**

Places Paid: **15 (See chart)**

Your Current Standing: **49th overall, 1st at your table**

Time Left in Round: **Expired**

Rebuys Allowed: **No**

Next Blind Level: **600-1,200**

This Tournament's Prize Money:

1st-10th:
Paid entry to
World Series of
Poker Main Event
(worth $10,000)
11th: $7,500
12th: $5,000
13th: $4,000
14th: $2,500
15th: $1,000

Total Prize Pool:

$120,000

Answer 109:

This actually has turned out to be a nice development for you. You would have liked to have raised out those behind you, but Queen-Jack suited wasn't quite a big enough hand to try it. Seat 4 did it for you with his raise, getting the next three players all to fold, leaving in only the original bettors. Additionally, Seat 4 is all in, which now makes you last to act for the remainder of the hand.

Another nice development is that you have four callers, a nice number for a drawing hand like yours. Further still, you have a huge chip advantage over the remaining three players who still have chips, an important factor if you decide the situation is right to bully some people. Call the 2,000 chips and take a deep breath and pay attention, Maynard, because everything is falling into place for you on this hand, and you should be able to sense it. If you don't sense it, don't fret, sometimes the cards talk to me. Really.

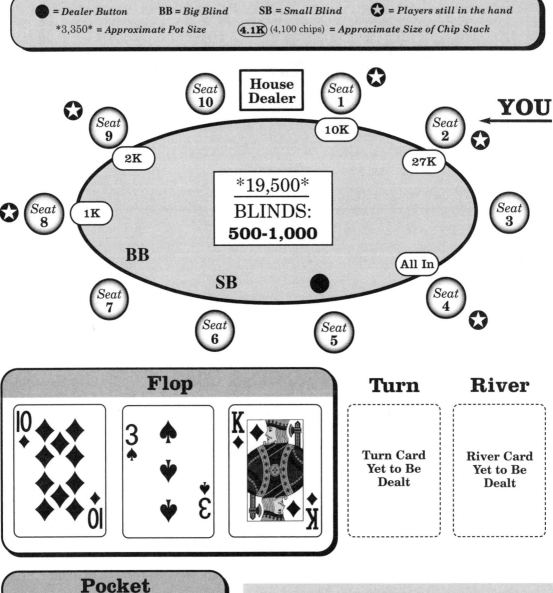

= Dealer Button   **BB** = *Big Blind*   **SB** = *Small Blind*   ⭐ = *Players still in the hand*

3,350 = *Approximate Pot Size*   **4.1K** (4,100 chips) = *Approximate Size of Chip Stack*

House Dealer

Seat 10 · Seat 1 · Seat 9 · Seat 2 · **YOU**

10K · 2K · 27K

19,500
BLINDS:
500-1,000

Seat 8 · 1K · Seat 3

BB · SB · All In

Seat 7 · Seat 6 · Seat 5 · Seat 4

Flop

Turn

Turn Card Yet to Be Dealt

River

River Card Yet to Be Dealt

Pocket

Situation 110:

After the flop, Seat 8 was first to act and he bet 1,000 chips. Seats 9 and 1 both called. It is now your turn to act. Do you fold, call the 1,000-chip bet, raise to an unspecified level, or go all in?

> ## Starting Hand (Pocket): **Q♦J♦**
> ## This Pocket's Win Rate: **44.2%**
> ## Win Rate Rank: **17 of 169 possible**

Tournament Situation:

Tourney: **Internet Qualifier**

Paid Entrys: **2,400 x $50**

Starting Chip Stack: **2,000**

Players Remaining: **1,120**

Places Paid: **15 (See chart)**

Your Current Standing: **49th overall, 1st at your table**

Time Left in Round: **Expired**

Rebuys Allowed: **No**

Next Blind Level: **600-1,200**

This Tournament's Prize Money:

1st-10th:
Paid entry to
World Series of
Poker Main Event
(worth $10,000)
11th: $7,500
12th: $5,000
13th: $4,000
14th: $2,500
15th: $1,000

Total Prize Pool:
$120,000

Answer 110:

Boy, what a nice flop, huh? You flopped an open-ender and four cards to a straight flush, the Royal, no less. Okay, okay, technically you don't have anything yet, but you have a lot of outs to make your straight or flush—fifteen to be exact. (Nine diamonds, four 9s, and four Aces for seventeen outs, but you have to take away two of them for the 9♦ and the Ace♦ because you counted them twice.)

Something else you have going for you is three timid bettors in front of you, two with very small stacks who didn't feel confident enough in the flop to bet more than the minimum amount. That tells me that if you were to raise now to say, 4,000 chips, you might get one, two, or all three of them to fold. And even if they all called, it wouldn't be the worst thing in the world since two of them can't do any more damage to you. Only Seat 1 presents any kind of a problem, and you've got nearly three times as many chips as he does. This is the time to start bullying. Raise to 4,000 now in a semi-bluff and let them know who's in control of this hand.

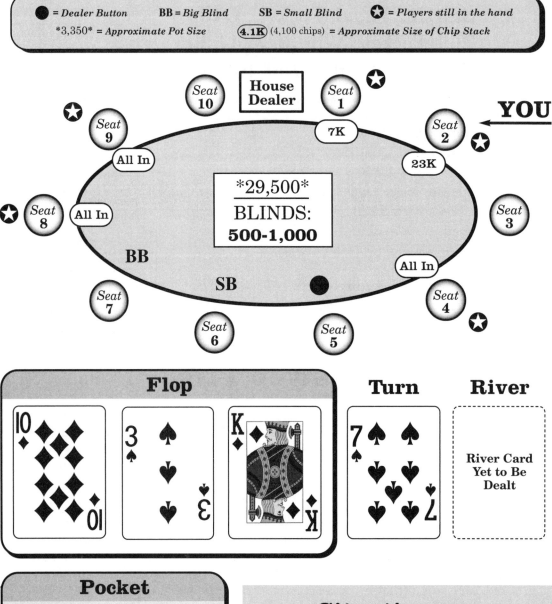

● = *Dealer Button*   BB = *Big Blind*   SB = *Small Blind*   ⭐ = *Players still in the hand*

3,350 = *Approximate Pot Size*   (4.1K) (4,100 chips) = *Approximate Size of Chip Stack*

Seat 10 — House Dealer — Seat 1 ⭐

YOU ←

Seat 9 — All In

Seat 2 ⭐ — 23K

7K

29,500
BLINDS:
500-1,000

Seat 8 ⭐ — All In

BB

Seat 3

SB

All In

Seat 7

Seat 4 — All In

Seat 6

Seat 5 ⭐

Flop

10♦   3♠   K♦

Turn

7♠

River

River Card Yet to Be Dealt

Pocket

Q♦   J♦

Situation 111:

All three players called your 4,000-chip raise after the flop, although Seat 8 was all in with 1,000 and Seat 9 was all in for 2,000. After the turn card was revealed, Seat 1 checked. (Seats 8 and 9 were already all in.) It is now your turn to act. Do you check as well, bet the minimum of 1,000 chips, bet a larger amount, or go all in?

Starting Hand (Pocket): **Q♦J♦**
This Pocket's Win Rate: **44.2%**
Win Rate Rank: **17 of 169 possible**

Tournament Situation:

Tourney: **Internet Qualifier**

Paid Entrys: **2,400 x $50**

Starting Chip Stack: **2,000**

Players Remaining: **1,120**

Places Paid: **15 (See chart)**

Your Current Standing: **49th overall, 1st at your table**

Time Left in Round: **Expired**

Rebuys Allowed: **No**

Next Blind Level: **600-1,200**

This Tournament's Prize Money:

1st-10th:
Paid entry to World Series of Poker Main Event (worth $10,000)
11th: $7,500
12th: $5,000
13th: $4,000
14th: $2,500
15th: $1,000

Total Prize Pool:
$120,000

Answer 111:

The turn missed you completely, leaving you with only the river card to come up with a made hand. You still have fifteen outs with forty-six cards unseen, meaning a ratio of 31-to-15, or about 2-to-1 odds of making a made hand. Thus, with nearly 30,000 chips in the pot, anything you bet up to 15,000 chips will be an appropriate call.

The question, however, is whether it's in your *overall* best interests to bet at this point. First, there is no real sidepot to shoot for, and if you miss, there is no way under the sun that you are going to beat three players who are already all in for the other pots. Second, you are now getting a free draw for a chance to win nearly 30,000 chips. Third, you lose nothing by checking, and if you make a hand, you may get more chips from Seat 1— maybe even all of them. If you put Seat 1 all in now and miss, you can say goodbye to 7,000 more chips. Finally, tournaments are about elimination and surviving elimination. A move that is the correct pot odds is not always the best move to make because you have more at stake in a tournament than an individual pot. Check this time.

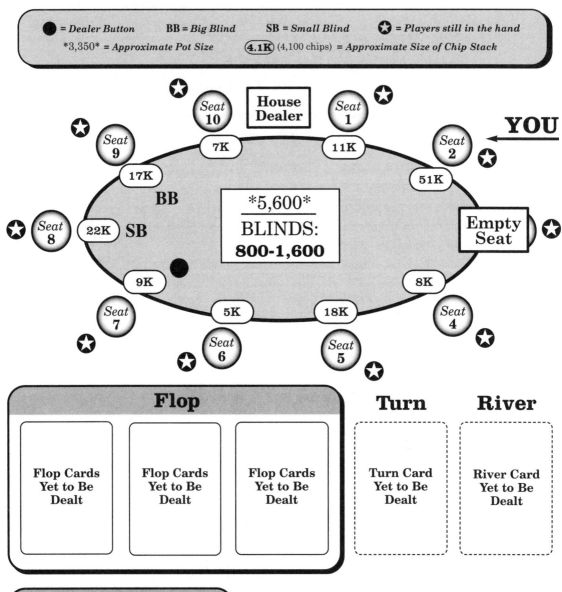

● = *Dealer Button*   **BB** = *Big Blind*   **SB** = *Small Blind*   ⭐ = *Players still in the hand*
3,350 = *Approximate Pot Size*   **4.1K** (4,100 chips) = *Approximate Size of Chip Stack*

House Dealer

Seat 10 — 7K
Seat 1 — 11K
Seat 2 — 51K (YOU)
Seat 9 — 17K
BB
5,600 BLINDS: 800-1,600
Empty Seat
Seat 8 — 22K — SB
Seat 7 — 9K
Seat 6 — 5K
Seat 5 — 18K
Seat 4 — 8K

Flop

Flop Cards Yet to Be Dealt

Flop Cards Yet to Be Dealt

Flop Cards Yet to Be Dealt

Turn

Turn Card Yet to Be Dealt

River

River Card Yet to Be Dealt

Pocket

A♦ A♦

10♣ 10♣

Situation 112:

As you'd hoped, Seat 1 folded in the face of your 7,000-chip bet on the previous hand. It is now about thirty minutes later in the tournament. You have received Ace-10 unsuited in your pocket. Seats 10 and 1 both called the 1,600-chip big blind bet. It is now your turn to act. Given the tournament situation presented above and on the opposite page, do you fold, call the 1,600, raise to an unspecified level, or go all in?

Starting Hand (Pocket): **A♦10♣**
This Pocket's Win Rate: **34.4%**
Win Rate Rank: **25 of 169 possible**

Tournament Situation:
Tourney: **Internet Qualifier**
Paid Entrys: **2,400 x $50**
Starting Chip Stack: **2,000**
Players Remaining: **822**
Places Paid: **15 (See chart)**
Your Current Standing: **4th overall,**
  1st at your table
Time Left in Round: **13 minutes**
Rebuys Allowed: **No**
Next Blind Level: **1,000-2,000**

This Tournament's
Prize Money:

1st-10th:
Paid entry to
World Series of
Poker Main Event
(worth $10,000)
11th: $7,500
12th: $5,000
13th: $4,000
14th: $2,500
15th: $1,000

Total Prize Pool:
$120,000

Answer 112:

You fold. Surprised? You shouldn't be. Look at Your Current Standing in the above chart. You're fourth overall in the tournament. There are only fifteen prizes being awarded, and the main reason you entered this tournament was to win a seat in the World Series of Poker in Las Vegas.

While Ace-10 is normally a playable hand in most instances, you are in early position, so you don't know what the six players yet to act after you are going to do. Also, your hand is unsuited, so it makes flushes harder to get. You don't have a pair, and if an Ace comes on the board, your 10 kicker isn't anything special. To make a straight, you need to hit a King, Queen, and Jack on the board (a tough proposition), AND avoid someone else's flush.

No, while this hand is certainly playable at the lower levels, and when you're in better position, now, with the blinds at the high level they've reached, and with your strong place in the standings, don't squander your chip stack on hands like this that look good but have a ways to go before they turn into anything decent. And don't forget, you had two players in front of you already call, so that indicates they have some sort of decent, playable hand. Fold this hand and come in when you've got a better one. Your chip stack will allow you to sit a while if you need to.

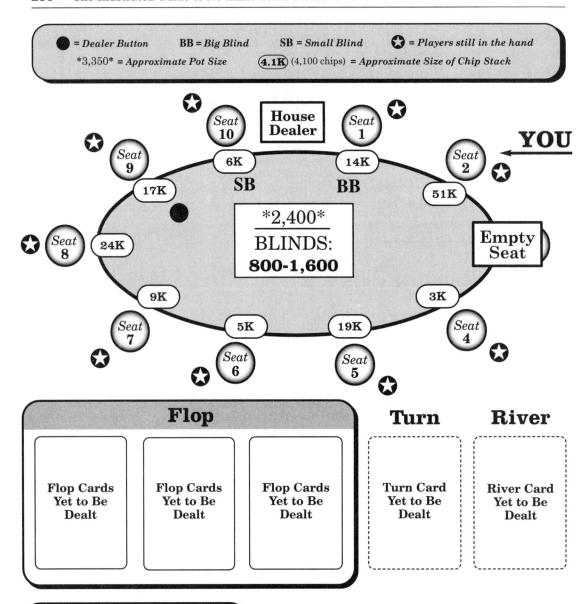

● = *Dealer Button*   **BB** = *Big Blind*   **SB** = *Small Blind*   ★ = *Players still in the hand*

3,350 = *Approximate Pot Size*   (**4.1K**) (4,100 chips) = *Approximate Size of Chip Stack*

YOU

Seat 10 — 6K
House Dealer
Seat 1 — 14K
Seat 2 — 51K
Seat 9 — 17K
SB
BB
Empty Seat
Seat 8 — 24K
2,400
BLINDS: 800-1,600
9K
3K
Seat 7 — 5K
19K
Seat 4
Seat 6
Seat 5

Flop

| Flop Cards Yet to Be Dealt | Flop Cards Yet to Be Dealt | Flop Cards Yet to Be Dealt |

Turn

Turn Card Yet to Be Dealt

River

River Card Yet to Be Dealt

Pocket

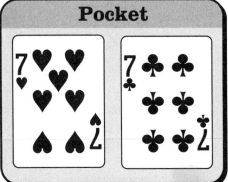

Situation 113:

Two hands later you receive a pair of 7s in your pocket. Given the tournament situation presented above and on the opposite page, do you fold, call the 1,600-chip big blind bet, raise to an unspecified level, or go all in?

Starting Hand (Pocket): **7♥7♣**

This Pocket's Win Rate: **28.6%**

Win Rate Rank: **30 of 169 possible**

Tournament Situation:

Tourney: **Internet Qualifier**

Paid Entrys: **2,400 x $50**

Starting Chip Stack: **2,000**

Players Remaining: **808**

Places Paid: **15 (See chart)**

Your Current Standing: **4th overall, 1st at your table**

Time Left in Round: **11 minutes**

Rebuys Allowed: **No**

Next Blind Level: **1,000-2,000**

This Tournament's Prize Money:

**1st-10th:
Paid entry to
World Series of
Poker Main Event
(worth $10,000)**
11th: $7,500
12th: $5,000
13th: $4,000
14th: $2,500
15th: $1,000

**Total Prize Pool:
$120,000**

Answer 113:

Once again, you should fold, and for most of the same reasons given in the answer to Situation #112. You are in early position, so anything could happen after you act. Are you really going to call with your pair of 7s if Seat 8 goes all in for 24,000 chips? Of course not. As for the pair of 7s themselves, the odds of catching a pair of anything in the pocket is 16-to-1, or about once every hand and a half when counting all the players at the table. This means that the odds are approximately 50-50 that someone else already holds a pair of something at your table right now, and the odds are 7-to-5 against you that their pair is higher. The point is, don't get too excited over a pair of 7s in first position. And even if no one else holds a pair before the flop, you can bet that anyone who decides to jump in on this hand with the blinds as high as they are will be holding big cards of some kind, and with five cards yet to come on the board, someone will likely pair up their Ace, King, Queen, Jack, etc., all of which will crush you if you don't hit a third 7. And what are the chances of you catching a third 7 if you don't hit it on the flop? Only 8.4 percent. This is one of those hands where if you don't have them beat going in, you're probably not going to have them beat at the end. And it's also a case where if you have them beat going in, you might not have them beat at the end either. Get rid of it. Your chip stack will let you ride things out a while.

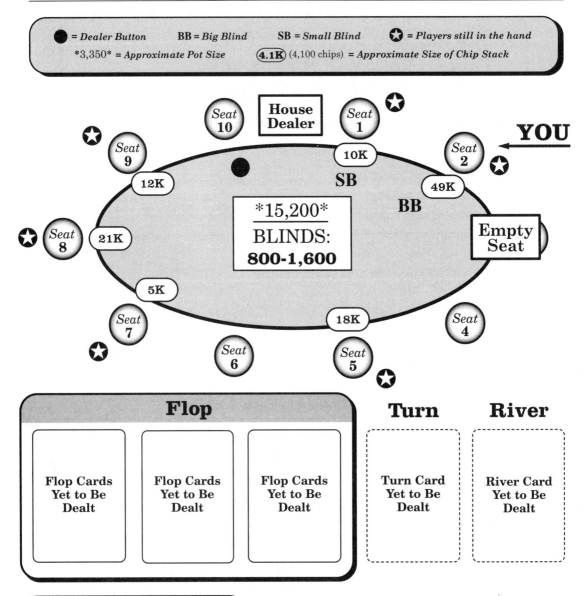

= Dealer Button   BB = *Big Blind*   SB = *Small Blind*   ⭐ = *Players still in the hand*

3,350 = *Approximate Pot Size*   **4.1K** (4,100 chips) = *Approximate Size of Chip Stack*

Seat 10

House Dealer

Seat 1

YOU

Seat 9

Seat 2

12K

10K

SB

49K

Seat 8   21K

15,200
BLINDS:
800-1,600

BB

Empty Seat

5K

Seat 7

18K

Seat 4

Seat 6

Seat 5

Flop

| Flop Cards Yet to Be Dealt | Flop Cards Yet to Be Dealt | Flop Cards Yet to Be Dealt |

Turn

Turn Card Yet to Be Dealt

River

River Card Yet to Be Dealt

Pocket

4♦   4♠

Situation 114:

On the very next hand, you caught a pair of 4s while in the big blind position. Seat 4 folded, then Seat 5 bet 1,600, the minimum. Seat 6 folded, Seat 7 called, and Seat 8 raised to 3,200 chips. Seats 9 and 1 called while Seat 10 folded. It is now your turn to act. Given the tournament situation presented above and on the opposite page, should you fold, call the 3,200, raise to an unspecified level, or go all in?

Starting Hand (Pocket): **4♦4♠**

This Pocket's Win Rate: **8.3%**

Win Rate Rank: **61 of 169 possible**

Tournament Situation:

Tourney: **Internet Qualifier**

Paid Entrys: **2,400 x $50**

Starting Chip Stack: **2,000**

Players Remaining: **805**

Places Paid: **15 (See chart)**

Your Current Standing: **4th overall, 1st at your table**

Time Left in Round: **10 minutes**

Rebuys Allowed: **No**

Next Blind Level: **1,000-2,000**

This Tournament's Prize Money:

1st-10th: Paid entry to World Series of Poker Main Event (worth $10,000)
11th: $7,500
12th: $5,000
13th: $4,000
14th: $2,500
15th: $1,000

Total Prize Pool: $120,000

Answer 114:

You should call the additional 1,600. What? I know, I know, you're thinking, "He just told me to fold a pair of 7s on the previous hand, why is he recommending that I now call a raise with a pair of 4s?" Because the circumstances of this situation are different. How? Well, first, and most important of all, your position is different. On the last hand you were first to act and had no idea yet what everyone behind you was going to do. On this hand you are LAST to act, and have a very good idea of what everyone is going to do. Seat 5 was first to act and only bet the minimum of 1,600 chips, even though he had nearly 20,000 in his stack. Seat 7 only called. Both of these players are highly likely to only call the 3,200 as well. If neither Seat 5 nor 7 raises, Seat 8 can't reraise. Seats 9 and 1 only called the original raise, so they aren't likely to reraise either. You are already in this hand for 1,600 big blind chips. It will only cost you 1,600 more chips to play for a likely pot of 20,000 chips, which is better than 12-to-1 pot odds for whatever you're trying to hit, which in this case is probably a set of 4s, of which the odds of hitting on the flop are about 8-to-1.

Two things to keep in mind: 1) if you don't hit this hand really strong on the flop, get out if anyone bets; 2) you have a much larger chip stack than your opponents, so it allows you to make this kind of a call with this kind of a hand in this position.

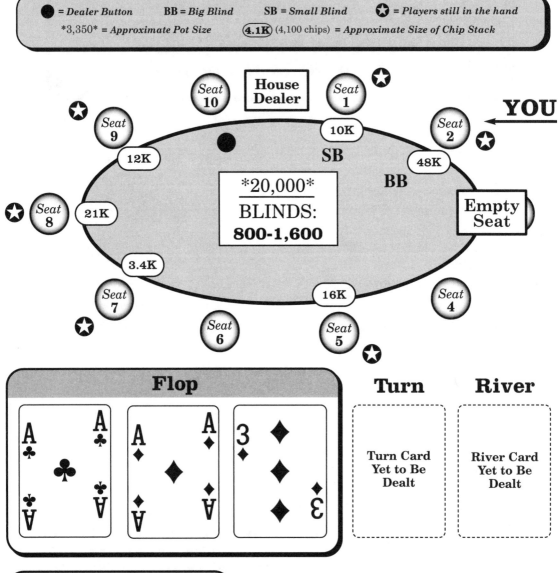

Situation 115:

After your call, the other players called as you expected. Following the flop, Seat 1 was first to act and he checked. It is now your turn to act. Do you check as well, bet the minimum of 1,600 chips, raise to an unspecified level, or go all in?

Starting Hand (Pocket): **4♦4♠**
This Pocket's Win Rate: **8.3%**
Win Rate Rank: **61 of 169 possible**

Tournament Situation:
Tourney: **Internet Qualifier**
Paid Entrys: **2,400 x $50**
Starting Chip Stack: **2,000**
Players Remaining: **805**
Places Paid: **15 (See chart)**
Your Current Standing: **4th overall,
1st at your table**
Time Left in Round: **10 minutes**
Rebuys Allowed: **No**
Next Blind Level: **1,000-2,000**

*This Tournament's
Prize Money:*

**1st-10th:
Paid entry to
World Series of
Poker Main Event
(worth $10,000)
11th: $7,500
12th: $5,000
13th: $4,000
14th: $2,500
15th: $1,000**

**Total Prize Pool:
$120,000**

Answer 115:

Well, the flop didn't hit you strong, so now what? The obvious answer would be to check, but let's think through this a bit. The flop that hit the board is the kind that will cause a lot of players to check. Why? First, the two Aces. Anyone not holding an Ace is going to be extremely wary of this flop, so they're going to check. Second, any player holding an Ace will realize that if they make a bet, they stand a good chance of scaring everyone out of the pot. Now, with a 20,000-chip pot, it might well be worth it to try and take it right now if you hold the Ace. On the other hand, a lot of players will get visions of a bigger pot and check, slow playing their three Aces. If they do this, then you might just get a free card on the turn. With this board, I have a feeling that you might get through it with a check.

If you bet this hand right now, you'll likely get everyone not holding an Ace to fold. But anyone holding an Ace will certainly at least call you, and maybe raise you. So, in this case, the obvious answer is the best answer, and that is to check. However, in situations like this, where I know I'm going to check, and am hoping that no one behind me bets so that I can get a free card, I'll make a move with my hand like I'm going to pick up some chips to bet with, then quickly pull my hand back and say, "Check." Many times the player(s) after me have said, "I was going to bet, but I saw you really wanted to, so I'll check."

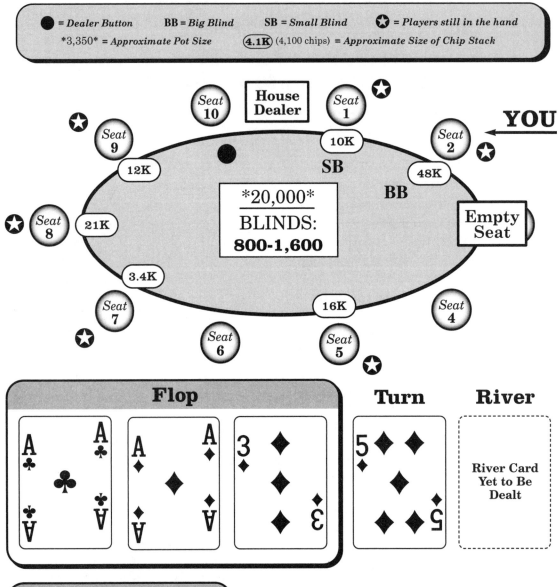

Situation 116:

As you'd surmised (and hoped!) everyone checked the flop. After the turn, Seat 1 checked. It is now your turn to act. Do you check too, bet the minimum of 1,600 chips, bet a larger amount, or go all in?

Starting Hand (Pocket): **4♦4♠**

This Pocket's Win Rate: **8.3%**

Win Rate Rank: **61 of 169 possible**

Tournament Situation:

Tourney: **Internet Qualifier**

Paid Entrys: **2,400 x $50**

Starting Chip Stack: **2,000**

Players Remaining: **805**

Places Paid: **15 (See chart)**

Your Current Standing: **4th overall, 1st at your table**

Time Left in Round: **10 minutes**

Rebuys Allowed: **No**

Next Blind Level: **1,000-2,000**

This Tournament's Prize Money:

1st-10th:
Paid entry to World Series of Poker Main Event (worth $10,000)
11th: **$7,500**
12th: **$5,000**
13th: **$4,000**
14th: **$2,500**
15th: **$1,000**

Total Prize Pool:
$120,000

Answer 116:

The 5 on the turn was a help. Sort of. It now means that any 2 will give you a straight, and the 2♦ will give you a straight flush—the nuts on this hand. Granted, a straight may not win this hand now that three diamonds are on the board, so you'll have to see how the betting develops to decide whether or not to say in.

You also still have a shot for a full house if either an Ace or a 4 comes on the river, although an Ace could also lead to someone holding quad Aces. And even if it doesn't, someone could be holding a pocket pair higher than your 4s, so the Ace would give them the pot. Hence, I don't think you can really count an Ace as an out for you. Any diamond will give you a flush, but since yours is only 4-high, you can't count on it holding up, especially with six players in the hand, but stranger things have happened.

It might be a good idea to make a small bet here since you have a commanding lead in chips. It will likely narrow the field considerably by the river and, if you get no more than a call, it will give you control of the betting, allowing you to check after the river card is dealt and maybe not get a bettor if you miss, since they might be afraid of being check-raised if they missed, too. Make a 2,000-chip bet, just over the minimum, and you can always fold if someone goes all in, especially if it's Seat 8 because of his stack size.

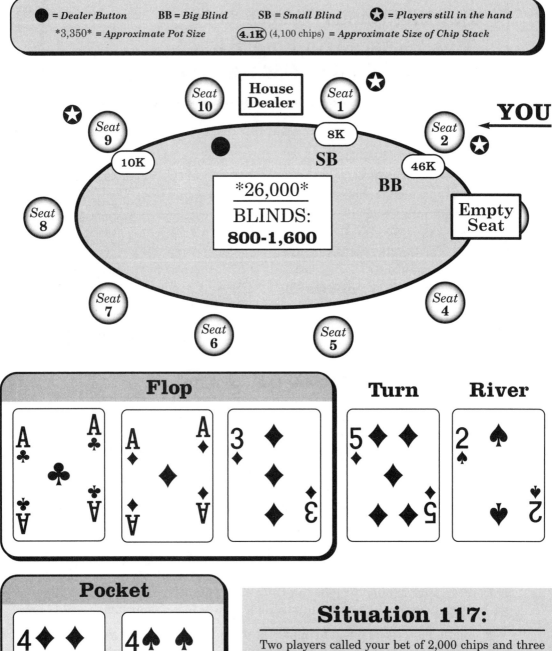

● = *Dealer Button*   BB = *Big Blind*   SB = *Small Blind*   ⭐ = *Players still in the hand*

3,350 = *Approximate Pot Size*   **4.1K** (4,100 chips) = *Approximate Size of Chip Stack*

Seat 10

House Dealer

Seat 1   ⭐

Seat 9   ⭐

YOU ←

Seat 2   ⭐

8K

SB

46K

10K

BB

26,000
BLINDS:
800-1,600

Empty Seat

Seat 8

Seat 7

Seat 6

Seat 5

Seat 4

Flop

A♣ A♣ 3♦

Turn

5♦

River

2♠

Pocket

4♦ 4♠

Situation 117:

Two players called your bet of 2,000 chips and three players folded, including the two biggest chip stacks (Seats 5 and 8). After the river, Seat 1 checked. It is now your turn to act. Do you check as well, bet the minimum of 1,600 chips, bet a larger amount, or go all in?

Starting Hand (Pocket): **4♦4♠**
This Pocket's Win Rate: **8.3%**
Win Rate Rank: **61 of 169 possible**

Tournament Situation:
Tourney: **Internet Qualifier**
Paid Entrys: **2,400 x $50**
Starting Chip Stack: **2,000**
Players Remaining: **805**
Places Paid: **15 (See chart)**
Your Current Standing: **4th overall,**
   1st at your table
Time Left in Round: **10 minutes**
Rebuys Allowed: **No**
Next Blind Level: **1,000-2,000**

This Tournament's Prize Money:

1st-10th:
Paid entry to World Series of Poker Main Event (worth $10,000)
11th: **$7,500**
12th: **$5,000**
13th: **$4,000**
14th: **$2,500**
15th: **$1,000**

Total Prize Pool:

$120,000

Answer 117:

The river brought you a straight, though not the nut straight. Anyone holding a 6-4 has the nut straight, but that's not too likely, especially since you hold one of the 4s. A flush, full house, and quad Aces will all beat you as well. It didn't seem like anyone was betting/playing a flush, although the two Aces on the flop could very well have prevented them from betting strong, since they obviously feared the full house possibilities. You might very well have the winner, but there are too many possible hands that could beat you, so you don't want to make a big bet. Just in case someone holds a flush, I'd make a small bet again, hoping to draw in those players holding a set of Aces or two pair. If you get raised, especially by someone going all in, you still probably have to call given the size of the pot and the size of your chip stack compared to your opponents, because they might be trying to ram through three Aces.

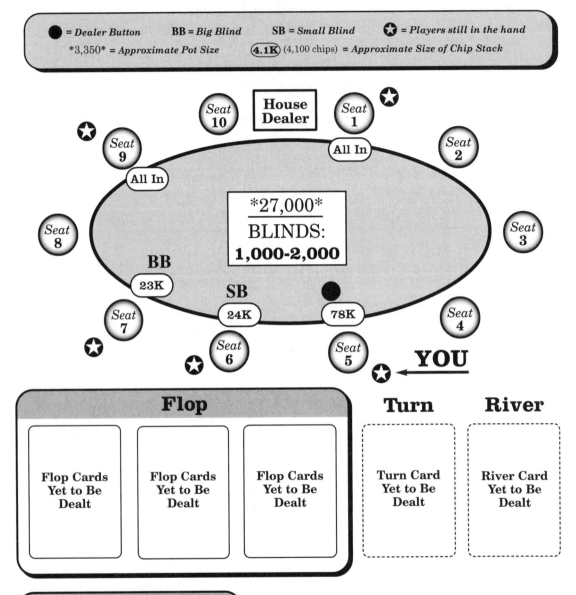

Flop

| Flop Cards Yet to Be Dealt | Flop Cards Yet to Be Dealt | Flop Cards Yet to Be Dealt |

Turn

Turn Card Yet to Be Dealt

River

River Card Yet to Be Dealt

Pocket

Situation 118:

You won the previous hand when your opponents showed pocket Kings and Ace-Queen. It is now the next round and you moved to another table as the tournament condensed. After Seat 8 folded, Seat 9 went all in for 12,000 chips and was called by Seat 1 who also had 12,000 chips. Seats 10, 2, 3, and 4 all folded. With pocket Jacks, do you fold, call the 12,000, raise to an unspecified level, or go all in?

Starting Hand (Pocket): **J♣J♠**
This Pocket's Win Rate: **64.5%**
Win Rate Rank: **7 of 169 possible**

Tournament Situation:

Tourney: **Internet Qualifier**

Paid Entrys: **2,400 x $50**

Starting Chip Stack: **2,000**

Players Remaining: **548**

Places Paid: **15 (See chart)**

Your Current Standing: **2nd overall,
    1st at your table**

Time Left in Round: **12 minutes**

Rebuys Allowed: **No**

Next Blind Level: **1,500-3,000**

*This Tournament's
Prize Money:*

1st-10th:
**Paid entry to
World Series of
Poker Main Event
(worth $10,000)**
11th: **$7,500**
12th: **$5,000**
13th: **$4,000**
14th: **$2,500**
15th: **$1,000**

Total Prize Pool:

$120,000

Answer 118:

You should fold. HUH? The fourth-highest ranked hand in Hold'em? Why? Here's why. Both players went all in while in early position. Yes, they could be going all in with a pair of 5s because the blinds are high and their stacks are relatively low. But they could easily be holding something that includes an Ace, King, or Queen, and maybe two of them. Also, you still have two players behind you with twice that many chips. They might hold an Ace in their hands and figure, "What the hell, now's as good a time as any to make a move." In the meantime, you're sitting there with a pair of Jacks, and if you don't improve on them, someone is likely going to take 12,000–24,000 chips away from you.

I know it's hard to fold a hand like this, but you've also got to remember your tournament situation. In the chart above, you'll notice that you are in second place overall. You've successfully built up a large stack of chips, a stack large enough to ride out expensive blinds for a while, and avoid mixing it up with larger stacks of chips until you want to. Now, it would be a different story if you either held pocket Aces or the betting was smaller, but this hand in this position the way the betting is shaping up, I'm outta here, putting my emphasis on the bigger picture: not wanting to blow my current tournament standing.

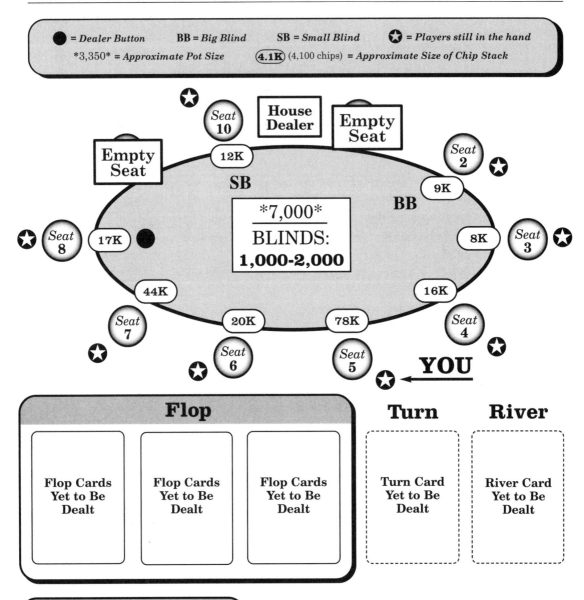

● = *Dealer Button*   BB = *Big Blind*   SB = *Small Blind*   ✪ = *Players still in the hand*

3,350 = *Approximate Pot Size*   (4.1K) (4,100 chips) = *Approximate Size of Chip Stack*

Seat 10 — 12K
Empty Seat
House Dealer
Empty Seat
Seat 2 — 9K
Seat 3 — 8K
Seat 4 — 16K
Seat 5 — 78K — YOU
Seat 6 — 20K
Seat 7 — 44K
Seat 8 — 17K

SB
BB

7,000
BLINDS: 1,000-2,000

Flop

| Flop Cards Yet to Be Dealt | Flop Cards Yet to Be Dealt | Flop Cards Yet to Be Dealt |

Turn

Turn Card Yet to Be Dealt

River

River Card Yet to Be Dealt

Pocket

K♥ 9♥

Situation 119:

It's several hands later now and your table is short two players, the result of Seat 7 having knocked them both out on the previous situation with a set of Kings. You have received a pocket hand of King-9 suited. Seat 3 was the first to act and bet the minimum of 2,000 chips. After Seat 4 called, it is now your turn to act. With five players yet to act after you, do you fold, call 2,000, raise to an unspecified level, or go all in?

Starting Hand (Pocket): **K♥9♥**

This Pocket's Win Rate: **20.0%**

Win Rate Rank: **37 of 169 possible**

Tournament Situation:

Tourney: **Internet Qualifier**

Paid Entrys: **2,400 x $50**

Starting Chip Stack: **2,000**

Players Remaining: **548**

Places Paid: **15 (See chart)**

Your Current Standing: **2nd overall, 1st at your table**

Time Left in Round: **9 minutes**

Rebuys Allowed: **No**

Next Blind Level: **1,500-3,000**

This Tournament's Prize Money:

1st-10th:
Paid entry to World Series of Poker Main Event (worth $10,000)
11th: $7,500
12th: $5,000
13th: $4,000
14th: $2,500
15th: $1,000

Total Prize Pool:
$120,000

Answer 119:

By now you should understand that this is an easy decision: you fold. Essentially a hand such as this is a drawing hand, and it's a weak one at that. You could make a straight, but you'd need to hit exactly a 10, Jack, and Queen somewhere on the board to make it, and it would be foolish to chase such a hand, spending who knows how many chips along the way in order to get there. If any Ace comes, your King is dead. And you certainly don't want to play a hand like this at this stage of a tournament that you're doing so well in.

About the only time you should play a hand like this is in a live limit game where the betting can be controlled, or in a no-limit game when you are in the right situation. Also, in either game you need to be in the right position, something that is clearly not the case with this hand as you have five players yet to act after you, any one of whom could go all in at a moment's notice, forcing you to risk a lot of chips on this weak hand, or forfeiting 2,000 chips if you've called. Throw it away, and don't lose any sleep over it. There will be another hand coming in a minute or two.

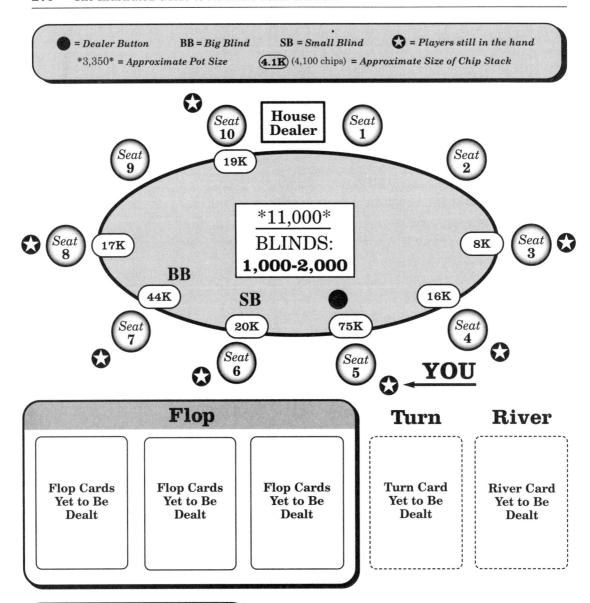

● = *Dealer Button*   BB = *Big Blind*   SB = *Small Blind*   ⭐ = *Players still in the hand*

3,350 = *Approximate Pot Size*   (4.1K) (4,100 chips) = *Approximate Size of Chip Stack*

Seat 10   House Dealer   Seat 1

Seat 9   19K

11,000
BLINDS:
1,000-2,000

Seat 2

Seat 8   17K   8K   Seat 3

BB
44K

SB
20K   75K   16K

Seat 7   Seat 6   Seat 5   Seat 4

YOU

Flop

| Flop Cards Yet to Be Dealt | Flop Cards Yet to Be Dealt | Flop Cards Yet to Be Dealt |

Turn

Turn Card Yet to Be Dealt

River

River Card Yet to Be Dealt

Pocket

A♠ Q♠

Situation 120:

Later in the same round, you receive Ace-Queen suited in your pocket. Four players all call the 2,000-chip minimum bet in front of you and three players fold. With only the two blinds to act after you, do you fold, call the 2,000, raise to an unspecified level, or go all in?

Starting Hand (Pocket): **A♠Q♠**
This Pocket's Win Rate: **64.9%**
Win Rate Rank: **6 of 169 possible**

Tournament Situation:
Tourney: **Internet Qualifier**
Paid Entrys: **2,400 x $50**
Starting Chip Stack: **2,000**
Players Remaining: **511**
Places Paid: **15 (See chart)**
Your Current Standing: **3rd overall,
    1st at your table**
Time Left in Round: **4 minutes**
Rebuys Allowed: **No**
Next Blind Level: **2,000-4,000**

*This Tournament's
Prize Money:*

**1st-10th:
Paid entry to
World Series of
Poker Main Event
(worth $10,000)**
11th: $7,500
12th: $5,000
13th: $4,000
14th: $2,500
15th: $1,000

Total Prize Pool:
$120,000

Answer 120:

Although you have a beautiful looking hand with a lot of potential, at this point it still holds more potential than actual clout. Just call the bet and see what the flop brings. There are already four callers in the hand in front of you and the big blind will be in, and possibly the small blind, so you have a lot of opponents facing you and you don't have a made hand yet. Certainly you will play this hand, but this is one of those times when it's best to see the flop as cheaply as possible, because you could easily get something like 9-6-2, all red, and then how are you going to feel about your two big black cards? When you look at your hand, don't just imagine what good things could come with the flop/turn/river; always be thinking of the potential danger that exists for you as well.

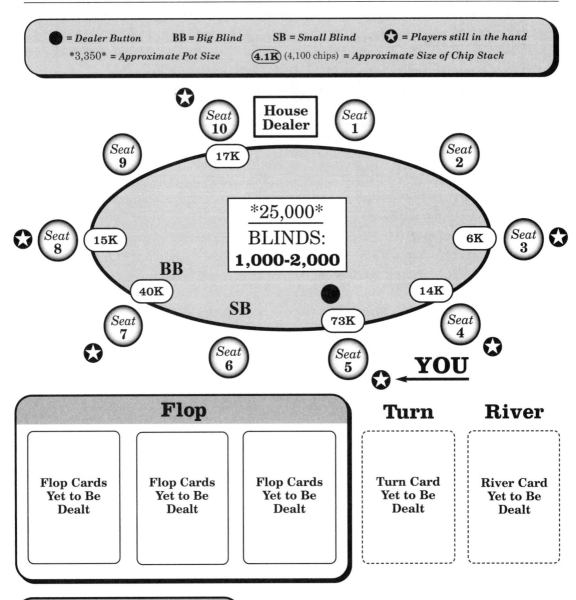

= Dealer Button   BB = Big Blind   SB = Small Blind   ⭐ = Players still in the hand

3,350 = Approximate Pot Size   **4.1K** (4,100 chips) = Approximate Size of Chip Stack

25,000
BLINDS:
1,000-2,000

Seat 10 — 17K
Seat 9
Seat 1
Seat 2
Seat 8 — 15K
Seat 3 — 6K
BB — 40K
14K
SB
73K
Seat 7
Seat 4
Seat 6
Seat 5
YOU

Flop

| Flop Cards Yet to Be Dealt | Flop Cards Yet to Be Dealt | Flop Cards Yet to Be Dealt |

Turn

Turn Card Yet to Be Dealt

River

River Card Yet to Be Dealt

Pocket

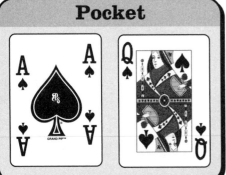

Situation 121:

After you called the bet, Seat 6 (the small blind) folded and Seat 7 (the big blind) raised to 4,000. The other callers all called the raise. It is now your turn to act. With no one to act after you, do you now fold, call as well, raise to an unspecified level, or go all in?

Starting Hand (Pocket): **A♠Q♠**
This Pocket's Win Rate: **64.9%**
Win Rate Rank: **6 of 169 possible**

Tournament Situation:

Tourney: **Internet Qualifier**

Paid Entrys: **2,400 x $50**

Starting Chip Stack: **2,000**

Players Remaining: **511**

Places Paid: **15 (See chart)**

Your Current Standing: **3rd overall,
    1st at your table**

Time Left in Round: **4 minutes**

Rebuys Allowed: **No**

Next Blind Level: **1,500-3,000**

*This Tournament's
Prize Money:*

**1st-10th:
Paid entry to
World Series of
Poker Main Event
(worth $10,000)**
11th: $7,500
12th: $5,000
13th: $4,000
14th: $2,500
15th: $1,000

Total Prize Pool:

$120,000

Answer 121:

Not much has changed for you except the slight increase in the betting level. Make the call, knowing that no one is behind you to raise it higher. With six of you in the hand, it promises to be a large pot, and you certainly want to be in on it as long as you have a chance, and with cards like Ace-Queen suited, you have a lot of potential, from a flush to a straight to big cards that can pair up.

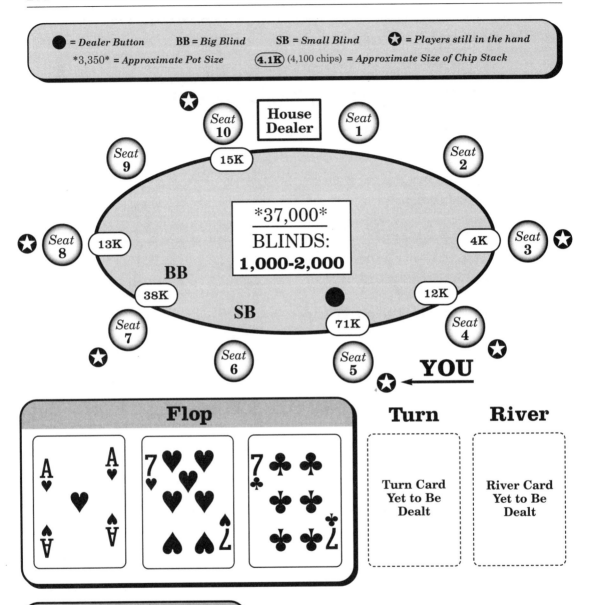

Situation 122:

After the flop, Seat 7 was first to act and he bet 2,000 chips. The other four players all called. It is now your turn to act. Do you fold, call the 2,000, raise to an unspecified level, or go all in?

Starting Hand (Pocket): **A♠Q♠**

This Pocket's Win Rate: **64.9%**

Win Rate Rank: **6 of 169 possible**

Tournament Situation:

Tourney: **Internet Qualifier**

Paid Entrys: **2,400 x $50**

Starting Chip Stack: **2,000**

Players Remaining: **511**

Places Paid: **15 (See chart)**

Your Current Standing: **3rd overall,**
1st at your table

Time Left in Round: **4 minutes**

Rebuys Allowed: **No**

Next Blind Level: **1,500-3,000**

This Tournament's Prize Money:

1st-10th:
Paid entry to
World Series of
Poker Main Event
(worth $10,000)
11th: $7,500
12th: $5,000
13th: $4,000
14th: $2,500
15th: $1,000

Total Prize Pool:

$120,000

Answer 122:

This is another one of those flops that makes it easy for everyone to check, or, as in this case, to do no more than call if there is a bet. The pair of 7s has to be scary, the Ace is threatening to all who don't hold one, and the two hearts are particularly dangerous because of the potential flush.

Since no one seemed inclined to challenge Seat 7's initial wager, it's time to use your big stack to separate the men from the boys (figuratively speaking, ladies!) on this hand. Make a modest raise to 6,000 chips, and make the players in Seats 8, 10, 3, and 4 trying to hit a flush decide how badly they want to risk their tournament on a draw, because if you take 6,000 chips from any of them, you'll be taking anywhere from almost half to all of their stacks. They'll have to know that if they miss their flush on the turn, you're going to come back with another bet before the river comes that will likely take all their chips, and if they miss on the river, they're done.

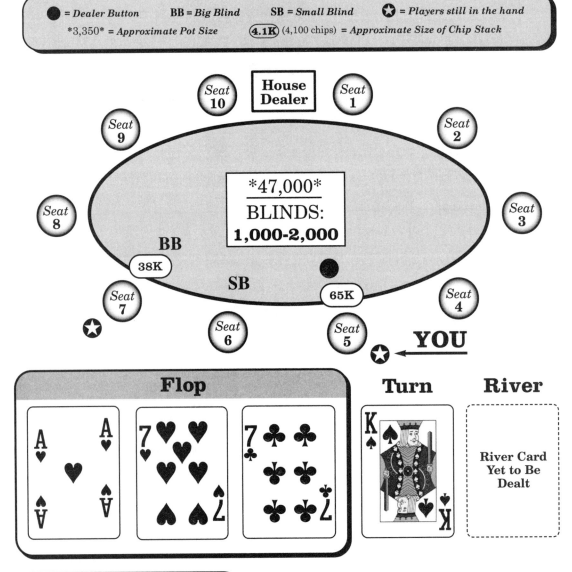

● = *Dealer Button*   **BB** = *Big Blind*   **SB** = *Small Blind*   ★ = *Players still in the hand*

3,350 = *Approximate Pot Size*   **4.1K** (4,100 chips) = *Approximate Size of Chip Stack*

Seat 10 — **House Dealer** — Seat 1

Seat 9 — Seat 2

47,000
BLINDS:
1,000-2,000

Seat 8 — Seat 3

BB 38K

SB 65K

Seat 7 ★ — Seat 6 — Seat 5 ★ — **YOU** ←

Seat 4

Flop

A♥ 7♥ 7♣

Turn

K♠

River

River Card Yet to Be Dealt

Pocket

A♠ Q♠

Situation 123:

As you had hoped, four of your five opponents folded after your raise; only Seat 7 (the big blind) called. After the turn, Seat 7 was first to act and he checked. It is now your turn. Do you check as well, bet the minimum of 2,000 chips, make a larger bet to an unspecified level, or go all in?

> ## Starting Hand (Pocket): A♠Q♠
> ## This Pocket's Win Rate: **64.9%**
> ## Win Rate Rank: **6 of 169 possible**

Tournament Situation:

Tourney: **Internet Qualifier**

Paid Entrys: **2,400 x $50**

Starting Chip Stack: **2,000**

Players Remaining: **511**

Places Paid: **15 (See chart)**

Your Current Standing: **3rd overall, 1st at your table**

Time Left in Round: **4 minutes**

Rebuys Allowed: **No**

Next Blind Level: **1,500-3,000**

This Tournament's Prize Money:

1st-10th:
Paid entry to World Series of Poker Main Event (worth $10,000)
11th: $7,500
12th: $5,000
13th: $4,000
14th: $2,500
15th: $1,000

Total Prize Pool:
$120,000

Answer 123:

It's important to keep in mind that you must be careful right now for a number of reasons. First, you are currently third overall in the tournament and a mistake could take you right out of the money. Second, the flop was dangerous with two hearts and two 7s hitting the board, none of which you hold in your hand. Third, the only opponent you still face was in the big blind and he didn't have to put any more money into the pot to see the flop, yet he raised, so he's probably got something very good in his hand. Fourth, after the flop, Seat 7 was first to act and he bet, apparently not afraid of the flop. Fifth, after your raise to 6,000, he called, unlike all the others who folded.

Now that the turn card has come, he's stopped betting, preferring to check. That might indicate that he's on a heart draw. If you check as well, you'll get to see the river card for free, but it will indicate weakness to him, maybe even giving him the belief that he can win with a bluff on the river.

I would make some sort of a modest bet here just to remind him that you are in control of the hand. Nothing so large that it would hurt you if you ended up losing it, though. Try 5,000 chips.

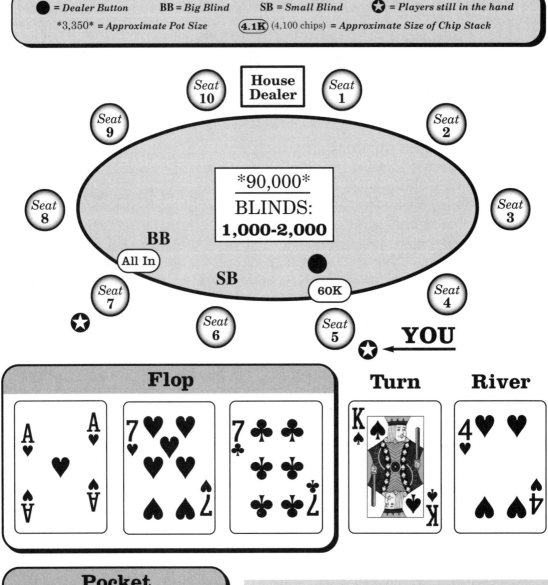

● = *Dealer Button*   **BB** = *Big Blind*   **SB** = *Small Blind*   ⭐ = *Players still in the hand*

3,350 = *Approximate Pot Size*   (**4.1K**) (4,100 chips) = *Approximate Size of Chip Stack*

Seat 10 — House Dealer — Seat 1 — Seat 2 — Seat 3 — Seat 4 — YOU — Seat 5 — Seat 6 — Seat 7 — Seat 8 — Seat 9

90,000
BLINDS:
1,000-2,000

BB — All In
SB
60K

Flop

Turn   ## River

Pocket

Situation 124:

Seat 7 called your bet of 5,000 chips after the turn. After the river card was dealt, Seat 7 acted first and went all in for 33,000 chips. Do you fold or call the bet of 33,000 chips?

Starting Hand (Pocket): **A♠Q♠**

This Pocket's Win Rate: **64.9%**

Win Rate Rank: **6 of 169 possible**

Tournament Situation:

Tourney: **Internet Qualifier**

Paid Entrys: **2,400 x $50**

Starting Chip Stack: **2,000**

Players Remaining: **511**

Places Paid: **15 (See chart)**

Your Current Standing: **3rd overall,
1st at your table**

Time Left in Round: **4 minutes**

Rebuys Allowed: **No**

Next Blind Level: **1,500-3,000**

*This Tournament's
Prize Money:*

**1st-10th:
Paid entry to
World Series of
Poker Main Event
(worth $10,000)**
11th: $7,500
12th: $5,000
13th: $4,000
14th: $2,500
15th: $1,000

Total Prize Pool:

$120,000

Answer 124:

What a #@!*&% river card, eh? So now what do you do? You could pick your nose and flick a booger at him, but that won't do much good. Is he bluffing or did he catch the flush on the river? The real question is, "Do you want to risk everything on this call?" If you call and he was bluffing, you'll have 150,000 chips and a lead so huge in this tournament, you wouldn't have to play a hand for an hour and would still be the chip leader. If you call and he wasn't bluffing, you could go home empty handed.

I believe it was Doyle Brunson—the godfather of Texas Hold'em poker—who once said that Texas Hold'em isn't a card game played by people, but rather it's a people game played with cards. Which speaks volumes about how he could win the World Series of Poker with a hand of 10-deuce.

Unfortunately, I would have to fold this hand. You still have 60,000 chips left, good enough to still be in the top handful of players in this tournament, and that ain't shabby. And don't forget, your opponent did raise preflop in the big blind. That could even mean Ace-King, which beats you even if he doesn't have the flush. It's tough to get out now, but as someone once said, discretion is the better part of valor. And don't forget, with 60,000 chips, depending on the hand and the opponent, you could double up in one hand to 120,000.

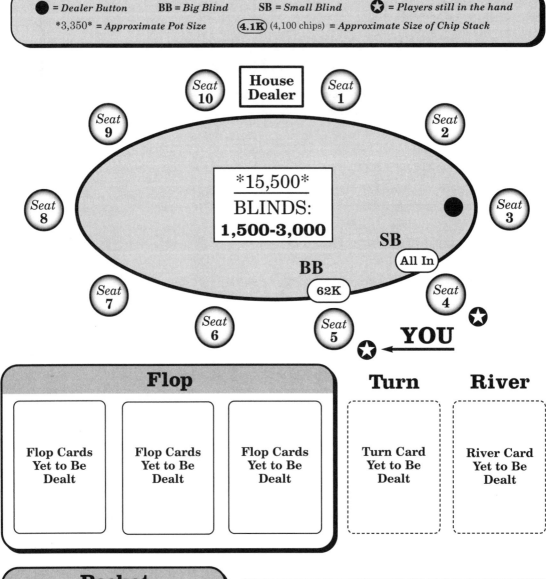

= Dealer Button   BB = Big Blind   SB = Small Blind   ⭐ = Players still in the hand

3,350 = Approximate Pot Size   (4.1K) (4,100 chips) = Approximate Size of Chip Stack

House Dealer

Seat 10
Seat 1
Seat 9
Seat 2
Seat 8
Seat 3
Seat 7
Seat 4
Seat 6
Seat 5

15,500
BLINDS:
1,500-3,000

SB — All In

BB — 62K

YOU

Flop

Flop Cards Yet to Be Dealt

Flop Cards Yet to Be Dealt

Flop Cards Yet to Be Dealt

Turn

Turn Card Yet to Be Dealt

River

River Card Yet to Be Dealt

Pocket

3♠   3♦

Situation 125:

It's now the next round and you caught two 3s in the big blind. Everyone folds to the small blind, who is steaming over a bad beat the hand before. After his bad beat loss, he text-chatted that he was going to go all in on the next hand no matter what his cards are, and he does for 11,000 chips. Do you fold or call his bet, since the odds are statistically about even that you will beat him, assuming he doesn't hold a higher pair?

Starting Hand (Pocket): **3♠3♦**
This Pocket's Win Rate: **4.5%**
Win Rate Rank: **66 of 169 possible**

Tournament Situation:
Tourney: **Internet Qualifier**
Paid Entrys: **2,400 x $50**
Starting Chip Stack: **2,000**
Players Remaining: **434**
Places Paid: **15 (See chart)**
Your Current Standing: **9th overall,**
   2nd at your table
Time Left in Round: **13 minutes**
Rebuys Allowed: **No**
Next Blind Level: **2,000-4,000**

This Tournament's
Prize Money:

1st-10th:
Paid entry to
World Series of
Poker Main Event
(worth $10,000)
11th: $7,500
12th: $5,000
13th: $4,000
14th: $2,500
15th: $1,000

Total Prize Pool:
$120,000

Answer 125:

A pair against two unpaired overcards is roughly a 50-50 proposition. If it were earlier in the tournament, I would say it's a no brainer to call, especially if we weren't talking many chips. But now, at this late stage, you're talking another 9,500 chips besides your big blind.

If you call him and lose, you'll fall from ninth place to somewhere around fortieth overall, and then you'll have to claw your way back up again. Now, if you held a pair of 8s, 9s, or 10s, and only had one overcard that could hurt you, the odds would be much more favorable and, for an even money proposition, I'd go for it, but not with two probable overcards. Fold the hand and let him have your blind.

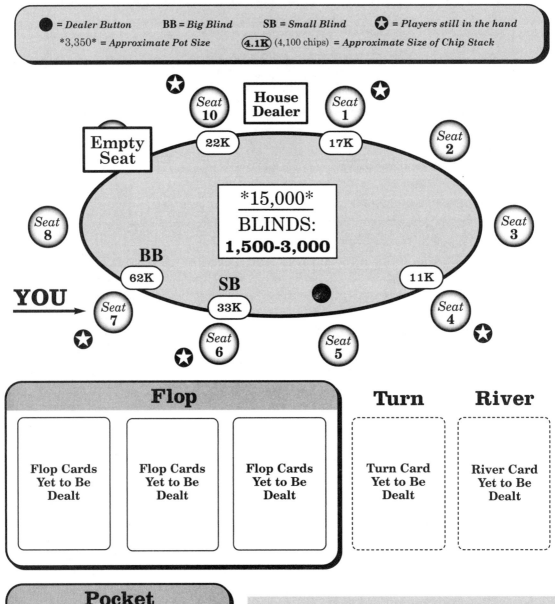

Situation 126:

It's later in the same round and you've been moved to another table as the tournament condensed. You received pocket Aces in the big blind position. Four players limped in for the 3,000 minimum bet in front of you. Do you tell the dealer, "Big enough," indicating a check, raise to an unspecified level, or go all in?

Starting Hand (Pocket): **A♣A♦**

This Pocket's Win Rate: **86.1%**

Win Rate Rank: **1 of 169 possible**

Tournament Situation:

Tourney: **Internet Qualifier**

Paid Entrys: **2,400 x $50**

Starting Chip Stack: **2,000**

Players Remaining: **398**

Places Paid: **15 (See chart)**

Your Current Standing: **10th overall,
1st at your table**

Time Left in Round: **6 minutes**

Rebuys Allowed: **No**

Next Blind Level: **2,000-4,000**

*This Tournament's
Prize Money:*

**1st-10th:
Paid entry to
World Series of
Poker Main Event
(worth $10,000)**
11th: $7,500
12th: $5,000
13th: $4,000
14th: $2,500
15th: $1,000

Total Prize Pool:

$120,000

Answer 126:

Well, these are cards you certainly like to see. Now the question is what to do with them now that you have them. Pocket Aces typically give rise to two schools of thought. Either bet them balls to the wall, hoping to drive out your opponents so they can't draw out on you, or slow play them, hoping to trap as many players for as much money as possible in the hand. There are occasions when both approaches are appropriate. In this instance, however, I think only one approach is correct: bet them big and try and drive out your opponents. I say this because the pot is already sizeable because of the large blinds. I say this, too, because it's starting to get into the late stages of the tournament and this is no time to get cute. Yes, it would be nice to slow play your Aces and trap all the players for at least 10,000 chips each, but you have to keep in mind that a Texas Hold'em tournament is a marathon, not a sprint. There are times in that marathon where you can coast, and times when you need to turn it on. This is one of those times. Make a bet of at least 15,000 chips. This will force at least three of your opponents to the brink of elimination if they call and lose, and the fourth is facing risking half his chips. If they all fold, fine. If any of them call, fine, you still have the best hand going in, and one of the cardinal rules in poker is to make your opponents pay when you have the best hand. Right now you know you're the best.

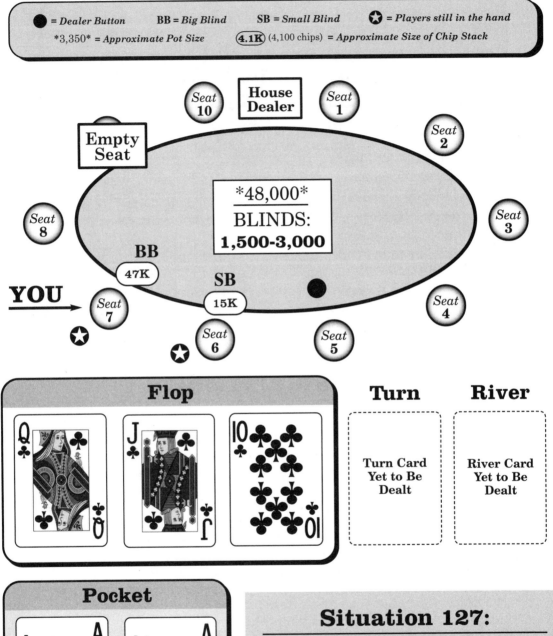

Situation 127:

Your 15,000-chip raise succeeded in getting all but one player to fold, Seat 6, who called your wager. After the flop, Seat 6 was first to act and he bet 3,000, the minimum allowed. It is now your turn to act in this heads up situation. Do you fold, call the 3,000, raise to an unspecified level, or go all in?

Starting Hand (Pocket): **A♣A♦**
This Pocket's Win Rate: **86.1%**
Win Rate Rank: **1 of 169 possible**

Tournament Situation:
Tourney: **Internet Qualifier**
Paid Entrys: **2,400 x $50**
Starting Chip Stack: **2,000**
Players Remaining: **398**
Places Paid: **15 (See chart)**
Your Current Standing: **10th overall, 1st at your table**
Time Left in Round: **6 minutes**
Rebuys Allowed: **No**
Next Blind Level: **2,000-4,000**

This Tournament's Prize Money:

1st-10th:
Paid entry to World Series of Poker Main Event (worth $10,000)
11th: **$7,500**
12th: **$5,000**
13th: **$4,000**
14th: **$2,500**
15th: **$1,000**

Total Prize Pool:
$120,000

Answer 127:

Geez, Louise, what a flop. Okay, time to hit the brakes for several reasons. First of all, your opponent bet first after seeing that flop, and remember, he called your 15,000-chip raise preflop (almost half his stack), so you've got to know he had some kind of a decent hand to begin with. Another reason to hit the brakes, though, is because the flop fit your hand beautifully. Not perfectly, but beautifully. You now have so many outs to improve your hand, it almost isn't fair. Are you invincible? No, of course not. But you have to like your situation.

As to your opponent's 3,000-chip bet, there must be a reason why he bet the minimum. Maybe the flop was okay for him, but not the greatest. Maybe his bet was a feeler, seeing what you would do. Maybe he flopped a straight but is afraid of the flush, but doesn't want to check and give you a free card in case you're chasing clubs, but also doesn't want to go all in because he has no clubs of his own.

In any event, with so many outs as well as top pair, I'd just call his bet at this point, partially because you're not quite there with the nuts yet, partially to milk more chips out of him, and partially because you may never get there and he may hold a set of Queens, Jacks, or 10s.

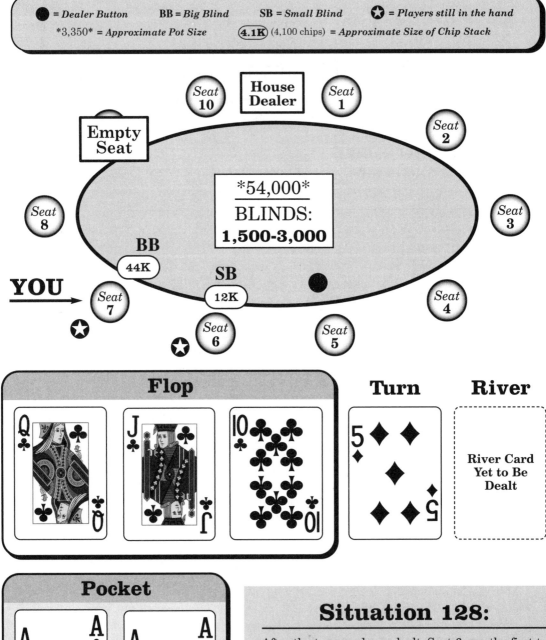

● = *Dealer Button*   **BB** = *Big Blind*   **SB** = *Small Blind*   ⭐ = *Players still in the hand*

3,350 = *Approximate Pot Size*   (**4.1K**) (4,100 chips) = *Approximate Size of Chip Stack*

Seat 10   **House Dealer**   Seat 1

Empty Seat

Seat 2

54,000
BLINDS:
1,500-3,000

Seat 8

Seat 3

BB
44K

SB
12K

YOU →   Seat 7   ⭐

Seat 4

Seat 6   ⭐

Seat 5

Flop

Turn

River

River Card Yet to Be Dealt

Pocket

Situation 128:

After the turn card was dealt, Seat 6 was the first to act and he again bet 3,000 chips, the minimum. Do you now fold, call the 3,000, raise to an unspecified level, or go all in?

> ## Starting Hand (Pocket): **A♣A♦**
> ## This Pocket's Win Rate: **86.1%**
> ## Win Rate Rank: **1 of 169 possible**

Tournament Situation:

Tourney: **Internet Qualifier**

Paid Entrys: **2,400 x $50**

Starting Chip Stack: **2,000**

Players Remaining: **398**

Places Paid: **15 (See chart)**

Your Current Standing: **10th overall, 1st at your table**

Time Left in Round: **6 minutes**

Rebuys Allowed: **No**

Next Blind Level: **2,000-4,000**

This Tournament's Prize Money:

1st-10th:
Paid entry to World Series of Poker Main Event (worth $10,000)
11th: **$7,500**
12th: **$5,000**
13th: **$4,000**
14th: **$2,500**
15th: **$1,000**

Total Prize Pool:
$120,000

Answer 128:

Since you clearly missed on the turn, and because of the possibility your opponent my hold a flush, a straight, or a set of something, you should just call. You can't get out at this point because the pot is too large, even if he had gone all in. What you must do now is get to the river as cheaply as possible.

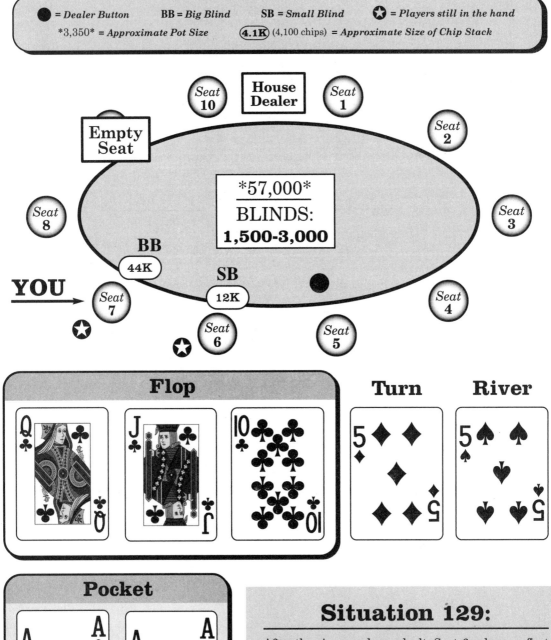

● = *Dealer Button*   **BB** = *Big Blind*   **SB** = *Small Blind*   ⭐ = *Players still in the hand*

3,350 = *Approximate Pot Size*   **(4.1K)** (4,100 chips) = *Approximate Size of Chip Stack*

Seat 10
House Dealer
Seat 1
Seat 2
Empty Seat
57,000
BLINDS:
1,500-3,000
Seat 8
Seat 3
BB
44K
SB
12K
YOU
Seat 7
Seat 6
Seat 5
Seat 4

Flop

Turn

River

Pocket

Situation 129:

After the river card was dealt, Seat 6, who was first to act, checked. It is now your turn. Do you also check, bet the minimum of 3,000, bet a larger amount, or go all in?

Starting Hand (Pocket): **A♣A♦**

This Pocket's Win Rate: **86.1%**

Win Rate Rank: **1 of 169 possible**

Tournament Situation:

Tourney: **Internet Qualifier**

Paid Entrys: **2,400 x $50**

Starting Chip Stack: **2,000**

Players Remaining: **398**

Places Paid: **15 (See chart)**

Your Current Standing: **10th overall, 1st at your table**

Time Left in Round: **6 minutes**

Rebuys Allowed: **No**

Next Blind Level: **2,000-4,000**

This Tournament's Prize Money:

1st-10th:
Paid entry to World Series of Poker Main Event (worth $10,000)
11th: **$7,500**
12th: **$5,000**
13th: **$4,000**
14th: **$2,500**
15th: **$1,000**

Total Prize Pool:

$120,000

Answer 129:

You didn't catch your Ace, King, or club as you had hoped, but the 5 on the river may not have been the worst card in the world for you. It did improve your hand to two pair. Since your opponent checked, it either means he didn't make or improve his hand, he did and he's waiting to check-raise you, or he just wants to see what you'll do. Unfortunately, you didn't hit your hand strong enough to bet, so just check and see what happens. If you were to go all in, you might run into a bad check-raise situation that could cost you dearly.

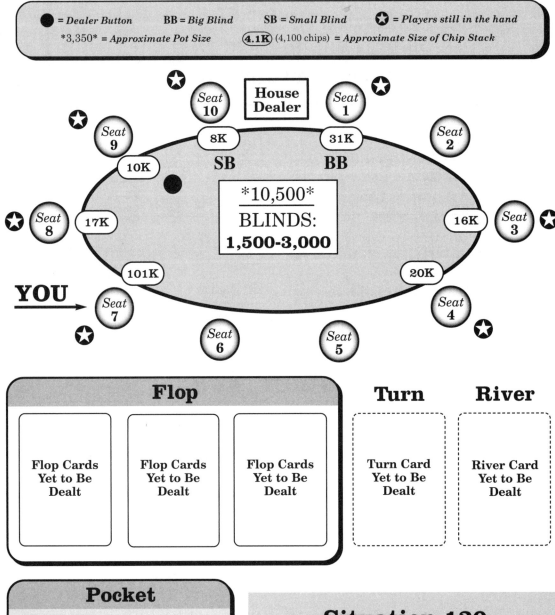

● = *Dealer Button*   **BB** = *Big Blind*   **SB** = *Small Blind*   ⭐ = *Players still in the hand*

3,350 = *Approximate Pot Size*   (**4.1K**) (4,100 chips) = *Approximate Size of Chip Stack*

House Dealer

Seat 10 — SB — 8K
Seat 1 — BB — 31K
Seat 9 — 10K
Seat 2 — 16K
Seat 8 — 17K
Seat 3 — 16K
Seat 7 — 101K (YOU)
Seat 4 — 20K
Seat 6
Seat 5

10,500
BLINDS: 1,500-3,000

Flop

| Flop Cards Yet to Be Dealt | Flop Cards Yet to Be Dealt | Flop Cards Yet to Be Dealt |

Turn

Turn Card Yet to Be Dealt

River

River Card Yet to Be Dealt

Pocket

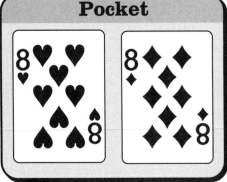

Situation 130:

You won the previous situation when your opponent showed two pairs, Queens and Jacks. It is now several hands later and you have received a pair of 8s in your pocket. Of the five players to act in front of you, two called the minimum bet of 3,000 chips and three folded. It is now your turn to act. With four players to act after you, do you fold, call, raise to an unspecified level, or go all in?

Starting Hand (Pocket): **8♥8♦**

This Pocket's Win Rate: **51.8%**

Win Rate Rank: **13 of 169 possible**

Tournament Situation:

Tourney: **Internet Qualifier**

Paid Entrys: **2,400 x $50**

Starting Chip Stack: **2,000**

Players Remaining: **362**

Places Paid: **15 (See chart)**

Your Current Standing: **1st overall, 1st at your table**

Time Left in Round: **3 minutes**

Rebuys Allowed: **No**

Next Blind Level: **2,000-4,000**

This Tournament's Prize Money:

1st-10th:
Paid entry to
World Series of
Poker Main Event
(worth $10,000)
11th: $7,500
12th: $5,000
13th: $4,000
14th: $2,500
15th: $1,000

Total Prize Pool:

$120,000

Answer 130:

A pair of 8s in the pocket is a decent, playable hand, but it's not enough to raise with at this point because you have four players to act yet after you. Stay in the hand with a call and try to see the flop as cheaply as possible.

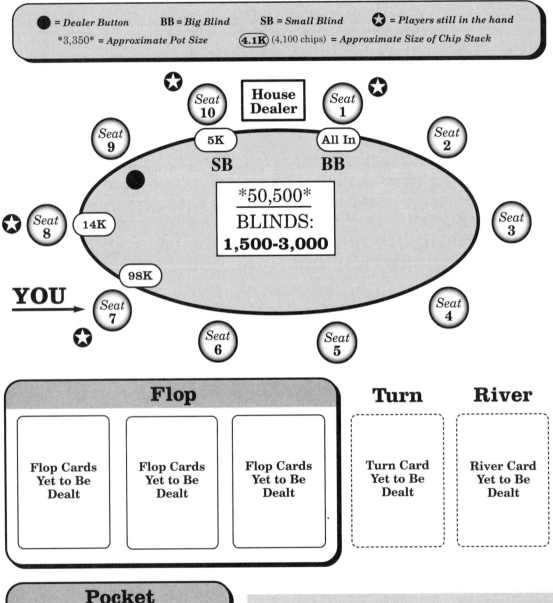

● = *Dealer Button*   BB = *Big Blind*   SB = *Small Blind*   ⭐ = *Players still in the hand*

3,350 = *Approximate Pot Size*   (4.1K) (4,100 chips) = *Approximate Size of Chip Stack*

Seat 10 | House Dealer | Seat 1
Seat 9 | 5K | All In | Seat 2
SB | BB
Seat 8 | 14K | *50,500* BLINDS: 1,500-3,000 | Seat 3
98K
YOU → Seat 7 | Seat 6 | Seat 5 | Seat 4

Flop

| Flop Cards Yet to Be Dealt | Flop Cards Yet to Be Dealt | Flop Cards Yet to Be Dealt |

Turn

Turn Card Yet to Be Dealt

River

River Card Yet to Be Dealt

Pocket

Situation 131:

After you called for 3,000 chips, Seats 8 and 10 also called while Seat 9 folded. Seat 1, the big blind, then went all in for 31,000 chips. Seats 3 and 4 then folded. It is now your turn to act. Given the tournament situation presented above and on the opposite page, do you fold or call the additional 28,000 chips?

Starting Hand (Pocket): **8♥8♦**

This Pocket's Win Rate: **51.8%**

Win Rate Rank: **13 of 169 possible**

Tournament Situation:

Tourney: **Internet Qualifier**

Paid Entrys: **2,400 x $50**

Starting Chip Stack: **2,000**

Players Remaining: **362**

Places Paid: **15 (See chart)**

Your Current Standing: **1st overall,
1st at your table**

Time Left in Round: **3 minutes**

Rebuys Allowed: **No**

Next Blind Level: **2,000-4,000**

*This Tournament's
Prize Money:*

**1st-10th:
Paid entry to
World Series of
Poker Main Event
(worth $10,000)**
11th: $7,500
12th: $5,000
13th: $4,000
14th: $2,500
15th: $1,000

Total Prize Pool:

$120,000

Answer 131:

A pair of 8s was a worthy hand when you had the chance to play it cheaply. Because of the all in bet for 31,000 chips, it's no longer cheap. As such, it is no longer worthy of playing, primarily because of your standing in the tournament: first place overall. Do you really want to risk another 28,000 chips on a pair of 8s in a heads up game? If your opponent has a higher pair or two overcards, you are at worst the underdog, at best about 50-50 in your chances to win this hand. There's still a long way to go, the blinds are high, and you, better than any other player in the tournament, are positioned to ride out poor and marginal hands. Throw this hand away now and wait for a better hand. Time is on your side.

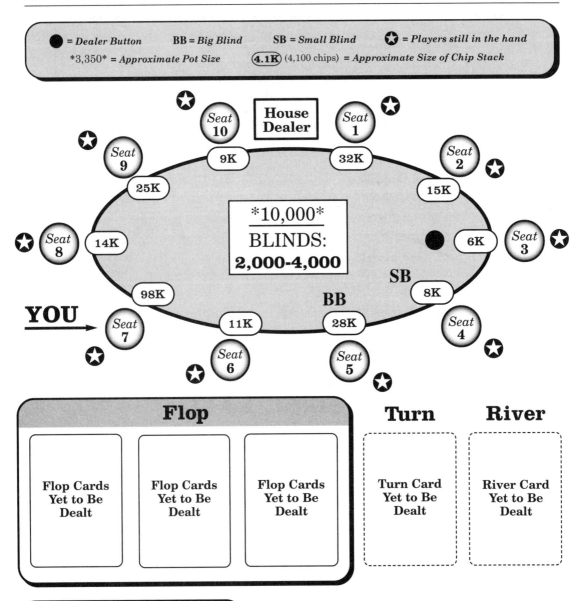

● = *Dealer Button*   **BB** = *Big Blind*   **SB** = *Small Blind*   ★ = *Players still in the hand*

3,350 = *Approximate Pot Size*   (4.1K) (4,100 chips) = *Approximate Size of Chip Stack*

Seat 10 — 9K
House Dealer
Seat 1 — 32K
Seat 9 — 25K
Seat 2 — 15K

10,000
BLINDS:
2,000-4,000

Seat 8 — 14K
SB
Seat 3 — 6K
98K
8K
YOU →
Seat 7 — 11K
BB
28K
Seat 4
Seat 6
Seat 5

Flop

| Flop Cards Yet to Be Dealt | Flop Cards Yet to Be Dealt | Flop Cards Yet to Be Dealt |

Turn

Turn Card Yet to Be Dealt

River

River Card Yet to Be Dealt

Pocket

A♥ 9♥

Situation 132:

It is now into the next round. You have received Ace-9 suited in your pocket. Seat 6 was first to act and called the 4,000-chip big blind bet. It is now your turn to act. Do you fold, call the 4,000, raise to an unspecified level, or go all in?

Starting Hand (Pocket): **A♥9♥**
This Pocket's Win Rate: **40.5%**
Win Rate Rank: **20 of 169 possible**

Tournament Situation:

Tourney: **Internet Qualifier**

Paid Entrys: **2,400 x $50**

Starting Chip Stack: **2,000**

Players Remaining: **339**

Places Paid: **15 (See chart)**

Your Current Standing: **1st overall,
    1st at your table**

Time Left in Round: **14 minutes**

Rebuys Allowed: **No**

Next Blind Level: **3,000-6,000**

*This Tournament's
Prize Money:*

**1st-10th:
Paid entry to
World Series of
Poker Main Event
(worth $10,000)**
11th: $7,500
12th: $5,000
13th: $4,000
14th: $2,500
15th: $1,000

Total Prize Pool:

$120,000

Answer 132:

As you get into the later stages of a big tournament, you'll start to notice two things happen. First, all those players with short stacks will do more picking and choosing when to go all in and when to fold. Because the blinds are so high, the short stacks won't be doing as much calling. They'll pick their spot and go for it. A second thing you'll start noticing is that the bigger stacks will start bullying the smaller stacks more and more.

What this means for you when you hold a hand like Ace-9 suited, a decent hand, is that if you call this bet for 4,000 (which I recommend doing) and one or two of the small stacks go all in for anywhere from 7,000—15,000 chips, it might not mean that their hand is all that powerful. It might have more to do with the fact that they're picking their spot to go all in with a marginally good hand, such as King-Jack unsuited, Ace-3 suited or unsuited, a pair of 6s, etc.

Now, if you get raised all in by a medium to large stack, it likely means they have a better hand than a small stack doing the same thing. So, I wouldn't fear an all in raise by a small stack late in the tournament with large blinds as much as an all in raise by a medium to large stack, in case you get raised after calling.

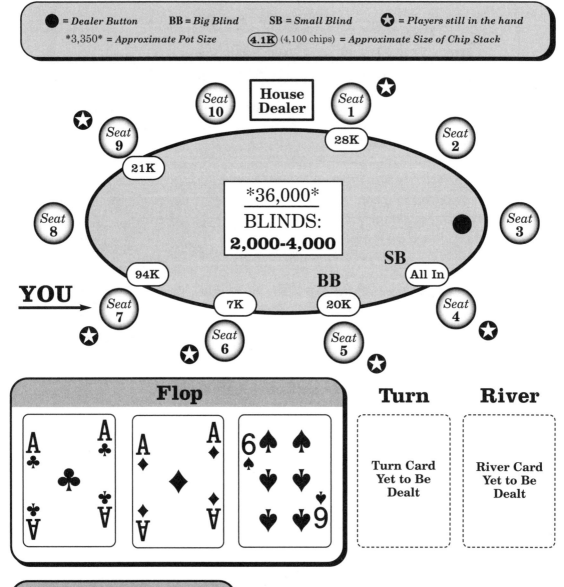

● = *Dealer Button*   **BB** = *Big Blind*   **SB** = *Small Blind*   ⭐ = *Players still in the hand*

3,350 = *Approximate Pot Size*   (4.1K) (4,100 chips) = *Approximate Size of Chip Stack*

Seat 10 — House Dealer — Seat 1 (28K)
Seat 9 (21K)
Seat 2
36,000 BLINDS: 2,000-4,000
Seat 8
Seat 3 ●
Seat 7 — YOU (94K)
Seat 6 (7K)
BB — Seat 5 (20K)
SB — Seat 4 (All In)

Flop

A♣ A♦ 6♠

Turn

Turn Card Yet to Be Dealt

River

River Card Yet to Be Dealt

Pocket

A♥ 9♥

Situation 133:

After you called, four other players called as well including the big blind. After the flop, Seat 4 went all in for 4,000 chips and Seat 5 called. Seat 6 called as well and now it is your turn to act. Do you fold, call the 4,000-chip bet, raise to an unspecified level, or go all in?

Starting Hand (Pocket): **A♥9♥**

This Pocket's Win Rate: **40.5%**

Win Rate Rank: **20 of 169 possible**

Tournament Situation:

Tourney: **Internet Qualifier**

Paid Entrys: **2,400 x $50**

Starting Chip Stack: **2,000**

Players Remaining: **339**

Places Paid: **15 (See chart)**

Your Current Standing: **1st overall,**
   1st at your table

Time Left in Round: **14 minutes**

Rebuys Allowed: **No**

Next Blind Level: **3,000-6,000**

This Tournament's Prize Money:

1st-10th:
Paid entry to World Series of Poker Main Event (worth $10,000)
11th: $7,500
12th: $5,000
13th: $4,000
14th: $2,500
15th: $1,000

Total Prize Pool:

$120,000

Answer 133:

What a great flop! This is what you live for: you're in control of the table and the tournament and the poker gods have blessed you with a flop like this. The problem now has shifted to one of trying to keep your opponents in the hand so you can win as many chips as possible. With a rainbow flop, flushes are going to be hard to come by. With Ace-Ace-6, straights are going to be just as tough to come by. A big bet by you now will likely scare most if not all of the players out of the pot. Just go along with the call and hope Seats 9 and 1 stay in the hand.

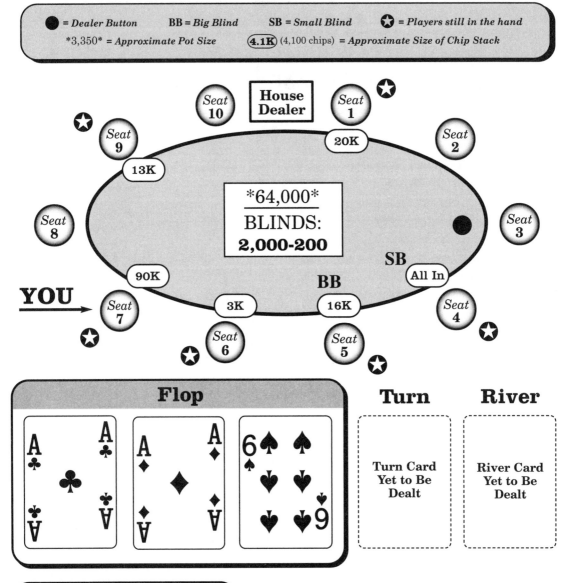

= *Dealer Button*   **BB** = *Big Blind*   **SB** = *Small Blind*   ✪ = *Players still in the hand*

3,350 = *Approximate Pot Size*   (**4.1K**) (4,100 chips) = *Approximate Size of Chip Stack*

House Dealer

Seat 10

Seat 1

Seat 9   13K

20K

Seat 2

64,000
BLINDS:
2,000-200

Seat 8

Seat 3

SB   All In

Seat 7   90K

3K   BB   16K

Seat 4

YOU →

Seat 6

Seat 5

Flop

A♣ A♣   A♦ A♦   6♠ 9♠

Turn

Turn Card Yet to Be Dealt

River

River Card Yet to Be Dealt

Pocket

A♥ A♥   9♥ 9♥

Situation 134:

After your call of 4,000, Seat 9 raised to 8,000 chips and was called by Seats 1, 5, and 6 (Seat 4 was already all in). With no one to act after you, do you now fold in face of this raise, call the additional 4,000 chips, raise to an unspecified level, or go all in?

Starting Hand (Pocket): **A♥9♥**

This Pocket's Win Rate: **40.5%**

Win Rate Rank: **20 of 169 possible**

Tournament Situation:

Tourney: **Internet Qualifier**

Paid Entrys: **2,400 x $50**

Starting Chip Stack: **2,000**

Players Remaining: **339**

Places Paid: **15 (See chart)**

Your Current Standing: **1st overall,
   1st at your table**

Time Left in Round: **14 minutes**

Rebuys Allowed: **No**

Next Blind Level: **3,000-6,000**

*This Tournament's
Prize Money:*

1st-10th:
Paid entry to
World Series of
Poker Main Event
(worth $10,000)
11th: $7,500
12th: $5,000
13th: $4,000
14th: $2,500
15th: $1,000

Total Prize Pool:

$120,000

Answer 134:

Boy, after this hand is over you'll have to remember to get the address of the guy in Seat 9 so that you can send him a Christmas card, 'cause he just gave you a gift by raising, in effect doing your work for you. Things are going quite well for you on this hand, so just call the additional 4,000 chips and keep everyone in the hand as long as possible.

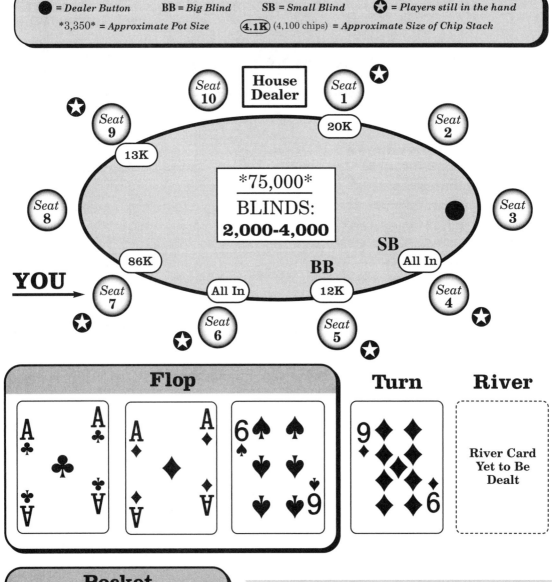

Situation 135:

After the turn card was revealed, Seat 5 was first to act and bet the minimum of 4,000 chips. Seat 6 called all in with his remaining 3,000 chips. It is now your turn to act. Do you fold, call the bet of 4,000, raise to an unspecified level, or go all in?

Starting Hand (Pocket): **A♥9♥**
This Pocket's Win Rate: **40.5%**
Win Rate Rank: **20 of 169 possible**

Tournament Situation:
Tourney: **Internet Qualifier**
Paid Entries: **2,400 x $50**
Starting Chip Stack: **2,000**
Players Remaining: **339**
Places Paid: **15 (See chart)**
Your Current Standing: **1st overall,
    1st at your table**
Time Left in Round: **14 minutes**
Rebuys Allowed: **No**
Next Blind Level: **3,000-6,000**

*This Tournament's
Prize Money:*

**1st-10th:
Paid entry to
World Series of
Poker Main Event
(worth $10,000)**
11th: $7,500
12th: $5,000
13th: $4,000
14th: $2,500
15th: $1,000

**Total Prize Pool:
$120,000**

Answer 135:

Boy, when the poker gods smile on you, they REALLY smile on you! This hand just keeps getting better and better, and sometimes that's the way it is in Texas Hold'em. The 9 on the river, among other things, means someone could hold a pair of 9s in the pocket for a full house, 9s over Aces, but that won't beat your full house because yours is Aces over 9s. It's a powerful feeling to know that nobody can possibly hold a better hand than you right now, and you can only be tied if someone else holds an Ace-9 just like you. And, with two diamonds on the board, maybe now someone holds a back-door diamond draw and will stay in the hand to the river in hopes of hitting another one for a flush, which of course means they are drawing dead.

Again, you're almost there, so play it cool and just call the bet of 4,000 and hope that Seats 9 and 1 stay in the hand for one more card. With the pot as large as it is, if they hold anything at all they'll likely stay in.

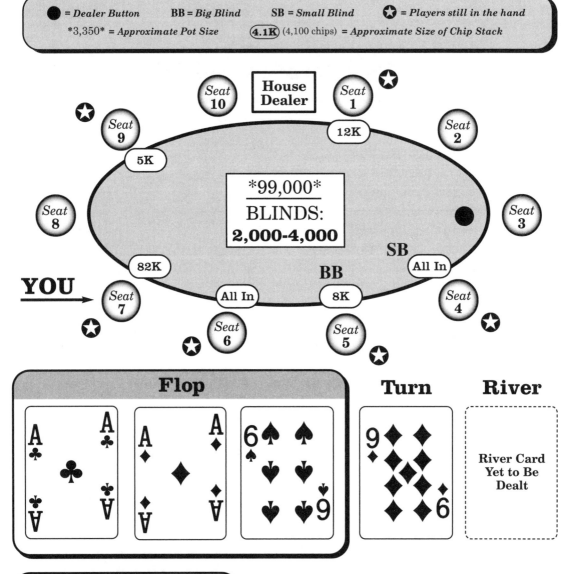

Situation 136:

After you called the bet of 4,000 chips, Seat 9 again raised to 8,000 and was called by Seats 1 and 5. With no one to act after you, do you fold, call the additional 4,000 chips, raise to an unspecified level, or go all in?

Starting Hand (Pocket): **A♥9♥**

This Pocket's Win Rate: **40.5%**

Win Rate Rank: **20 of 169 possible**

Tournament Situation:

Tourney: **Internet Qualifier**

Paid Entrys: **2,400 x $50**

Starting Chip Stack: **2,000**

Players Remaining: **339**

Places Paid: **15 (See chart)**

Your Current Standing: **1st overall, 1st at your table**

Time Left in Round: **14 minutes**

Rebuys Allowed: **No**

Next Blind Level: **3,000-6,000**

This Tournament's Prize Money:

1st-10th:
Paid entry to
World Series of
Poker Main Event
(worth $10,000)
11th: $7,500
12th: $5,000
13th: $4,000
14th: $2,500
15th: $1,000

Total Prize Pool:

$120,000

Answer 136:

Forget about sending the guy in Seat 9 a Christmas card; send him a nice present and his wife a BIG bouquet of flowers. He's making your job so easy it's almost a poker crime. Obviously you should just call again, keeping everyone in the hand as long as possible. By the time this is over, there are going to be a bunch of players bled dry and sent packing. The stranglehold you're going to have on this tournament is going to be so...well, you're almost there. We'll talk about your strategy of how to play with a stranglehold lead shortly.

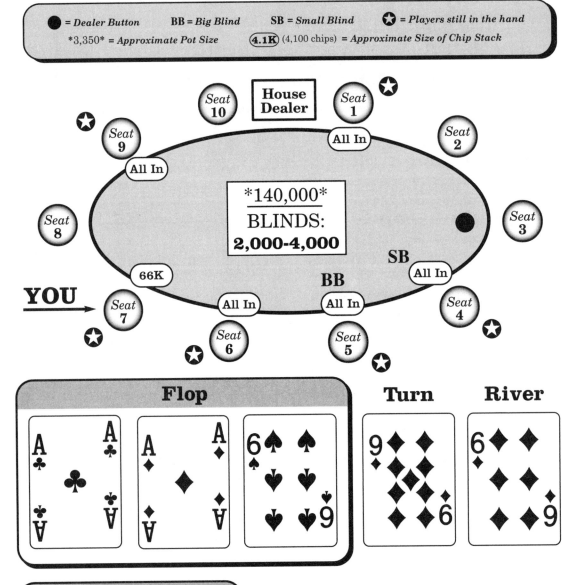

Situation 137:

After the river card was dealt, Seat 5 went all in for his remaining 8,000 chips. When it was your turn to act, you called the bet. Seat 9 then went all in for his last 5,000 chips. Seat 1 then raised all in for his last 12,000 chips. You called the additional 4,000 chips, putting everyone in the hand all in, and turned over your full house. Seat 1 turned over his pocket 6s to win the hand, dealing you a horrible bad beat. What do you do now?

Starting Hand (Pocket): **A♥9♥**

This Pocket's Win Rate: **40.5%**

Win Rate Rank: **20 of 169 possible**

Tournament Situation:

Tourney: **Internet Qualifier**

Paid Entrys: **2,400 x $50**

Starting Chip Stack: **2,000**

Players Remaining: **339**

Places Paid: **15 (See chart)**

Your Current Standing: **1st overall, 1st at your table**

Time Left in Round: **14 minutes**

Rebuys Allowed: **No**

Next Blind Level: **3,000-6,000**

This Tournament's Prize Money:

1st-10th:
Paid entry to World Series of Poker Main Event (worth $10,000)
11th: $7,500
12th: $5,000
13th: $4,000
14th: $2,500
15th: $1,000

Total Prize Pool:

$120,000

Answer 137:

Number one, you get ready to play the next hand, because it will be dealt in a matter of a few seconds. Two, you make sure you play the next hand properly, and not out of anger over having suffered a horrible bad beat. Three, you have to accept the fact that sometimes bad beats are just that...bad beats, and they happen to everyone. Four, when you have time, reflect on the hand to try and figure out if you did anything wrong. In this case, about the only thing you could say you did wrong—and this is just nit-picking—was raise Seat 1's raise after the river card was dealt because the possibility did exist that quad 6s could be in someone's hand.

As to everything else you did in the way of betting strategy, you shouldn't have done it any differently. When you flopped a set of Aces, Seat 1 already had you beat with a full house, so you actually caught up with him and passed him when the 9 came on the turn, giving you the highest possible hand on the board. All your calling of initial bets and later raises was entirely proper in your attempt to maximize the amount of money you expected to win. Unfortunately, the river card filled his miracle need. The last thing you need to do is cross Seat 9 off your Christmas list and let Seat 1 send the damn flowers to his wife. You've got another hand to play. Keep your head in the game that is yet to come.

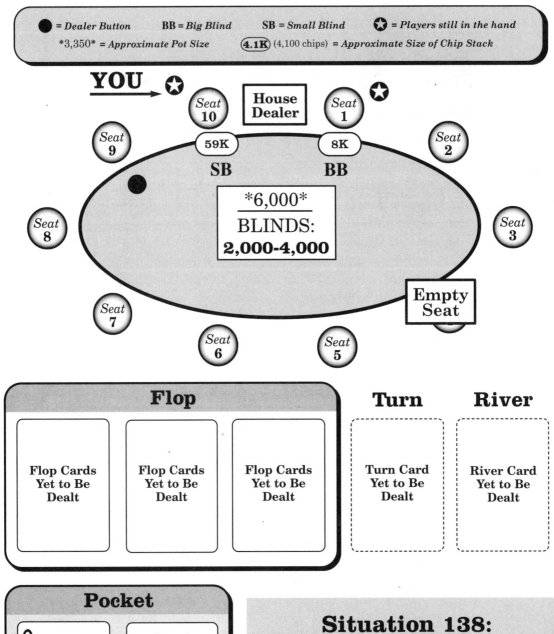

Situation 138:

It is now near the end of the same round you suffered the bad beat in and you've been condensed to another table. While in the small blind position, you received Queen-9 suited. Everyone folded to you, leaving you alone in the hand with the big blind. Given the tournament situation presented above and on the opposite page, should you fold, call the 4,000 big blind bet, or bet 10,000, forcing Seat 1 to go all in to play?

Starting Hand (Pocket): **Q♣9♣**
This Pocket's Win Rate: **19.1%**
Win Rate Rank: **38 of 169 possible**

Tournament Situation:

Tourney: **Internet Qualifier**

Paid Entrys: **2,400 x $50**

Starting Chip Stack: **2,000**

Players Remaining: **221**

Places Paid: **15 (See chart)**

Your Current Standing: **12th overall,
2nd at your table**

Time Left in Round: **1 minute**

Rebuys Allowed: **No**

Next Blind Level: **3,000-6,000**

*This Tournament's
Prize Money:*

**1st-10th:
Paid entry to
World Series of
Poker Main Event
(worth $10,000)**
11th: $7,500
12th: $5,000
13th: $4,000
14th: $2,500
15th: $1,000

Total Prize Pool:

$120,000

Answer 138:

As you can see in the chart above, this hand's relative win rate rank is 38 out of 169 possible hands when played against one other random hand, and that is exactly the situation you find yourself in here. There is nothing more random than a big blind hand. When everyone else folded, it left you isolated with Seat 1. You have a much larger chip stack and you have the advantage of position over him, so long as you bet first. Put the 10,000 chips into the pot and force him to fold or go all in. Statistically there are 131 pocket hands that fare worse than the one you currently hold. In the worst-case scenario, he's only going to ding you another 8,000 chips over what he would if you just called and later folded.

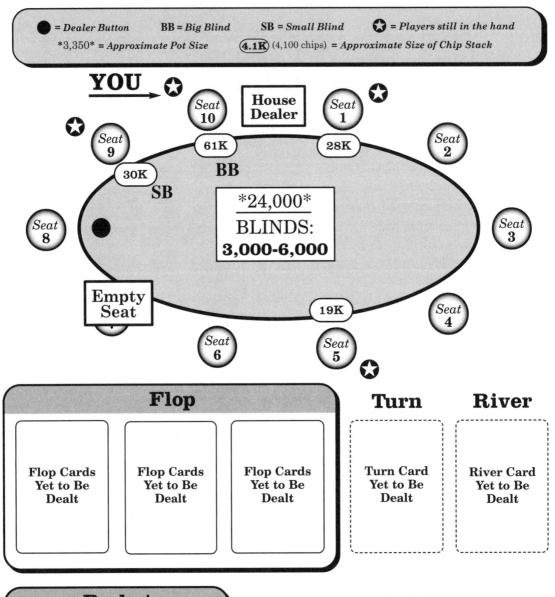

● = *Dealer Button*   BB = *Big Blind*   SB = *Small Blind*   ★ = *Players still in the hand*

3,350 = *Approximate Pot Size*   (4.1K) (4,100 chips) = *Approximate Size of Chip Stack*

YOU →

Seat 10   House Dealer   Seat 1

Seat 9   Seat 2

61K   28K

30K   BB

SB   Seat 3

24,000
BLINDS:
3,000-6,000

Seat 8   Seat 3

Empty Seat   19K   Seat 4

Seat 6   Seat 5

Flop

| Flop Cards Yet to Be Dealt | Flop Cards Yet to Be Dealt | Flop Cards Yet to Be Dealt |

Turn

Turn Card Yet to Be Dealt

River

River Card Yet to Be Dealt

Pocket

2♦   2♣

Situation 139:

It is now early in the next round and you have received pocket 2s in the big blind position. Seats 1, 5, and 9 have all called the minimum bet of 6,000 chips. You are last to act. Do you announce, "Big enough," indicating you are checking, raise to an unspecified level, or go all in?

Starting Hand (Pocket): **2♦2♣**
This Pocket's Win Rate: **4.0%**
Win Rate Rank: **72 of 169 possible**

Tournament Situation:

Tourney: **Internet Qualifier**

Paid Entrys: **2,400 x $50**

Starting Chip Stack: **2,000**

Players Remaining: **188**

Places Paid: **15 (See chart)**

Your Current Standing: **15th overall, 2nd at your table**

Time Left in Round: **10 minutes**

Rebuys Allowed: **No**

Next Blind Level: **4,000-4,000**

This Tournament's Prize Money:

1st-10th:
Paid entry to World Series of Poker Main Event (worth $10,000)
11th: **$7,500**
12th: **$5,000**
13th: **$4,000**
14th: **$2,500**
15th: **$1,000**

Total Prize Pool:

$120,000

Answer 139:

Let's get one thing clear right now, the only reason you're playing this hand is because you're already in the pot because of your big blind and because no one raised. Had they, you would have folded, right? RIGHT? Right. So, check it to the flop and see what comes, but there had better be another deuce or it had better be free or you're gone. Right? RIGHT!

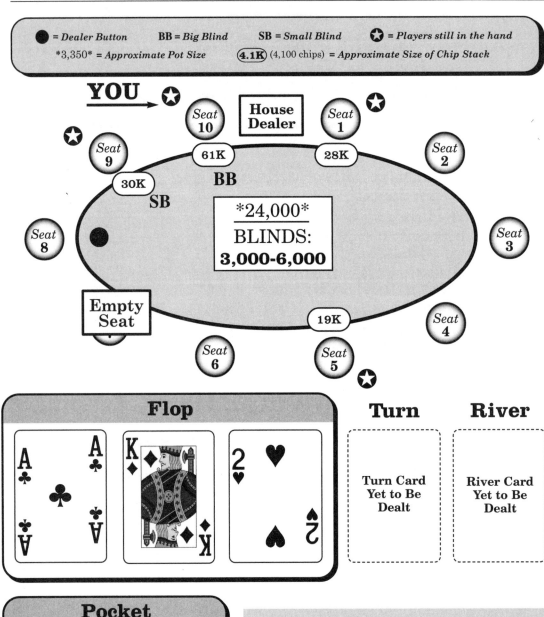

● = *Dealer Button*   **BB** = *Big Blind*   **SB** = *Small Blind*   ★ = *Players still in the hand*

3,350 = *Approximate Pot Size*   **4.1K** (4,100 chips) = *Approximate Size of Chip Stack*

YOU → ★

Seat 10   House Dealer   Seat 1

Seat 9   61K   28K   Seat 2

30K   **BB**

SB

Seat 8   *24,000*
BLINDS:
3,000-6,000   Seat 3

Empty Seat   19K   Seat 4

Seat 6   Seat 5

★

Flop

A♣   K♦   2♥

Turn

Turn Card Yet to Be Dealt

River

River Card Yet to Be Dealt

Pocket

2♦   2♣

Situation 140:

After the flop, Seat 9 is first to act and he checks. It is now your turn to act. Do you check as well, bet the minimum of 6,000, bet a larger unspecified amount, or go all in?

Starting Hand (Pocket): **2♦2♣**

This Pocket's Win Rate: **4.0%**

Win Rate Rank: **72 of 169 possible**

Tournament Situation:

Tourney: **Internet Qualifier**

Paid Entrys: **2,400 x $50**

Starting Chip Stack: **2,000**

Players Remaining: **188**

Places Paid: **15 (See chart)**

Your Current Standing: **15th overall, 2nd at your table**

Time Left in Round: **10 minutes**

Rebuys Allowed: **No**

Next Blind Level: **4,000-4,000**

This Tournament's Prize Money:

1st-10th:
Paid entry to
World Series of
Poker Main Event
(worth $10,000)
11th: $7,500
12th: $5,000
13th: $4,000
14th: $2,500
15th: $1,000

Total Prize Pool:

$120,000

Answer 140:

You caught what you needed on the flop, so you can stay in the hand but you need to be careful, because Aces and Kings are most likely lurking out there somewhere, you just don't know where. With a flop like this, players who don't have an Ace or King are likely going to check. Players with an Ace or King might also check in an effort to disguise their hand. Since you have the true stealth hand, any bet by you will almost certainly be attributed to an Ace or King. Go ahead and give your opponents what they want, a bet that indicates you likely have an Ace or King. This will help you gain information on who's got the real hands at the table. If you get raised, you're obviously going to call. Keep in mind that at this late stage of the tournament, many players won't get cute or monkey around with slow playing power hands, and no one bet huge preflop like they had pocket Kings or Aces that they didn't want to get snapped off by a player drawing out on them, so it doesn't appear anyone held either of these hands.

Now, it very well could be that several players hold either an Ace or King, and if they catch another for a set, that's great, because you'll have a full house, an unbeatable hand so long as they don't hold pocket Kings or Aces and don't pair the board on the river. Make the minimum bet of 6,000 and see what transpires.

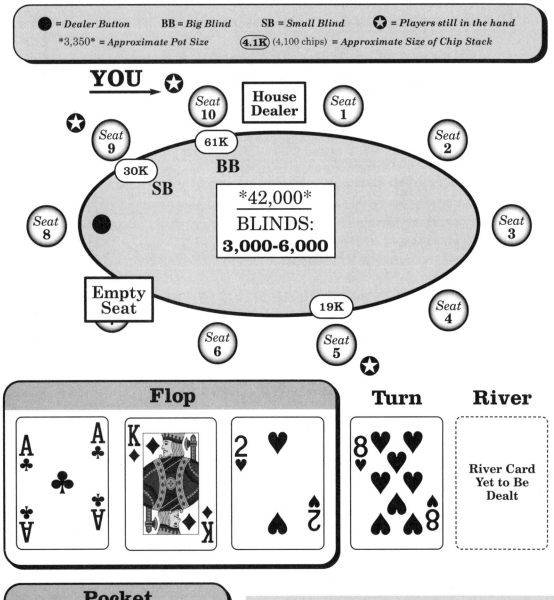

= *Dealer Button*   **BB** = *Big Blind*   **SB** = *Small Blind*   ⭐ = *Players still in the hand*

3,350 = *Approximate Pot Size*   **4.1K** (4,100 chips) = *Approximate Size of Chip Stack*

YOU ➡️ ⭐

Seat 10   House Dealer   Seat 1

⭐ Seat 9   61K

30K   BB

SB

42,000
BLINDS:
3,000-6,000

Seat 8   Seat 2   Seat 3

Empty Seat   19K   Seat 4

Seat 6   Seat 5   ⭐

Flop

A♣ K♦ 2♥

Turn

8♥

River

River Card
Yet to Be
Dealt

Pocket

2♦ 2♣

Situation 141:

Two of your three opponents called your bet of 6,000 chips and one folded. After the turn card was dealt, Seat 9 was first to act and checked. It is now your turn to act. With only Seat 5 to act after you, do you check as well, bet the minimum of 6,000 chips, bet a larger unspecified amount, or go all in?

Starting Hand (Pocket): **2♦2♣**

This Pocket's Win Rate: **4.0%**

Win Rate Rank: **72 of 169 possible**

Tournament Situation:

Tourney: **Internet Qualifier**

Paid Entrys: **2,400 x $50**

Starting Chip Stack: **2,000**

Players Remaining: **188**

Places Paid: **15 (See chart)**

Your Current Standing: **15th overall, 2nd at your table**

Time Left in Round: **10 minutes**

Rebuys Allowed: **No**

Next Blind Level: **4,000-4,000**

This Tournament's Prize Money:

1st-10th:
Paid entry to World Series of Poker Main Event (worth $10,000)
11th: $7,500
12th: $5,000
13th: $4,000
14th: $2,500
15th: $1,000

Total Prize Pool:
$120,000

Answer 141:

Not much has changed after the turn card unless someone holds one or two 8s in their pocket. The only thing other than concealed 8s to worry about (besides the obvious slow played pocket Kings or Aces) is the potential heart flush draw on the board.

There are several ways you can approach the betting right now. You could check, playing conservatively in case the heart flush comes on the river and you don't pair the board for a full house; you could go all in, hoping to discourage any player on a heart draw or holding a big pair from staying in the pot, but I doubt it would work at this stage of the tournament with the pot as big as it is now; or you could do something in between.

I think I would bet the 6,000 again, keeping the pressure on your opponents and reminding them again who has control of this hand.

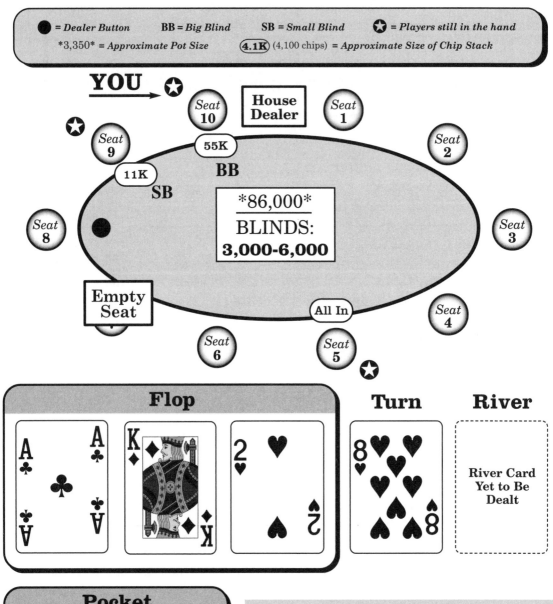

● = Dealer Button **BB = Big Blind** **SB = Small Blind** **★ = Players still in the hand**
3,350 = Approximate Pot Size **4.1K (4,100 chips) = Approximate Size of Chip Stack**

YOU →

Seat 10 — House Dealer — Seat 1
Seat 9 — 55K
11K — BB
SB
Seat 8
Empty Seat
Seat 6 — Seat 5 (All In) — Seat 4 — Seat 3 — Seat 2

86,000
BLINDS:
3,000-6,000

Flop

A♣ K♦ 2♥

Turn

8♥

River

River Card Yet to Be Dealt

Pocket

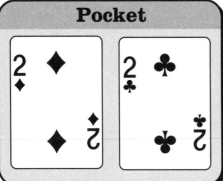

2♦ 2♣

Situation 142:

After you bet 6,000 chips, Seat 5 quickly went all in for 19,000 chips. Seat 9 took a long time to call the bet. It is now your turn to act with no one after you. Do you now fold, call the additional 13,000 chips, or raise to 24,000, forcing Seat 9 to go all in if he wants to continue in the hand?

Starting Hand (Pocket): **2♦2♣**

This Pocket's Win Rate: **4.0%**

Win Rate Rank: **72 of 169 possible**

Tournament Situation:

Tourney: **Internet Qualifier**

Paid Entrys: **2,400 x $50**

Starting Chip Stack: **2,000**

Players Remaining: **188**

Places Paid: **15 (See chart)**

Your Current Standing: **15th overall, 2nd at your table**

Time Left in Round: **10 minutes**

Rebuys Allowed: **No**

Next Blind Level: **4,000-4,000**

This Tournament's Prize Money:

1st-10th:
Paid entry to
World Series of
Poker Main Event
(worth $10,000)
11th: $7,500
12th: $5,000
13th: $4,000
14th: $2,500
15th: $1,000

Total Prize Pool:

$120,000

Answer 142:

Well, with a set of 2s and this board, and with the pot as large as it is, you can't fold now. The speed with which Seat 5 went all in is certainly a bit disconcerting, but maybe he just holds an Ace or Ace-King and is worried about the heart draw himself. Maybe he's got two other pair, such as King-8 suited, or something weird like that.

Then of course you have to worry about Seat 9. He seemed reluctant to call, but in an Internet tournament, you never know. Maybe he was trying to open a box of Cocoa Puffs or something and it took him a while to get back on his mouse. Maybe he was feigning reluctance. Maybe he really has pocket Aces and is getting ready to...oh, just call the bet already and see what the river brings. Sometimes you just can't worry about what the other players are holding in their hands as much as you should concentrate of what YOU have in your hands, which is a set of deuces. Right now I still like your chances.

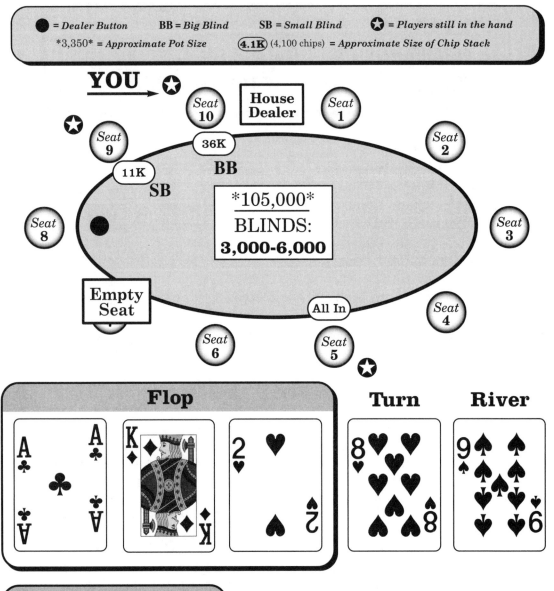

Situation 143:

After the river card was dealt, Seat 9 checked. It is now your turn to act. With no one to act after you (Seat 5 was already all in), do you check as well, bet the minimum of 6,000 chips, bet a larger unspecified amount, or bet 11,000 chips, forcing Seat 9 to go all in to continue in the hand?

Starting Hand (Pocket): **2♦2♣**

This Pocket's Win Rate: **4.0%**

Win Rate Rank: **72 of 169 possible**

Tournament Situation:

Tourney: **Internet Qualifier**

Paid Entrys: **2,400 x $50**

Starting Chip Stack: **2,000**

Players Remaining: **188**

Places Paid: **15 (See chart)**

Your Current Standing: **15th overall, 2nd at your table**

Time Left in Round: **10 minutes**

Rebuys Allowed: **No**

Next Blind Level: **4,000-4,000**

This Tournament's Prize Money:

1st-10th:
Paid entry to World Series of Poker Main Event (worth $10,000)
11th: **$7,500**
12th: **$5,000**
13th: **$4,000**
14th: **$2,500**
15th: **$1,000**

Total Prize Pool:

$120,000

Answer 143:

Well, unless someone was holding pocket 9s, the river card was a blank for everyone. There is no way to make a straight with this board and the heart flush just got busted. Seat 9 hasn't seemed too anxious to bet the last several rounds, so if you bet the 11,000 and he missed, he'll probably fold. He might fold no matter what you bet. The real thing to consider is whether or not he was truly slow playing Aces or Kings. It sure doesn't seem like it to me. If you bet just the 6,000, he might call, holding out hope for a miracle, like you playing a single pair of something, but I doubt it. Consequently, I'd bet the 11,000 and trust my instincts that a set is enough on this hand, and maybe he'll interpret your bet as a bluff and call you.

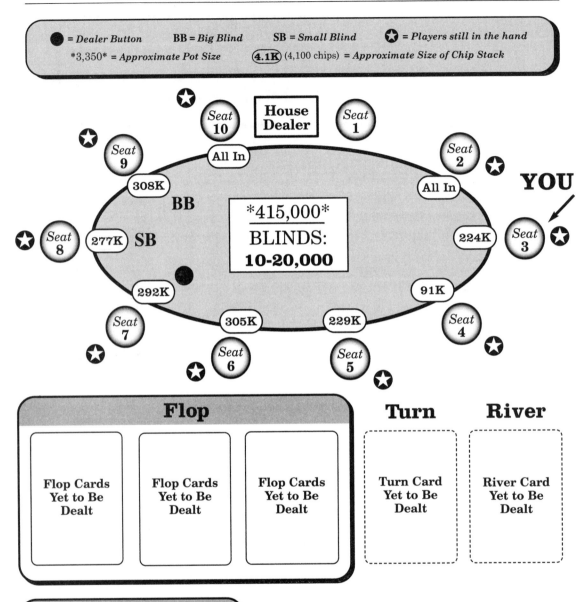

Flop

Flop Cards Yet to Be Dealt

Flop Cards Yet to Be Dealt

Flop Cards Yet to Be Dealt

Turn

Turn Card Yet to Be Dealt

River

River Card Yet to Be Dealt

Pocket

Situation 144:

It is now very deep into the tournament and the average chip stack is 240,000 chips with only twenty players left. You received Ace-10 suited in your pocket. Seat 10 was first to act and went all in for 182,000 chips. Seat 1 folded and Seat 2 went all in for 203,000 chips. It is now your turn to act. Do you fold, call the 203,000, raise, or go all in?

Starting Hand (Pocket): **A♣10♣**

This Pocket's Win Rate: **50.7%**

Win Rate Rank: **14 of 169 possible**

Tournament Situation:

Tourney: **Internet Qualifier**

Paid Entrys: **2,400 x $50**

Starting Chip Stack: **2,000**

Players Remaining: **20**

Places Paid: **15 (See chart)**

Your Current Standing: **13th overall, 6th at your table**

Time Left in Round: **6 minutes**

Rebuys Allowed: **No**

Next Blind Level: **15,000-30,000**

This Tournament's Prize Money:

1st-10th:
Paid entry to World Series of Poker Main Event (worth $10,000)
11th: $7,500
12th: $5,000
13th: $4,000
14th: $2,500
15th: $1,000

Total Prize Pool:

$120,000

Answer 144:

Ace-10 suited is a very good hand, as you can see in the chart above with its fourteenth relative win rate rank. A suited Ace-10 may be pretty to look at, it may have a good performance rating, but you also need to consider— no, put EMPHASIS on—your current situation in the tournament. Right now you are thirteenth overall of the twenty remaining players, barely high enough to make the cut into the prize money if you can hold on.

Frankly, you didn't enter this tournament to take home $4,000, which is what you'll get if you end up in thirteenth place. Every move you make right now is critical. With two players with approximately equal chip stacks all in ahead of you already, you know that one of them is most likely going to take the other out, barring a tie hand. Also, with so many players yet to act behind you, one or more of them may jump in as well, which means it will be harder for your Ace-10 suited to win. But what it also means is maybe two or more players will get knocked out on this one hand, improving your chances to go further in the tournament. And remember, the top ten prizes are all the same, so it isn't necessary to finish higher than tenth place. Fold this hand and let the other guys fight it out.

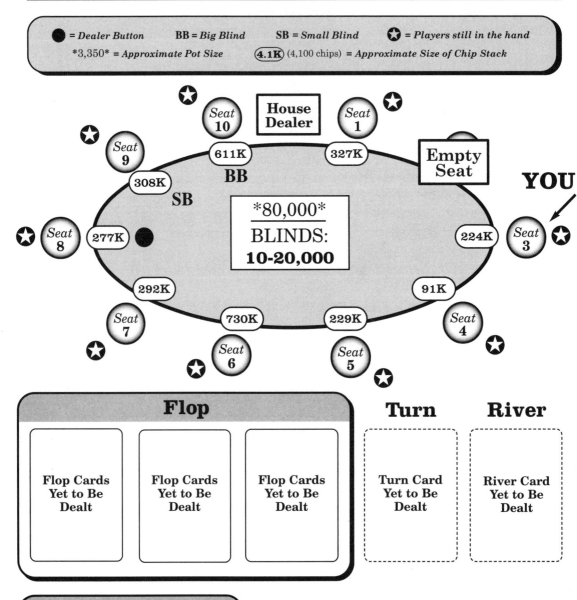

= Dealer Button   **BB** = Big Blind   **SB** = Small Blind   ⭐ = Players still in the hand

3,350 = Approximate Pot Size   **(4.1K)** (4,100 chips) = Approximate Size of Chip Stack

House Dealer

Seat 10 — 611K — **BB**

Seat 1 — 327K

Seat 9 — 308K — **SB**

Empty Seat

YOU

80,000
BLINDS:
10-20,000

Seat 8 — 277K

Seat 3 — 224K

Seat 7 — 292K

Seat 4 — 91K

Seat 6 — 730K

Seat 5 — 229K

Flop

| Flop Cards Yet to Be Dealt | Flop Cards Yet to Be Dealt | Flop Cards Yet to Be Dealt |

Turn

Turn Card Yet to Be Dealt

River

River Card Yet to Be Dealt

Pocket

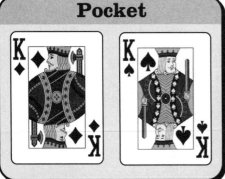

Situation 145:

Two players got knocked out on the previous situation and one new player was brought over from the other table to equal them out with nine players each. After receiving a pair of Kings in your pocket, Seat 1 was first to act and bet 50,000 chips. It is now your turn to act. With seven players yet to act after you, do you fold, call the 50,000-chip bet, raise to an unspecified level, or go all in with your remaining 224,000 chips?

Starting Hand (Pocket): **K♦K♠**
This Pocket's Win Rate: **74.6%**
Win Rate Rank: **2 of 169 possible**

Tournament Situation:

Tourney: **Internet Qualifier**

Paid Entrys: **2,400 x $50**

Starting Chip Stack: **2,000**

Players Remaining: **18**

Places Paid: **15 (See chart)**

Your Current Standing: **13th overall, 8th at your table**

Time Left in Round: **5 minutes**

Rebuys Allowed: **No**

Next Blind Level: **15,000-30,000**

This Tournament's Prize Money:

1st-10th:
Paid entry to World Series of Poker Main Event (worth $10,000)
11th: $7,500
12th: $5,000
13th: $4,000
14th: $2,500
15th: $1,000

Total Prize Pool:

$120,000

Answer 145:

Touchy one, this hand. You caught a great hand, but it's certainly vulnerable, especially if an Ace hits the board. The problem is, though, that you still haven't qualified for one of the top ten prizes. Even though two players were knocked out on the previous hand, you didn't move up in the standings any because they both had fewer chips than you. The average chip stack is now about 267,000 chips, and you're below that.

Still, you aren't going to catch a hand like this that often, especially in critical "must-have" situations. You're two hands away from the blinds, which means if you don't catch a hand there, you'll drop another 30,000 chips.

You could just call the 50,000-chip bet from Seat 1, but that could open the door for someone behind you getting in relatively cheaply and drawing out on you. As tough as it may seem to do, you've got to slow down those behind you. You also need to think about leaving yourself a little wiggle room in case you totally miss the flop, especially if an Ace comes. If you go all in and get called by a bigger stack, you'll have to win or you go home— without the coveted World Series seat. Make a raise to 100,000 chips and see what the other players behind you do. If you're forced to go all in, then so be it. For now, try to accomplish both goals of getting those behind you to fold and keeping some chips just in case the flop is bad.

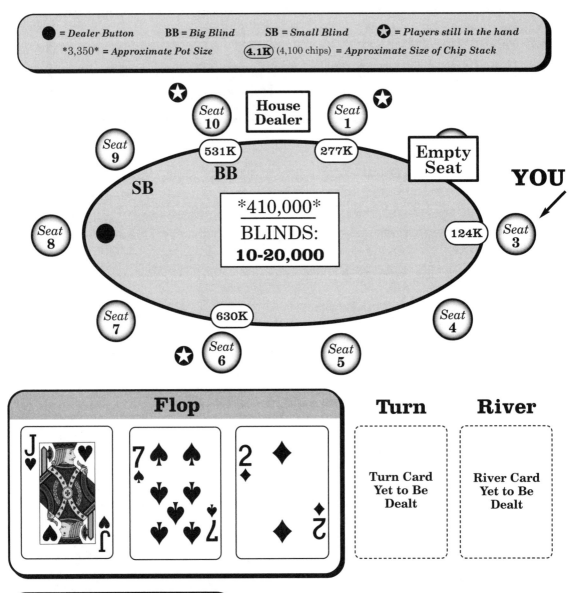

● = *Dealer Button*   **BB** = *Big Blind*   **SB** = *Small Blind*   ⭐ = *Players still in the hand*

3,350 = *Approximate Pot Size*   (**4.1K**) (4,100 chips) = *Approximate Size of Chip Stack*

Seat 10 — 531K
House Dealer
Seat 1 — 277K
Seat 9
Empty Seat
YOU
Seat 8
Seat 3 — 124K
SB
BB

410,000
BLINDS:
10-20,000

Seat 7
Seat 4
Seat 6 — 630K
Seat 5

Flop

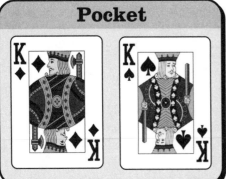

Jʜ 7♠ 2♦

Turn

Turn Card
Yet to Be
Dealt

River

River Card
Yet to Be
Dealt

Pocket

K♦ K♠

Situation 146:

Seats 6, 10, and 1 all called your raise to 100,000 chips. After the flop, Seats 10 and 1 both checked to you. With only Seat 6 yet to act after you, do you check as well, bet the minimum of 20,000 chips, make a larger bet to an unspecified level, or go all in?

Starting Hand (Pocket): **K♦K♠**
This Pocket's Win Rate: **74.6%**
Win Rate Rank: **2 of 169 possible**

Tournament Situation:

Tourney: **Internet Qualifier**

Paid Entrys: **2,400 x $50**

Starting Chip Stack: **2,000**

Players Remaining: **18**

Places Paid: **15 (See chart)**

Your Current Standing: **13th overall, 6th at your table**

Time Left in Round: **5 minutes**

Rebuys Allowed: **No**

Next Blind Level: **15,000-30,000**

This Tournament's Prize Money:

1st-10th:
Paid entry to World Series of Poker Main Event (worth $10,000)
11th: $7,500
12th: $5,000
13th: $4,000
14th: $2,500
15th: $1,000

Total Prize Pool:

$120,000

Answer 146:

The flop would appear to have been kind to you. The flop is important because so many of your final cards will have been revealed after the flop (five of your seven). This means you have a strong indication of how the hand is going to go. For example, with three different suits on the board, you have to believe anyone hoping for a flush before the flop is now ready to get out. Most possible straight draw combinations appear to have faded as well, although you can't completely discount someone having played a 10-9 or 9-8, especially suited. I wouldn't imagine that so close to making the final ten Seat 1 played pocket 7s or 2s before the flop since he raised in first position, although pocket Jacks is certainly a possibility. I also can't believe either of the other two would have played pocket 7s or 2s. Again, Jacks is a distinct possibility, especially the way they all bet.

Since the flop—the most dangerous time for someone holding pocket Kings—came without bringing an Ace, I would now feel much better about going all in. Push it all in right now, and get the fence-sitters out of the hand.

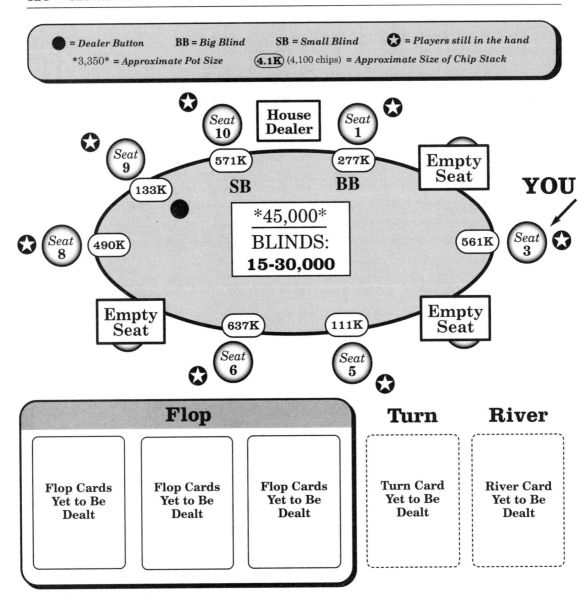

● = *Dealer Button*   **BB** = *Big Blind*   **SB** = *Small Blind*   ⭐ = *Players still in the hand*

3,350 = *Approximate Pot Size*   **4.1K** (4,100 chips) = *Approximate Size of Chip Stack*

House Dealer

Seat 10 — 571K — SB

Seat 1 — 277K — BB

Seat 9 — 133K

Empty Seat

YOU

Seat 8 — 490K

Seat 3 — 561K

45,000
BLINDS:
15-30,000

Empty Seat

Empty Seat

Seat 6 — 637K

Seat 5 — 111K

Flop

| Flop Cards Yet to Be Dealt | Flop Cards Yet to Be Dealt | Flop Cards Yet to Be Dealt |

Turn

Turn Card Yet to Be Dealt

River

River Card Yet to Be Dealt

Pocket

K♣ Q♦

Situation 147:

You succeeded in getting everyone to fold with your all in bet on the previous hand and have improved your chip stack significantly. It is now into the next round and the average chip stack is 343,000 chips with fourteen players left. You received King-Queen unsuited and are first to act. Do you fold, call the 30,000-chip big blind bet, bet a larger unspecified amount, or go all in?

Starting Hand (Pocket): **K♣Q♦**

This Pocket's Win Rate: **39.2%**

Win Rate Rank: **23 of 169 possible**

Tournament Situation:

Tourney: **Internet Qualifier**

Paid Entrys: **2,400 x $50**

Starting Chip Stack: **2,000**

Players Remaining: **14**

Places Paid: **15 (See chart)**

Your Current Standing: **4th overall, 3rd at your table**

Time Left in Round: **14 minutes**

Rebuys Allowed: **No**

Next Blind Level: **20,000-40,000**

This Tournament's Prize Money:

1st-10th:
Paid entry to World Series of Poker Main Event (worth $10,000)
11th: $7,500
12th: $5,000
13th: $4,000
14th: $2,500
15th: $1,000

Total Prize Pool:

$120,000

Answer 147:

Even though this is a solid starting hand, especially in a game that no longer features ten players, I would fold this hand. Why? Because you're in first position and have no idea yet what the other six players are going to do and two of them have larger stacks than you. Also, you are now into the money for sure, with a guaranteed prize of at least $2,500. If you look around the table you'll see two players with very small stacks. All you have to do is sit and wait and they should go by the wayside in the not-too-distant future, which would move you up to at least a $5,000 prize. And undoubtedly there are several players at the other table who are short-stacked as well. You have well over the average stack, so be patient and let your stack work for you, even if you have to fold the next two hands when you'll have your two blinds. You easily have enough chips to ride out the loss of 45,000 on your next two hands if need be. Finally, you don't even want to get tempted to play this hand at this point, because if it gets you close and you lose 100-200,000 chips, it could put you on the bubble in short order and you'll risk missing the top ten finishers.

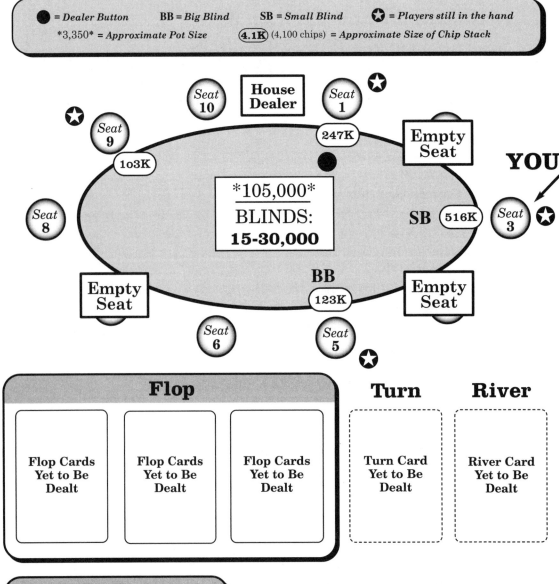

= *Dealer Button*   **BB** = *Big Blind*   **SB** = *Small Blind*   ⭐ = *Players still in the hand*

3,350 = *Approximate Pot Size*   (**4.1K**) (4,100 chips) = *Approximate Size of Chip Stack*

Seat 10   **House Dealer**   *Seat* 1   ⭐

Seat 9   247K

⭐   1o3K

105,000
BLINDS:
15-30,000

YOU ↙

Seat 8   **SB** 516K   *Seat* 3 ⭐

Empty Seat   **BB** 123K   **Empty Seat**

Seat 6   *Seat* 5   ⭐

Flop

| Flop Cards Yet to Be Dealt | Flop Cards Yet to Be Dealt | Flop Cards Yet to Be Dealt |

Turn

Turn Card Yet to Be Dealt

River

River Card Yet to Be Dealt

Pocket

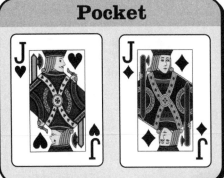

Situation 148:

Several hands later you are in the small blind and catch a pair of Jacks. Seats 9 and 1 both called the 30,000-chip big blind bet while Seats 6, 8, and 10 all folded. With only Seat 5 (the big blind) yet to act after you, do you fold, call the 30,000, raise to an unspecified level, or go all in? (Note: Pay particularly close attention to the Tournament Situation on the opposite page before deciding.)

Starting Hand (Pocket): **J♥J♦**
This Pocket's Win Rate: **64.4%**
Win Rate Rank: **7 of 169 possible**

Tournament Situation:

Tourney: **Internet Qualifier**

Paid Entrys: **2,400 x $50**

Starting Chip Stack: **2,000**

Players Remaining: **13**

Places Paid: **15 (See chart)**

Your Current Standing: **4th overall,
3rd at your table**

Time Left in Round: **12 minutes**

Rebuys Allowed: **No**

Next Blind Level: **20,000-40,000**

*This Tournament's
Prize Money:*

1st-10th:
Paid entry to
World Series of
Poker Main Event
(worth $10,000)
11th: $7,500
12th: $5,000
13th: $4,000
14th: $2,500
15th: $1,000

Total Prize Pool:

$120,000

Answer 148:

Yes, a pair of Jacks is a nice hand, but should you play it when the three small stacks are all going against each other? At least they will be if you fold. And if you fold, perhaps two of them will get knocked out and move you that much closer to the desired top ten finishers.

While there is some merit in folding this hand, consider something else: what if you stay in and knock all three of them out? If you'll notice, you have more chips than the three of them combined. Certainly Jacks are vulnerable to Aces, Kings, and Queens. But since you're already in for 15,000 chips anyway, and since you have the bully stack between the four of you, I'd call this hand for 15,000. I wouldn't raise it because I'd be trying to keep the big blind in. You can push him around later if you need to, so long as the cards cooperate.

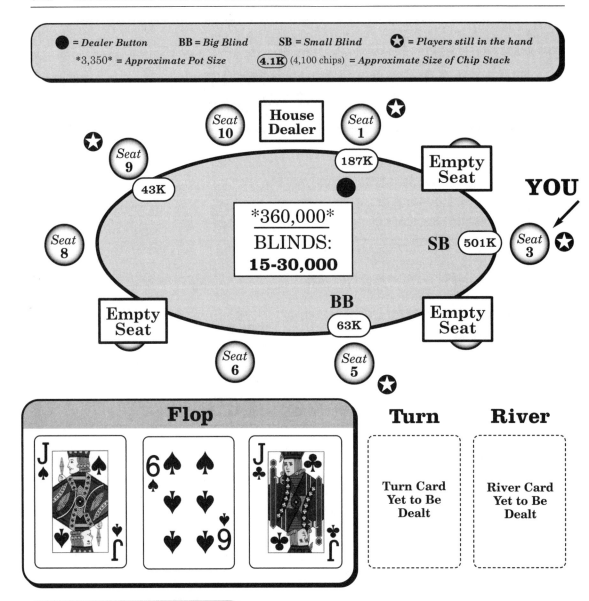

Situation 149:

After the flop, you are first to act and check, hoping to keep everyone in the hand as long as possible. Seat 5 bets 60,000 and Seats 9 and 1 both call. It is now your turn to act. Do you fold and let the three of them fight it out, knowing that one and possibly two are going to get knocked out, or do you call, raise to an unspecified level, or go all in right now?

Starting Hand (Pocket): **J♥J♦**

This Pocket's Win Rate: **64.4%**

Win Rate Rank: **7 of 169 possible**

Tournament Situation:

Tourney: **Internet Qualifier**

Paid Entrys: **2,400 x $50**

Starting Chip Stack: **2,000**

Players Remaining: **13**

Places Paid: **15 (See chart)**

Your Current Standing: **4th overall, 3rd at your table**

Time Left in Round: **12 minutes**

Rebuys Allowed: **No**

Next Blind Level: **20,000-40,000**

This Tournament's Prize Money:

1st-10th:
Paid entry to World Series of Poker Main Event (worth $10,000)
11th: $7,500
12th: $5,000
13th: $4,000
14th: $2,500
15th: $1,000

Total Prize Pool:

$120,000

Answer 149:

You just call again. You still want to be in this hand so you can manipulate it—if possible—in order to knock out all three players on this one hand. You don't want to raise it yet because you might scare out one, two, or all three of them as they cling to the hope that they can make the top ten.

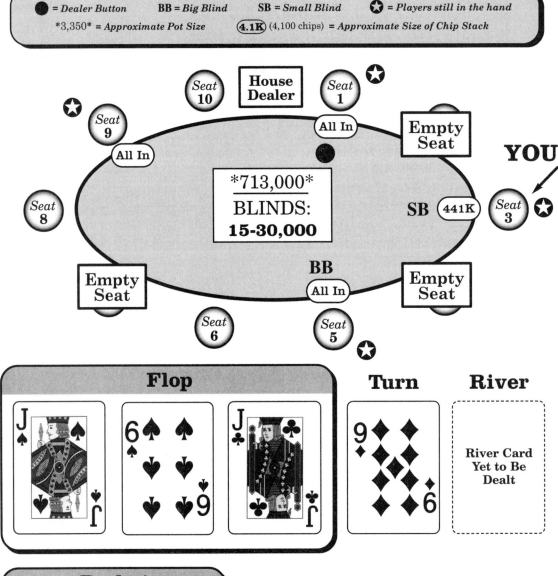

Situation 150:

After the turn card came, you checked. Seat 5 then went all in for 63,000 chips and was called all in by Seat 9 for 43,000 chips. Seat 1 then went all in for 187,000 chips. What do you do now?

Starting Hand (Pocket): **J♥J♦**
This Pocket's Win Rate: **64.4%**
Win Rate Rank: **7 of 169 possible**

Tournament Situation:
Tourney: **Internet Qualifier**
Paid Entrys: **2,400 x $50**
Starting Chip Stack: **2,000**
Players Remaining: **13**
Places Paid: **15 (See chart)**
Your Current Standing: **4th overall,
 3rd at your table**
Time Left in Round: **12 minutes**
Rebuys Allowed: **No**
Next Blind Level: **20,000-40,000**

*This Tournament's
Prize Money:*

1st-10th:
**Paid entry to
World Series of
Poker Main Event
(worth $10,000)**
11th: $7,500
12th: $5,000
13th: $4,000
14th: $2,500
15th: $1,000

Total Prize Pool:

$120,000

Answer 150:

You make three calls. The first call is of Seat 1's bet. The second call is to your travel agent, 'cause *you're going to Las Vegas to play in the World Series of Poker, baby!*

There is no possible card that could come on the river that will allow any player still in the hand to beat you. It would take a straight flush or four of a kind higher than Jacks, and neither is possible with this board. When the 9♦ came on the turn, it mathematically eliminated the possibility of any straight flush or quads higher than Jacks from occurring. You successfully knocked out all three of these players on this one hand, reducing the tournament to ten players, the magic number needed to win your seat in the World Series. When you get there, be sure and tell everyone you meet that this book helped get you there. (Sorry, couldn't help it!)

Oh yeah, that third call? *Call your mother and tell her you love her.*

The Terminology of No-Limit Texas Hold'em

Ace The highest or lowest card in the deck. When played as the lowest, it is used to make a 5-high straight, as in A-2-3-4-5 of mixed suits.

Ace high A no-pair hand in which the highest card held is an Ace.

Aces full A full house made up of three Aces and a smaller pair.

Ace-high straight A straight consisting of A-K-Q-J-10 of mixed suits.

Aces over Two pair, the higher of which are Aces.

Aces up See Aces over.

act To bet, call, fold, or raise in turn at the appropriate time. When it's your turn to play, the dealer (or another player) might say to you, "It's your turn to act."

action 1) Similar to act. When it's your turn to play, someone might say, "It's your action." 2) A term used to describe the liveliness (or lack thereof) of a game. If there are a lot of bets and raises, someone might say, "There's a lot of action in this game tonight." Conversely, if it's a slow game without a lot of betting, you might hear, "There's not much action tonight." 3) That portion of a pot that a player qualifies for. For example, if on the river player A bets $16 and player B calls the bet for $16, and then you go all in for your remaining $5, then a side pot is created for $22 for players A and B. You are said to only have action for the first $5 each of you placed into the pot.

active hand A hand which is still in contention for a pot.

active player A player who is still in contention for a pot.

add-on 1) One last optional chip buy offered to all players in a re-buy tournament, usually with no minimum chip requirement, and usually at a specified time. 2) In live play, when a player's current chip count is less than the minimum buy-in and he purchases additional chips that are less than the minimum buy-in amount but brings his new total to more than the minimum buy-in is considered to have purchased an add-on.

advertise The intentional showing of one's cards in order to set up the other players at the table for a planned future action. Typically a player who is advertising will turn over a hand in which he bluffed his opponent(s) out of a pot in order to make them think he bluffs a lot, hoping then to trap them with a good hand the next time. Less typically, a player will show his good cards in order to make his opponents think he only plays good cards, thereby setting them up to be bluffed later on.

aggressive This term relates to a style of play that is represented by much betting, raising, and reraising. This should not be construed as the same thing as loose play. Some very good players who don't play a lot of hands will, when they get good hands, bet, raise, and reraise aggressively.

ahead Having more chips than you started with. If you bought in for $100 and after two hour's play your stack was at $135, then you would be $35 ahead.

air ball A card that is of no help to you. See blank.

all black Having a Club or Spade flush.

all in Placing all of one's chips into the pot on one bet. In tournament play, this can represent a huge amount of chips, as you might witness on television. In live play, this represents a final bet, call, or raise of one's remaining chip(s), typically representing less chips than one's opponents have at the table.

all red Having a Diamond or Heart flush.

ammunition A slang term for chips.

announce Declare, as in one's hand.

announced bet A verbal declaration by a player of his intended bet which is binding if made in turn.

ante One or more chips put into the pot by each player before the cards are dealt and which do not constitute part of a player's bet, like a blind. While antes are used in all major tournaments, they are not usually used in a live limit Texas Hold'em game.

backdoor When a player catches two cards on the turn and river that gives him a hand that he only had two or three cards of on the flop, and typically either didn't expect to catch, or wasn't originally trying to catch. Examples: catching the last two cards of a straight, flush, or four of a kind.

backdoor flush Catching two cards on the turn and river for a flush.

backdoor straight Catching two cards on the turn and river for a straight.

backer Someone who financially backs another player in either a live game or a tournament.

backs The reverse sides of the cards, as opposed to the faces, or fronts of the cards that show the ranks and suits.

back-to-back Catching two of the same cards in a row, as in, "I caught back-to-back Aces."

bad beat When a strong hand is beaten by a long shot hand, especially when the holder of the eventual winning hand should not have been in the pot to begin with (at least if playing correctly, or according to the disgruntled loser).

bad beat jackpot Typically a large house jackpot that is awarded when a particularly high hand of minimum qualifications is beaten by an even higher hand of minimum qualifications. Although it varies from poker room to poker room, the typical bad beat would consist of a full house of at least Aces over 10s being beaten by four of a kind or better. Usually the house rules require that both pocket or hole cards must play. The usual breakdown of the jackpot would be to award 50 percent of the jackpot to the loser of the bad beat, 25 percent to the winner of the bad beat, with the remaining 25 percent being divided equally among the players at the table who were dealt in the hand.

bad beat story The sad tale of someone who suffered a bad beat on a hand, usually a big pot. Typically no one else at the table wants to hear the story.

balanced games The philosophy employed in some poker rooms of keeping tables with the same betting limits balanced with the same number of players rather than unequal numbers. For example, in a poker room with two active $3-$6 games going on, rather than have one table with nine players and one with five, the house will seat seven players at each game.

bankroll The money a player has available to gamble with.

bar To officially ban someone from playing in an establishment.

beat the board To have a hand that beats the five community cards displayed on the table, as in, "I can beat the board."

behind Having less chips than you started with. If you bought in for $100 and, after two hour's play you had $30, then you would be $70 behind.

bet for value To bet a hand with the intention of getting called by one or more lesser hands, as opposed to making a bet in order to get others to fold.

bet into To make a bet before another player, often one who potentially holds a better hand, as in, "You only had a pair and you bet into a straight draw?"

bet on the come To make a bet hoping that the card(s) you need will eventually come.

bet out of turn To make a bet before it's one's turn to do so. In most poker rooms betting out of turn is not binding and the player is required to take his bet back. Betting out of turn is often an honest mistake, either because the player is new or because the player couldn't see the cards of one or more players between himself and the last player to have acted. Sometimes, however, it is a ploy utilized by savvy players to influence the action of other players in the hand. Some poker establishments consider such a bet unethical which might result in either a penalty or barring from play.

bet the limit To bet the maximum amount allowed.

bet the pot To make a bet equal to the size of the pot in a no-limit or pot-limit game.

betting level The limit currently being played at in a tournament. The betting levels increase at appointed times, or rounds. For example, a tournament may start off with blinds of $10-$20 but after fifteen minutes they will increase to $20-$40. After another fifteen minutes the blinds might go to $40-$80, and so on.

betting limit In a limit Texas Hold'em game, there are four rounds of betting and each round has a structured, required betting limit. For example, in a $4-$8 game, after the two pocket cards are dealt there is a round of betting. All bets and raises must be in increments of $4. After the flop, there is another round of betting, again at required $4 increments. After the turn, another round of betting takes place, this time in $8 increments. And after the final card is turned up, a final round of betting takes place, again at the required $8 increments.

betting round In limit Texas Hold'em there are four betting rounds, one each after the dealing of the pocket cards, the flop, the turn, and the river.

bicycle Slang term for a 5-high straight in which the Ace is played as the low card. Also called a wheel.

big bet In limit Texas Hold'em, there are two limits of betting, one small and one big. For example, in a $4-$8 game, the $4 betting level would be considered a small bet and the $8 level would be considered a big bet.

big blind In a typical Hold'em game, the big blind (see also large blind) represents the largest mandatory blind required on each hand. The required big blind rotates around the table from player to player. The blind structure can vary from casino to casino. In a $4-$8 game, for example, the big blind would typically be $4, or the amount of a full small bet. Sometimes three blinds are used. In this case, there might be two small blinds of $2 and one big blind of $4. If there are only two blinds being used, then the small blind is the player one seat to the left of the dealer button and the big blind is one seat to the left of the small blind. Blinds are utilized to get the betting action going.

big hand A strong, powerful hand.

big player A player who plays in big-limit games.

big slick The name given to a player's pocket hand when he holds an Ace and a King.

black Meaning clubs or spades. If, for example, there are three hearts on the board with just the river yet to be dealt, and a player holds a hand (such as three of a kind) that he believes will beat anything currently out there but will lose if a fourth Heart comes up (thereby probably giving an opponent a flush) you might hear the player say, "Bring black!"

black chip A $100 chip at most casinos.

blank A card that adds no value to a hand. For example, let's say you hold a Queen and a Jack unsuited. The flop comes up King-10-3 of different suits. With no chance of a flush, you're now hoping for either an Ace or a 9 for a straight. If a 4 comes on the turn, that is said to be a blank as it is no help to you at all. Also called an air ball.

blind Either as a small, middle, or big blind, this is money that is required to be put into the pot before the cards are dealt and which becomes part of a player's bet should he decide to stay in the hand. If the player decides he doesn't like his hand, he may forfeit his blind. In Texas Hold'em, blinds are mandatory, the amount of which can vary from casino to casino, and will vary from level to level.

blind bet A bet made without looking at one's cards.

blind game A game which utilizes blinds (like Texas Hold'em).

blind off In a tournament, when a player either hasn't shown up yet or is gone from the table when it's his turn to post a blind, his chips are placed into the pot by the dealer to cover his blind(s). If the player never shows up, his chips will ultimately be blinded off.

blind raise A raise in which the player to the left of the big blind raises before receiving any cards.

bluff To make a bet with a weak hand hoping the remaining players in the hand will fold their hands. Sometimes a good player will bluff on a hand actually hoping he's called in order to show his hand as advertising, thereby setting up the other players at the table for a later hand in which he won't be bluffing.

board 1) In Hold'em, the board represents the community cards turned up on the table. The board consists of five cards: the flop, the turn, and the river. 2) The sign-up board used by the poker room to make a list of waiting players who either want to play or active players who want to change tables or seats. Most poker rooms have an actual blackboard or large dry erase board on which to make their lists. The board will also usually list the games currently being played and their limits as well as jackpot amounts.

board man The person employed by the casino to operate the board and who will call out the waiting players' names when they have a seat in a game.

boat Slang term for a full house. See also full boat.

bone Slang term for a $1 chip.

book The mystical set of rules that supposedly apply to the proper play of poker. While there may be certain obvious smart plays in Hold'em, there is no actual "book" that is all encompassing.

boost To raise. A player might say, "Boost it up."

bottom pair A pair that is represented by one of your pocket cards and the lowest card of the flop. For example, if you have a K-6 in your pocket and the flop comes up A-J-6, you have flopped bottom pair.

bounty A premium paid in some tournaments for busting another player out of the tournament.

bounty tournament A tournament in which bounties are utilized.

box 1) The house dealer's location at the table. 2) The actual chip rack that the dealer operates out of while at the table. If the dealer is actually dealing, he is said to be in the box.

boxed card A card turned the wrong way in a deck. Upon discovery, this will usually lead to a reshuffle.

break 1) To win all of another player's chips, either forcing him out of the game or to buy more chips. 2) To break down a stack of chips into commonly used increments for ease of counting.

break even To end a session not having won or lost any money.

bring it Oftentimes said by a player who is hoping the dealer brings the one card he needs, especially on the river.

bully Said of a player who is running over the game by betting aggressively whether or not he has the best cards. Sometimes said affectionately among friends at the table.

bump it Slang term for a raise. A player might be heard to say, "Bump it up."

buried A term for losing heavily. A player might say, "I'm buried three hundred."

burn To take the top card of the deck out of play, usually by placing it face down on the table in the burn pile. In Hold'em, a card is burned before each round of cards are dealt.

bust 1) To break a player out of a game. 2) To go broke yourself in a game. 3) To draw to a hand and miss. 4) A worthless hand.

busted flush To miss on a flush draw.

busted straight To miss on a straight draw.

bust out To lose all one's chips and be forced out of the game or tournament.

button 1) The actual dealer button used in a house dealt game that is placed in front of the player who is in the acting dealer position. It is usually a large white plastic disc with the word "DEALER" stamped in black on both sides. 2) The player represented by the button. A player might ask, "Who's the button?" or "Where's the button?"

buy 1) To purchase chips. 2) To bluff and win a pot simply by betting. Another player might ask, "Did you buy that pot?"

buy-in 1) The minimum amount required to get into a game. In many casinos, the minimum buy-in is ten times the small blind. For example, if you are looking to join a $3-$6 game, the minimum buy-in would usually be $30. 2) The cost of entering a tournament.

cage The cashier's area, usually behind glass or bars in which the cage person will buy and sell casino chips. At the end of a playing session, this is usually where you will take your chips to cash them in before leaving the casino.

call To match a bet made before you. You would say "call," or, "I call."

called hand A hand that someone bet and someone else called.

caller Someone who calls another player's bet or raise.

calling hand A hand with which a player feels he must call under almost any circumstances, even if he feels his opponent has already made his hand.

calling station A term used to describe a player who rarely raises but seems to call every bet, even with weak hands. Such a player should never be bluffed.

can't beat the board Said of a hand that can't beat the five community cards on the board. Thus, the player is playing the hand on the board.

cap To put in the maximum number of bets allowed in a round. Usually said, "Cap it."

capped A dealer might say, "It's been capped," meaning that the maximum number of bets and raises in a round has been reached.

capper The chip or other item used to cover one's cards to protect them from accidentally being mucked, either by the dealer accidentally scooping them up or when another player's discarded cards touch an unprotected hand.

cappuccino A slang term used by some dealers to indicate that the betting has been capped.

card down What is announced by the dealer to attract the attention of the floor person to apprise him that a card has fallen to the floor. Usually the dealer or other players are not allowed to pick up the card. Whether or not the card that fell to the floor is still in play is subject to the individual card room's policies.

card room sometimes **cardroom** 1) The section of a casino where poker is played. 2) An establishment where poker is played. 3) The room inside a club where poker is played.

card sense An acute awareness of what is going on in the entire game, not just one's own hand, and the ability to adapt one's play to the ever-changing game situation.

card shark An expert or professional card player. Not to be misconstrued as a card cheater.

card sharp A card cheater.

cards speak The rule that says that no matter what a player may say about his hand, the cards themselves speak for what the hand actually is.

cash in To leave the game and cash in one's chips with the cashier.

cash out See cash in.

casino An establishment, usually larger and more opulent, devoted to gambling games of all kinds.

casino cage The cashier's cage where players go to buy and sell casino chips and conduct all matters financial.

catch To receive a card, usually in the context of making a good hand. "Nice catch," you might hear an opponent say.

center pot Another term for main pot.

chance Odds, as in, "You had a one in four chance of making that hand."

change list A list kept by the floor person, usually on the board, of which players have requested seat or table changes.

chase To bet recklessly, usually when losing, in order to get even. One is said to be chasing cards when undertaking this poor strategy.

cheat To play dishonestly. If caught cheating in a licensed poker establishment you will be barred from playing there again and might even face criminal charges. If caught cheating in a private game you might be physically assaulted.

check 1) To make no bet but still retain your cards. If someone bets after you, you will then either have to fold your hand, call the bet, or raise the bet if the betting limits permit. 2) The technical term for a casino chip.

check blind To check your hand before receiving or looking at your cards. Also called check in the blind.

check in the dark Another term for check blind.

check rack A rack that holds one hundred casino checks or chips. A rack of one hundred $1 checks, which are usually white chips, is called a rack of white. A rack of one hundred $5 checks, which are usually red, is called a rack of red.

check-raise To check, usually with a good hand, and then, when someone bets and it gets back to you, to raise.

chips The common term for casino checks.

chip rack Another term for check rack.

chop the blinds When, after all the other players have folded before them, the two blinds each take their blind bets back. They are said to be chopping it up.

chop the pot When two (usually) players split a pot equally.

cinch An unbeatable hand. Also called a cinch hand.

cinch player A player who only plays the nuts.

circle A pot boundary. In some casinos there is an actual line drawn around the table. If a player's bet crosses that line it is committed to the pot. In casinos without an actual line, the dealer can determine if a bet is actually committed or not, depending on where the player places his bet or potential bet.

clear the rail A request by either a player or the dealer for all uninvolved persons hanging around a poker table to step back to a designated distance away from the table.

clip joint A casino that either uses crooked dealers or works in confederation with crooked gamblers to fleece unsuspecting players.

close Also called close to the vest. A conservative player, as in, "He plays it close."

Club flush A hand with five cards, all clubs.

clubs One of the four suits of cards, the symbol of which is the shamrock: ♣ clubs are black in the traditional deck, green in the four-color deck. A single card in the clubs suit is called a Club.

cold No good cards coming out. If a particular player isn't catching any good cards, he is said to be cold. If no one seems to be catching any good cards, the deck is said to be cold.

cold call To call a bet and one or more raises without yet having any money in the pot.

color change To exchange checks of one color for checks of another color. Typically this occurs when a player is leaving the table and exchanges a lot of lesser value chips for a fewer number of higher value chips.

color up See color change.

come This means to bet and stay in a hand with the hope and/or expectation of getting the card you want in order to win the hand. A common example in Hold'em is when you hold two cards of one suit in your pocket and flop two more of the same suit. You then either bet or call on the come the next two rounds with the expectation that the fifth card of your suit is going to come.

come back at To reraise.

come in on the blind To sit down and join a game at the exact moment it is your turn to put in the big blind.

come over the top To raise a raise.

community card One of the five board cards that all players can make use of with their two pocket cards in the making of their best five-card hand.

community pot See family pot.

complete the bet When a player goes all in with less than the amount of the required bet, the next player can complete the bet by bringing it up to the limit. In a $4-$8 game, for example, if on the last round one player goes all in with his last $3, another player may complete the bet by putting the whole $8 in the pot. Under standard poker rules, a player may only complete the bet if the all-in player bets less than half of the specific bet. If the all-in player bets more than half a bet, the next player must either call that amount or raise a full bet.

concealed hand A hand that, because of the way it was played, was concealed from being a good hand. This happens sometimes when three or more players are involved in a hand and two of them are actively raising each other. The player with the concealed good hand just keeps calling, letting the other two players do the work of building a pot he is likely to win. For example, if a player holds 8-8 in the pocket and the flop comes up A-K-8, he now holds a set of 8s, likely the best hand. Then, if the turn and river come up something like 5-5, he now has a full house, 8s over 5s, and can only be beaten by pocket Aces, pocket Kings, or pocket 5s, none of which are impossible, but none of which are statistically likely.

connectors Usually refers to two unsuited pocket cards in sequence, such as 9-10.

conservative player Description of a tight player who doesn't bet unless he has a good hand, and usually the best hand.

corner seat Either of two seats next to the house dealer in a house-dealt game. Also called Seat 1 (the first seat to the dealer's left) and Seat 10 (the seat to the dealer's immediate right).

count down The act of the dealer counting down a player's chips to arrive at his total so that another player, contemplating a call, can make the decision to call or not. Usually associated with a no-limit game.

cowboy Slang term for a King.

crank it up To start a poker game in a card room.

crimp A bend in a card. Sometimes it's accidental, but sometimes it's done intentionally by a card cheat in order for him to spot it from a distance when it's dealt out. This is one reason card decks are replaced quite often in casinos.

cut Also called cutting the deck. To separate the deck into two packets after they've been shuffled and place the former bottom packet on top before dealing the cards.

dark Without looking at your cards. To bet in the dark is to bet without looking at your cards. To call in the dark is to call without looking, and to raise in the dark is to raise without looking at your cards.

dead card Any card not in play or a card which, according to rules of play, cannot be played in a hand, such as a card which falls to the floor.

dead game Term used to describe a game without much action.

dead hand A reference to a hand which, for a variety of reasons, might be declared legally unplayable, such as when it is touched by another player's discarded hand.

dead man's hand Two pair, Aces and 8s. So called because this was the hand Wild Bill Hickok was alleged to have been holding when he was shot in the back by Jack McCall in a Deadwood, South Dakota, saloon in 1876.

dead money 1) Money put into a pot by a player or players who subsequently fold their hands and therefore cannot win. 2) A term used to designate players of lesser ability who are unlikely to win in a game or tournament.

deal To distribute the cards to the players.

dealer The person who physically deals the cards to the players.

dealer button The large round plastic disc that is placed in front of the player who is designated as the acting dealer.

deal in To be included in a specific hand. A player might tell a dealer to "deal me in," as he gets out of his chair to get a cup of coffee or perform some other quick errand. He wants to let the dealer know that he'll be back in his seat before it's his turn to act. Also, a dealer may ask a player if he wants to be dealt in after missing his blinds, in which case the player would have to post the blind(s) he missed while gone from the table.

deal out To skip a player during the deal, usually because he's gone from the table or has announced he's leaving the table for a short while.

decision The resolution of a dispute, usually by the poker room's floor person.

deck The complete pack of fifty-two cards used in a Texas Hold'em poker game. The Jokers are not used.

deck change Changing the deck in the game. Sometimes a dealer will ask the floor person to change the deck due to damage to one or more cards in the deck. It is also not unusual to hear a player ask for a deck change, either because he's noticed something physically wrong with some of the cards or he's just having a bad run of luck and feels a new deck will change his luck for the better.

declaration The verbal announcement at showdown of one's hand. For example, a player might say, "I have a King-high flush."

declare To make a declaration.

deep stack A stack of chips a player starts off with in a tournament that is larger than normal. For example, most tournaments, both Internet and live, start a player off with anywhere from one to two thousand chips. In a deep stack tournament, a player will start off with anywhere from five to ten thousand chips.

denomination A card's rank, such as Jack or 7.

deuce The 2 card.

deuces full A full house consisting of three 2s and another pair.

dewey Another name for the 2 card.

Diamond flush A hand with five cards, all diamonds.

diamonds One of the four suits of cards, the symbol of which is shaped like the rhombus: ♦ diamonds are red in the traditional deck, blue in the four-color deck. A single card in the diamonds suit is called a Diamond.

dimestore A term used to describe a pocket hand of 5-10 (five and dime).

discard To throw one's hand away.

discard pile The place on the table where the dealer puts all of the cards that have thrown away, or discarded, by the players.

discards All of the thrown-away cards, which are sometimes combined with the undealt cards at the end of a deal.

Dolly Parton A term used to describe a pocket hand of 9-5, so called after the movie *9 to 5*.

donate To throw one's chips into the pot not really expecting to win. The player might say, "Okay, I'll donate," or "Here's my donation."

double gutter or **double gut shot** A hand with two holes in it that if either are filled will give the holder a straight. For example, a hand of 7-9-10-J-K has two holes in it, the 8 and the Queen. If the player catches either of these two cards he makes a straight.

double bluff A bluff that is performed by betting, being raised, and by reraising.

double up Said of a player who goes all in during a tournament and wins an equal amount from an opponent who calls his bet. He is said to have doubled up his chip stack.

down Behind, or losing. A player might say, "I'm down two hundred."

down to the felt An all-in bet or busted out of a game.

Doyle Brunson A term for a pocket hand of 10-2. So called because professional poker player Doyle Brunson twice won the World Series of Poker (1975 and 1976) with those two hole cards.

drag 1) To remove the house cut from a pot before the dealer pushes the pot to the winner. 2) The act of a player scooping in a winning pot.

draw In Hold'em, a hand that is not yet complete, such as a straight or flush draw, but if made complete on the turn or the river will likely beat one's opponent(s).

draw dead Drawing to a hand that cannot win even if made and not usually recognized as such by the player hoping to hit the draw. For example, if you hold A-J and the flop comes up 6-5-5, you're hoping to draw another Diamond on the turn or river for a flush. But if another player holds a pair of 6s, a pair of 5s, or a 6-5, you're drawing dead because he already has either a full house or four of a kind, either of which will beat your Ace-high flush.

draw for the button When the dealer, at the start of a game, deals one card, face up, to each player. The high card gets the dealer button to start the game.

drawing hand In Hold'em, with four cards to a flush or straight with one or two cards yet to be dealt, you are said to have a drawing hand.

draw out To beat an opponent by drawing a winning card on the turn or river. A player might say, "I had him beat on the flop but he drew out on me."

draw to To have a hand that you are hoping to make on the turn or river. If, for example, you have two diamonds in the pocket and catch two more on the flop, you are drawing to a flush.

drink pot An agreement between two or more players that whichever of them wins the next pot will buy a round of drinks for all involved in the agreement.

drop The amount taken from each pot by the dealer and (usually) physically dropped into a box located underneath a slot on the poker table next to the dealer's chip tray. The drop amount funds the house's expenses for running the game. Anything left over is the house's profit.

drop box A box which is usually connected to the underside of a poker table and slides in place into which the dealer will drop the house rake from a pot or the collections from the players who pay by time.

drum A term used to describe a tight player, as in, "He plays tighter than a drum."

duck Another name for the 2 card.

dust The term used to describe the action a dealer takes when he either claps his hands together or rubs his palms together before turning his palms upward so the security cameras can see his hands are empty and that he is not stealing chips.

early position Usually considered to be the first three positions to act in a Hold'em game.

easy money 1) An inexperienced or poor player 2) money won from such a player.

edge The advantage that one player has over another in a poker game.

eights full A full house with three 8s and another pair. Also called eights over or eights up

eighty-sixed To be barred from an establishment, as in, "He's been eighty-sixed."

end bet A final round of betting in some Hold'em games in which a higher amount (usually double the big bet) is allowed to be bet and raised.

even To be even, as in not winning or losing. A player might say, "I'm even for the night," or "If I win this pot I'll be even for the night."

expectation 1) In the long run, the average expected profit or loss from a particular bet 2) the average expected win rate of a particular hand 3) the average number of times you expect to hit the hand you're drawing for.

exposed card Any card which is turned face up on the table, either intentionally such as when the board cards are dealt, or unintentionally as when a player discards his hand and accidentally or purposely flips his cards up.

face The front side of a card which depicts the rank and suit of the card.

face card Any King, Queen, or Jack. Also called picture cards or painted cards.

family pot A pot in which all players at the table are participating. Also called a community pot.

fan To spread the cards out on the table face up, usually to inspect that all cards are present in a new deck being used for the first time.

fast game A game that either moves along quickly or one with a lot of betting and raising.

fatten the pot To put more chips in the pot. Also called sweeten the pot.

favorite The hand or player that has the best chance of winning.

feed the pot Putting money in the pot, especially when done foolishly. Also called feeding the kitty.

feeler bet A small bet made to see if anyone else will call or raise. A bet made to gain information.

felt The cloth surface that covers a poker table.

fifth street The fifth and final board card in Hold'em.

filled up 1) To make a full house 2) To make a specified hand. A player might say, "I filled up my flush."

final table In a tournament consisting of multiple tables, as players are eliminated the remaining players are combined on lesser and lesser tables until only one table of players remains. This is called the final table. In most tournaments of size, anyone making the final table can usually expect to place in the prize money.

first Ace At the start of a new game, the dealer will deal all players one card to see who starts with the dealer button. If two players each draw an Ace, the first Ace wins.

fish A term used to describe a loose or poor player who usually loses.

fives full A full house consisting of three 5s and another pair. Also called fives over and fives up.

fixed limit In Hold'em, the betting increments are fixed limit, meaning the players have no option on how much they wager. The bet and raise limits are fixed.

flash To inadvertently expose one of your hole cards.

flat call To just call another player's bet when you could (and maybe should) have raised because you have a good hand. Also called a smooth call.

floor 1) The proximate area of the poker tables. 2) The floor person in charge of the dealers, players, and tables on a given shift. If a dealer has a question, or if a dispute between two players arises, the dealer might say, "Floor!" meaning she wants the floorperson to come to her table. Also called floorman and floor person.

flop In Hold'em, the first three community cards turned face up on the table by the dealer. The flop comes immediately after the betting is completed after the pocket cards are dealt. After the three-card flop, another round of betting takes place before the dealer brings a fourth up card. If, for example, you hold two 7s in your pocket and the three-card flop brings another 7, you are said to have "flopped a set of 7s."

flush Five cards of the same suit but not in consecutive sequential order. A flush outranks a straight and is just below a full house. A flush is typically called by its highest card, such as "Queen-high flush."

fold To throw one's cards away and no longer be involved in a hand.

fold out of turn The act of folding before it's one's turn to do so. Not only is this practice against the rules, it is heavily frowned up in poker rooms because it could affect the play of others at the table.

forced blind A mandatory blind that is required to be put into the pot, on a rotating basis, before the cards are dealt to stimulate the betting in a hand.

forced-move game Also called a must-move game. When a casino or card room has more than one table playing the same limit game, there is usually one table that is considered the main game. The other tables are known as feeder tables, in which players can be forced to move to the main game when a seat comes open in order to keep the main game full. This is different from a balanced game in which an equal number of players are kept at each table and players are not allowed to move to another table unless someone at another table volunteers to switch with them.

four-card flush To hold four cards to a flush.

four-card straight To hold four consecutively ranked cards of various suits to a straight.

four-color deck As opposed to the traditional deck which uses only red and black for the suits, a four-color deck employs black for spades, red for hearts, blue for diamonds, and green for clubs.

four-flush Four cards to a flush.

four of a kind Also called quads. Four of a kind means four cards of the same rank, such as four Kings or four 6s. Four of a kind ranks above a full house and below a straight flush.

fours full A full house consisting of three 4s and another pair. Also called fours over and fours up.

four spot A 4 card.

fourth street In Hold'em, the fourth community card dealt face up on the table. Also called the turn card. After this card is another round of betting before the fifth and final board card is brought by the dealer.

free card When no one active in a hand bets after the flop or the turn, then the next card is brought by the dealer without costing the players any money, in essence a "free card."

free-roll tournament A Hold'em tournament which costs the player nothing to play, the prize money being put up by the house. Usually players must qualify to play in the tournament by some predetermined house policy, such as number of hours played in the previous week, month, quarter, or year. Oftentimes players with more hours played are awarded more chips at the beginning of the tournament.

freeze-out tournament A tournament in which players cannot re-buy. Once they've lost all their chips, they're out. Prizes are awarded based on the order of elimination.

front Having a position at the table that is to another player's left, meaning you act after the other player. You are said to be "in front of the other player."

full bet A bet that is as large as the current limit. For example, in a $4-$8 game, on the river $8 is a full bet. Anything less, such as a player who goes all in for his remaining $3, is not a full bet. Card rooms vary on their rules as to whether or not a partial bet can be raised or not.

full boat Another term for full house.

full buy A buy-in equal to or greater than the minimum amount required to join a game.

full house A poker hand consisting of three cards of one rank and two cards of another rank, such as three Queens and two 10s. This would be called a full house, Queens over 10s, or maybe Queens full of 10s. A full house ranks just above a flush and just below four of a kind.

full table A poker table in which every available seat is occupied. A full table consists of either nine, ten, or eleven players, depending on the card room.

gamble To play loosely or even recklessly. Among poker players, this is a specific term applied to the play of a loose player, or one who is not playing by "the book." It does not have the same meaning as the traditional understanding of the word.

game The specific kind of poker game being played. For example, when you first arrive at a card room and ask the floor person what games are going on, he might say, "We have both a $3-$6 game and a $10-$20 game going on right now."

gap A missing card in a hand, usually when referring to straight. For example, if you hold a 7-8-9-J, the gap is where the 10 should be.

gapper Also called one-gapper. This refers to one's pocket hand when the cards are separated by just one rank in the middle, such as 6-4, or K-J.

garbage 1) The discard pile. 2) A poor hand.

get a hand cracked To have one's hand beaten, usually late in the hand and usually when one's opponent was drawing against the odds.

get out To fold a hand.

get well To win a big pot that puts you even or ahead.

give away A poker tell; to reveal your hand by some manner or obvious play.

go all in See all in.

good hand A legitimate, playable hand.

good game A game in which you expect to win a lot of money, usually because you're better than all the players in the game.

green chip A $25 casino check.

grift To cheat.

grifter A cheater or swindler.

grinder A player who grinds out his wins (or a living) at poker by only playing when getting the correct odds on his hands, or when it is at his advantage to do so.

grind out To win at poker gradually, but consistently. Sometimes said disparagingly of a conservative, winning player who never wins big but also rarely plays risky hands.

gut shot The card that fills an inside straight draw. For example, if you hold a 10-9-8-6 of mixed suits, and draw a 7 on the turn or river, you have made a gut shot straight.

half kill A game in which the betting limits increase 50 percent when one player wins two or more consecutive pots. For example, if a player wins two pots in a row in a $4-$8 game, the betting increases to $6-$12 until that player fails to win a pot, at which point the betting returns to $4-$8. The dealer will place a kill or half kill button in front of the player responsible for the half-kill situation until he fails to win a pot at which point the dealer will return the button to his tray. In a half-kill $4-$8 game, the player winning the half-kill button must place a $6 bet into the pot, so he is automatically in the hand unless another player raises to $12. The player on the kill button may then either call or fold, in which case he forfeits his $6 half-kill bet.

hand One deal around the table in which all players involved are dealt two pocket cards which, when used in combination with the five community cards to form one's best five cards, comprise a player's hand.

heads up A situation when only two players are left competing for a pot. They are said to be going heads up.

hearts One of the four suits of cards, the symbol of which is shaped like a heart: ♥ One of the four suits of cards, the symbol of which is shaped like a heart: ♥ hearts are red in both the traditional deck and the four-color deck. A single card in the hearts suit is called a Heart.

heater Hot streak.

help To improve one's hand. A player awaiting the turn or river cards might be heard to say, "I need some help."

high card The card that determines the winner at the showdown between two hands with no pairs or better, or when two flushes or straights are being compared. In these situations, the hand with the higher card wins the pot. If the two hands are exactly tied, then the pot is split.

hit To make a hand by receiving a card you need.

Hold'em Officially known as Texas Hold'em. A form of poker that originated in the American Southwest, spread to the Nevada casinos, and eventually became the nearly universal form of poker played around the world. Two cards are dealt face down to each player at the table and five community cards are dealt face up in the middle of the table. Each player's hand is represented by the best possible five cards of the seven. There are four rounds of betting, the first after the two down cards are dealt, the second after the simultaneous three-card flop, the third after the fourth up card, and the last after the fifth up card. After all betting is complete, players still active in the hand turn their two down cards over and the dealer declares a winner.

holding The cards in your hand. A player might ask, "What are you holding?"

hole Also called hole cards. The term used to describe the two down cards each player is dealt at the beginning of the hand. Also called the pocket. You

might hear a dealer say, "You didn't qualify for the jackpot because both hole cards didn't play."

honest or **keep you honest**. The act of calling another player's bet even though you feel you are beat just so you can see their hand to see if they are bluffing or not. The calling player might say, "Okay, I'll call. Someone's got to keep you honest."

hot Catching good cards; winning a lot of pots.

house 1) Another term for an establishment such as a casino or card room. 2) A shorter term for a full house.

house cut The portion of each pot that a dealer removes and places into the drop box before paying the winner of the pot. The house cut pays for the establishment's expenses and provides its profit. See also rake.

house rules Rules that are specific to a particular establishment. Usually the establishment's complete list of house rules is posted for public viewing somewhere in the establishment.

hustler Someone who makes his living playing cards. He might do so ethically or unfairly.

idiot end of a straight The low end of a straight which can or does lose to a higher straight. For example, if your two pocket cards are 7-8 and the flop is a 9-10-J, you have the idiot end of the straight because anyone holding 8-Q or Q-K has you beat. And even if they only hold the Queen, if a King comes up on the turn or river they'll make their straight and beat you. You have to proceed very cautiously when holding the low end of a straight. Also called the ignorant end.

implied odds The calculated ratio of what you should win on a particular hand to what the current bet is costing you. This also includes what money is likely to be bet in subsequent rounds.

improve To make one's hand better, especially by catching the one particular card you are hoping for.

in for The amount of action a player in a hand is entitled to. This usually comes into play when side pots are involved. A player who went all in for less than other players is only in for that portion of the pot, usually the main pot. He is not in for the side pots because he has no monetary stake in them.

inside straight Four cards to a straight with one hole in it, such as a 9-10-J-K of various suits. This will become a straight upon catching a Queen and filling the hole. Also called a gut shot straight.

in the air The term used to describe the dealing of the cards. At the start of a tournament, you might hear the floor person say, "Okay, dealers, let's put them in the air."

in the blind Being in one of the two or three blind positions of a hand.

in the dark Betting, calling, or raising without seeing one's cards. You might hear a player say, "I'm raising in the dark."

in the money Having lasted long enough in a tournament to receive some of the prize money.

in turn The act of playing in order, when it is one's turn to do so.

isolate To bet in such a way, usually aggressively, in order to drive opponents out of a pot so as to isolate yourself against one particular player, usually a poor player, thereby increasing your odds of winning.

Jack The face card that ranks just above the 10 and below the Queen.

jack it up To raise. You might hear a player say, when raising, "Okay, let's jack it up."

jackpot Any of a variety of extra cash prizes awarded by the establishment to a player who attains, usually, a specified high hand. Jackpots vary from house to house so it's always best, when playing in a new establishment, to ascertain what the jackpot hands are so you don't accidentally discard a jackpot winner without collecting the prize. Some common types of jackpots are the bad beat, Monte Carlo style, high hands for the day, etc. The jackpots are usually player funded by a dollar taken out of each pot and dropped into a slot in the table into a second drop box (besides the house rake drop box). The establishment is responsible for keeping this jackpot money on account so that it can be paid out any time it's won by a player.

Jacks full A full house consisting of three Jacks and another pair. Also called Jacks over and Jacks up.

Joker The fifty-third and fifty-fourth cards in the deck which are not used in Hold'em.

keep someone honest To call them even though you believe you're going to lose just to see if they were bluffing on their bet or not.

kicker The highest unpaired card in your hand. Many times the kicker will determine who wins the hand. For example, if you have A-J in the pocket and your sole opponent at the showdown has A-10, and the community cards are A-K-8-4-2 and neither of you made a flush, then you will win. You both have a pair of Aces with a King, but you have a Jack-8 and your opponent has a 10-8 for your last two cards. Your Jack is better than his 10, thus, your kicker was better than his. This is also called having your opponent outkicked.

kicker trouble Getting into a hand with a low second card, such as when you play an Ace-4. Since most low limit Hold'em players will play Ace-Anything, if you play an Ace-4 you're likely to lose since more kicker cards will beat your 4 than your 4 will beat (only a 3 or 2). A player who gets himself into such a position might be heard to say, "I've got kicker trouble," once the community cards come out and they're all higher than his kicker.

kill The act of deliberately making a hand dead by the dealer so that there will be no argument as to whether or not the hand was live. For example, if Player A bets on the river and Player B calls, Player A will then toss his hand away because he knows he was bluffing and cannot beat Player B. Player C, who was not in the hand but has the right in most card rooms to request to see any called hand, then requests to see Player A's cards. The dealer will then take Player A's cards, tap them against the discard pile (thus killing the hand), and turn them over for everyone to see.

kill pot Betting limits which are double the normal limits. In some card rooms, when a player wins two consecutive hands the pot becomes a kill pot. In a $4-$8 game, for example, after a player wins two pots in a row the dealer will place a kill button in front of that player and the betting limits now become $8-$16 until that player fails to win a pot. The player must place an $8 bet into the pot. This does not remove

the obligation of the players in the blinds to post their normal $2-$4 blinds. The purpose of the kill pot is to stimulate higher betting activity. See also half kill.

King The face card that ranks just above the Queen and just below the Ace.

Kings full A full house consisting of three Kings and another pair. Also called Kings over and Kings up.

kitty Another name for the pot.

lady Another name for the Queen.

large blind Another name for the big blind.

last position The last position to act in a particular round. This is a very powerful position in Hold'em because it allows you to gain information by seeing what everyone else does before you.

last to act The player who acts last in a particular round. This is, generally speaking, the best position to be in.

late position In Hold'em, when the table is full, late position is generally considered to be one of the last three positions to act at the table.

laydown To fold one's hand. This term is often used as a compliment as in, "Good laydown," because it implies that the person who folded probably folded a good hand that most players would have called with but realized he was beaten by a better, unseen hand.

lie To bluff. Lying is an integral part of poker, whether subtle or blatant.

limit The amount of the betting increments in Hold'em. In a $4-$8 game, the increments, or limits, are $4 the first two betting rounds and $8 the last two betting rounds.

limit game What the vast majority of casino Hold'em games are. Whether a game is $3-$6, $4-$8, $10-$20, or $100-$200, it is still structured by betting limits. The rest, such as most of the games you see on television, are no-limit games.

limp in 1) To get into a pot cheaply because no one raised. 2) To call reluctantly, usually with a mediocre or poor hand and because no one raised the bet which would have forced you to fold a hand that was less than desirable.

line Sometimes actual, sometimes imaginary, this is a pot boundary that determines whether or not a player's bet is committed to the pot. In casinos without an actual line, the dealer uses his or her own judgment as to whether or not a bet is actually committed, depending on where the player places his bet or potential bet.

little blind Also called the small blind, this half (or other less-than-full) bet is placed as a bet by the first player to the dealer's left at the beginning of each hand. The little blind (and all blinds) rotate after each hand so that all players are in the blinds an equal share of the time.

live A live, actual game in which real actual dollar-valued chips are being bet as opposed to a tournament. Also called a ring game. When you go to a casino or card room, you will be playing in a live game.

live hand A hand that is still eligible to win the pot.

long shot A hand that has little chance of winning.

look To call a bet.

loose game A game filled with loose players.

loose-passive game A game with lots of action but little raising.

loose player A player who plays almost any hand that has even a prayer of winning. The opposite of a tight player.

loser A losing player.

Low-limit game A poker game played for small amounts of money. The lower stakes Hold'em games you'll find in casinos and card rooms will be along the lines of $1-$2, $2-$4, $3-$6, and $4-$8.

luck A pure illusion that bad players think is responsible for their losing and which good players realize will only determine the outcome of their play in the short run.

made hand A complete hand, such as a straight, flush, or full house.

main game In a casino with more than one poker table of the same limit, the main game is the one the house keeps filled up as long as possible, even feeding it players from the other tables when seats come open.

main pot The pot that all players have a stake in when a side pot has become necessary due to a player or players going all in for less than full bets.

make To catch the specific card you need to complete your hand. For example, a player holding four spades would need to catch another Spade in order to make his flush.

make up the blind To post whatever blind money is necessary after having missed a hand that included one of your blinds.

marked cards Cards that have been marked or altered in some way by a cheater in order to tell their rank when held by other players.

marker An IOU, usually held by the casino, which represents money owed by a player and against which the player plays.

mechanic A card sharp, usually a dealer, who cheats by manipulating the cards.

middle Another name for the main pot when there is a side pot involved in a hand.

middle blind The second blind in a three-blind game, coming after the small blind and before the big blind.

middle pair When a player has paired one of his two pocket cards with the second highest card on the board. For example, if you have 9-8 in your pocket and the flop comes up K-8-3, you are said to have flopped middle pair.

middle position In a nine-handed Hold'em game, middle position is generally considered the fourth, fifth, and sixth seats to act in a hand. If it's a ten-handed game, then the seventh player to act is also in middle position.

misdeal Any of a number of situations that arise causing the dealer to redeal the cards before any action has been taken. Many times this happens when a dealer notices he has accidentally skipped a player, or has given a player three cards, or notices that he began dealing without one of the players having returned his cards from the previous hand, etc.

miss To not draw a needed card.

missed blind To be absent from the table when it was your blind, such as during a bathroom or meal break.

miss the flop A situation said to occur when the three-card flop completely fails to improve your hand.

money plays An announcement, usually by the dealer, that a player's cash money on the table will cover any bets he makes until the floor person brings the player chips equal to the cash money so that he can participate in the game. This situation may occur when a new player first sits down at a table or when a player already in the game busts out and requests more chips.

monster Also called monster hand. A very high hand.

motion The act of betting. Some establishments have a house rule that states that if you make a motion toward the pot with chips in your hand like you are betting, it constitutes the intention of betting and will be binding.

move all in To go all in with your remaining chips.

muck 1) The discards or discard pile. 2) To fold one's hand. You might hear a player ask about another player, "Is he still in the hand?" to which the dealer might reply, "No, he mucked his hand," or, "No, he tossed them in the muck."

multiway pot A pot involving more than two players.

must-move game A Hold'em game that requires players to move to a different game in order that the house can keep as many tables full as possible.

nice hand A frequent comment, usually meant as a compliment but occasionally sarcastically, heard at the table, most of the time directed by the loser of a hand to the winner of the hand.

nines full A full house consisting of three 9s and another pair. Also called nines over and nines up.

no-limit The other form of Hold'em poker besides limit poker. In no limit Hold'em, a player may bet any or all of his chips at any time, unlike limit Hold'em in which a player may only bet according to the structured limits.

nuts Also called the nuts, and, if a flush or straight is involved, nut flush or nut straight. The nuts is the highest possible hand, at any point in the hand, given the community cards displayed. It is unbeatable. For example, if you have two Aces before the flop, then you have the nuts since no hand (at that point, anyway) can beat two Aces. If the flop then comes K-J-4 of mixed suits, then any player holding two Kings would have the nuts since the best possible hand at that point would be three of a kind. As another example, if the five community cards displayed were A-Q-J-8-3 of mixed suits (meaning no flush possible), then a player holding K-10 would have the nuts because an Ace-high straight would be the best possible hand.

odds The probability of something occurring or not occurring, as in the catching of a needed card, usually expressed in numerical form, one number to another, such as 4-to-1.

offsuit A term used to describe your two pocket cards when they are of different suits. Also called unsuited.

on Describes whose turn it is. Example, if the dealer says, "Dennis, it's on you," that means it is Dennis's turn to act.

on a heater On a hot streak.

on a rush In the middle of a hot streak.

one-card draw A hand that needs one card to become complete, such as a straight or flush.

one-gapper Also called gapper. This refers to one's pocket hand when the cards are separated by just one rank in the middle, such as 6-4, or K-J.

one pair A poker hand that contains only one pair.

on the board 1) The face-up community cards in Hold'em. 2) To have your name listed on the poker room's board as wanting a seat in a particular game. It is common for players to be listed as wanting to play in more than one game, such as $3-$6 and $4-$8, and then take a seat in whichever game opens up first.

on the button The player who has the dealer button in front of him. This is a powerful position because it allows the player to be the last to act in the last three betting rounds of a Hold'em hand.

on the come The act of betting on a hand that isn't yet made, as when a player bets when he has only four cards to a flush or straight after the flop with the expectation (hope!) of making the straight or flush. Such a player is said to be betting on the come, or what is yet to come.

on the end To catch a needed card on the river.

on the side In reference to a bet that goes into the side pot as opposed to the main pot because an opponent still in the hand doesn't have enough money to match the bet.

on tilt Description of a player who starts to play recklessly and more poorly than usual because he's become upset. This typically occurs when a player has lost a number of hands in a row, usually due more to bad luck than to his own bad play.

open-ended straight Holding four consecutive cards to a straight, such as 9-10-J-Q. Hitting either an 8 or a King will give you a straight. Also said to be a straight that is open on both ends. Also called an open-ender.

open seat A vacant seat at a poker table.

option 1) The opportunity of the player in the big blind to raise the bet if no other player has raised before the action gets back to him. 2) In a kill game, the opportunity of the person who killed the pot to raise the bet if no one else raised before him. He has this option to raise even if he is the first to act.

oral declaration When a player verbally announces his intention on his turn before actually placing the chips in the pot. Such a declaration is considered binding.

out 1) Not participating in a hand. 2) Folding a hand. You might hear a player say, "I'm out."

out of turn The act of a player who bets, raises, or folds when it is not his turn to do so. In most establishments acting out of turn is not binding.

outs The total number of cards that could yet come to improve one's hand.

overcall To call a bet after one or more other players have already called the bet.

overcard A card on the board that is higher than either of your pocket cards. If, for example, your pocket consists of a pair of 8s and the board shows K-J-7-5-2, then there are two overcards to your pair, the King and the Jack. Any opponent holding either a King or a Jack has you beaten. This is why it is dangerous to bet or call in an overcard situation.

overpair A pocket pair that is higher than any card on the flop. For example, if you hold a pair of 10s and the flop is 8-7-3, you hold an overpair.

overs button A button placed in front of any player at the table who is willing to play for a higher limit than the regular game. Playing overs is not required. As few as two players at the table may agree to play overs.

over the top A raise, generally when done on top of a previous raise.

paint A face card. Also called painted card.

pair Two cards of the same rank, such as two 6s, or two Kings.

pass Loosely construed, to check.

pat hand A hand that needs no other cards for improvement. Usually made on the first five cards dealt.

pay off To call a final bet in order to see the other player's cards just to make sure he wasn't bluffing, usually with the belief that you're already beaten. A player might say, as he's calling the bet, "Okay, I'll pay you off."

percentage call A call in which a player is the decided underdog in the hand but does so because he is receiving such good money odds for making the call. In other words, the pot is so big in relation to what he's being asked to bet, he's making the smart play in doing so.

player Any participant in the poker game.

play the board A situation in Hold'em when a player's hole cards are not used and the player's best hand is formed from the five community cards. If two players end up playing the board (not an uncommon occurrence), the pot is split.

pocket The first two cards dealt face down to each player in a Hold'em game.

pocket pair Two cards of the same rank dealt to the player's pocket. A pocket pair can be especially powerful when a third card of the same rank comes on the flop for two reasons. First, because it gives the player three of a kind, which is a strong hand. Second, because the hand is well hidden from your opponents because two of the three cards are hidden away, face down.

pocket rockets A slang term for holding two Aces in one's pocket hand.

poker A card game in which players try to make the best five-card hand possible and place bets against other players projecting that they indeed have the best hand possible, try and convince them they have the best hand possible, or attempt to drive them out or bluff them out with wagers in order to win the communal pot.

poker face To maintain a consistent, unchanging facial expression during the game so that opponents are not able to tell whether you've got a good hand or bad hand, hit the card you were after or missed it, or are making a serious bet or are bluffing.

poker hand The five cards that a player ultimately ends up playing when contesting for a pot.

poker table In Hold'em, the poker table is oblong in shape and usually seats nine or ten players plus a dealer.

position Where a player sits in relation to all the other players in the game in the context of where the dealer button is.

position bet A bet made more on the strength on one's position in the betting scheme rather than on the strength of one's hand. For example, if everyone in the hand checked after the flop and after the turn, if the player who is first to act makes a bet after the river card comes even though it doesn't help his hand, he is said to be making a position bet because he thinks everyone else has weak hands as well based on the previous two rounds of checking, and will fold if there's a bet.

post If a player misses his blinds for some reason, he can either wait until the blinds come around to him again and join the game, or, if he wants to join in again immediately after returning to the table, he can post the amount of his missed blinds. In effect, he's just making up for what he missed while he was away from the table.

pot The chips in play on a given hand. The pot is located in the middle of the table in front of the dealer and is formed when the dealer scoops in the bets of all players and places them together in a pile.

Pot A! Sometimes said by a player who wins their first pot of the night.

pot limit Hold'em A form of Hold'em in which the maximum betting limit is always equal to the size of the pot.

pot odds A term you'll hear used by the better players, pot odds is the ratio of the size of the pot compared to the size of the bet a player must call to stay in the hand. For example, if the pot contains $30 and you are asked to make a

$6 call, then the pot odds are 5-to-1. If the odds on making the hand you need to win are 10-to-1, then you are not getting the correct pot odds and you should fold the hand.

pre-flop The situation or the bet before the flop is dealt.

private tournament A tournament in which players must get the permission of the tournament director in order to play. Private tournaments are also hosted by various Internet sites, usually when the tournament director wants to schedule an online tournament for a group of his friends or a group of like-minded players with some sort of rules understanding and/or variation. Also called *restricted tournament.*

protect 1) As in to protect your hand, this means to cover your two pocket cards with a chip or some other object so that the dealer doesn't accidentally scoop them in. Also, to prevent another player's discards from touching your cards which, under Hold'em rules, requires that your hand be declared dead. 2) A strategy of aggressive betting by a player other than you that helps you win the main pot when you're all in because it drives out other bettors not willing to contest the aggressive bettor for the side pot. This other player, then, has protected your hand. 3) A strategy of aggressive betting that drives other players out of a pot because they are unwilling to match higher bets on a drawing hand.

puck Another name for the button.

pump To raise. Also said pump it up.

put Also called put you on it. This is when you make an educated guess as to what another player is holding. You might hear a player say, "I put you on a pair of Kings."

put the clock on A request by a player to the dealer to turn the stopwatch on a notoriously slow player. Once so notified, the slow player has one minute to act. If he fails to do so, his hand is considered to pass, or fold if the situation calls for it.

quads Holding four of a kind.

Qualifier tournaments A tournament in which players usually are playing for the right to play in another tournament, either with a higher entry fee (which is paid for by winning a seat in the qualifier), or with a special prize fund available only to qualifying players. For example, it is possible on some Internet sites to win a seat in the World Series of Poker ($10,000 entry fee) by winning or placing highly in a qualifier tournament that had an entry fee of only $25 or so. Some Internet sites also make use of "step-ladder" qualifiers in which you can start off by buying a seat in a qualifier for a small amount, e.g., $5. If you win your table, then you get an automatic entry, or "ticket," into the next level of the qualifier tournament in which the entry fee is $50. If you win your table again, or place high enough in the overall of that round, you win a ticket to the next level in which the entry fee is $500, and so on.

Queen A face card that ranks just above the Jack and just below the King.

Queen high When you hold no pairs or better and your highest card is a Queen.

Queen-high flush A flush in which the Queen is your highest card in that suit.

Queen-high straight A straight consisting of a Q-J-10-9-8 of mixed suits.

Queens full A full house consisting of three Queens and another pair. Also called Queens over and Queens up.

quorum The minimum number of players required to start a game. This varies from casino to casino, but is generally six.

rabbit hunt To search through the undealt cards after a hand is over to see what you would have drawn had you not folded. Most card rooms frown on such a request by a player and in many it's not allowed. Only poor or beginning players make such a silly request.

race off In a Hold'em tournament when the betting levels have increased to the point where lower denomination chips are no longer used, a race off occurs. In this scenario, all players place their soon-to-be excluded lower denomination chips in front of them. The dealer will break them down and exchange as many as possible for higher denominations. The few remaining chips that do not comprise enough to make for another higher denomination chip are left in front of the player. The dealer will then deal one card to the players for each chip they have in front of them. In most casinos, whichever player gets the highest card wins all the small chips, which are then exchanged for the higher denomination chips which are about to be used in the next betting level.

rack A chip rack, typically that holds five rows of twenty chips each.

rag A poor hand.

rail An actual or imaginary barrier that is used to separate the players from onlookers and those waiting to play.

rainbow The term used to describe a flop which reveals cards of three different suits.

raise 1) To increase the bet to the next permitted level. 2) The amount of the increase.

rake 1) The percentage of the pot that the dealer removes and puts into his drop box. The rake accounts for house expenses, profits, and the jackpots. 2) The act of taking the rake.

rank The denomination of a card. The fourteen ranks, in order, from high to low: Ace (when played as high card), King, Queen, Jack, 10, 9, 8, 7, 6, 5, 4, 3, 2, and Ace (when played as low card).

rap The physical act of rapping ones knuckles (or tapping one's fingers) on the table to indicate your intent to check.

read To come to a conclusion about another player's hand based on his actions, remarks, betting patterns, or other tells.

reach for one's chips To make a move toward one's chips, presumably in preparation for making a bet. This often has the effect of causing other players who had checked previously to fold; they only needed to see you go for your chips before throwing away their hands.

re-buy In Hold'em tournaments where it is allowed, the purchase of chips after going bust or nearly bust.

red Hearts or diamonds. You might hear the player say, "Bring red!"

redeal To deal again, usually because of a misdeal.

release To fold a hand.

represent To bet in such a way as to indicate a particular hand. When you see a raise before the flop, the bettor is usually representing a powerful hand, such as pocket Aces, Kings, or Queens, or maybe an Ace-King suited. Watch his subsequent betting because if an Ace comes on the river and he checks, it might be because he holds something like pocket 10s or 9s, for example, and now a pair of Aces beats him.

reraise To raise a raise.

restricted tournament See *private tournament.*

riffle To shuffle the cards.

ring game Any non-tournament game.

river The fifth and last community card placed face up on the board by the dealer. There is a round of betting after the river card is dealt.

rock An extremely tight player who takes few chances. When he bets, he has something.

roll Winning streak.

round Once around the table in which everyone has had the opportunity to be on the button and in the blinds.

rounder A slang term for a poker player.

royal Short for a royal flush.

royal flush The highest hand in Hold'em. This hand consists of an A-K-Q-J-10 of the same suit. How rare is the hand? Statistically speaking, if you hit a royal flush today, then played poker forty hours a week thereafter, it would be about eleven years until you got your next one, assuming it came exactly at the time statistical probabilities say it should.

runner A flush or straight card that arrives on the turn or river after holding only three cards of that particular hand after the flop.

runner-runner Flush or straight cards that hit on both the turn and the river when you held only three of that particular hand after the flop. It is particularly galling to a player to have a hand seemingly won only to lose to a player who hits runner-runner to beat him, especially if the river card fills a gutshot straight.

run over the game To bet in an aggressive and intimidating manner toward the other players.

rush A winning streak in which a player will win several hands in a row.

sandbag To pass or check a good hand with the intention of raising later. Similar to check-raising.

sandbagger One who sandbags. Sometimes met with disapproval by other players.

satellite tournament A tournament whose prize is oftentimes a paid entry into a larger tournament. In 2003, Chris Moneymaker won his $10,000 seat into the World Series of Poker by winning a satellite tournament for which he'd paid about $40. He eventually won the World Series and its $2.5 million first prize. The 2004 champion, Gary Raymer, who won the $5 million first prize, won his seat by winning a $180 satellite.

scheduled tournament A tournament that takes place at a certain scheduled time, regardless of the number of players, unless one requirement of the tournament is that a certain minimum number of players have to register or the tournament is cancelled. Scheduled tournaments can range from small (one table with ten players) to large (nearly six thousand people played in the 2005 World Series of Poker tournament in Las Vegas). Different from sit 'n' go tournaments in which the tournament begins immediately upon getting the required number of players.

scramble Prior to shuffling the cards, a dealer will turn all the cards upside down on the table and fan them out over a large area. He will then thoroughly mix the cards before collecting them up and shuffling.

seat A chair at a poker table.

seat change Sometimes players will change seats, either because they think the other seat is luckier, their seat is unlucky, the lighting is better, or they just have a favorite seat position at a table. To request a seat change, a player should tell the dealer who should then make sure that the seat change request is written on the board. This eliminates disputes later as to who is entitled to which open seat.

seat position The seat next to the dealer's left is seat #1. Going clockwise from there, the seats are numbered up to 9, 10, or 11, depending on how many chairs the establishment chooses to have.

second pair A pair that consists of one of your hole cards and the second-highest card on the flop. Same as middle pair.

see A called bet.

semi-bluff A bet made on a hand that is likely not the best hand at the table when the bet is made, but which has definite possibilities of improving when subsequent community cards are dealt out. If everyone else folds, then the bet succeeded as a bluff. If it doesn't, it might still improve.

send it A remark said by an ungracious winner at the showdown when he wins the pot.

session A period of playing poker that begins from the time a player first sits down at the table until the time he cashes in his chips and leaves the game.

set Three of a kind. A set is achieved when holding a pocket pair and having another card of the same rank coming on the flop, turn, or river.

set over set One player's set as compared to another player's set.

setup A box containing two decks of cards. Either a dealer or a player might request a new setup. The dealer would request it of the floor person if she felt there was a defective card, for example, and a player sometimes requests it of a dealer if he feels his luck is running badly.

sevens full A full house consisting of three 7s and another pair. Also called sevens up or sevens over.

shill A player who is playing for the house to help get a game started or keep a shaky game going. Actual shills do not keep any of their winnings. They are paid an hourly wage and play with house money.

short buy A buy-in of less than the usual minimum buy-in. Sometimes the house will allow this to keep action going in a shaky game. At other times, when there is a waiting list of players, short buys either will not be allowed or only one short buy will be allowed between full buys.

short handed A game with less than the normal amount of players. Some card rooms will not offer short-handed games. In those that do, some players will not play in short handed Hold'em games because it doesn't allow them to get the correct odds on many types of bets.

short stacked Low on chips.

show To show one's cards on the show-down.

show both cards At the showdown, sometimes a player will only turn up one of their two hole cards. The dealer will then tell the player to "show both cards," since the rules require it and the dealer is not permitted to touch a player's live hand.

showdown The point in the hand when, after all betting activity has taken place, all players turn their two pocket cards face up and compare them to everyone else's to determine who has the best hand.

show one, show all The unwritten rule in almost all poker rooms that says if a player shows his cards privately to one player, that all other players have a right to see the cards if challenged by a player in the game.

shuffle To mix the cards before dealing them.

side pot Often referred to as on the side. A secondary pot that is created when one or more players still active in the hand have run out of chips while others remain who have enough chips to continue to bet. The additional bets go into the side pot.

sign-up board See board.

sit 'n' go tournament A tournament that begins immediately upon filling up with the required number of players, occasionally used in cardrooms and casinos but most often found on the Internet. For example, if the tournament host lists a single-table $5 sit 'n' go tournament, it will begin immediately after the tenth and final player needed to fill up the tournament registers.

Sometimes sit 'n' go tournaments will consist of two tables (twenty players), three tables (thirty), or more. Different from scheduled tournaments, which begin at an appointed time, regardless of the number of players.

sixes full A full house consisting of three 6s and another pair. Also called sixes over and sixes up.

small bet The lower betting limit in a double-limit Hold'em game. For example, in a $4-$8 game, $4 is the small bet.

small blind Another name for the little blind.

smooth call To call with the intention of raising if anyone else raises. A form of slow playing one's hand similar to check-raising.

snap off To win a hand you were behind on by drawing a needed card on the river. Or if you were on the losing end of such a situation, you might say, "My Aces were good until they were snapped off on the river by that third 4."

soft break The exchanging of cash for part chips, part money. For example, a player may give the dealer a $100 bill and ask for $40 cash and $60 worth of chips.

spades One of the four suits of cards, the symbol of which is shaped like an inverted valentine with a stem: ♠ spades are black in both the traditional deck and the four-color deck. A single card in the spades suit is called a Spade.

splash the pot To throw one's chips into the pot rather than placing them in front of you, thereby mixing your chips in with those already in the pot. Splashing the pot is highly unethical as it makes it difficult or even impossible for the dealer or other players to tell how much you put into the pot. Some establishments will even remove a player who splashes the pot as it can be used as a form of cheating.

split pot A tied pot that is divided equally among all players with the same hand.

spread 1) To start a poker game. You might hear a floor person say, "We're just about to spread a $4-$8 game." 2) To fan out the cards of a new deck in front of the players to give them a chance to see that all fifty-two cards are in the deck.

square the table A request by either the dealer or a player to have the chairs at the table aligned properly so that all players are equally spaced at the table. Typically called for when one or more players are being crowded.

stack 1) All of one's chips. 2) A stack of twenty chips. 3) To arrange one's chips in neat piles after scooping in a pot.

starting hand A player's first two cards in Hold'em, also called pocket or hole cards.

steal a pot To win a pot by bluffing.

steal the blinds To win only the two blinds by making a bluff bet, usually in late position.

steam To be on tilt.

stiff the dealer Failing to tip the dealer after winning a pot.

straight A poker hand which consists of five cards of consecutive rank of mixed suits. A straight ranks just above three of a kind and just below a flush.

straight draw A poker hand that contains four cards to a straight.

straight flush A poker hand which consists of five cards of consecutive rank all of the same suit. A straight flush ranks above four of a kind. An Ace-high straight flush is also known as a royal flush.

string bet A bet which is either illegal or can be challenged as illegal by another player because all of the chips were not put into the pot at the same time.

strong hand A hand that has a high likelihood of winning.

structured-limit game Limit Texas Hold'em is a structured-limit game because the betting levels and limits are proscribed. There is no deviation of betting limits allowed in limit Hold'em.

stuck Amount one has lost. You might hear a player say, "I'm stuck two hundred."

sucker A loser or poor player.

suck out To draw out on an opponent.

suit One of the four groups of cards: clubs ♣, diamonds ♦, hearts ♥, or spades ♠.

suited Holding two pocket cards of the same suit.

suited connectors Holding two pocket cards of the same suit and consecutive in rank.

sweeten the pot To raise.

table change A request by a player to move to another table.

table charge 1) The portion taken out of each pot for house expenses and profit. Also called the rake. 2) In some casinos, players pay an hourly table charge instead of participating in a rake game. Sometimes referred to as time or time collection.

tell A mannerism that another player can pick up on that gives away your hand.

tens full A full house consisting of three 10s and another pair. Also called tens over and tens up.

Texas Hold'em The official name of Hold'em.

three of a kind A poker hand consisting of three cards all of the same rank, such as three Jacks. Three of a kind ranks just above two pair and just below a straight.

threes full A full house consisting of three 3s and another pair. Also called threes over and threes up.

tight Playing very conservatively.

tilt See *on tilt*.

time charge A fee charged by the establishment for the privilege of playing in the establishment, which provides the premises, licenses, cards, other players, etc.

toke A tip.

top pair A pair made by matching one of your hole cards with the highest community card on the board.

tournament chips Chips with no actual cash value and used only in tournaments.

trap To catch one or more players by playing your hand in such a way as to disguise its strength, usually by checking, underbetting, or check-raising.

tray The dealer's chip rack.

trey The 3 card.

trips Three of a kind. Shortened from the word triplets. Trips are usually considered to be made when holding one of the cards in your pocket and making two more on the board. Similar to a set, which is made when holding two of the cards in your pocket and making the third card on the board.

turbo tournament A tournament in which the rounds are much shorter than in a normal tournament. For example, most Texas hold'em tournaments utilize rounds of ten, twelve, or fifteen minutes, with some bigger-money tournament utilizing thirty-minute rounds. The typical turbo tournament uses three-minute rounds, thus the tournament concludes much, much faster than a regular tournament. Turbo tournaments with twenty-four hundred players can conclude in an hour or so, where the same size tournament using ten to fifteen minute rounds can take up to six to eight hours to conclude.

turn The turn card, which is the fourth card dealt face up on the board. After the turn, the betting level increases to twice the limit of the first two rounds.

two bets The first raise after a bet.

two pair A poker hand consisting of two cards of one rank and two cards of another rank. Two pair ranks just above one pair and just below three of a kind.

twos full A full house consisting of three 2s and another pair. Also called twos over and twos up.

uncalled bet A bet that is made by one player and not called by any other player, thereby giving the pot to the player who made the bet.

underbet To make a smaller bet than one might normally make, or to call instead of raising, in order to entice another player into raising for the purpose of reraising him later when one holds a powerful hand. One of the strategies used in trapping other players.

underpair To hold a pocket pair whose rank is lower than any of the three cards on the flop. For example, if you hold two 6s in your pocket and the board flops K-J-9, you hold an underpair.

under the gun The first player to act in a hand.

unlimited re-buys A tournament in which players who bust out are allowed to take an unlimited number of re-buys during a certain time period.

unsuited A term used to describe your two pocket cards when they are of different suits. Also called offsuit.

upcard In Hold'em, the five community cards are upcards–cards dealt face up.

upstairs To raise. Can be said, "Take it upstairs."

up to The person whose turn it is to bet. For example, if the action gets to a player who's not paying attention, after a few seconds that dealer might say to the player, "It's up to you."

value Getting paid off for a good hand. Also called full value.

value bet To bet for full value of one's hand.

varying one's play To occasionally play differently than you normally do so as to throw off opponents who think they know your style.

verbal bet An oral bet, which is binding if made in turn in most, but not all, card rooms.

verbal declaration An oral declaration of one's hand.

wager A bet.

wait To check.

weak hand A poker hand with a low probability of winning.

wheel A 5-high straight when the Ace is played as the low card.

white A $1 chip in most casinos. A stack of white is $20 and a rack of white is $100.

winning hand The best hand at showdown.

wired Holding a pair, usually as one card in the pocket and one on the flop, but occasionally used as a term for a pocket pair. You might hear a player say, "I had wired Kings but lost on the river to a set of 5s."

World Series of Poker Oftentimes written as **WSOP**. The game's grandest tournament was held at Binion's Horseshoe Casino in Las Vegas in late spring of each year through 2004, but has moved from downtown to the strip at the Rio starting in 2005. The tournament actually consists of numerous smaller tournaments featuring all kinds of poker, capped off by a No Limit Texas Hold'em tournament with a $10,000 buy-in. With the explosion of Hold'em worldwide, first place prize money grew to $7.5 million in 2005, up from $5 million in 2004, and $2.5 million in 2003 from $1 million just a few years before that. The winner of each of the World Series events also gets a coveted gold bracelet.